Who We Are
The Code of Creation

The link between science, healing and spirituality

SUSANA COR DE ROSA

Copyright © 2019 Susana Cor de Rosa
All rights reserved.

This book may not be reproduced, totally or in part, by any mechanical, photographic, electronic method or voice recording or added to a database, or shared in any form or copied for public or private use—other than legal short quotes in articles and reviews—without previous written permission of the author.

The author of the book does not intend to substitute medical advice and does not dispense any technique as a form of treatment for physical, emotional, mental or medical problems without the advice of a medical specialist or other healthcare professional. The aim of the author is to offer information of a general nature to assist in issues of spiritual and emotional well-being. In case you use any information contained in this book for yourself, which is your constitutional right,

you do so at your own risk. Neither the author nor the publisher assume any responsibility for your actions.

Title: Who We Are: The Code of Creation
Original Title - 3rd Edition: Quem Somos Nós - O Código da Criação
Author: Susana Cor de Rosa
Translator: Isabel Alfaiate
Reviser: Paul Alfonso Soto
Cover Design: Talita Romão & AlfaPrint (Portugal)
ISBN:978-989-98155-4-4
Printer: Create Space
Publisher: Susana Costa

To my mother Maria da Anunciação and Karen Blossom for your courage to live, your unconditional love and your altruism.

CONTENTS

Preface I
Acknowledgements II
The Awakening III
Introduction 1
   Reading Orientation 2
1 The Web of Life 4
2 The Senses 18
   The sense of vitality 20
   The sense of movement 20
   The sense of equilibrium 20
   The thermal sense 21
   The sense of empathy 21
   The sense of clairvoyance or remote vision 22
   The sense of clairaudience 24
   The sense of telepathy 26
   The sense of intuition 27
   The sense of inspiration 28
   The sense of self 29
3 Who Constructs Reality? 31
4 Attention 37
   Attention and Perception 41
   Using Attention 45
   Living Attention 49
   The Principle of Attention 52
5 Intention 57
   Intention in Movement 60
   Linked Intention 62
   Intention in Health 64
   Multifunctional Intention 70
   Coherent Intention 74
   In the Footprint of Intention 80
   Intention Practical Guide: 84
6 Thought 88
   Thought in Process 90
   Directed Thought 91
   The System of Beliefs 98
   Reconnecting Thought to Health 103
   Genetic Thought 109
   Thoughts Entwined in the World 113
7 Image 119
   Images in Process 121
   Imagetic Multifunctionality 127
   Impression by Image 132
   Self-image 140
   Reformulated Image 143
8 Word 147
   On the Path of Words 150
   Declarations of Life 160
   Words with Impact 162
   Beyond Linear Words 169
9 Emotion 174
   The Discovery of Emotions 176
   In the Steps of Emotion 178

- More than Emotion 183
- Emotional Impact 186
- 10 Feeling 202
  - Discovering Feelings 206
  - On the Pathway of Feelings 208
  - Finding Positive Feelings 215
  - Feelings in Movement 219
  - The Timing of Feelings 225
- 11 Action 234
  - The Discovery of Action 237
  - Unfulfilled Action 244
  - Give 250
- 12 The Quantum Leap 254
- Bibliography 260
- Susana Cor de Rosa's bio and activities 264
- Synopsis 267

Preface

A tale, passed from generation to generation by the Dogon people of Mali, says that we are all born with a certain number of words inside our bellies and, one day, when these are finished, we die.

Luckily, every day we can store hundreds of new words, through our contact with the world, through conversation with friends, reading, attending the theatre and going to the cinema. Everything adds more and more words to our life and in that way, we increase our stock, postponing the ultimate end.

The tale of the belly that fills up with words in order to keep us alive makes us think of the importance of sharing words and not just being alone, gazing at our navels, tattooed on the inside with a thousand words, which can only lead us to death. I imagine a belly full of words shriveling on the inside because they are not pampered, because there are no new seeds growing there.

Words are, for me, a precious commodity. I work with them. I know how important each one is, when I want to transmit ideas or pass information on. However, since I met Susana, I realized that there is much more to that than words: the intentions, emotions, feelings... all, in harmony, can be worked in favor of self-knowledge.

With Susana, I became aware of my connection with everything around me, and the infinite possibilities that the universe presents to me daily. This discovery has been so good, and I am always grateful for Susana being "placed" in my path more than eight years ago. Thanks to her and her teachings, I have optimized and improved my way of thinking and feeling the world that surrounds me, changing in this way my perception and relationship with the Other.

You will certainly feel identified with much of what you read throughout various chapters of this book. This is what happened to me when I heard Susana speak for the first time. I thought: at long last, someone speaks a language that says so much that I thought was merely a figment of my imagination... My intuition told me, the moment I found her (or found her again?), that less than ten years later I would be here with her discussing a book on this subject. And here it is.

I hope that when reading this book, you will also feel the need to Change, because it is guaranteed it will be for the Better.

Fernanda Freitas, March 2012

Acknowledgements

God, thank you for your hand in mine… and for your love and joy, always supporting me.

To Elsa Bolou, my dearest friend, you are amazing. Thanks, girl. When we met, the whole universe moved us into a new territory of ourselves and towards a journey to find more love, joy, compassion, friendship, victories and wisdom. It is a blessing be with you and grow to higher realms of awareness.

To Louis Moore, my deepest gratitude for your light and altruism. You are so inspiring, my friend. Keep doing what you love most.

To Nita, beloved friend: thank you. You are a treasure and a beautiful soul.

To Ruth, my dearest friend, thank you. You are a light in my life and in the world. The universe gave me a huge present by placing you in my life.

To Cátia Antunes, a wonderful heart and a precious jewel in my life.

To **Verónica Orvalho**, many blessings, my friend.

To Fernanda Freitas THANK YOU for your presence in my life.

To the translator, dear **Isabel Alfaiate** and to the reviser **Paul Alfonso,** my profound thanks.

Tiago, my dear, you are pure love. Thank you.

Thank you **Talita Romão**, for your work, light and creativity.

Dear **Mother, Maria,** I love you. Thank you for your love, energy, and strengths. You are such a blessing.

Dear **Father, Brothers, Family and so many friends**, namely Luísa Crespo, Ana Barreto, Joaquim Alegria, Lauro Trevisan e Maria Odete, and so many others, thank you as well.

The Awakening

"Everything that comes, comes for a reason."
Fernando Pessoa

"The happiness of the soul is the beautiful days of life, whatever the season."
Socrates

Late one August afternoon, while lying on the beach, I nodded off. I don't know how long I slept, but I do know something happened when I woke up. I found myself in a state of grace. Profoundly relaxed and connected with the All. I felt at one with the sea and sand, the sky and the sun, at one with totality. Joyfully alive.
The sensation was so overwhelming that I simply surrendered to what was happening, feeling connected to something much greater than me. I dissolved into all that exists. My reality changed in the blink of an eye. I knew who I was and what everything was. It was such an enriching experience that even thinking about it today still has the same impact after so many years.
At the time, I longed to live better, more in harmony with myself and the people I had around me. I wanted to learn how to deal positively with events and circumstances, and to live happily, with love, enjoying the abundance around me, and *helping* people to be happy. I wanted an existence full of meaning. I believe everyone wants to experience this and, I must confess, at that moment, on the beach, it seemed to me to be the easiest thing to achieve. Through this experience, I had internalized what I had only known in theory: the connection with primordial energy, with unity. Since this defining experience, I have had several other moments of connection with unity that have influenced my life.
Life had not always been this way. Until I was 28, I felt unhappy, disoriented, full of apprehension. I felt tense and internally split. For many years, I juggled a job as a hemodialysis technician while studying law. I began to feel that there had to be something more than work, family or money that could make me feel whole. I wanted to get to know myself as a being, broaden my horizons, free myself from prejudices, feel connected and, ultimately, be happy.
It was so strange: after achieving what I wanted with so much effort, nothing made sense. Then I went in search of the meaning of life. I did not know where to find the answers. The questions were so pertinent and clear that messages came in numerous ways. I was attentive and prepared to take risks. Susie, a work colleague, began to talk to me about "energy," showing me very different books than the enormous law books I was studying. Later, a patient who did hemodialysis spoke about the vital energy of reiki. It was 1996 and everything was new.
Eventually I found myself attending a talk about healing. I asked so many questions! (I still do not understand how the speaker managed to be so patient with me). That year I went on holiday to Paris, where I stayed in the home of my dear friend Georges. He lent me the book *The Power of your Subconscious Mind* by Dr. Joseph Murphy. With the questions I asked, the answers arose as well. For this reason, I ask so many questions in the book—to evoke the replies. Questions open pathways.
During this formative time, I fell in love with life, healing, physics and quantum mechanics. I even earned a new surname. During a seminar attended by various

Susanas, they started calling me Susana Cor de Rosa (pink Susana). I accepted it and became known by it. Later when I understood the significance of the pink energy (universal love in movement). I began to believe that this is my way: having a surname like Love helps to be *it* at each moment. This name has brought me many blessings and that is why I use it.

As my way of thinking, speaking, feeling and behaving was being transformed, I noticed that the universe wisely supported me. I was, and continue to be, the creator/co-creator of my reality, and as my travel companion, the universe enriched it. The inner calling and the realization that my transformation is to be shared with the world, together with healing, made me even more curious, asking more intimate, soul-searching questions, leading the mind to search and work more in this direction. It is here that physics and quantum mechanics come in, because that which my intuition and inspiration tell me and what I put into practice, has a scientific explanation. What I do is to permeate the mental work with the sensibility of the heart. After learning mentally, I have to release all the information so that my heart sorts and channels it as the heart is the most powerful energy field we have, and it is the heart that performs miracles.

Questions from the quantum point of view that continue to broaden my horizons (bilocality—being in two places at the same time; the possibility of "travelling" in time—past and future; instantaneous communication and obtaining information independently of the matrix point), become more evident as I practice unified quantum healing, the quantum intelligence and the quantum from the heart and for the soul. The connection with the field of unified consciousness—the information field—which will be shown in a while, is real and allows us to perform what we call miracles, the impossible —what we could only conceive of in dreams.

Working with the Unified Quantum Healing, the Quantum Intelligence or Quantum from the Heart and for the Soul and other energetic soul matrixes in seminars, consultations and with myself, has led me to witness and participate in many extraordinary events: for example, the disappearance of a tumor, the vision for a project or professional success. These have happened to a great number of people and although the process is beyond me—because it in itself is grandiose—the truth is that from a quantum perspective they are infinite possibilities existing in the field of the unified consciousness being actualized. Quantum physics/mechanics accepts them as possible tendencies of the movement of consciousness in itself. And consciousness is everything; we are it already.

We are linked to the field of infinite possibilities and we have the most advanced technology for the evolution of humanity—that is the *"technology of our consciousness"*—which is also available to you. In this book you will understand it and feel it and you will be able to use it from now on.

This book is the result of an intense passion for life, my search for self-knowledge, a way of testing myself as freely as possible. It is the result of my love for sharing ideas, visions of the world, feelings and experiences, as well as the profound desire to contribute so that each human being awakens to their real dimension, believing that together, we will build a better world for all. I sincerely believe that this is possible. Thank you for being united for the same purpose.

Susana Cor de Rosa

Introduction

"A human being is a part of a whole, called by us 'universe', a part limited in time and space He experiences himself, his thoughts and feelings as something separated from the rest...a kind of optical delusion of his consciousness. This delusion is a kind of prison for us, restricting us to our personal desires and to affection for a few persons nearest to us. Our task must be to free ourselves from this prison by widening our circle of compassion to embrace all living creatures and the whole of nature in its beauty."
Albert Einstein

You are beginning to read an extraordinary book.
You are entering a new dimension of yourself, the world and even of the universe.
What you have conceived to this moment up to NOW about who you are, who others are and what the nature of reality is all about to change. Once your perception is changed, the world will never be the same for you: both you and the world will expand.
Presently, we are living in the information and communication era. We have so much information and so much technology available to us that very often we do not know what to do with it—or even without it. We are connected to the internet; we work in a network at the office; we speak on cell phones at any time, and we can keep up with the news wherever we are; not to mention using social networks to communicate with "friends." Increasingly we have more stimuli to look to the exterior and look for solutions "outside" to resolve our daily and global problems. This communication and technology revolution has substantially changed our lives and the world.
What if there was still another information and communication revolution for us? One that instead of being done externally would operate internally, affecting everything?
What if a profound transformation is needed within the paradigms that we have accepted as valid until now and which made us understand Who We Are?
Something that would allow us to understand our position in the universe and how we can create a full life—from relationships with our family members, to our health, success, and the extinction of poverty and famine. The revolution which has already started inside you has drawn you to this book.
The first perception that changes the established information system is the fact that we are linked to each other and to nature, sharing the network of life.
The second is that we are unlimited beings.
The third is that we are information and we are permanently in communication with one another, with the planet and with the field of unified consciousness. There is a quantum conversation occurring on a fundamental and intimate level between us and this field of unified consciousness—our quality of life, the way we develop, and the way the planet develops also depend on it.
Finally, the fourth perception points out that we are in fact the creators of our reality. We are therefore responsible for what we experience individually or collectively.
From the moment we understand and apply these four basic perceptions to our everyday life, we will become different. Our family members and friends will notice the transformation, and the world and the universe will be different, as a result of our change.
The truth is that we already have all the resources to make this new revolution of information and communication; the "technology" is already available too.

It is the "subtle technology of our consciousness" operating: we are gifted with intelligence and sensibility; we capture information and we communicate it the highest level. The sixteen senses that we have—rather than the five that are presented as the only ones that exist—capture information on various levels, allowing us to communicate in a surprising and effective manner with ourselves, with others and with the field of unified consciousness, challenging all the concepts of what we thought was possible.

Communicating telepathically and knowing how our child's first day at school is progressing is real. It is possible to feel or connect empathetically with the people who are dear to us; to support, comfort, love, guide and assist them even though we are not physically present. This innate ability is always available to us.

It is true that any information can be accessed by us via intuition, solving a work issue at the right time or being inspired to create a project. It is absolutely possible to heal ourselves within a heartbeat, immediately and change the paradigm of a whole life. We truly affect everything and everyone at each moment and we can feel and create the synchronicities in our lives.

The power to perform small and big "miracles" is always available and works with any one of us, at any place, time or in any circumstances. We are not separated from them; we are miraculous and operate in the field of infinite possibilities.

We are infinitely powerful and unlimited beings. We function multidimensionally. We are creators and actively participate in life, giving it meaning and substance at every moment. We construct reality through attention, intention, thought, image, word, emotion, feeling and action. This is the language of creation—The Code of Creation.

Using this language, we inform and *enform* life. We construct our own reality of professional success, love, personal and family fulfillment. But also divorce, failure or illness. We are also builders of triumph, of facilities, of that profound love that we feel, the loss, the shame, the fear, and also the wish for world peace. What we are will be imprinted on the screen of life. It is possible to change at any time, and co-create, step by step or in great leaps, realities we are proud of and for which we are deeply grateful.

Because everything is possible, this book will give you answers that have not been given before, and it is part of a grand purpose for the growth of humanity.

Feel it as a good friend, a benevolent presence conceived to walk with you through life.

Thank you for being in the process of READING THIS BOOK, for making a revolution of the senses, and for discovering and sharing "Who We Are."

Reading Orientation

This book is interactive: it was designed to communicate with you and you with it.

The book has information that will be captured at various levels, and it is therefore important to open your channels to the messages that this book provides for you.

You can read it through in one go, or maybe you feel that you need to stop, breathe and connect yourself more deeply and feel the love. There are notes (♥ Stop, Breathe, Love) that suggest those moments for you to mindfully pause. However, feel comfortable to stop or start reading when you feel the need.

Each chapter tells a story. You may read it again each time you return to the chapter. You will notice that words and ideas are sometimes repeated throughout the chapters.

This is so you can become familiar with them and then establish deeper connections in yourself.

Trust. The author thought about this and worked towards your wellbeing.

The book contains exercises, which you are advised to do. There are cases of people who when reading the book and doing the proposed exercises, solved health issues (for example the disappearance of a lump in the breast), relaxed, found professional answers, and felt profound love, amongst other experiences. They have gone on to attend consultations, workshops and retreats to find out Who They Are and proceeded on their way.

If it is easier for you, you can download questions from: www.susanacorderosa.com, print them and write as much as you wish.

In this book, I make many references to God. This does not imply, at any time, that I wish to impose God's existence onto the reader. Instead, it is merely to give you a sense of inclusiveness and transcendence.

Read it with pleasure and joy and be open to changing your perceptions as you read further.

If you like, you may place the book on your chest and open it on a page at random and see the suggestions for your day.

This book is written referring to *us*, on purpose. On a second reading or whenever you decide, I suggest you change "us" to "I" and whenever it says "I" change that to "us." It is a way of holding us responsible, both individually and collectively.

This book has twelve chapters and within these are subchapters and testimonials of people who are familiar with "Who We Are."

Share the book confidently with your friends, knowing deeply that a transformation force is in movement for the good of all.

I will be grateful if you send me your testimonial to: susana@susanacorderosa.com

Feel wanted, loved and blessed
Susana Cor de Rosa

1 The Web of Life

Story
Space and time did not exist, yet love was already pulsating. Being love, in love and giving itself up for love. Concentrated in a spot so full and still, where only love could fit, it exploded overwhelmingly. A web of love was formed and with it, light and darkness, the particle and the antiparticle, the sunrise and sunset, space and time, action and rest—and the unlimited possibilities of love became available. The web stretched, deepened, occupied space, time and beyond, connecting all possible creatures to one another and to itself. Time—and yet no time—passed and the web of love, as a result of so much crisscrossing over itself, formed droplets of love. In each connection of the web, a droplet of love was formed, reflecting the totality of itself and of all the other droplets on the web. Wherever the droplets looked, they only saw love, emanated love, spoke of love and made love and the whole web moved in it. When any droplet thought love, felt love and touched love the whole web undulated in it and the droplets at each point glowed with love... and behold, a droplet of human love emerged and the web of love expanded, continuously connected to it to this day...

"Therefore I know myself completely and through knowing myself totally, I know the whole of humanity, totally."
Fernando Pessoa

The question of your origin, of where you came from, and where everything originated, is present in the mind and in the heart of every human being. This question may emerge when we behold a starlit sky, when we contemplate an ocean or listen to the heartbeat of our sleeping child. This natural act of curiosity and our connection with existence, throws us into an internal journey that could last a lifetime—or maybe in a single moment, in an epiphany, we understand the mystery profoundly—and life expands intensely.
What if we could unveil, rephrase or intuit the origins of life and with that knowledge and feeling, could we also know Who We Are and occupy our place with wholeness in the universe?
Could we envision new connections to existential issues which have always preoccupied us as human beings; could we find solutions to the challenges we face daily, from health, the upbringing of our children, everyday safety, to experiencing a loving relationship or earning money to honor our commitments? And what about creating profound links with life and, at the same time, always feeling protected by it, in the constant company of a friendly and intimate presence.
What a deep sense of peace we would feel. What a sensation of being home, amongst loved ones, at each moment... what freedom to be, do or have, could we experience... what confidence and joy our faces would show in the wise knowledge that, effectively, *everything is possible*.
Is there actually a point where we all came from the source of life? Is it possible that there is something that has knitted us to all that exists and even all that can potentially be brought into existence, and into which we are all interwoven in a magnificent web of life?

Perhaps it is possible to know how the source of all life functions, sharing information and communicating with it in a specific language or code and interacting with it?
What point would that be, where everything originated?
In the beginning, only pure consciousness was. Some call it the void of pure potential, full of possibilities, from which reality will emerge—a uterus of primary energy that breeds all, accepts all, moving and recreating itself at each moment: from the birth of a supernova, a volcanic eruption, a meeting with the love of our lives, winning the lottery, toothaches, unemployment or the most beautiful symphony. The endless possibilities of reality, of any reality, are conceived here.
The great secret to interact with this womb of primary energy is in the first place to sense/know that it is real and recognize that there are laws governing it in order to communicate and interact with it. The knowledge of this secret opens all the doors of creation to us.
Perhaps you, the reader, are asking yourself, "what is the primary energy?" You probably already know the word *energy* and use it frequently. However, I am going to show you a more precise definition so that you gain a better understanding of it while reading and will be able to feel it better. The word energy comes from the Greek *energeia* meaning act and potency. Energy can also mean force, from the Latin root *vis* or from the Chinese root *chi*. Energy can be understood as force in action, force in movement, or still, as a possibility and a manifestation.
Max Planck, the father of quantum physics, understood at the beginning of the twentieth century that energy was not released continuously, but rather in the form of freestanding packets of energy—"quanta". The "quantum" is the smallest quantity of energy that two particles can exchange between them. According to him, the universe was made of energy of quanta, and matter, on a fundamental level, was seen as a wave of probability and not as a fixed thing. In other words, the objects that we have in our lives, from a cell phone, to a car, and even a tree, a virus, a human body or a shooting star are at their utmost, elementary level waves of probabilities, which are energy[1].
Since the end of the nineteenth century, the existence of energy fields has been scientifically accepted. Thus, in the twentieth century, the idea of a unified field of energy, an all-embracing field that supports and interlinks with all the rest, has also been theorized.[2]
In order to understand the idea underlying the field of unified energy, we need first to understand what a field is. A field is a mathematical construct that scientists use to represent a medium that connects several points in space, normally via a force such as electromagnetism. It can be represented as a kind of broad sheet in which interrelations and its effects can be detected. In addition, a field can be understood as a zone of influence, a coherent structure interacting with everything existing within it. A field can be what generates, supports and allows interrelations and energy exchange between each quantum entity on it, also with itself.
The field of unified energy is the medium through which everything connects; it is the web, the organized and coherent structure that manifests and supports existence in various forms, (for example, galaxies, bacteria, flowers, human beings) and

---

[1] Max Planck - Quantum theory.
[2] James Maxwell and Michael Faraday. See electromagnetic theory.

interrelates them, interacts with them and with itself. It is also supreme intelligence, pure energy, and formless energy, uncreated potential and transcendent life. This is the primordial field of energy where everything originates: the quantum womb of reality. We call this field the field of unified consciousness. It is the protagonist of life.[3]

Each human being has lived, felt, thought or perhaps even searched for proof of this field of unified consciousness—the quantum womb of reality. It may have been in a moment of pain or despair when pleading for the help of a higher power to solve a crisis. It may also have been at a special occasion in your life when your heart was beating intensely and you felt profoundly linked to something higher than you and were bursting with love and joy, intuitively understanding everything.

In fact, we want to understand and feel what we and everything else are made of. Many of us have already understood that we are more than matter, more than bodies, that we are energy and that events, objects and everything else are also energy.

Effectively, we want answers about the nature of reality and the essence of life, and we also wish to know, feel and apply that knowledge daily so that we may have a better life. On a deeper level, we long to know who we are—We Are Consciousness—and we use this consciousness systematically for our happiness, which is after all, the purpose of our life.

Those answers, the knowledge, are found in this field of primordial energy—the field of unified consciousness—and also within you. It is your source, as well as mine, and that of the totality.

This field of unified consciousness can be perceived as an ocean of infinite energy, a sea of minute vibrations oscillating in "empty" space, interconnected by "invisible threads" and united by consciousness. We are the quantum waves within this ocean of energy. Even when these waves are dissolved in it, we are always connected to it because we have the same nature. In a certain way, all that we perceive in reality, however small, medium or large, is also the same: a wave of energy from this quantum ocean and connected to it.

The field of unified consciousness is the genesis of everything that is visible and invisible. It is pure potential and expressed act is what creates matter and nonmatter. It is what is beyond form and what creates all forms. The field of unified consciousness is what observes, what witnesses life and at the same time creates it, intervening in it with us. It is the creator of space and time and it is beyond space and time and yet between them. The field of unified consciousness is the infinite presence, our essence and that of the All. It is the creator of reality and everything is possible for it.

Max Planck considered consciousness to be the genesis of all reality. *"I regard consciousness as fundamental. I regard matter as derivative from consciousness. We cannot get behind consciousness. Everything that we talk about, everything that we regard as existing, postulates consciousness."*[4]

And even what we consider "matter" was also in his perception, consciousness: *"All matter is originated and exists only as a result of a force (...) we have to assume that*

---

[3] This term has come to me through intuition. I am grateful that other authors before me were also exploring the concept field of unified consciousness; establishing the connection between unified field theories, consciousness and spirituality.

[4] Quoted in The Observer (25th January 1931). Cited in Joseph H. Fussell, 'Where is Science Going?: Review and Comment", Theosophical Path Magazine, January to December 1933 (2003), 199.

behind this force there is a consciousness, an intelligent mind (...)"[5]

Now, by acknowledging the existence of the field of unified consciousness, as well as understanding that science supports it, we can broaden our perception of it. For many of us, it is understood as the Source, the Matrix, God, Buddha, Allah, Great Spirit or simply Force. For others it is understood as Pure Mathematics, Supreme Order or Emptiness.

The quantum physicist Max Planck is able to express this in a superb manner in his famous lecture Religion and Science (May 1937). *He wrote: "Both religion and science need for their activities the belief in God, and more over God stands for the former in the beginning, and for the latter at the end of the whole thinking. For the former, God represents the basis, for the latter – the crown of any reasoning concerning the worldview."*[6]

The truth is that independently of the name, faith in God or the absence of it, this field of consciousness is real; it exists, supports us, links us and communicates with us and us with it. That is our starting point and our destination. Being Who We Are—a point of creation, linked to all of creation, constructing reality at each instant through The Code of Creation. And as such, making all the difference for the better in our lives.

The field of unified consciousness can be perceived also as the field of information. The word information, whose Latin root is *information + onis* means idea, conception or plan, as well as the action of forming or doing. The word "information" contains in itself both the possibility (idea) as well as the act (doing).[7]

The field of unified consciousness is primordial and timeless information[8] that can be in a potential state, as well as being manifested information, existentially visible, throughout time in numerous facets, shapes, dimensions and contexts, for example as a comet, a dinosaur or an iPad.

Simply, life can be seen as information in potential state (without form) or information in a manifested state (with form).

It is the field of information that contains and connects, like a gigantic web, the information from all creatures (or things), all dimensions, all places and all times (past, present and future), as well as, being the information field containing in itself endless possibilities of information, limitless probabilities of quantum interconnections.

The truth is that potentially, at every moment, everything and everyone is connected to the information field; we are part of the information field; we inform the field and we also create, as consciousness, the information and the form of the field.

I will share with you an experience from one of my seminars, where a participant felt connected to the information field—the field of unified consciousness—and changed her perception of who she was.

Testimonial

My name is Ana and I am an artist. I express my gifts through voice, movement and feeling. I went to the workshop of *Unified Quantum Healing* during a very delicate

---

[5] "Discourse of Max Planck about the nature of matter," Archiv zur Geschichte der MaxPlanckGesellschaft, Abt. Va, Rep. 11 Planck, Nr. 1797.
[6] Max Planck, Religion und Naturwissenschaft, Leipzig: Johann Ambrosius Barth Verlag, 1958, 27.
[7] Portuguese dictionary, Porto Editora
[8] If you would like to know more about an In-formation Theory please see the work of David Bohm. Wholeness and the Implicate Order. London: Routledge & Kegan Paul, 1980. Please see also the work of John Wheeler regarding information.

stage in my life. I wanted to find answers and tread new paths in my life, starting with my profession, health and affections. I must confess: I had no idea what the seminar was about or what I would be doing. I simply felt that I had to go...

In one of the exercises of healing, I felt my whole body vibrating and expanding. I was totally connected with the universe and shined brightly. I felt immense light and dots of information undulating. I was totally transparent, immense and one with all.

The sensation was one of a reencounter with myself, like I was caring for myself and at the same time I was both in my own and in God's lap at the same time. I was fulfilled, whole for the first time and with the sense of "returning home"...

My consciousness changed—I found my essence—I became aware that I had no limits, that I was connected to all and was all. After all, I was and am the creator of my reality.

In this state, a sense of completeness came over me, a vastness of love so great that I felt like singing, jumping, running, shouting, hugging, kissing... and every pore in my body throbbed with gratitude. I was in a state of grace because I knew who I was and understood the origin of life. We are one with the field of consciousness; I know it by my own experience and that is magnificent.

Ana Cosme, singer

♥ Stop, Breathe, Love

The perception that we are all connected to the field of information, the field of unified consciousness, is natural. It is our origin. There is a fundamental interdependence, a basic connection and a constant partnership between us and the information field. We are one with it and it with us.

We are life in movement, information vibrating just like everything that surrounds us. We are a point of information in the information field transmitting data, sharing ideas, states of the soul, music, love and action, creating realities and are also a part of the All. Moreover, we are something that is constantly becoming, recreating itself indefinitely in tune with the field of information.

The human being is conscious information endowed with the capacity to affect and create the information/reality. In effect, humans are simultaneously the creation and the creator in the field of information.

We are a creation because we are a manifestation of the field; we are the creator because we have the creative potential, the conscious potential, to choose how reality is going to manifest itself by focusing our attention.

In the energy web of life, the human being is at the same time a thread of the web and someone who moves on the web, changing it by an act of will. The web conforms to that act, with that human sovereign decision, moves and reflects it in reality, in the global web. Effectively, at each moment we crystallize realities through wishes, fears, beliefs, dreams, words, images and attitudes that we nurture and we see these results in our lives and also in the All.

Here is the story of the experience of a creator of reality, who understood her connection and power to construct different results in her life.

Testimonial

During the Who We Are workshop, I clearly understood that I am a consciousness responsible to choose the life that I truly want to live. This awakening of consciousness was extraordinary and opened several possibilities to change my life leaving behind any past worries.

At the time, I had applied for a job moved by the fear that I might not be able to get work soon in my desired position. Then, I understood that this decision was indeed going to separate me from myself (meaning from what I really wanted as a job) and from other projects that I really wanted to engage at that time, and probably, would bring me more of the same. As such, after the workshop, I began to practice what I had learned and decided to change my destiny, to be who I am, directing my focus to my wished results. What happened was very special; it enabled me to gain confidence and trust life, feeling supported by this field of consciousness, as well as, choosing to have what I really desired for myself, such as engage in new projects and returning to live in the place I wished for. This act of trusting and following my heart's desire, gave me a new stability and a fresh vision of the possibilities before me. I am now living in the place I chose; I feel renewed and in harmony with the All.

Ruth Silva, consultant

Through focused attention, the human being chooses a set event, crystalizing that which was only potential into a real event. When the human being chooses and brings something to life, the information field mirrors the chosen event, because it works in partnership with us.

Without any type of judgment, the information field "uploads" whatever we consciously selected. Reproducing in the cosmic "net" what we coagulated energetically, based on a thought of success, or an emotion of fear, or a behavior of aggressiveness or of great generosity and love. The information field reproduces the level of consciousness of our creations and through this reproduction, it not only gives us the power to understanding what we actually did, but also gives us the possibility to improve our creativity in our next act of constructing reality.

♥ Stop, Breathe, Love

As we already know that the field of unified consciousness —the information field— exists and we acknowledge its role as founder of life, the next step is knowing the laws ruling it, that is, how it functions. When we understand how something works, we can interact with it and even affect it.

Although we have to use technical language in this first chapter, which is short, it is worth explaining so that the book may flow. Read it with serenity and at the same time effortlessly. You do not have to memorize anything; we are merely showing concepts and putting information into context. All is well.

Classical physics suggests a more materialistic, objective and compartmentalized vision of reality in the dimension of space and time and is based on the mechanisms of cause and effect and predictability. In the vision of classical physics, the human being is just "another piece" of nature separated from the universe, with a role of little relevance in the universe. Reality is not affected by the human observer. The world and the objects in the classical view are objectively real; they exist whether we are observing them or not. "The moon is there even if we do not look at it," as Einstein stated.

The assumptions of conventional science, which I describe below, have influenced our vision of the world and our way of experiencing life, since the seventeenth century. They explain macroscopic phenomena such as the movement of the planets and are useful to build spaceships, X-ray equipment or to understand the biochemistry of the liver.

1) Mechanicism/Determinism: The universe is mechanical. We can compare it to a gigantic clock, seeing that all is ascertainable, and predictable, as long as we know all the initial conditions and the causal sequences. The concepts of space and time are absolute.

2) Causality: Causality describes how subatomic activity occurs related to a cause and subsequent effect in time, a sequential order in time. According to this principle, an effect cannot occur before its cause, and it is not possible that what happens at the end of an experiment to impacts what occurs at the beginning. There is a sequence in time: it is linear, moving forward (past, present, and future). Subatomic activity and events obey this law.

3) Continuity: In the universe, all the change or movement occurs in a continuous manner. Natural phenomena occur according to a sequential order in a defined and compartmentalized space and time. There are no discontinued leaps or unpredictabilities.

4) Locality: Any event or phenomenon has a local cause and effect, propagating itself in space and time, at a finite speed. The speed of light cannot be transcended and it is not possible for communication and action at a distance to exist simultaneously.

Consequently, in order to affect an object, direct action on it is essential and the effects of this action are circumscribed in space and time, i.e. it is not possible to communicate and interact instantly.

5) Objectivity (extreme): Material reality is independent of the subject perceiving it. The observer/human consciousness does not participate in the world.

According to quantum physics/mechanics, which studies events on a microscopic level (the forces underlying our physical world), the universe is a field of infinite probabilities and reality, on a fundamental level, is energy— waves/particles—in movement, seeing that these waves/particles are not isolated entities per se or independent entities. They diffused, a pulsation of energy that sometimes appears and disappears and that is always in a relationship with all the possible waves/particles and with possible locations or movements. Furthermore, these waves/ particles are always potentially connected, communicating with each other and with everything at every instant and in any place. The universe is communication in the true sense of the word.

From the point of view of quantum physics, instead of being considered as something substantial, matter is something insubstantial, a wave of probabilities in movement. Reality is a construction being systematically actualized, dependent on observation and human will. Each human being has a role in the universe and intervenes in it.

Space and time are not closed frontiers; on the contrary, they can be transcended as there is a potential and constant connection in the here and now with all the possible points in space and time and beyond it.

The scientific dogmas of conventional physics (determinism, causality, continuity, locality and objectivity) can be deconstructed in a radical manner. Let us see:

1) The uncertainty principle: this denies the determinism and the causality set out by conventional physics. The quantum physicist Werner Heisenberg revealed through the uncertainty principle that there exists a deep form of indetermination/uncertainty in the physical world when he asserted that it is impossible to know simultaneously the position of a particle and its speed, or know where the particle is and simultaneously to know where this particle is going. That is, we cannot know/measure with total accuracy all the properties of a particle at the current moment, and inevitably, we are unable to know with total certainty (rigor) where it will be in the future; therefore the future of that wave/particle is undetermined and conventional determinism falls. However, it is possible to predict the possibilities and the probabilities of the wave/particle being there or here.[9]

Does this principle create "space" in our lives for flexibility and openness to difference since the uncertainty is part of the essence of life?

2) Discontinuity: The principle of continuity in classical physics assumes that all movement is continuous. Yet, the movement of subatomic entities is discontinuous, nonlinear. One of the experiments that better focuses discontinuity is the quantum leap in the atom, by Niels Bohr. An electron, moving around the nucleus of an atom, jumps from a higher orbit to a lower one without passing through the intermediate space between the two orbits and is crystallized in one single place instantaneously. Due to the fact, that an electron can assume the behavior of a wave, it can potentially be in many places at the same time, for example, simultaneously in various orbits around a nucleus. When the consciousness of the observer focuses on the electron, it instantaneously becomes crystallized and becomes immediately in one position only. However, the passage from the wave of probabilities of an electron to a "real" electron/ particle occurs instantly.

Does this principle open the door to many possibilities for us, so that we can jump to new horizons of life and be "greater" than we have ever been?

3) Non-locality: This principle breaks the principle of locality, stating that it is possible to affect quantum objects (waves/particles) simultaneously without direct/local influence on them or something (a force) mediating the action, transcending space. This principle was first explained by John Bell (Bell's Theorem—John Bell 1965).
Non-locality describes how two subatomic particles, separated in space by thousands

---

[9] Goswami, Amit, *Visionary Window: A Quantum Physicist's Guide to Enlightenment*, Portuguese edition (Editora Cultrix), pg. 42 and following

of kilometers or even by millions of light years, or separated in time, 20 seconds or 1 million years, "communicate" with each other, interact instantly, in a coordinated and concerted way, as if each knew what the other is "thinking" or doing.

In 1982, the scientist Alain Aspect proved Bell´s theorem, the principle of non-locality, by carrying out a laboratory experiment: "the experiment concerned the behavior of two photons or particles of light flying off in opposite directions from a source, and separated by 12 m between each other. The two photons, from the same source, can be observed by two detectors that measure a property called polarization; these two particles were sent at the same time in opposing directions and when a change was made to the polarization of one of the moving particles (+ to -), instantly the other particle changed its polarization to the opposite of the first particle (- to +)."[10]

Through this experiment, it was made clear that it is possible for subatomic particles to "communicate" and interact instantaneously with each other, in spite of the distance that may separate them, in this case 12m.

This experiment violated the principle that no communication could travel faster than the speed of light, as assumed by Einstein, because it shattered the barrier of local action and that of space-time. The time estimated for this interaction between particles was less than a billionth of a second—twenty times faster than the velocity at which light travels in empty space.

Taking the evidence for the principle of non-locality further, in 1997 an experiment was carried out by various scientists at the University of Geneva, where the aim was to find out if quantum correlations are maintained over long distances. Simply put, the scientists sought to find out whether instant "communication"/interaction between subatomic particles was possible at long distances.

To that effect, a single photon was divided in two equal particles and each was sent in opposing directions about ten kilometers apart, without the possibility of any signal being emitted or any type of force intervening between them and it was proven that they were non-locally interacting.

"Two entangled photons are sent into all-fiber interferometers using a telecommunications fiber network. The two interferometers are located 10.9 km apart from one another.(...)

The correlated photons choose both short arms or both long arms through the interferometers(...)

Two-photon fringe visibilities of up to 81.6% are obtained.(...)

"In conclusion, this experiment gives evidence that the spooky action between entangled photons does not break down when separating the particles by a physical distance of 10 km"

In 2004, this principle was proven once again (by the same scientist and a new team), only this time, the distance between the particles was fifty Kilometers. For further details, please see the publications referenced here.[11]

Is it possible that this principle shows the way to another type of communication,

---

[10] Aspect, A., Dalibard, J., and Roger, G., "Experimental Test of Bell´s Inequalities Using Time-Varying Analyzers", Physical Review Letters 49 (1982), summarized from pgs 1804-7.
[11] " Tittel, W., Brendel, J., Gisin, B., Herzog, T., Zbinden, H., Gisin, N., (1998) "Experimental Demonstration of Quantum Correlations over more than 10 km," Physical Review A, Vol. 57, No. 5, 1998. Marcikic, I, de Riedmatten, H., Tittel, W., Zbinden, h., Legré, M., e Gisin, N(2004). Distribution of timebin entangled qubits over 50km of optic fiber. Physical Review Letter, 93.

more subtle, global and universal and even more intimate sharing of who We Are?

4) The participation of the subject in the creation of reality: This principle refutes the absolute objectivity professed by conventional physics in which the subject does not participate in or affect reality. On a quantum level, reality is susceptible to being influenced and configured according to the observer´s conscious decision.

In accordance with Niels Bohr´s principle of complementarity, subatomic reality can assume an undulating character (be a wave of possibilities), just as it can assume a corpuscular characteristic (be a particle) and even be both a particle and a wave.

Subsequently, what determines if an electron appears in the form of particle or a wave when observed depends on how it is observed/measured. Bohr stated, *"An electron is a wave if you observe it through an apparatus for measuring waves. And it is not a wave if you observe it through an apparatus to measure particles."*[12]

Now this is possible because there is a consciousness observing the electron. Therefore, the human observation influences the quantum object.

This is even better expressed by the quantum mathematician Pascual Jordan: "The observations do not only disturb what has to be measured, they produce it... We *force (the electron) to take a set position... We ourselves produce measurement results.*"[13]

In fact, the consciousness of the observer subjectively creates interferences with the state of infinite possibilities and through the observation, measuring and intention, causes a collapse (breakdown) in the entity observed, which will assume a certain state as a result of the interference. In this sense, the human being creates reality because it has the power to choose how it is going to be through observation.

Is it possible through this principle to observe life from a new point of view and be responsible for the changes that we want to live? After all, we create reality.

5) A holographic vision of the universe: During the 70s, the quantum physicist David Bohm theorized that the universe functions like a gigantic cosmic hologram. The nature of reality is one and is interconnected and affects itself mutually at each point of the cosmic hologram, being that each piece of the universe represents exactly the whole and contains information about the constitution of the totality. That is, each piece of the hologram can be used to reconstruct the whole hologram and each change to one point of the hologram affects the hologram in its totality.[14]

The word hologram has its origin in the Greek prepositive *holo* which means "all" or "complete." The idea that underlies a hologram is that a whole, in spite of being able to be divided into smaller parts, continues to be represented as a totality.

But what is a hologram? It is a special kind of photograph that produces a three-dimensional image created by patterns of interference of energy.

This photograph is generally obtained using the coherent radiation of a laser.

"The laser light is divided in such a way that one part illuminates the object and the other part shines directly on a photographic plate... The result of the interference of these two laser beams of light produces a three-dimensional photograph, spread over the photographic plate, where any part of the photographic surface has the full image,

---

[12] Goswami, *Visionary Window*, Portuguese edition (Editora Cultrix), 53
[13] Mermin, D., Boojums All the Way Through: Communicating Science in a Prosaic Age. Cambridge University Press, 1990, pg. 119.
[14] Bhom, David, Wholeness and the Implicate Order (London: Routlegde & Kegan Paul, 1980).

but on a smaller scale.
Said simply, each part of the photograph is a hologram, showing the All."[15]
For example, in a holographic photograph of a daisy, the greater the spreading of the image of the flower and reduction of the size of the daisy, the flower would always be shown as complete—whole in itself.
Accepting this holographic vision, in which the universe is a dynamic and coherent whole both in a potential state as well as in a manifested state, represented in numerous forms, contexts and dimensions it is possible to understand that any of those possible manifestations contains the totality in itself, but only on a smaller scale.
In the cosmic hologram, each point of the hologram, whether we call it a planet, a flower, an earring, a cell, a proton or neutrino, mirrors the integrity, the whole and it is intimately connected and in communication, being that any alteration to a part of the hologram, causes a change in the whole hologram, affecting all the cosmos.

Do we understand that through this principle one small change in us can totally revolutionize our life and affect the universe integrally?

6) Interconnectivity: A network of life in which entities are interdependently connected, whether internally or externally, to a field, a system, a cell, an atom, or an object.
The origin of life is unity—the field of unified consciousness. The unity links us inexorably and coherently to one another and to all that is, in a gigantic and multidimensional tapestry. Effectively, the threads are interlaced and woven, mutually affecting each other and the tapestry, and creativity is all developing.
What interconnectivity reveals is that — which is one is inseparable —, and that once connected, we are potential and indefinitely connected. Additionally, we find that interrelations and interactions in the field and between all expressions of life are creatively evolving, expanding our perception of the universe.

Is it possible that through this principle we become aware that after all, We Are One, always connected, creative by nature?

♥ Stop, Breathe, Love

So, what does this mean? It means that the field of unified consciousness—the information field—has an all embracing and genial way of functioning, challenging us to look towards the "outside" and towards the "inside" in the same "place," which is the unity. To understand the way it works we have to be intimate with nature and with ourselves.

Observing life from an ordinary perspective, objectively and deterministically speaking, we live in a mechanical universe, of which we are separate entities. Reality exists independently of my observation or participation.
This universe is ruled by laws of cause and effect that determine and fix reality in time and space in an absolute manner. The phenomena are conditioned by continuous and

---

[15] Langford, Michael, *Fotografia Básica*, (Basic photography), Portuguese 5th edition, Dinalivro, 2003.

localized movement. Anything that occurs, or any action that we do, needs time and has to travel a distance.

On the other hand, this perception of a physical separation between me and others, animals, plants or objects, prevents me from consciously being in communion and intervening in life, not being liable for what happens to me, or to others, to the planet or to the universe. The sensation is of isolation and separation, because life happens to me, and apparently I have no power to participate in it and to fulfill myself in my own way. I am probably at the mercy of a hostile universe that does not know me, and does not take into account what I think, wish or feel and the magic of life, the miraculous and the sacred are illusions.

What is the meaning of life like this? Who are we here? Are we mere coincidences, fruit of evolution, without a purpose or mission in the world?

Being attentive in life in an extraordinary perspective and "tempering" objectivity with subjectivity. We live in an intelligent and sensitive universe—the field of unified consciousness—with which we are connected on a fundamental level and with whom we are a team. Reality is also riddled with us and we take part in it at each moment.
In the field of unified consciousness—the information field—transcending space and time is possible, and whatever we wish, think or feel can occur instantly because it was and will always be within the field.
We are interwoven with each other, in nature, in the stars and, in essence, we are just one. Each one of us is responsible for ourselves\ and for all of life and has in himself the whole universe.
Quoting the quantum physicist David Bohm *"In some sense man is a microcosm of the universe; therefore what man is, is a clue to the universe. We are enfolded in the universe."*[16]

♥ Stop, Breathe, Love

What quantum physics is showing us is that, on a microscopic scale, the rules of conventional science are transcended. On a quantum level, reality exists in a state of pure potential, being that the subatomic particles do not exist in set places, they are in movement, they sometimes appear and sometimes disappear, showing only tendencies to exist.
There is a super luminal coherence that functions beyond causality, continuity, locality, determinism and strong objectivity. Subatomic particles behave in an unpredictable manner, able to be in two places at the same time, communicating beyond space and time, transcending the speed of light and interacting non-locally, and showing us the possibilities of being infinitely connected.
Well, on a fundamental level, we are energy. We are also quantum compounds, made of waves, particles and more — We Are Consciousness-— and it is our consciousness that will decide how a quantum object (for example, an electron, a photon) will be manifested and where.
In agreement with this, if the subatomic particles can, then we who are capable of

---

[16] http://www.brainyquote.com/quotes/quotes/d/davidbohm392793.html.

affecting them, can too. We are creators of reality, on a full time basis.
Yes, we can do things that challenge the linear logic, the laws of conventional physics and transcend ourselves infinitely. That is our quantum nature. Therefore, a change in our perception is essential.

The perception has to be of inclusion. Of being intimately connected to all and to everything—to the field of unified consciousness, the information field — and of being simultaneously an information field informing and forming life.
This perception about Who We Are is so radical that it places us on top of the world, with open arms for life and for ourselves. We are available to take part in a journey where we are whole, with our feet well set on the ground, connected to nature, with an expanded heart and connected with the cosmos. The feeling is one of belonging and of vitality because we are the power of realizing ourselves and affecting the All.
The repercussions are many, starting with our family or work relationships, to health, politics, or ecology; everything changes.
With the perceptual lenses clarified, we understand and experience that we are unlimited, as is the field of unified consciousness—the information field.
We can communicate with an aunt in Brazil, without using the telephone or Skype, because that which we are made of is with us and with that aunt, immediately and always. We are all connected to all points in space and so is the aunt and us as well, sharing information. We can decide the result of an experience, for example, at work and in our favor, even before it has happened, because we focus and feel it as accomplished. Our observation, desiring a result, causes the manifestation.
We are integrated in a web of light that acknowledges and dignifies each desire, idea, advice or gesture, transforming it also in its will and the collective and cosmic realization.
We leave our mark on everything we do, think, feel or are. After all, we are the magicians and the magic, the synchronization and perfection is the natural state of our life, the planet and the field of unified consciousness that operates with us and us with it.
We give sense, form and significance to life because we are one with it. Who We Are is present and communicating at each moment, on the highest level. We are the sensibility and the intelligence, creating, and recreating itself, and developing purposefully, in unison with the field of unified consciousness.
Think about this: what is one, unites—that is the fundamental contribution that we have to share with humanity.
Through the perception of inclusion, we feel immensely powerful and also greatly responsible for the good as well for the not so good, which is happening in our lives, in the world and in the cosmos.
The possibilities already exist in the field of unified consciousness—the information field—we only need to know how to use them and what will we construct.

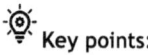 Key points:

- Consciousness is the genesis of everything.
- The void is full of possibilities. The quantum womb gives birth to all life.
- There is a field of unified consciousness that creates all reality. This field

is the creator of space and time and it is beyond it. Is what creates all forms, and is formless; also transcend all forms. It is what observes, what witnesses life and at the same time creates it, intervening in it with us.
- Matter on a fundamental level is not a thing, is energy, quanta.
- Quantum Physics, which studies events on a microscopic level (the forces underlying our physical world), presents the universe as a field of infinite probabilities and reality, on a fundamental level, is energy, waves/particles, in movement.
- Each human being has a participatory role, interfering with this quantum world creating reality also.
- Understanding six principles related with quantum physics can help us to have a different view about what is reality and Who We Are.
- Changing our perception, being included in the universe, connected to all, and naturally to the field of unified consciousness, the information field, is essential.
- Effectively, we give meaning and give form to life because we are one with it, and it communicates with us, showing us what we are creating and giving us the opportunity to recreate anew.

Self-reflection:
❶ Have you ever perceived energy or fields of energy?
❷ What aspects of quantum physics have aroused your interests?
❸ Today, are you aware that you are connected to life?

Exercise:
Sit with your back straight, close your eyes, and breathe deeply nine times.
Be aware of yourself.
Be aware of your energy at this moment.
Be still.
Focus on the stillness that already exists within you, through you and all around you.
When you feel ready you may open your eyes and maintain the stillness within you.

If it is easier for you, you can download the questions at:
www.susanacorderosa.com

2 The Senses

Story
A long time ago, in a distant kingdom, lived a miller. This man led a quiet life. His days were spent working and some were so lonely, that his only company was the sound of the grinding mill. One day, he sat in silence at the mill, watching the grain when he began to hear sounds coming from inside him. It was a melody that sounded like a stream running on a summer's day.
Another day, while working, there was a sudden flash and a clear image of himself occurred to him. Only it was very strange—He was older, married with children, and had many horses. In actuality, he only had a donkey. How could this be?
One sunny morning, he was talking to his neighbor José and understood him so well it was almost like being inside of him. He even knew what exactly what José would say next. The miller was stunned with what was happening to and thought: I must be going mad. How can this be?
In order to understand what was happening to him, the miller went to speak to a wise man in the village and told him about his experience. After listening to the miller, the wise man said:
"Rest, dear soul, because life runs through us in many ways and you are in tune with it."
After saying this, he said no more and looking the miller in his eyes, bade him farewell.

"It is only necessary for me to see clearly, with the eyes or the ears, or with any other sense, for me to feel that it is real. I may even feel two things that are unconjugable at the same time. It does not matter."
Fernando Pessoa

"Each of us contains the information about the entire universe and all of existence, ... all of its parts, and in a sense is the whole cosmic network, to the same degree..."
Stanislav Grof

Have you ever felt that what you were capturing of reality was beyond the five senses? Did you ever experience a situation in which you had no idea how to interpret or even store it in your mental boxes? It is very probable. Just like the miller in our story, did you think you had gone totally mad? Or did you even try to better understand what was happening? Possibly both.
The issue is that we start from the assumption that we only have five senses, which is an outdated concept, and we limit our observation of the world and our understanding of it through this old and reductive idea.
In effect, we are a field of information, linked to the field of unified consciousness, which is the source of all information and we are systematically receiving data from it at a high speed. However, we are not always aware of it, considering that the information is multidimensional, and we condition ourselves to receiving it through the usual channels—the five senses.
What to do then? First, we should expand the perception that there are more senses, understand their function, and try to engage with them on a daily basis. Since the

Ancient Greek civilization, it has been believed that we have five senses (vision, taste, touch, hearing and smell) with some acceptance of intuition as the "sixth sense". However, the range of senses was extended, namely by Physiologist Wolfgang Von Buddenbrock, who considered there to be nine senses (temperature, pain, balance and muscular sense),[1] and by Rudolf Steiner who considered the existence of twelve senses (life, movement, balance, heat, speech, thought and I).[2] In this chapter, we will consider the ideas of both authors.

We assume that there are sixteen senses: hearing, vision, smell, taste, touch, vitality, movement, equilibrium, thermal, empathy, clairvoyance, clairaudience, telepathy, intuition, inspiration and the sense of self.

Before approaching them, we need to better understand what is information and the information field. Therefore, we will start there.

Information for the majority of people is perceived as data, however this only one of the perspectives to understand information. *In-forma-tion* can be seen as potential, something that as within itself the possibility to become a form. And *en-forma-tio*n, is the act of getting a form, putting a form into something, the materialization. Information and enformation are two faces of the same coin and are inseparable. The unified field of consciousness is information in potential state and is also enformation what gives form to everything.

The information field is a self-conscious entity. This means that it has consciousness of itself and is also conscious of the relationships that are established between itself as the subject and the object.

The field is both self-referential and the reference of all its creations, establishing dynamic and interactive relationships with them. It is potential information, as well as enformation manifested holographically, mirroring the information that it has already contained, contains and will contain, and communicates it actualized in the all and for the All.

♥ Stop, Breathe, Love

Human beings are conscientious information in human form and are continually enformed and informed by the field of information, the unified field of consciousness and informing and enforming the field.

This informational symbiosis between the field of unified consciousness and the field of human consciousness is automatic, since the field of unified consciousness is the matrix of all the creations and the informational origin of manifested and non-manifested life.

The field of unified consciousness is in constant dialogue with us and with all creations. We are also having a quantum conversation with the field of unified consciousness at all moments of our life.

Subsequently, the human being "receives" and processes the information from the field of unified consciousness, from his field and other fields, namely, those of other people, animals, plants, objects and Earth, through the senses. The senses are organs of multidimensional perception, which capture the visible and invisible reality.

---

[1] Mora, José Ferrater, *Dicionário de Filosofia* (Philosophy dictionary, Portuguese edition), Allianza Editora, pg. 2997.
[2] Steiner, Rudolf, "The Riddle of Humanity," (GA 170), Conference at Dornach (1916).

With the senses, we capture mostly images, smells, sounds, movements, temperatures, intuitions, and a great amount of information existing in the world.

As the information we receive is immense (to understand this immenseness, we need only consider the information of the whole universe), we were provided with different senses.

Some capture the more subtle information, such as intuition; others that which is "denser," such as the sense of smell. It is still information, it just moves more "rapidly" than the other.

One originates in the field of unified consciousness (intuition) and the other could originate in the human or planetary field. As example is the smell (classical sense) of something good. Its origin can either be the first field, if it comes from the perfume we are wearing, or from the second field in the case of the smell of wet earth.

Some of the senses will capture information in an apparently linear, continuous form, locally and objectively. Other senses capture information on a quantum level, being in automatic communication and correlation with the field of unified consciousness—the information field.

We reiterate that the function of each sense is to capture reality. More appropriately, the "material" or "immaterial" reality and make it present for the human being and once he is in possession of the information, man decides what to do with it. For example, I may receive the inspiration for a symphony and accept it or not. However, that information reached me through the sense of inspiration.

We will explain here only the senses of vitality, movement, equilibrium, thermal, empathy, clairvoyance, clairaudience, telepathy, intuition, inspiration and the sense of self, totaling eleven, because the other five are already familiar.

The sense of vitality

This sense permits us to perceive the state of natural harmony, of health and when we are moving away from it. It is this sense that gives us information about the levels of energy, mood and information about feeling strong or weak or if something is not right with us, especially if we are getting ill.

We receive information from the human energy systems and the consciousness/brain matrix processes it, defines it, interprets it, organizes it and memorizes it, giving us information about the level of vitality.

The sense of movement

This sense captures information about changing energy, whether this is felt in terms of an internal change, a new creative impulse, a sense of circulation of energy, speed, agitation, a sensation of stillness or slowness, a change of place in space and time, the degree of liveliness, etc.

We receive information through the sense of movement and the consciousness/brain matrix processes it, defines it, interprets it, organizes it and memorizes it so that later the mechanisms of internal self-regulation work.

The sense of equilibrium

This sense allows us to have the perception of verticality and being in harmony.

Underlying the human condition, is the notion of being erect, having a vertical axis on which all structure rests. In equilibrium, in the verticality, the energy flows, passing through this vertical channel.

In the inner ear, we have sensors that detect the information of equilibrium, which is processed, defined, interpreted, organized and stored at the consciousness/brain matrix level.

The thermal sense

This sense allows us to perceive temperature, not only internally but externally as well. We collect thermal information through the thermal sense, and the consciousness/brain matrix processes it on the level of the hypothalamus (deep brain area) which, upon receiving this information, coordinates the internal activity from the nervous system to the endocrine system, so that the temperature is regulated.

For example, if the temperature is high, it provokes vasodilation of the capillaries permitting the blood to cool, or provokes the sense of thirst, urging us to drink water. I am sure the senses that I have just mentioned (vitality, movement, equilibrium and thermal), can be easily recognized as the information they provide is already familiar. We will now look at another level with the senses of empathy, clairvoyance, clairaudience, telepathy, intuition, inspiration and the sense of self, which receive the information directly from the field of unified consciousness—the information field— making it available in the consciousness/brain matrix instantaneously.

The sense of empathy

Do you remember the miller in the story, who understood his neighbor so well that he seemed to be inside him? The character was so scared that he wanted to understand what was happening... and readers, have you ever felt empathy with someone? Who knows if you felt it when you fell in love, or even with a stranger?

How is it possible to be who we are and be able to understand or observe what another person sees, if we are separated and different from them? And what if we are always connected to one another and are on a fundamental basis, the same being?

Then it would naturally be possible to "receive this information" without having to change roles because we would only be "reading-sensing" information and we would be grateful for that.

The truth is that you already have the sense of empathy to capture that information and use it as you wish to.

The sense of empathy allows us to have a perception of the "I" of the "other" in a broader and deeper sense. Through empathy, we connect with the energy field of the "other" being and we receive it. We can feel what the other feels, think what the other thinks, and see life as the other sees life, even though there is no physical, verbal or visual contact with the other.

Through the sense of empathy, we are "reading" what is happening in the energy field of the "other" being in a direct manner, and we receive that information in accordance with our quantum nature. We are a point of the whole and we are always potentially interconnected with it.

Perhaps you are thinking "This is far too strange or esoteric for me. How can I know if this is true? Is there scientific proof of empathy?".

There are scientific experiments that show that it is possible to feel empathetically what another feels (good or bad) or what another sees or hears.

In his book *The Whispering Pond*, Dr. Ervin Laszlo points out that it is possible for *"identical twins to feel the pain, the traumas and the crises of their twin, even if he is on the other side of the world."* We accept this as the sense of empathy working. It is also possible for one entity to see what another sees or feels, even if the subjects are separated and isolated electromagnetically.

The scientist Jacobo Grinberg Zylberbaum proved that it was possible to have communication and transfer of information between separated subjects. He conducted an experiment with a couple in which each of them was sent into a separate room, electromagnetically isolated and were connected to an electroencephalogram. One of them was subjected to a set of stimuli (flashes of light, sounds or short and intense electric shocks on the right ring finger) and when these stimuli occurred, these were represented in the electroencephalograph of the subject in question. It was found that there was communication at a distance of what the other person was seeing and feeling: *"The couple, who were deeply in love, revealed patterns intimately synchronized in the electroencephalogram feeling (...) a deep unity."*[3]

The psychologist, Charles Tart in Berkeley, carried out an experiment to see if it was possible to empathetically feel the pain of another person. For that effect, he monitored various people on the level of blood volume and heartbeat, etc. When the psychologist gave himself electric shocks, without the people who were the object of this experiment being aware, *"on a non-conscious level, they registered drops in the blood volume and increase of heartbeat revealing an empathic connection."*[4]

It is truly disconcerting to think about the capability we have to feel what another feels. Have you thought of the implications this has for your life?

♥ Stop, Breathe, Love

The sense of clairvoyance or remote vision

We return to the miller, our dear character whose senses worked so well. Do you remember that he saw things in the future (that he was married with children) and did not understand where these visions came from?

Perhaps the reader may also have seen images or visions that cannot be explained in the present moment? Maybe you did not even pay attention to these because it was a dream or because the images you saw did not seem to fit with reality.

Is it possible to receive images of future moments? And images of the past? And what do we do with this highly classified information?

Yes, it is possible, and we will explain why.

The sense of clairvoyance or remote vision allows us to capture image information, without needing to use our eyes to physically see. We see internally, in the mind. The consciousness/brain matrix is the holographic station, reproducing the images that this sense has captured and mirrors them like a big screen.

Through the sense of clairvoyance, we access image information independently of its

---

[3] Laszlo, E. *The Whispering Pond: A Personal Guide to the Emerging Vision of Science*, Element, 1996, summarized from pgs. 135 - 136 of the Portuguese edition.

[4] Tart, C., "Physiological Correlates of PSI Cognition," International Journal of Parapsychology, Vol. 5, No. 4, 1963, summarized from pgs. 375-86.

dimension, its nature, the type of experience or event, state or type of entity, etc.

In effect, we receive data instantaneously from any "place" that exists in the universe and from any time (past, present or future). This information is obtained directly and instantaneously from the field of unified consciousness and communicated simultaneously to the consciousness/brain matrix that reproduces it.

The consciousness/brain matrix functions in a network with the field of unified consciousness, where correlation and communication exist and are instantly actualized.

It seems like science fiction, or something so mystical that we hesitate to believe that it is possible to access information in this way. But it is true: we do have this sense and there is scientific proof of this.

There were scientific experiments carried out at Stanford Research Institute in California and also in American and ex-Soviet Union military bases that showed, through what the scientists called remote vision, that it was possible to see places where people and things would be in advance. The scientists Russell Targ and Hal Puthoff carried out various experiments in this field. In one of them an individual named "Harold Sherman was able, through remote vision, to know information about planetary conditions on Mercury and Jupiter, which were previously considered invalid by astrophysicists, but later, these conditions were confirmed and validated by NASA."[5]

According to the quantum physicist Dr. Amit Goswami, paranormal phenomena such as remote vision, involve non-locality—instant communication and interaction, at any distance and at any time—and result from a quantum leap beyond space-time and *"this is possible due to the quantum nature of our brain, which allows it to automatically know the information"*.[6]

In another experiment carried out by the above mentioned scientists, Ingo Swann (an artist) was asked to use remote vision to identify a place which would not be on a conventional map and to describe the weather conditions of that place, at that time. Ingo Swann entered into an altered state of consciousness, where he focused on and began to give information about an island in the Indian Ocean, only identifiable on military maps. Furthermore, he stated that the American army was unaware of the existence of a secret Soviet weather station, and he was even able to describe the weather conditions on the island at that moment in time.[7]

What the studies carried out by Russel Targ and Hal Puthoff also showed was anyone can use remote vision if they are in a state of altered consciousness, relaxed, and aligned with the field of unified consciousness.

Using the sense of clairvoyance, where information is obtained instantaneously, is the result of a correlation between the brain and the nonlocal consciousness. A form of resonance occurs through the field of unified consciousness, and the field of the individual works as a receptor and reader of the information which is stored and available to be accessed.

On another level, the sense of clairvoyance can also be used to make medical diagnoses

---

[5] Targ, R. and Puthoff, H., MindReach: Scientists Look at Psychic Abilities, Delacorte Press, 1977, summarized from text, and Targ, R., and Harary, K., The Mind Race: Understanding and Using Psychic Abilities, Villard Books, 1984.

[6] Goswami, A., *The Self-Aware Universe: How Consciousness Creates the Material World*, Putnam´s Son, 1995, pg 130.

[7] Targ, R., and Harary, K., The Mind Race: Understanding and Using Psychic Abilities, Villard Books, 1984, and Targ, R. and Puthoff, H., MindReach: Scientists Look at Psychic Abilities, Delacorte Press, 1977, summarized from text.

at a distance. In his book *The Whispering Pond*, Dr. Ervin Laszlo describes experiments carried out by the American surgeon Norman Shealy, who works in partnership with a medical clairvoyant, Caroline Myss. He gives her the name and date of birth of the patient over the phone, so that a diagnosis can be made. In spite of a distance of many kilometers, the diagnosis is made accurately, using the sense of clairvoyance, *"with a success rate of 93%, in a 100 cases."*[8]

The power that each human being has to access the image library of the field of unified consciousness is unbelievable. We can see images of the whole or any part of the whole, at any moment and in any place. After all, we are unlimited and we have unlimited access to the information of the field.

The hologram is real and is always available to be accessed.

What would change in our lives if we used this sense more often?

Would we understand beforehand what would happen at work meeting and assume the correct attitude? Or when looking at someone and having a perception of a brilliant zone in his/her body, would we tell them?

And who knows, would we observe the interior of our own body before going to the doctor? There are so many possibilities available to us...

♥ Stop, Breathe, Love

The sense of clairaudience

Do you still remember the character in the story? The miller who could hear inside himself a melody of running water like a stream on a summer day.

Who knows if you, the reader, have already perceived an internal sound? A sound very different from all others that flows through you in a very clear manner and resonates within you. It may be just a musical note or another sound. It is also possible that it is a voice transmitting information that is confirmed to be accurate, normally retrospectively.

The sense of clairaudience allows us to perceive an internal and/or external sound, and this information may be known or unknown.

When using the sense of clairaudience, we place ourselves in tune with the field of unified consciousness, the consciousness matrix, which contains unlimited and instantaneously accessible information. This information is communicated simultaneously to the brain, which functions as a quantum data receptor, reproducing the sound information and making it available and accessible.

We can receive data from the past, present, or future, and also receive information that can be contextualized spatially on planet Earth, or maybe from another planet or solar system. We can receive sound impressions from people, objects, plants, mountains and other entities.

We can hear the music of the spheres and the singing of our soul.

The reception of this information can occur in an altered state of consciousness (for example, in meditation), or when we are anaesthetized, unconscious, in a coma or even going through a near death experience.

Here are some scientific experiments and other materials that corroborate what we

---

[8] Laszlo, E. The Whispering Pond, Portuguese edition, summarized from pgs 135 - 136.

have been exposing:

For example, Dr. Bernie S. Siegel, in his book *Love, Medicine and Miracles*, attests that there are surgeons who, during lumbar region surgeries, transmit messages to the patients when they are under anesthesia so that after the surgery the patients are able to relax their pelvic muscles and urinate normally. It was confirmed that the patients not only listened, but reacted, conforming with the instructions given, as they urinated without a probe.[9]

This would only be possible if at a non-conscious level, they captured the information and were listening. In reality, they were capturing the information, through the sense of clairaudience, which works in a nonlinear manner, and captures information in a quantum manner.

On the other hand, people who went through experiences of near death and then came back to life—namely in situations of heart attacks or during surgeries— are still hearing. They mention besides the feeling of being outside their bodies and very light, they also heard voices speaking in the room and were aware, in some cases, that they heard the voice of an angelic being who communicated with them. The sense of clairaudience is active even in these conditions.[10]

In this case, I remember a situation when, in an altered state of consciousness, I also captured information directly from the field of unified consciousness via clairaudience. A friend called me from the Algarve, saying that she needed to help her doctor's son. The boy of seventeen had been involved in an accident and was in a coma. My friend asked me if I could do something to bring him back.

I did not know the father or the son, and I knew nothing of their lives. I entered into a state of altered consciousness and tuned into the field of unified consciousness and simultaneously with the consciousness of this boy. I asked him what I should know.

The darkness was immense but the universal consciousness, which is all, answered me, telling me the reason for the accident, which was family problems between the parents. The boy felt the need to break with everything, especially with the lies and also explained how tempted he was to disappear to end his suffering. I asked him to consider other possibilities and informed him that he would be helped. I stressed that whatever his decision, he would be respected and loved. I thanked the universal consciousness and returned to my normal state of consciousness. This process was very intense for me.

Two days later my friend phoned me to thank me, saying that the boy had come out of the coma. I shared with her the experience I had had and imagine the mix of surprise and gratitude I felt when I realized that every thing the universal consciousness had told me coincided exactly, verbatim, with what my friend was telling me about this family.

It sounds like fiction or supernatural phenomena, to be able to capture information in this manner, but it is real and it is happening every day. This is the result of our quantum nature, and of living in the field of unified consciousness, where we are linked to one another and are part of the web of life. It is possible to communicate instantaneously through different systems of energy, independent of their spatial or temporal location.

---

[9] Siegel, B.,"Love, Medicine and Miracles", Harper & Row, 1986, Summarized from pg. 76 of the Portuguese edition.
[10] Moody, R., *Vida depois da Vida* (Life after Life), 1st Portuguese edition, Editora Pergaminho, 2006.

♥ Stop, Breathe, Love

The sense of telepathy

Do you remember the TV series *Space 1999*, where one of the characters communicated telepathically?
The character was able to read thoughts and used that information to make decisions. Have you ever had a conversation with either a friend or someone else, when even before they had spoken, you knew what they were going to say and said it for them? I am sure you have. It is common for people to say "You must have read my mind".
Or have you ever been about to phone your beloved, when suddenly the telephone has rung? In fact, the information was captured through the sense of telepathy and instantaneously data appeared in the consciousness/brain matrix.
The sense of telepathy allows us to perceive what another person is thinking, no matter where they are or when the thought occurred. The brain works like a quantum entity, in correlation with the field of unified consciousness, with an instantaneous interaction and transfer of information between the two entities.
A scientific experiment, carried out by the neurophysiologist Jacobo Grinberg-Zylberbaum and his team, describes how the sense of telepathy could function. Two volunteers "were introduced to getting to know each other and then to feel one another in a meditative silence for 20 min". Then these two people were separated, into two different rooms, electromagnetically isolated and each person was connected to an electroencephalogram.
One of them was subjected to flashes of light at regular intervals. The receiver of the information did not have any stimuli. The one who was stimulated with the flashes of light showed this on the electroencephalograph. Simultaneously, the same type of brain activity was also registered on the electroencephalogram of the other person, who was not subjected to the same flashes of light.[11]
On another experiment, Dr. Giulio Ruffini and Alvaro Pascual-Leone, proved telepathic communication. "They connected one person in Mumbai, India, to a wireless headset linked to the internet, and another person to a similar device in Paris. When the first person merely thought of a greeting such as "ciao", Italian for "hello", the recipient in France was aware of the thought occurring. The subject receiving the message could not comprehend the word itself, but could report flashes of light in their brain that corresponded to the exact moment when the word "ciao" was being thought."[12]
The automatic communication between these two brains is possible due to the quantum nature of the brain and thought" with the field of unified consciousness, forming a single quantum system that allows entities to be in communication and interaction instantaneously. The wave of possibilities is superimposed, potentially everywhere (non-locally) and timelessly, and this wave can be crystallized in a moment in time defined by the consciousness of the subject in the act.[13]

---

[11] GrinbergZylberbaum, J., Delaflor, M., Attie, L., and Goswami A., "The EinsteinPodolskyRosen Paradox in the Brain: The Transferred Potential," Physical Essays, Vol.7, No 4, 1994 (summarized from pgs 422-428).
[12]   http://www.dailymail.co.uk/news/article2745797/Scientistsclaimtelepathysuccesssendingmentalmessageoneperson4000milesaway.html
[13] Goswami, A., The Self-Aware Universe: How Consciousness Creates the Material World, Putnam´s Son,

This act of consciousness is a unique act between energy systems, which are unified into a single entity by the conscious intention in the field of unified consciousness. They show coherence and the information is transmitted instantaneously.

It is extraordinary that we are able to communicate telepathically. A network like the internet is already inside us. We can receive and send information wherever we wish; we have unlimited traffic and we are not dependent on a cellphone or a computer, a pen drive or a wireless connection.

On the other hand, because we are all connected and are able to find out everything at any time, there are no more secrets. Even the things that we possibly wish to keep to ourselves are in fact available as information in the field of unified consciousness and can be known by a person who we are having lunch with, or an attendant at a clothes shop.

♥ Stop, Breathe, Love

The sense of intuition

Imagine what it would be like if we decided to accept that for every question in our lives, the answer was already available and we could access it directly? Actually, all concerns could be swept away from our minds, because their solutions already exist. Sounds like fantasy? But it is true. Through the sense of intuition, we are able to capture the information we need and relax.

The sense of intuition allows us to have a direct perception of the truth, without having to go through a process of analysis or reasoning. The information "comes" to us in an unpredictable manner and contains the essence of what we need to know, at the right moment.

This sense is already familiar to many people, at least by name. For example, some people call it the sixth sense. Others define intuition as something that they cannot explain, but they feel, or are sure is correct.

Probably everyone has already experienced a situation when their sense of intuition has warned them about a particular situation and was absolutely correct. For example, I remember being on the telephone to book a seminar in the Azores and suddenly I realized that it would not be the best date; my head shook, I groaned and I felt my heart palpitating.

Immediately, I changed the date, without understanding exactly why. A month and a half later, I realized that I already had another commitment, which I could not change. This had been booked for me without my knowledge, and it would have coincided with the first date.

I thanked my intuition for making this information available so clearly beforehand. In fact, intuition functions perfectly. It is an accurate, discontinuous, nonlocal, quantum leap of consciousness without spatial or time limitation.

The information is made available immediately and is mirrored holographically, in the field of unified consciousness. Since each one of us is also multidimensional information, we can, at any time, access the information, because it is always there. The consciousness/brain matrix is the quantum receptor of this information from the

---

1995.

field of unified consciousness, as there is a correlation and instantaneous communication between them.

Intuition is always sudden information, and may be expressed in various forms, for example, a bright idea, a feeling of happiness or love or a sensation that can be felt in the body, namely, feeling good, warm, or a localized, unpleasant feeling (for example, tinnitus, or tightness in the stomach).

It differs from person to person how the message is transmitted and understood, but the information is there, brilliant and ready to be accepted or rejected. If our consciousness accepts intuition, our life can jump on a gigantic trampoline of simplicity.

Have you thought that, from now on, you will become more receptive to your intuition? It is your internal GPS that is always available to lead and guide you, at each moment. Trusting it saves lives and allows us to be successful in all areas of our life.

♥ Stop, Breathe, Love

The sense of inspiration

Now imagine that every time you needed ideas or wanted to create something new, you would go to a "place" and you would get whatever you needed.

It could be the plan for a new bridge over the Tagus River, the spring-summer fashion collection, writing a thesis, or composing a piece of music.

Well, that place already exists; it is the field of unified consciousness and each one of us has a password to enter it, because we are already there. The inspiration we need is present in a quantum manner. All we need is to be open to our own sense of inspiration.

The sense of inspiration allows us to have a creative and direct perception of reality. Inspiration is the creative breath of the field of unified consciousness that we receive unexpectedly and which updates our consciousness and sheds light on life.

Just as with intuition, the information emerges unexpectedly. There is a quantum leap that occurs discontinuously and non-locally without going through the intermediate spaces of linear and temporally located knowledge.

Einstein stated *"I did not discover relativity just with thought."* He was inspired.

Inspiration is the unusual creative impulse, which provides not only ideas, but also the enthusiasm to create a project (a life, a book, a painting, music, a child, an invention, a building, social work, etc.). The information is revealed to us spontaneously, providing a revolutionary sense of direction or new possibilities, within that which we already knew, but with a creative and metamorphosing impulse.

Inspiration is simultaneously the creative potential and the creative action that impels the human consciousness to mold the world.

This sense captures the multidimensional information of the field of unified consciousness and is processed instantly in human consciousness. Inspiration is a springboard for consciousness that allows a human being to have a creative enlightenment on any subject, in a surprising manner.

Today is a good day to inspire and be inspired.

♥ Stop, Breathe, Love

The sense of self

Have you ever experienced a moment in your life, when for an instant, perfection was real, present, in front of you? A time when you were connected and felt the totality of yourself?

The sense of self allows us to directly perceive the One consciousness. It is the sense of being. This sense has a clear understanding (cognition) of the origin of life, its stages of development, the potential life choices, or the possibility of energy encounters, and the transitions between lives. It is the knowledge of the portals between birth and death, the communication between spiritual entities, the celestial spheres and their influence, the supra-sensitive knowledge and changes of state.

The sense of self is the total vision of being, the perfect unity of both potential and act. It is consciousness recognizing consciousness.

Accept the possibility of opening yourself to be who you really are; an unlimited and magnificent being and let life flow totally in you and through you.

Once here, I am sure that our perception of life will have changed in a huge way. After all, instead of five, we have sixteen senses, and some of them capture reality in such a way that we would not even dare to dream of. However, this is possible and can be proven and the various scientific experiments shown here are only a few of the many carried out in this field.

The vastness and scope of this multidimensional perception of the senses such as empathy, clairvoyance, telepathy or intuition is so great that it astonishes us.

After all, the universe holds no secrets for us, and shares itself so generously that we can at most enjoy the endless potential and at least, can remain receptive to the fact that we are more than what our regular senses show us.

The sixteen senses that we have listed above are tools of human perception which receive and process multidimensional information. The senses we habitually use give the appearance that there is a separation between us and the object of perception, as well as the field of unified consciousness (for example, vision). They function in an apparently linear and continuous manner, locally, inside space at a given time and at a defined speed.

On the other hand, the senses that capture information directly from the field of unified consciousness, such as intuition, clairaudience or inspiration, show us the truth about our quantum nature.

They reveal the principle of infinite possibilities, instantaneous communication and omniscient (all-knowing) information, such as discontinuous and nonlocal movement, and the transcendence of space, time and the speed of light. This forces us to accept inseparability as our real nature. That is, the consciousness in us and in everything, is omnipresent and limitless.

After all, Who Are We? We are born communicators in a constant dialogue, unlimited beings participating in life, with keen senses for transcendence.

Key points:
- Contrary to the traditional belief, we have sixteen senses: hearing, vision, smell, taste, touch, vitality, movement, equilibrium, thermal, empathy,

clairvoyance, clairaudience, telepathy, intuition, inspiration and the sense of self.
- The senses are organs of multidimensional perception, which capture the visible and invisible reality.
- Some of the senses like vision apparently show us the world, reality as linear, local and objective;
- Others, like intuition or telepathy capture information on a quantum level, and shows us how we, and everything, are interconnected and life has magic
- Our potential to communicate is limitless and we are in a constant dialogue with the field of unified consciousness, with others and the planet.
- We are always being heard and answered and we can use our sixteen senses to transform our lives. We have keen senses for transcendence.

Self-reflection:

❶ Describe an experience where you were aware of your senses, for example, the smell of wet earth.

❷ Which of the senses described in the chapter were previously unknown to you and which ones were of greater interest to you?

❸ And how does this discovery change the way you face reality?

Exercises:

❶ Write 2 experiences that you have had regarding your intuition.

- How did the intuition come?
- Did you feel any sensation or a hint about something?
- How can you be more aware of your intuition?

❷ Have you ever noticed that you are communicating telepathically with a person, an animal or plant? Describe how it was.
Make an experiment with someone you love. One of you will think about something intentionally and emit this idea to the other. Think about this for 30 seconds. Then relax. Do these 3 times.
The other person is just open, not thinking or trying to do anything. Afterwards ask the person what came into his or her mind or what kind of feeling he or she had.
Change places; now the person that was emitting becomes the receiver.

❸ Take a moment to breathe deeply. Close your eyes and focus your attention on a point near your hair line, in the center of your forehead. Stay focused there for 3 min. and ask yourself. What do I need to know? Be receptive to images, a "dejá vue", or a vision that can come to you.

3 Who Constructs Reality?

Story
A long time ago, in an enchanted place, lived a genie. Because his life was simple and pleasant, the genie was always smiling. He knew how to create reality and enjoyed doing this so much that he believed he was the happiest of beings.
One day, a little girl with big eyes and a beating heart entered his world. The genie was so happy to have company that he decided to give her all his attention.
The little girl had never seen a place like this before. It was magical. Everything she wished for appeared. Her thoughts echoed and had life. What she felt, grew, and when she moved, everything moved with her.
What kingdom was this? The child thought that she could only be dreaming, but her eyes were open. She could touch, smell and she felt that it was real. Curious, she asked the genie where she was, and he replied that she was in "The Land Where Everything Is Possible."
The little girl said, "Wow! ´The Land Where Everything Is Possible´ is fantastic! I have never heard of this place. Is it possible to take it with me?"
The genie told her that she had always been living there, but she just could not remember it.
"But how can I remember?" asked the child. The genie then decided to offer her a magic wand of creation so that she could put it into action immediately.

"In the beginning there were only probabilities. The universe could only come into existence if someone observed it. It does not matter that the observers turned up several billion years later. The universe exists because we are aware that it exists."
Sir Martin Rees

"The human observer is not only necessary to observe the properties of an object, but is necessary even to define these properties."
Fritjof Capra in the "The Tao of Physics"

Have you ever felt that you entered into another world even if it was only for an instant? Have you ever felt that life had magic, and that you were linked to that magic? And what if, like the little girl, you already lived in The Land Where Everything Is Possible, and only needed to open your eyes and heart to it? Remember that you have the power of creation inside you. Would you like to stop being a character in your life story, apparently at the mercy of others or the world? Wouldn't you rather be the director, directing the film of your life, knowing that you are more than the film? So it is. It makes you think.
I understand that I am a wave in a gigantic ocean and the way I perceive myself, the fish, the algae and the ocean, makes reality appear to me in a particular way. The way that I observe and ponder reality allows me to interfere with it. This perspective has helped me throughout my life.
Quantum physics helped me to understand that the consciousness of the observer interferes with subatomic reality through the act of observing it. Our observation brings the qualities of the subatomic world to life that go from potential to real just

from the act of focusing on them. We caused the emergence of those properties from the *"quantum gelatin[1]"* giving shape or color to the gelatin through observation or by measuring that subatomic phenomenon.

The quantum physicists understood, as they carried out experiments with subatomic entities, that human consciousness affected the experiment itself.

In 1927, Niels Bohr and Werner Heisenberg theorized that, on a fundamental level, subatomic entities existed as waves of infinite possibilities in a quantum soup. They saw that such entities did not have a precise location or defined state, until something happened and converted them into one of the possibilities, into a determined quantum object with a determined location. And that *something* was observation by a human being. The simple act of looking, and of having a certain intention, thought or feeling, interferes with the execution of a given experiment.

Is it possible to admit that the subatomic world is also waiting for us in order to be realized? And that our acts of observation are really important? Effectively yes, on a quantum level the act of observing a quantum entity affects it, i.e., we cannot separate the observer from what is observed.

One of the most intriguing experiments which can explain this point of view is the double slit experiment. Here is a simple explanation:

1) A light source illuminates two narrow adjacent slits in a screen. The light (waves) passes through the two slits and it is projected on a second screen. The waves interfere like ripples in a pond. They appear as a series of dark and light fringes on the wall, revealing an interference pattern.

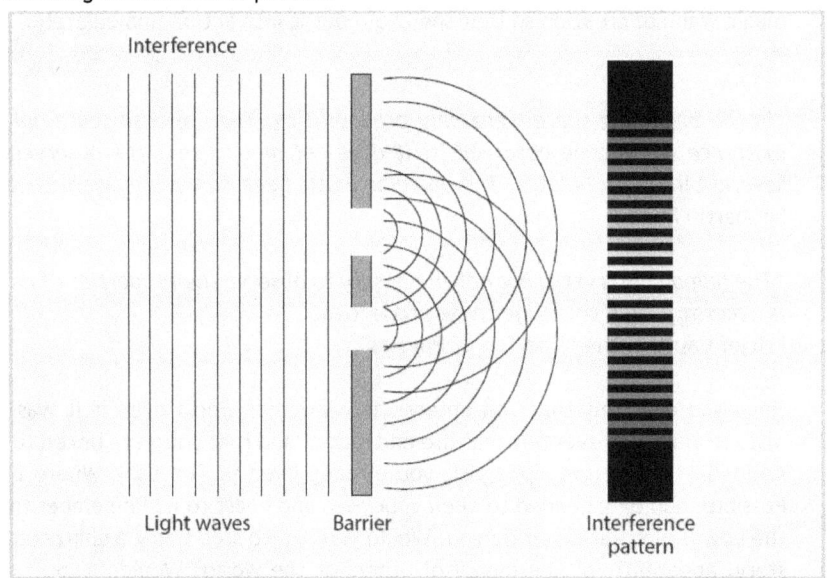

2) Imagine now doing this but instead of waves, using particles/electrons like" tiny balls", passing through the two slits. If the particles behave accordingly with classic physics, each particle will either pass through one slit or the other. And on the second screen we will have only two lines, two peaks, representing particle behavior. But it is

---

[1] Lynne Mctagart also uses this concept on her book "The Field" HarperCollins Publishers

not the reality in the quantum realm. The particles will present a pattern of interference, which is not logical at all. How could this be?

3) So, the scientist thought, what if instead of sending a big amount of particles, he would only send them one by one, slowly, and see what happens? Does the interference pattern shows up again? In this scenario, the particles were sent one by one and passed through the slits. Firstly, they appeared randomly on the screen. But, gradually, the pattern of interference appears again. How can this be? They were particles/electrons, individualized entities; how can they behave as waves, producing an interference pattern?

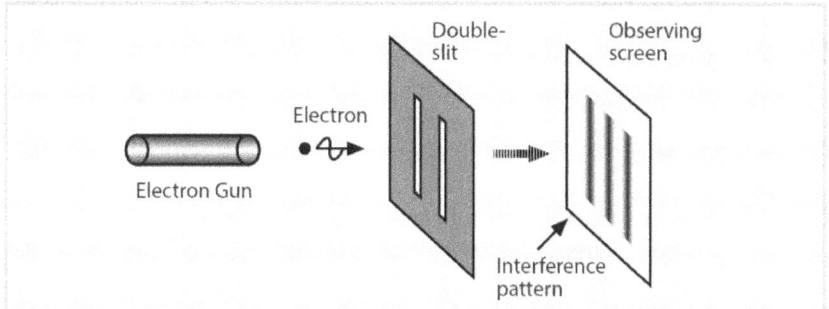

4) How can a small particle, which had arrived as localized point on the screen, become something different?

The particle must be aware there were two slits, not one, giving birth to this interference pattern, and changing their "natural" behavior. But how?

5) The scientist needed to investigate more and put a detector, spying through which slit the particle would go through. The detector was put above the upper slit designed to flash or beep when the particle passes through the upper slit. 50% of the time the detector will beep. The other 50% of the time the detector would not beep, assuming the particle would go through the lower slit. So, each particle indeed passed through one slit or the other. The result was a particle pattern, completely different. Strange, isn't it? Again, it seems like the particles knew someone was observing them.

6) Now the intriguing part. The scientist decided to maintain the detector but unplugged to see what would happen. The results were completely abnormal. The interference pattern appeared again.

So, what can we infer from this? The subatomic world is altered by the human observer. When we observe an electron, and we want to know, for example, through which slit it has crossed, this intentional observation affects the behavior of the electron. The quantum reality that we are observing at that moment is the product of what we focused on. The consciousness of the observer interacts with what is observed and affects it.[2]

Einstein already stated that *"observing means we have constructed some connection between a phenomenon and our conception of the phenomenon"*. This suggests that nothing in the universe is independent of our observation/perception of things. It

---

[2]

https://images.search.yahoo.com/search/images;_ylt=A2KIbZzfAltb8.wA6yFXNyoA;_ylu=X3oDMTEyanNv NWYzBGNvbG8DYmYxBHBvcwMxBHZ0aWQDQjQ4NTNfMQRzZWMDc2M?p=free+images+interference+patter ns&fr=mcafee_uninternational

suggests that our consciousness, when observing, is giving life to that which is being observed, and in accordance to this, at each moment we are creating a reality (a house, an interview for a job, a recovery of health, the relationships we have, etc.).

It is absolutely incredible to understand that, after all, we are a part of the subatomic world and that it is concerned with us. It is true; it is concerned with our observation, desire or meaning and accepts it. We are creating reality moment by moment, from dealing with a technical issue with our computer, to the act of making love, to earning more money, or creating safety.

If however, your perception is stubbornly attached to the solidity of objects, and you cannot understand how you interfere with them or create them, simply become open to the idea that, fundamentally, objects are energy, just like you are. Both have the same origin: the field of unified consciousness. Quantum physics states that even solid objects are energy, they are waves of probabilities in movement, that is, they are probabilities of things and the observer has a participative role in the creation of reality.

It is human consciousness that gives form to an experience and delivers it to the field of unified consciousness which accepts it totally, making it present at the exact time that we are living it. Like an enormous screen, the field of unified consciousness mirrors everything that our consciousness is focused on. This is true for good things, adversities, illnesses, miracles, debts, abundance, love, joy and happiness; the consciousness reflects everything without any judgment or interference. It only gives us the possibility to continuously create, over and over and over again.

♥ Stop, Breathe, Love

Now that we understand that we are the creators, **working in partnership with the field of unified consciousness,** we may ask ourselves what can we create.

The truth is that we can create everything. Remember that we live in The Land Where Everything Is Possible... From a quantum point of view, we live in a universe with unlimited possibilities; therefore, the creations that are possible are also unlimited.

We were conceived to create and the field of unified consciousness provided us with a special language, a system of communication to share information with it and it with us, so we can build reality together. This is the language of creation—The Code of Creation.

You know this language innately. You have always communicated with it. The language of creation is attention, intention, thought, image, word, feeling, emotion and action. This language is simultaneously information and enformation. In other words, it transmits data and gives form, embodying life. This language is common to the field of unified consciousness and human beings. We share the information in the field of unified consciousness—and it is available to build reality.

Each one of these energies (attention, intention, thought, image, word, feeling, emotion and action) is, by itself, creative and capable of bringing experiences to life. That is, a thought creates reality, just as an image or a feeling, because they are energy. However, it is also important that they are all aligned in the same direction, like a laser, so that the results are manifested.

Together, these energies are a cohesive whole, highly efficient in the creation of life. They are interconnected and cooperate so that you can fully realize your potential.

These energies move through you, causing the field of unified consciousness to actualize itself.

I am certain that you are already using the language of creation because it is part of you and part of the whole universe. Up to now, you may not have had a clear perception of its role in building your life. From the moment you begin to use it on a daily basis, you will experience a quantum leap. I know this from my own experience, and there are many other people whose lives have changed radically for the better by using this information.

It is true; you will become a deliberate creator instead of a disoriented creator. You will understand that you can lead your life while being guided at the highest level and that it is fun to work in a team with the field of unified consciousness.

By using the array of energies, we are also using the "material" that composes everything—energy in movement, light and information — Consciousness vibrating. That which constitutes everything will resonate with you and respond to you.

This is the language used by the field of unified consciousness to communicate with you. It recognizes when you use it. Through the Field, each one informs and enforms life with a contour, dimension, texture, color, giving a unique form to it. In response, the field of unified consciousness informs and enforms you. This is because human beings and the field of consciousness are fundamentally connected, communicating directly and permanently; they are one.

The system of reality creation through the 8 energies is a grand process in each human being participating in life, writing his signature and leaving their mark on the world in partnership with the marking of the field of unified consciousness—the information field.

This system of reality creation of reality through the 8 energies—that are in fact only one: the energy of all—is intelligent and sensitive, available to you at every moment. 365 days a year, twenty-four hours a day. It is free and powerful.

You are using it in any place, at any time, in any situation or event. It works with you or any other person and also with animals, plants, objects or any reality.

You can only use this system of reality creation because your quantum nature only allows you to create reality at each moment. Effectively, it is not possible to resign from what you are: Consciousness in movement, a field of information in constant communication, linked to the field of unified consciousness and with the function of creating reality. You use this language—The Code of Creation—each instant.

It is now time to build reality knowing that there is a field of infinite possibilities available to you and that you already live in The Land Where Everything Is Possible. This is fantastic for you and everyone, the planet, and for the field of unified consciousness—your origin.

In the next chapters, we will address the creation language—the creation system—on the level of attention, intention, thought, image, word, feeling, emotion and action in more detail. We are going to relearn to use The Code of Creation so that we remember Who We Are: powerful creators essentially connected to life and others, capable of making existence progress. In the meantime...be happy!

Key points:
- Human beings have an active and creative role in the universe.
- We are natural influencers of the quantum world.
- What we observe is affected by our observation which brings to life characteristics, forms, colors, experiences.
- Because we are always observing the quantum world, reality is also dependent upon us.
- We constantly live and participate in the universe as we create it.
- The human consciousness shapes experiences: good things, adversities, illnesses, changes, debts, abundance, love, joy, etc., and the field of unified consciousness mirrors, like an enormous screen, everything that our consciousness is focused on.
- We have the opportunity to change reality itself.
- We were conceived to create and the field of unified consciousness provided us with a special language —The Code of Creation.
- The Code of creation is constituted by eight energies: attention, intention, thought, image, word, feeling, emotion and action, and each of these forces are by themselves creative and capable of bringing to life events, objects, experiences, meetings.
- You were born a creator of realities. You can make changes. Use your consciousness and your observations wisely.

Self-reflection:
❶ Have you ever thought that you can build reality?
❷ What, in the language of creation, drew your attention the most?

Exercise:
❶ Focus your energy on a positive outcome. Something simple for you.
Embrace the possibility that the quantum world is going to show you that result.
Have fun: make a drawing of it, sing something you like while you focus on it, be curious. When you see it manifested say to yourself: I am a creator of this and other realities. Stay aware.

4 Attention

Story
Long ago, a very rich and powerful king lived in China. The king frequently asked his councilors, "What will make my life change for the better?". But the answers he received never satisfied him.
One day the king heard from one of his friends that there was a person that could give him the answer that he had been searching for—a very wise Zen master, who lived in the mountains, about a month's travel away.
The king decided to secretly make the journey, accompanied only by his closest servant. After the month of travel, the king finally found the Zen master's house, deep in the forest. The king immediately went to the master's door and sought him out. As soon as the master appeared, the king asked him what would finally change his life for the better. The master stared at the king for a long moment, thinking. The master simply invited him to chop wood. He said,
"Concentrate on the wood, on the axe and become one with them: there you will find the answer."

"Men go forth to marvel at the heights of mountains and the huge waves of the sea, the broad flow of the rivers, the vastness of the ocean, the orbits of the stars, and yet they neglect to marvel at themselves."
Saint Augustine, *Confessions*

It is probable that each one of us has already undertaken a journey searching for something profoundly valuable and, just like the character, longed for answers. Inside of each human being there is a powerful king who desires a full life. In order to conceive it and enjoy it, we need to use attention.
In a broader sense, attention is energy, light vibrating, and information in movement in the field of unified consciousness—the field of information. It is also a language through which the field of consciousness communicates with us and us with it. Attention is an instrument at the service of the human consciousness that allows us to create reality. It is extremely important, because without attention there is no manifestation.
The field of unified consciousness is the foundation of life, both visible as well as invisible, and naturally, attention is its creation.
In order to refresh central ideas so far—there are three "origins" of attention. However, the energy of attention is unique because there is only one.
❶ Unified consciousness
❷ Individual consciousness
❸ Planetary consciousness
We will now look at each of these.

❶ Attention from the field of unified consciousness

The field of unified consciousness is the quantum womb of life. It is very probable that we have been generated by the consciousness as a result of an act of attention on itself, generating even more life, in human form.

The field of unified consciousness has endless information in potential state, as well as information already materialized in numerous forms. Because of our connection on a fundamental level, it is possible to access quantum data that vibrates in the field and simultaneously know on which *"focal point"*[1] of the matrix of the field it will direct its attention. That is, it is possible to follow each footstep of the field, where it will place the attention in the next creative instant and create in partnership with it.

When in conscious resonance with the field of unified consciousness, the consciousness/brain matrix captures this data and reveals it instantly within us and if we accept the information, it becomes available in our lives, and simultaneously, in the All.

The attention of the field of unified consciousness—the field of information—is used by the field to create reality at any nanosecond and is always accessible to us.

❷ Attention from the individual consciousness

Attention can be defined as the act or effect of us concentrating on something. We direct our attention to people, events, ideas, sentiments or objects. We capture information through the senses and give it attention, understand it and attribute it significance and worth.

The process of attention/perception happens at a great speed within us and the information that we concentrate our attention on can come from both the exterior (for example, hearing a sound or music, the taste of ice cream, someone winking) and from the inside (for example, empathizing with someone or intuiting something, etc.).

Through attention, we choose what to concentrate on, for a short or a long time, on one or various persons or things, or on what we like or dislike. The possibilities are vast.

When being attentive, we use the language of creation, irradiating that energy inside our energetic field and simultaneously to the field of unified consciousness, manifesting in our life that which we concentrated through attention, as well as the field of consciousness mirroring in the reality around us what we are bringing to life with attention.

❸ Attention from the planetary consciousness

Earth is a field of energy in movement, irradiating energy to all forms of life existing on it and to the field of unified consciousness. It receives energy and information from all people, the human collective, and from the field of unified consciousness.

When the planet accepts the focus of Humankind's attention, it processes it and retransmits it in the same vibrational frequency to the human community and the field of unified consciousness. When receiving this planetary information, each individual or group has the capacity to accept, alter or reject it, systematically feeding the planetary consciousness once again.

♥ Stop, Breathe, Love

---

[1] The author Dr. Joseph Murphy uses this term also but I use it in a different perspective.

Now that we understand attention from a broader perspective, we will focus specifically on human attention, which we—as individual consciousnesses—all produce. We will explore this in detail and from now on, when we speak of attention, perception is necessarily included because one does not occur without the other. I am also going to use the word '*observe*' and this often means, in the strict sense of the word, to observe and other times in a wider sense, which means to comprehend; it could be, for example, to listen, feel, think, wish, intuit, etc.

To begin, let's remember that attention is an instrument placed at the service of human consciousness so that it can create reality.
Attention can be defined as the act or the effect of our focus. In a broader sense, it is a process of concentration realized by the consciousness/brain matrix at a given moment and that focus on something (material or immaterial), makes it present.
Attention is a function of the consciousness/brain matrix that selects what to focus on through a multistep process of observation.
In other words: we capture information through the sixteen senses and process it internally. Through one or more acts of observation, we then selectively choose to concentrate on one piece of information amongst many others. Through attention, we elect one piece of information as being more important than the other.
Attention is closely linked to perception. They are two inseparable sides of the same coin. We consider perception to be the act or the effect of understanding the world. Perception is a dynamic web in which information and interpretation are interrelated. It is information with meaning—what that information or reality means for me.
The process of perception involves the act of directly receiving information through the sixteen senses, from observing it, selecting it, paying attention and processing it, as well as giving significance, context and a sense of adequacy to the data received. This is done in light of what we are from a mental, emotional, and behavioral point of view, but also as a soul inserted in a social, cultural and spatial-temporal context. For example: A person with a 4th grade education who is a shepherd has a different perception of reality compared to the financial director of a corporation. The perception will also be different, for example, between two brothers who have lived through the same traumatic experiences. One of them has overcome it and learned to be a better person and the other clings to what happened to him and feels like a victim of circumstances.
The perception of reality is also differentiated between a man living in Iran who professes the Koran and another man living in the West who is agnostic. It is natural that the perception of reality that we had in the 80s and the one we have now is different; we have changed and so has life.
The act of perceiving, of understanding reality, is based on information, the selection of data that attention has established, and a set of judgments, interpretations, memories, associations, emotions and experiences that can be taken into account so that the information makes sense to us.

❤ Stop, Breathe, Love

Returning to attention, we understand that it has to do with the information that we observe (internally and externally) and the information that we selectively choose to

value or give more importance to, concentrating on it for a nanosecond, minutes, hours or even years.
The question that naturally emerges is "What is attention for in life and how does it work?"
Attention serves to create reality, more appropriately, limitless possibilities of reality.
The field of unified consciousness is pure information vibrating and we are the information of that same field with a human form, living in the field, interacting and participating in the quantum information of the field of unified consciousness.
On a quantum level, matter and reality exist in a state of infinite possibilities vibrating indefinitely in the quantum soup and for this reality to go from potential to act, (being manifested) it needs a conscious entity that participates and intercommunicates with the field of unified consciousness. That entity is the human being.

When Man observes information, he observes a vast number of quantum data and in that act of observation, stops himself at one of the informational possibilities, that is, pays attention to it, and this act of concentrating on a specific piece of information crystallizes what was just potential information into "real" information and becomes manifested.
Attention is then the act of observation of the conscious/brain matrix focused on information and that focus brings to life that which was only a probability and makes it emerge as reality for us.

♥ Stop, Breathe, Love

On a quantum level, the participation of the consciousness of the observer in bringing to the fore the properties and qualities of a quantum object (electron) has attention underlying it, because it is the link that transforms the potential and concentrates it into the real.
The conscious/brain matrix observes and processes the information systematically and chooses to focus through one or successive acts of attention on one or various data that are in movement in its field of energy, showing these and giving them life, that is, making them present.
When we fix our attention, even if just for an instant, we are selecting from the possibilities to which we want to give importance and our perception focuses on an idea, emotion, person, object or event. It is this act of attention or concentration that coagulates the information that represents the idea, the person, the sentiment, the behavior or event, making it present, available for the manifestation. And it is in this sense that attention is the creator of reality.
Attention enables the-creation of observed and focused reality in tune with the field of unified consciousness and the planet, manifesting that which the consciousness/brain matrix focused on.
When changing the focus of attention, that is, when selectively paying attention to certain information, we create life and inclusively change the way life appears to us. Therefore, attention must be used intelligently, sensibly and responsibly, so that what we bring to life is good for us and for the All.
If, at this moment, our attention is on the problems with our children, the bills to be

paid, an argument with your spouse, or if God (for those who are believers) will punish us for doing something wrong, it is wise to reconsider what we are paying attention to. After all, does it make sense to bring it to manifestation?

In reality, what we actually wish is to find solutions for those issues about our children, having more money, living our relationship with our spouse harmoniously, and feeling the love of God. Therefore, it makes sense to sharpen attention on what is really good for us, creating the realities that resonate with our heart in partnership with the field of unified consciousness.

Attention and Perception

"There are those who go through the forest and only see firewood."
Leo Tolstoy

"The eye through which I see God is the same eye through which God sees me; my eye and God's eye are one eye, one seeing, one knowing, one love."
Meister Eckhart

As we said before, attention is the act or set of acts that the consciousness/ brain matrix realizes when observing and focusing selectively on one or various pieces of information, giving it momentary, or repeated prominence.

This act of consciousness creates because it interferes with the subatomic wave on the potential level and permits the coagulation of the subatomic wave as a determined and localizable particle.

Is all attention the same? Or can attention be given in various ways? There is only one attention and strictly speaking, it is a process. A dynamic activity that is carried out and occurs in our consciousness/brain matrix in accordance with the information that the sixteen senses systematically shows. It is also a process because of the mental, emotional, experiential and spiritual information that we have in memory, as well as information that is being created or recreated in our energy field and the energy that we are perceiving.

All this is magnificent and happens very quickly inside us.

In order to reply to the questions above, we will show a linear possibility of the process of attention, keeping in mind the explanation of that which is complex and that which we wish to simplify.

When faced with information, which is a constant, the consciousness/brain matrix selects:

❶ **What** to pay attention to
❷ **When** to pay attention
❸ **How** to pay attention

❶ Faced with vast information, the consciousness/brain matrix decides **What** to pay attention to, and as a result of that act of attention, we have an immediate perception of the idea, person, event, object, emotion or experience that consciousness focused on.

❷ Faced with information, the consciousness/brain matrix decides **When** to pay attention; the 'when' of attention is in the **now**, but here, as a general rule, the perception of linear time intervenes (past, present and future) and we perceive the information in a defined spatiotemporal moment.

It is common to be aware of what we are thinking, writing, speaking, imagining, feeling or experiencing at a given moment and context. For example, how often do we realize that we are now paying attention to an event that has already passed and we have the sensations of the past?

The 'when' of attention/perception can also be anchored beyond space-time. This happens when we experience states of unity with the field of unified consciousness and immediately access actualized information non-locally. We may feel that time has stopped or that time does not exist, that we are beyond Earth or the solar system, or still, we may feel we are the All or emptiness. This is an extraordinary experience.

❸ In conformity with the information, the consciousness/ brain matrix chooses **How** to pay attention and this, in turn, can be in a concentrated or distributed manner.

Attention is provided in a concentrated manner when the consciousness/brain matrix chooses to be focused exclusively on a piece of information and the rest becomes secondary at that moment, or in the following moments. Attention is in line with the information observed and is fixed on it in a unique manner. This information is edited and perceived in the energetic field with priority.

Attention is provided in a distributed manner when the consciousness/brain matrix chooses to distribute its attention on different pieces of information at that time, giving similar importance to the different pieces of information simultaneously. Attention is fragmented in respect to the information that is being observed and is distributed by various points in a plural form. This information is edited and perceived in the energetic field as equally important information.

Answering the questions "Is all attention the same? Or can it be provided in various ways?" the answer is that although attention is a unique process, it can be provided in different forms.

♥ Stop, Breathe, Love

Continuing further with what we have been explaining about attention, **do the What, When and How of attention affect perception?**

Effectively—yes, when paying attention to something we necessarily perceive. Attention and perception are closely linked: one does not happen without the other; both are part of the process of capturing reality realized by the consciousness/brain matrix.

Therefore, **What** we focus on, **When** we focus, and **How** we focus feeds perception and affects it, along with the reality that has been observed and perceived.

For example, if we are venting about an argument many hours after it happens, we are still exclusively focused on the argument, the perception of reality is naturally affected by the argument. On the other hand, if we focus on the sweet words of our husband, and we mention them to our sister and we just think how nice it is to love, this focus of attention has necessarily affected our perception and we see life with love and sweetness.

❤ Stop, Breathe, Love

I believe we understand that attention affects perception. **And does perception also interfere with attention?**

Human perception is the marriage between what is information 'in itself and personalized information—what does this information mean for me, at this moment—translating the worldview of that being.

The act or effect of giving meaning, of understanding the information, underlies attention. When we change perception, we also change attention, since we are sending different pieces of information that in turn are fixed by attention, feeding back the perception.

Each time perception is changed, we have a new possibility to focus our attention on another informational point that changes reality. For example, a friend of mine had the perception that she was too short and needed to wear high heels at work to feel right. One day, she decided to try flats. She realized that these suited her. She looked at herself various times in the mirror and liked what she saw. From that new perception of herself, she began to wear the shoes at work that she felt most comfortable with.

This can be translated from a perceptual point of view. We can say the following: First, this friend had a perception—*I only look nice if I wear high heel shoes*—then, she changed her perception—*I also look nice wearing flat shoes*—she focused her attention on the information, looking various times in the mirror—new information—the flat shoes—perception: *flat shoes also make me look good*—and reinforced that perception—*I like to see myself wearing flat shoes; I will start wearing them, etc.*

When we change perception, a variety of possibilities become available in our field of information, which are fixed by attention, reinforcing or creating new perceptions and with them distinct realities. This makes all the difference in our life, because the change of perception not only changes attention, it also changes the creation.

I am sure that we have experienced, at least once in our lifetime, a conflict with a colleague, a friend, a relative or a neighbor and we got the perception that the situation was not good. As it happens, if we change the perception—because we thought more about the issue—we give attention to other aspects and consequently, the perception of reality changes, giving us the possibility of another attitude. We may receive an apology or forgive the person in question—and that happened because we changed the perception and the attention, and we created a different reality in tune with the field of unified consciousness.

Below is a testimonial of that change with a gigantic impact.

Testimonial

I went to a consultation with Susana because I had difficulties in my relationship with my mother. Very serious things had happened between us and I felt attached to what "she had done to me." I was full of resentment and heartbreak and could not get on with my life, even though many years had passed. It was almost my birthday and I decided to give myself this consultation as a present.

During the consultation, I understood my role in the process. My attention was focused on the wrong thing—I could only see darkness and evil. I dwelled mentally on the film, the words, the pain, what she "did to me" instead of what I did to myself, for many years, giving attention to the worst and causing myself more harm with this attitude.

I felt I was no longer me... It was a staged repetition for my mind, which wanted to suffer.

With Susana, I opened my heart and began to feel love for my mother; I forgave her and found a place for her inside me. I changed my perception about her and about myself, and my reality changed 180 degrees. Now I understand that the principal role regarding my mother is mine. The way I see her and how I feel is my responsibility. What I now give my attention to is going to build the present and the future for my family and me.

Maria Emilia, nurse

♥ Stop, Breathe, Love

The next issue then is "How to change attention or perception, given that they mirror each other?"

We change **attention** by choosing other information to focus on. For example, we focus on a different thought or a feeling, on a distinct person, a different scenery or event. That is, having a differentiated thought, a word, an image or emotion and a distinct behavior.

We also change attention by choosing another perception—changing the meaning that an idea, a word, an image, a feeling or action represents for us. Or what a person, event or object means for us.

The differentiated perception will move information that attention will meanwhile focus on.

We change **perception** by modifying the meaning that an idea, word, image, feeling or act represents for us.

We change perception by changing thoughts, images, words, emotions and behaviors.

Furthermore, we change perception by changing the attention regarding ideas, people, objects, events or circumstances. A new focus of attention will bring new data that will feed perception.

♥ Stop, Breathe, Love

Reaching this point, we ask the following: in our daily life, what is the importance of how attention and perception mutually affect each other? It is immense. Our quality of life is affected directly by the attention and significance that we give to people, objects, events or circumstances.

We have all experienced that the more attention we direct to something (be it good or bad), the more evident it becomes and the more importance we give to one particular situation, the greater dimension it gains.

In addition, from the quantum point of view, the participation of the consciousness of the observer who focuses, perceives or measures the subatomic reality, influences the quantum object, causing it to assume a determined state and manifests it. In conformance with this, we are potentially always affecting and creating the reality that we give attention to and we perceive (good, bad or indifferent) in line with the field of unified consciousness.

Therefore, the fact that attention and perception mutually affect each other constitutes a blessing for us because when we modify one, necessarily, the other one changes and we change the reality that is susceptible to being created by it.

Using Attention

"I like to see," he said, "because only by seeing can a man of knowledge know."
Carlos Castañeda in *"A Separate Reality"*

Do you still remember that attention is a tool at the service of the human consciousness so that it can create reality and it is also the language of creation? Yes. Then let us continue.

Attention is an activity of the consciousness/brain matrix that makes information present through focus.

Before attention is focused, we have information in virtual state. After attention is fixed, we have information in a real state, crystallized and "materially" available. That is, we have probabilities of reality emerging, becoming alive.

The real issue then is using attention in the best way so that reality appears in accordance with the ideals, wishes or feelings we have.

The truth is that there is so much information that it is not easy to understand what we are giving attention to and therefore bringing to creation.

Very often, it seems that we are on autopilot in relation to what we focus on, repeating the same scheme of thought, feeling and behavior, perpetually attracting similar types of energy, people and events to our life. What should we do then?

First, understand that real attention implies being aware of what we are focusing on. Attention is a present act and an act of presence because we conscientiously select **What, When and How** we will focus. Evidently, this happens at such an exorbitant speed that we are almost unaware of this process. The consciousness is aware of what it is observing and focusing on and how it is being focused. We could call this action *conscious attention*.

The automatic pilot is an unconscious way of being, where the attention is asleep.

Conscious attention allows us to witness life and live it because we are aware of what appears in reality. We take possession of the world and we participate in it in an authentic form. Only by being attentive can we decide consciously if we want to change, readjust or create new possibilities amongst endless possibilities.

As a result, Who We Are depends on what we give attention to. We build our identity based on what we have been giving our attention to over the years and change is only possible by paying attention distinctly. For example, if a relationship has had our daily attention and we identify ourselves as being a person with relationship issues, it is necessary to change our attention regarding the thoughts, emotions, words and attitudes and also the manner we give attention to those concerned. In the first instance, it is very strange because we are on unknown ground. It appears we do not quite know who we are; there is no relationship of identity. It is something new. But this open space, not knowing who we are, gives the possibility of choosing who we wish to be. We cease to be the person with the relationship issue and we become the person who chooses the relationships that he/she wants to have. And this makes all the difference in life.

Saying this in a simple manner: **The change of attention revolutionizes the creation, letting us be who we choose to be.**

♥ Stop, Breathe, Love

Remember we said earlier that we can pay attention in a concentrated or in a distributed manner? Let us resume this topic.
In concentrated attention, we focus on one piece of information only. In distributed attention, we focus on a variety of information at the same time. **Does the fact that attention is focused in a concentrated or distributed manner make any difference?** More specifically, does it affect how reality is going to be presented to us, or not?
Concentrated attention means that the focus of attention is fixed exclusively on a given piece of information, whether it is a person, event, object or idea. That is, the consciousness/brain matrix and the respective energy field are united with that information and the probability of it appearing in the physical world as a thing, person, event or feeling is vast.
On the other hand, evenly distributed attention means that the focus is spread over various information. For example, we are focused on our spouse, work, what happened to the neighbor or on the money in our savings.
The consciousness/brain matrix and the respective energy field are distributing attention amongst the various pieces of information and the probability of this information emerging on the physical plane as events, objects or feelings is lower than in the concentrated attention because the act of attention is shared.
Let us use a simple metaphor to better understand concentrated and distributed attention. Let us imagine one person playing a musical instrument through a great tube, and the tube is placed on our ear. When the person plays, a horn for example, the sound comes directly to our ear and has a very powerful impact: not only is it heard beautifully, but also the sound seems to be amplified by the tube, as well as, producing strong, echoing sensations. This occurs because the sound is directed exclusively. On the contrary, if we hear the horn, at the same distance, but without the tube, the sound is going to spread, distributed over the space of the room, and reaches our ear more diluted, lower, and does not produce the same auditory sensations because the sound focus is fainter and the sound potential was distributed.
Answering the issues above, is there a difference between focusing in a concentrated or distributed manner in how reality is presented to us?
Yes, there is a difference. Although both manners of paying attention produce effects in our energy field—that is, they have the potential of bringing to reality, events, objects, situations or persons—the difference is that concentrated attention is stronger in the creation of reality than distributed because the attention focus is one.

♥ Stop, Breathe, Love

Now other questions emerge. **Would it be possible to pay attention to a person, event or object and make it emerge immediately through our attention? Or does it take some time? And which way of paying attention creates faster? Is it concentrated or distributed attention?** These are interesting questions and there are replies at various levels. They follow:
1- On a quantum level, space-time can be transcended and the exchange of information and interaction between the particles can occur instantly. This phenomenon is based on the scientifically proven principle of non-locality, which I

discussed at the beginning of the book. So, on a fundamental level it is possible for the focused human consciousness to make an object present in physical reality in an instantaneous manner.

That happens because the exchange of information and the interaction between the subatomic vibration and the human consciousness is processed in a vibrational pattern beyond space and time. I remember a friend who was undergoing cancer treatment and when formulating her intention of a cure in a group, and **focusing her attention on the cure,** she immediately felt the presence of the Divine Holy Spirit, who was healing her and at that moment she was cured (her testimonial is in the following chapter).

From a quantum point of view, what happened was the information already existed in the field of unified consciousness, but only in a virtual state, and from the moment when the human consciousness focused on it, communicated it and interacted with it, this information, at that moment, actualized itself in physical reality—manifested a result. Therefore, it "takes no time," simply emerges from the quantum potential and manifests it in act.

Besides this example, I am sure we have lived through the experience of focusing our attention on something, such as a wish and the manifestation happened immediately. It could have been a coffee, a phone call, a compliment or a present.

2 - On another level, the consciousness can be focusing on a certain object, event or person, but it "takes time" to appear in physical reality. Why?

In the field of unified consciousness, the information is already available and able to be materialized, but perception is aligned with the dimension of space and time and things tend to be perceived in a continuous and linear form before our eyes.

The manifestation is apparently happening in a gradual and sequential way, and we only become aware that it has really happened when the results are visible. It is like a spiral tightly entwined around itself that stretches and collapses. The spiral, which is the event or the object in depth, which we are focusing on, is only one. But when we stretch the spiral we get the impression of the space and time it takes for the event to appear. And, when the spiral collapses it seems that the event or object is there.

Both movements of the spiral are possible to manifest reality and it is common for us to perceive in-depth and becoming aware of the space and the time that things take until they are visible (spiral stretched), instead of accepting them as being manifest and that we are already experiencing them (collapsed spiral).

3- On an additional level, it is also possible that the manifestation "needs" hours, days, months or even years to appear on the physical plane by virtue of an attachment that the person focusing has. Although attention is focused and is constant on a given situation or object, there is an attachment energy that blocks the manifestation.

The attachment is a perception that could have the underlying need to control, distrust, fear or even an obsession for a determined result that has to emerge, in a certain manner, in a given context in time. The attachment is an interference that fixes attention on a limitation instead of releasing it to the possibility, preventing the materialization of what is being focused on.

The act of focusing in a free and clear manner is ideal to bring to life what we are focusing on. Let us give a simple example: A couple is obsessed with having children. They are always focused on children, on when they will have children, on what they will do to have children. They make love in that manner, at the best time, they eat healthily, take the vitamins and yet still the baby does not appear.

How many of them, as soon as they give up and relax, permit the baby to emerge? In my family this happened. After ten years of medical tests, attempts and more attempts, my brother and sister in law were confronted with the verdict of the doctor: they were unable to have children. Disillusioned and profoundly upset, on the eve of St. António (the Feast Day in Lisbon) they decided to forget the whole situation and went to the celebrations, danced, ate and drank a lot. The night ended well and in love. The next month, my sister in law was pregnant. As soon as they decided not to focus on the issue, they let go and a baby girl was the result.

4- On the other hand, the manifestation may not be immediate, may take time to happen, because attention is distributed on a great amount of information or events. Although each focus of attention is potentially suitable for manifestation, attention has still not reached a critical point, critical mass, so that the manifestation is possible. One of the possible solutions is for attention to become concentrated exclusively on one piece of information until it becomes materialized as an event, object, sensation or behavior, amongst others.

5 - Still on another level, although attention is focused on a particular event or object, it could take some time until it is manifested: minutes, hours, days, months or years. Why? It is possible that while attention is well focused, perception could be interfering with attention, sabotaging the manifestation. That is, the perception that we have of reality, namely, the beliefs regarding what we are focusing on—if it is possible or not, if it can be immediate or not, the manifestation of our focus (the values, the rules, the emotions or passed experiences)—could be interfering subtly and preventing the manifestation. For example, if we are focusing on having a new job, but we believe that it cannot happen from one day to the next (when in fact it can and there are a great number of people who have experienced this), the probability that it may take some time before you have a new job is greater because we focused on the new job and on the idea that time is needed before it happens.

To overcome this situation and sustain the possibility of a new job from one day to the next, attention and perception must be aligned. In this case, we focus attention on the new job and allow it to happen from one moment to the next, or still, we leave open the perception of when it will happen, not even thinking about it, to facilitate that it happens quickly. Better still, we feel already employed; all this is going to change the situation.

Some other example, we are focusing on being cured of an illness, but then we think that we have to return to a job that we do not like and we do not want to do that. This thought creates interference with the focus of attention, which is to cure, as well as, fixing attention on what is not desired. There is a latent opposition that prevents the manifestation. An additional example, we focus attention on having professional success, but then we feel insecure when faced with so much public exposure. The emotional insecurity is blocking the manifestation of professional success.

What will we do to manifest what we have been focusing on? We maintain the focus of our attention on what we decide to create (health and success) and we also change perception—we give a new interpretation or a new meaning to the perceptions we have had and release negative emotions that just hindered, assuming another way of being in life.

In the case of the job, for example, we can find positive things at work, take on responsibilities or change attitudes. Or then we change our perceptions, for example, we think about changing jobs because we want to do new things, or own a business and we feel different things. It is also very important that we act in relation to the job, namely to plan what we will do, to contact people, ask for financing, etc. and change our way of being in relation to the job for joy and well-being, always maintaining our focused attention on healing so that it can be manifested.

In the example of professional success, in order for it to be achieved, we keep our attention focused on success and we change our perception regarding the insecurity of public exposure. We modify the meaning of public exposure, or find positive points regarding public exposure and activate thoughts, images and emotions of security that will change the perceptions and we focus on success and on the security together. We are internally successful. Once there is vibrational clarity and the attention is coherent, the probability of success being manifested is very high.

Living Attention

"What is the use of looking without seeing?"
Johann Wolfgang Goethe

It is through attention that we take part in life, holding onto people, things, events, sensations or ideas and, through it, we make them vivid and real at that moment. Said in a simple manner: **that which we focus on, we make probable and materialize**
Before paying attention, the information is in a potential state. From the moment we focus with attention, we move in line with what is being focused on and that information acquires a determined state, which has to do with us, bringing to life what we have imprinted.

If attention was not a highly potential tool in our lives, would anyone bother to draw our attention to anything? After all, incredible amounts of money are spent each year on advertising campaigns just to draw our attention. Why is that? It is because attention is important. It moves the world and crystallizes realities. **Without attention, there is no manifestation.**

Attention is powerful. It is the language that the field uses to give life, and that we also possess in order to create individual, planetary and cosmic reality. It is an instrument of the consciousness, able to realize profound transformations wherever it is focused. **Attention is presence, incarnating that which is focused on.**

On another plane, attention is a "necessity" that human beings have and shows many facets, such as dedication, interest, participation or involvement. By being attentive, we are connected to what we are observing, feeling or doing. If we are not attentive, we are not present. Things or persons go unnoticed and we do not live them intensively.

Any one of us can be present, attentive, giving life to whatever we wish through the focusing of attention. The practical applicability of this tool is limitless. It can build an improvement in your child´s performance at school, family harmony or the bond of a couple, total health, financial status or having more free time.

Here is a testimonial that shows the importance of attention in the construction of reality.

Testimonial

My life has changed, as well as my son Miguel´s life and my family since I changed my beliefs and attention regarding his capacities.

In preschool, my son´s teacher said that I should not expect much from Miguel because he could not learn well. Unaware, I accepted this verdict, I gave it attention, I told my husband and family...

In primary school, the teachers felt that Miguel was not very productive, inattentive and that I should not expect him to be successful at school. My son was always unhappy, and nothing seemed to change him. I paid attention to this; speaking about it to my husband, friends and to the family. Evidently, Miguel did not improve his school performance.

In my consultation with Dr. Susana, I mentioned this issue that worried my mind and my emotions so much. During the session she immediately told me: "Carla, did you believe what they told you about your son?... With those lenses, with that limited perception of your son, you will get nowhere."

We unblocked my mind, emotions, energy, and the energy of the family amongst others. I brought "homework" to do. One of them consisted in seeing, thinking, and loving my child as a capable, intelligent child and giving him positive reinforcement for everything he did well. The key word was persistence.

As I worked internally on myself and on Miguel, he began to get stronger. Getting good grades, being participative in class, making friends and gaining self-confidence. The previous academic year he had negative grades for everything. Now, he got excellent grades, even in mathematics he got a four (out of the possible five). But above all, he is happy, he smiles, walks proudly and all of his teachers like him. It is not a miracle, it is real and it was necessary to persist with him.

I changed my energy and I used it, focusing attention on what was good, to what I wanted and felt in my heart as true, every day, and every hour. Do you want your child to change his performance? Then change your lenses and support your child with love.

Carla Sebastião, mother and consultant

It is arguable that the universe was created due to an act of attention on itself and that we have been brought to light as a result of this same act. We are the fruit of the attention of the field of consciousness and it provided us with the capacity to pay attention and also create that which we are focused on.

Every day, through attention, we are adding aspects to our personal and collective universe and affecting other universes. So, be careful with what we are paying attention to, because it is productive. We reiterate, what we focus on, we manifest. Rather than being carried away by the focus of attention, which, in general, is disorganized, burdened with distorted perceptions and the excess of external stimuli, we can guide our attention. Yes, stop paying attention to what does not make sense or that is no good for us and guide it to what we wish to bring to life in a conscientious and responsible manner.

Choosing what to focus on, paying attention (or not) to things, people, ideas, sensations or attitudes, is a conscious act with a gigantic impact on our life and on the lives of other beings. This is because attention creates reality.

The question that follows is **"how do we guide attention?"** because sometimes or very often, we get the sensation that we are on autopilot.

Firstly, we should remember that attention is an instrument that we possess; it does not possess us. We are sovereign regarding our attention; we are able to decide—always—what to pay attention to, when to pay attention, and how to pay attention; that is in us and not in the exterior.

I am sure that we have all been through the experience of having great disorganization or confusion all around us and, for an instant, various minutes or even hours, we focused our attention on something else to feel better and we achieved it. *If we were able to focus our attention once, it is more than natural to achieve it over and over again. Attention, like everything else in life, requires practice. The more we practice guiding attention, the easier it becomes, the better the results achieved, the more enthusiastic we will be, and the more willing we will be to practice, raising the vibration in a virtuous cycle of creation.*

We have to actively select the information that we wish to focus our attention on, when we want to focus and how we want to focus our attention. For example: we choose to give our complete attention to our husband when we arrive home, without dividing our attention at all with matters such as the kitchen, or the telephone, or with putting the groceries away. And really practice this. That may imply stopping, being in silence, listening, looking into the eyes of our husband, talking, playing music that he likes, etc. Each one of us finds the best way.

An alternative way of guiding attention is meditating regularly (passive or active) or finding another procedure that works for us. It could be done when waking up or going to sleep and when we do housework, on the bus, or during our coffee break at work, however we wish.

What is important is that the decision to pay attention is implemented regularly. The more we practice it, the more results we find. At the end of the chapter, I will show a few simple exercises.

♥ Stop, Breathe, Love

Regarding attention, **is there a way of knowing if we are paying attention to what is "right" for us?**
How can we establish guidelines for this?

In the first place, we are going to understand what "correct" is—an idea or a set of ideas, rules, values, customs and beliefs that are contextualized in a social, cultural, political and religious environment at a given space-time and that has significance for us. As it happens, what is "right" also develops throughout our life and is a mental, emotional and behavioral construction, permitting us to take a position when faced with situations.

You can always check in with your internal guidance, such as your feelings, when you are focusing your attention. Emotions and feelings translate the internal environment and guide us in relation to the vibrational quality of the information, allowing us to make choices. As a rule, the first impression gives us the key to that situation. We notice if the emotional answer brings us good sensations or the sense of being connected, which indicates that our attention is being correctly focused, or if the sensation is an ill feeling, fear or pain. The probability of an ill feeling indicating to us that there could be a better path is great. Also tells it is time to focus attention on another piece of information or change the perception or accept another challenge. It is highly recommended to listen to our hearts or intuition to perceive if we are focusing our attention on what is right for us, or not, because we will get the answers in a broader and more accurate manner for each situation.

The Principle of Attention

"Where there is attention ends the unconsciousness."
Sufi Proverb

"Let's plant a tent on every star..."
Eça de Queirós

Does human attention have an underlying principle that guides the way it functions, or is it random? Yes, attention has an underlying way of functioning and we can even speak of a possibility regarding the principle of attention: **what we place attention on becomes evident.** *This is possible because, by the act of fixing our attention, we are selecting, communicating and inter-acting with the information on which we are focused, causing this information to become present. It becomes an integral part of us, and we of it, manifesting itself internally and externally.*

We are potentially connected with all information, but when we give it attention, the connection is actualized and the manifestation of what is being focused on appears in reality.

Giving a simple image to understand better, imagine that reality in a quantum state is a gelatinous soup, inform (without form), undetermined, or having qualities, characteristics or dimensions, only in a potential state.

The *"quantum gelatin,"* after being fixed by our attention, gains color, form and taste, manifesting what the act of attention concentrated.

The principle of attention means, then, that where the attention is placed causes the emergence of the qualities or properties of what is being focused on and makes them real.

To summarize:
Attention is life. He who is attentive is awake and produces more life. This means:
1- Attention is a creative act of our consciousness.
2- Our attention gives life to what we observe, how we observe and when we observe it.
3- We are the owners of our attention.
4- We decide always what to focus on; how and when to focus on;
5- The way we give our attention to people, things, events, environments affects them and us.
6- Attention creates links to all life and because life is interdependent, we are recreating all life at each instant.

♥Stop, breathe, Love

We add still that underlying attention is the **principle of resonance.** This principle is the regulator of communication and interaction between energy and information systems.

In accordance with the principle of resonance, there is communication and interaction between two or more systems of energy or systems of information when they vibrate in the same frequency or wave, are on the same phase, and resonate harmoniously or sub-harmoniously. When that happens, these energy or information systems cease to be "separate" entities, becoming cohesive, one, and emitting vibrations or information together, which that vibrates potentially in the infinite.

Let us give an example so that it becomes clearer. In a room, we have two cellos placed on opposing sides. If we play the musical note B on one of them only, the other cello is going to emit the same sound, the note B. This happens because there is communication and interaction between the energy waves of one cello with the other and they become united with the same purpose, emitting the sound B.

Each piece of information the consciousness faces, and/or emits, is vibration, energy. The vibration moves at a set speed or cadence. The number of times that this movement occurs can be measured, and then we obtain a frequency. As a rule, we measure the movement in cycles per second and we get the unit of measurement in Hertz (Hz) 1Hz is one cycle per second), but there are other units of measurement.

Each piece of information is a frequency of energy, and in the field of unified consciousness, the seat of life, there are innumerable frequencies of energy of which the human being, the plant, the planet or a bacteria is an expression. These frequencies of energy can communicate and interact with each other, which is, being in resonance—in that case, they are on the same wave frequency.

Our consciousness/brain matrix captures these pieces of information or frequencies through the sixteen senses and enters into resonance with them when these vibrate in the same coordinates or vibrational tone, with the information it has, as well as, with that which it is systematically creating, recycling and imitating. This process of resonance occurs at an incredible speed.

In the process of attention, we observe the information and select data that are in tune with the frequency of the wave that is vibrating in us at that moment. We focus and are focused on what is vibrationally compatible with us, be it totally new information or information that is in memory.

Let us give a simple example to make it clearer. We are walking on the beach, relaxed, looking at the sea. We feel good. Vibrationally, we are on a good vibe. Suddenly, we get an idea to write a book; we focus our attention on it; we feel it is an excellent idea and make a mental note of it. The sensation is good and we continue to walk.

Translating this into another language, we are in a certain vibrational state and are in tune with the new information. We capture it via the sense of inspiration. The information is available, internally we are observing it and we focus on it via attention. It is the idea for a book and it makes a lot of sense for us. We feel good, continue in resonance with the information regarding the new book; we make mental notes; we give it more attention; we maintain ourselves in tune with the vibration of the idea for the book. We feed back the vibration for as long as we want, giving it attention in the same frequency as the wave.

This information—idea for the book—can vibrate indefinitely, as long as the initial frequency and attention given continues in vibrational tune.

For the book to emerge through us, it is necessary to maintain the initial vibration in tune and get into action—to write.

Another example: We wake up with the alarm clock and think about an argument from the previous night. We continue to hear what our mother said "you are a difficult person; no one can put up with you," rattling in our head. At work, things are not going that well. It appears that everyone has decided to pick on us and complications occur one after the other.

Translating this into another language: the vibration of the beginning of the day is still in tune with what happened the previous night. When remembering what happened, we focused attention on past information and made it present again, feeding the vibration of discomfort and ill feeling.

The energy field continued to emit vibrations of misalignment and any other field that emits information in the same frequency of the wave is captured and comes into communication and interaction with ours, again we give attention to that which is disorganized and shows itself perceptually as a complication or a problem, feeding back the system. As long as we do not change the vibration and the attention of the information on which we are focusing, the probability of maintaining the same vibrational state and having ideas, emotions and or behaviors that have a tendency for disorder is enormous.

♥ Stop, breathe, Love

Who Are We then? Revolutionaries of creation through attention. The act of fixing attention is the chisel that is carving the quantum sculpture of our lives at every instant and has an impact on a universal scale. In fact, each point of individual attention interferes with the quantum reality, concentrating not only on one face of that same reality, as well as fixing the human collective and the field of unified consciousness.

We are all connected on the network of life and the concentration we carry out, moment after moment, be it in need, unemployment, or abundance, in peace or social solidarity, affects us immediately, as individuals, as well, making it possible for the global community to share that same reality.

After all, we can be the saviors of ourselves, our neighbor, or even of the Prime Minister or the Secretary-General of the United Nations when dwelling, namely, on solutions, opportunities, clear communication and the hope of the resolution of conflicts, through peace.

It is unquestionable that we have the power to choose **What** to focus on, **When** we will focus and **How** we will give attention to ideas, to people, things or events in our day to day. Furthermore, our quantum nature, connected with the field of unified consciousness, knows that it has infinite possibilities available for changing the attention/perception and that, however small the change is on the part of the whole, it changes the whole, immediately.

It is so simple, the secret of creation of reality, speaking to the field of unified consciousness, the language of attention and listening to it.

The formula for transforming our lives and all humanity is completely accessible and easy to realize. Using attention/perception in a conscious and directed manner, recreating ourselves and the world in the image and likeness of each one (in their fullness) and in totality.

A great power like this comes with the respective responsibility, and this is both personal and collective. Instead of perceiving that someone else or others can or should carry out the redirection of attention, we will accept it now and we will carry out a small shift in our focus of attention/perception.

We focus on peace and on changing one behavior, per day, towards peace, and on a global scale, we have a completely different planet and are decisively more peaceful. And it all started with the small step that we took, leading us to greatness as a community, a planet and even affected galaxies and the very universe in a magnificent web.

🚀 Reprogramming your attention practice:

In order to change your energy levels and what you are living ask yourself these two questions as often as you can throughout your day:

- Do I want to experience this in my life?
- What consequences does this have in my life and in the lives of others?

If you consider or feel it is not the "right" thing for you, then it is time to deliberately change focus. Use your will and attention consistently to do the practices below:

☺1- **Change the focus of attention by looking at something else**—for example, a flower, an object, a finger and focus on this new information, for a moment or a few minutes, breathing deeply. It is like changing the television channel.

☺2- **Focus on thoughts that oppose that which we've been focusing on**. For example, if we are focusing on a past experience of weakness, we can now focus on the strength we've gained. We changed the attention and the perception.

☺3- **Modify the meaning that this situation, event or person has for us**. For example, we did not say anything sensible in a job interview. Instead of considering this event as a disaster, we can consider it as practice that will bring us great success next time. *Yes, there are always more opportunities to be successful.*

☺4- **Make mental questions, or speak them aloud, in order to interrupt the flux of thought**. For example, what different things can I find? Or, show me something positive here? Or, how many correct, intelligent, good or fascinating things have I already realized? The objective is to make the mind perform a neural search for other possibilities and focus on them.

☺5- **Get out of your mind and focus on the body**. For example, put your hand on your heart, changing your position (seated to standing) or moving your body in an unusual manner, shaking yourself vigorously. Or, simply get some exercise. The body and the mind are a connected component of the human energy field. When we change the position of our body, not only does our attention shift to that movement, but also the information kept on the level of the cell memory for that bodily position emerges and attention is fixed on that different information. Then there is space to focus on what we consider "right" and attention becomes fluid.

☺6- **Meditate**. Meditation changes brain frequencies and helps us to perceive reality differently.

Use the **zero-point meditation to become detached.** To be detached is to inhabit an interior status of neutrality in which we can observe things without judgment and enable the flow of the intrinsic connection between us, others, and life. We are present, in the here and now, and in that sacred instant, everything is. This extensive attention, based on a state of receptivity, totally present and covering infinite possibilities in alignment with the field of unified consciousness, allows the manifestation of any reality without any kind of effort. If you would like to have this meditation, please send us an email.

Key points:
- Attention creates reality.
- Without attention, there is no manifestation.
- We participate in the world through attention. Our acts of observation bring to life what we focus on.
- Before you pay attention, you have quantum data. After you pay attention, you crystalize one possibility and it is able to manifest as a reality in your life.
- Our consciousness when faced with information selects:

❶ **What** to pay attention to
❷ **When** to pay attention
❸ **How** to pay attention

- You are the one who decides to what, when and how to pay attention to reality.
- You fix your attention to people, things, events and environments all day long. When you change the quality and the kind of attention you gave them you change your world and the planet.
- What you focus on becomes evident, and sooner or later it will materialize in your life.
- Attention shapes who you are.
- Your identity is connected to what you give attention to at each instant. Changing your attention will change you and those around you.

Self-reflection:
❶ What impacted you the most in this chapter?
❷ Indicate an idea, a subject or behavior to which you will give your concentrated attention.
❸ Describe three ideas, three subjects, three images and three positive emotions to which you are going to give attention in a distributed manner.

Exercises: Practice Attention
❶ Listen to a sound and remain totally attentive through its duration.
❷ With your eyes open, focus on an object, for example, a vase, for three minutes. Observing each detail of the vase, the form, the material, the color, the light on the object, etc. Then with closed eyes remember everything you have observed.
❸ Pay attention to the present moment. For example, when drinking water be aware from the movement of holding the glass, bringing it to the mouth, feel the water flowing through the throat, the sensation of quenching the thirst, etc. Be totally present in each act.

5 Intention

Story
A long time ago in a small village in Persia, there lived a washerwoman. One day, she was taking the laundry out of the basket by the riverbank, when she saw a beautiful frog lying sunbathing on a stone. The washerwoman looked at it and thought: "What a good life that the frog has. If only I was like it."
After soaking and scrubbing some of the laundry, she noticed the frog was still lying in the sun and she said to herself: "the frog does not work, does not have a family to feed and has time for everything... I wish I was that frog." The washerwoman was beating and rinsing the washing vigorously in the river, giving a sigh of weariness, when she said: "What a life I have. I want a better life!"
Later in the day, as she hung out the laundry over some stones and grass for it to dry, she saw that the frog was still in the sun. Without knowing exactly why, she spoke to the frog saying: "You are a queen, and you have the life of a queen. I also want to be and live like you..."
As soon as she had said these words, the frog jumped towards her and said:
"Be careful what you wish for because it could happen."
The washerwoman was so stunned by what she heard that she stopped hanging out the clothes...

"The first step in getting something is desiring it."
Mother Teresa of Calcutta

Have you ever desired that your life could be different and, like the character in the story, said: "I wish!" Or have you dreamt or had a vision of yourself so grand that you were anxious to achieve it and share it with those you love and the world? Is there a possibility of life showing you that whatever you wish, your intentions, might happen? Is it more than probable that this is true?
The use of the creation language of intention allows us to realize big and small miracles. To do this, it is first necessary to understand intention.
In a broad sense, intention is information, light and energy in movement, vibrating in the field of unified consciousness. It is still a language through which the field of unified consciousness communicates with us and us with it.
Intention is also a tool placed at the service of the human consciousness, for it to construct reality.
As we have been saying, the field of unified consciousness is the basis of all being[1] and the basis of both, that which is potential, and that which is materialized, and naturally, the basis of intention as well.
In order to facilitate the understanding and the organization of the exposition, we confirm that there are three origins of intention. However, the energy of intention is one.

---

[1] Amit Goswami in his book Visionary Window... states also this idea of "consciousness as the ground of all being". See pg. 79 of the Portuguese edition (Editora Cultrix).

❶ Unified consciousness
❷ Individual consciousness
❸ Planetary consciousness
We will now address them one by one.

❶ Intention arising from the field of unified consciousness

The quantum maternity of life is the field of unified consciousness and it is in it that the endless information, plans, dreams and infinite potentialities have their source.
We are linked on a fundamental level to the field, and it is possible to access that information, make it ours—as Einstein said "knowing God's mind"—and discover the tendencies of life. Or we can know the probabilities of the connections on a subatomic level, even before these are particularized.
When we are consciously in resonance with the field of unified consciousness, the consciousness/brain matrix captures this data and instantly reveals it inside us. We can access any data in the quantum library, namely dreams, inspirations, inventions, perfect health, and purposes of life that are the potential of life, which we can actualize or not.
The human being accesses and receives information from the field of unified consciousness making it theirs, through the focus of the consciousness and the acceptance of the information. Intention as energy, light and information from the field of unified consciousness is always available to us, at any *focal point*, or moment.

❷ Intention from the individual consciousness

As human beings, we produce intentions. In a wider sense, the act of thinking, deciding or desiring something is an intention. And it is normal to do it. We think about how Monday is going to turn out, and that is an intention for the day. We wish to earn more or that the head of department gets better, and those are also intentions. A desire of the heart that enlivens the will, for example, ending poverty, getting married or speaking with a guardian angel. Or a resolution that leads us to have an objective, for example, go on holiday or earning €50,000.00 per month, *leading us to action.*
In a stricter sense, intention is a united force which enables us to modify reality. It is an internal calling for us to participate and imprint our mark on life.

Intention is a subtle force focused on the transformation of reality.
When we formulate intentions, we emit that energy inside our energy field in tune with the field of unified consciousness and we manifest in our life what we intend; in addition to this, the field of consciousness mirrors into the reality around us that which we are bringing to life with our intentions.

❸ Intention from the planetary consciousness

The planet is a living entity, a field of energy in movement, emitting energy for all beings that live in it and for the field of unified consciousness. It receives information from the human community and from the field of unified consciousness.
Earth welcomes the intentions of all Humankind's processes them and retransmits them

in the same vibrational frequency to the human community and the field of unified consciousness. Each person and community receives this information and has the capacity to accept, change or reject the intentions being formulated, feeding once again the planetary consciousness.

Intention is energy in movement in the field of unified consciousness and can be manifested multidimensionally in any plane of existence. It is also human energy vibrating, which that can be materialized individually and collectively, affecting the planet and also the field of unified consciousness. It is a powerful force in the creation of reality.

♥ Stop, Breathe, Love

From now on, we will give the principal role to human intention, that is, the intentions produced by the individual consciousness.
Human will is based on internal impulses that propel us to redefine Who We Are. That purpose, internally defined, is an intention; for example, forgiving a sibling, discovering the cure for cancer, attending a retreat or going to developing countries as a missionary.
In parallel, a human being can be permeated by external stimuli that can trigger a resolution regarding something; for example, seeing a lovely motorbike or a house and formulating the intention to acquire it.
In one way or another, **intention is the force that propels us towards the realization.** *Intention is then the subjective attitude of transforming the world with a purpose, modeling it in accordance with our will: an internal disposition for the concretization of something material or immaterial, causing a change in our being and in the state of things.*
Intention is a tool of the human consciousness that, when formulated, moves the whole universe towards a manifestation. Before intention, we have the natural state of indetermination of the subatomic particles, moving themselves in the field of unified consciousness. *When we have an intention, our consciousness concentrates on a point of vastness and actualizes it, causing the crystallization of the particles into a specific form.*
Effectively, intention is the quantum laser that evokes the possibility and engraves it into reality. It is a language that the field of unified consciousness understands when we communicate with it, and through which it communicates with us and with the planet, permitting us to create together with it.
The applicability of intention in daily life is limitless, be it for creating harmony in the home, or changing the results of a medical test, curing a disease, finding a satisfying job, speaking to our friend, forgiving our mother, but also for building tension at work, falling into financial problems, and social exclusion.
Human intention is focused energy with a purpose and what we already know is that each time that our consciousness is focused, it creates. In the act of focusing on something, we actualize the connection with something and bring it to life.
In truth, we imprint the fingerprint of our will in the wave of possibilities of quantum reality, and this will is interconnected with the will of the totality and emerges, manifesting itself physically. Things such as the recovery of a friend that was in

hospital, getting pregnant, receiving the desired birthday present, or having time to eat ice cream between two important meetings, can happen.

It does not matter what we are focusing on, its dimension, its form, its context or even time and space. Intention always works in the scope of the endless possibilities that the field of unified consciousness shows us, therefore, the choices and the manifestations are limitless. We can always create and recreate anew, successively, through our intentions.

Intention in Movement

"Therefore it follows, that we as human beings must consist of nothing more than a geometric collection of the harmonic waveforms of light—guided by intelligence."
Bruce L. Cathie in "The Energy Grid"

"Intention is the point of contact between Heaven and Earth in the heart of Man."
Maria Costa

How is the act of formulating an intention processed and what manifestations does it bring?

Although intention is an indefinable subatomic dance, I am going to explain it in a linear manner so that we can understand it better.

In our consciousness/brain matrix, we are systematically processing information: we perceive data instant by instant, we give it meaning and make decisions. This data can emerge perceptually as ideas, sensations or images and we focus on them.

Intention is information that has a purpose, which we consider valid, and we pay attention to. It can be an internal calling for a vocation (be a doctor), a wish from the heart (live by the sea), to make a dream come true (have a music room), a desire to change (change living conditions) or simply a thought (find a parking space).

In this act of intending, one bit of information pulsates in our energy field, and simultaneously, in the field of unified consciousness, actualizing the information field automatically. From the moment that we emit that information, or energetic instruction, the field of consciousness, which is in constant dialogue with us and all the life, is configured so that our expression of sovereignty occurs, giving it substance and form.

When formulated, the energy of the intention is an order for the subatomic world to reconfigure itself. Numerous subatomic particles that were in an undetermined state immediately actualize themselves, to form a defined entity. That is, a particle or group of particles, joining in a particular and determined form, at a point of the matrix, which we call physical reality.

Intention is the subtle technology of our consciousness, which allows us to reorganize the quantum world according to our subjectivity and particularities, and reality appears in a way that has been defined by us. **Intending is enforming, giving body to life.**

In the act of intending, of formulating a purpose, wishing or thinking about someone, a thing, a situation or an event, the quantum tapestry instantly models itself and shows itself with the contour, the color and the quality of what has been intended by us, showing us that reality.

We participate in life and create the world, moment by moment through our intentions, and the realities that we can evoke are unlimited because life is expanding and so are we. We must intend, and in that act, we are creating reality. Any reality. It can be breakfast in bed, a harmonious meeting of apartment owners, the presence of a guardian angel, the spontaneous remission of a tumor, the success of a surgery, the cleaning up of an ocean or the feeding of a nation. Everything and anything is possible.

♥ Stop, Breathe, Love

Having an intention is a simple process. We inform ourselves about a will, a desire or an idea and communicate it internally and the field of unified consciousness listens to us and feeds its realization, aligning people, circumstances, resources and the planet for its manifestation.
The field of consciousness interlinks and synchronizes the movements of all the actors in the process, so that we live the experience of what we intended.
For example:
We have the desire to forgive our father or to free ourselves from a relationship. The moment we became aware of it, the father or the boyfriend calls us and we have a serious conversation that solves the issue.
It is also possible to have a heartfelt wish for building a society that is more just, and in that sense, we notice an email from UNICEF suggesting that we make a donation, sharing our wealth.
It can be an idea or thought that emerges at the time and we follow it immediately, or a recurring thought: namely, intending to have healthier eating habits and a friend suggests a vegetarian restaurant, and we accept the invitation. We intend to arrive at work every day at ten to eight and it happens.

♥ Stop, Breathe, Love

It really is possible to intend, focus for an instant and acknowledge the immediate emergence of what we focused on.
From a quantum point of view, all possibilities exist simultaneously and are present in the field of unified consciousness, in the absolute now. When we make an intention, we communicate on a subatomic level and information that exists in a potential state emerges from the field of unified consciousness in a determined state, manifested in reality.
This process is instantaneous because the subatomic entities only have to actualize their state. They were already overlapping "everywhere" and "over all time"; it was only necessary to assume a precise location, which they were already occupying but only in a virtual state. Therefore, the manifestation does not take "any time" because it was already present and available to be realized on a physical level. It is only needed for the effect to be raised through intention.
Intention is a subtle energy that vibrates inside us and in the field of unified consciousness, able to manifest immediately the purpose that is felt internally, the desire in our heart or thoughts that we have in the meantime been focusing on. It

simply emerges.

Intention is the tool that allows us to create reality in partnership with the field of unified consciousness. Any reality is manifested through its force. The focus of intention leads to the emergence of worlds, shapes or contexts so that we live through experiences in line with what we intended. This force, united with the field of unified consciousness, can turn what we intended into reality, even in an immediate manner; it could be a dream job, a scholarship to enter university, the disappearance of a phobia or even a romantic meeting with the love of our life.

The applications for this power, which we already have, are vast. It is a subtle yet advanced technology, which we have from birth and forms part of our basic software. All we need to do is use it with consciousness and responsibility for the good of all.

Linked Intention

"Possibilities and Miracles mean the same thing."
Prentice Mulford

"Ask and you shall receive."
The Bible

"The now is what is done all the time and in no time at all."
Jean Paul

I am sure you have used your intention to create small or great achievements in your life. Actually, you are doing it at this very moment while reading this book.

Which conditions, circumstances or people could appear or disappear in your life so that your internal will, your realization could happen? And what about broadening your horizons? Allowing yourself to be, do or have what effectively make sense for you? Intention is the way to realization and it is available to be used. Let us look at it further.

The field of unified consciousness has limitless possibilities of reality, and so do we. We are consciousness experimenting states of consciousness and realities, updating the infinite probabilities at each instant.

Intention is simultaneously the information that the field recognizes (the data we transmit, is already known to it), as well as the enformation (the form) that the information can be coated when being achieved: for example, health, a computer game or holidays.

In truth, life has all that we need and in the act of intending what makes sense for us, we update a great number of probabilities of reality already existing, and we create with the field the concretization. An event, a person or circumstance, is a result of our intentions.

It is us communicating with the essence of life and it is answering us in tune. In this fundamental dialogue, immanent to the very nature of reality, everything is possible. Illnesses can disappear miraculously, relationships can be transformed, things and events can emerge in the wink of an eye. It seems unreal but it is true. We house the key to creation we just need to reactivate it in the lock so that all the doors open. "Ask and you shall receive," it is just an internal command for us to remember again that what we ask for already exists in the kingdom of the potential. In the act of

evoking, it is automatically present.
There is no separation between asking and receiving, because these are two sides of the same face. We and the field of consciousness are one, and when we emit the vibration of intent, it is already linked to the field that simply reflects it in reality.

♥ Stop, Breathe, Love

For some, the miraculous is extraordinary, because it is perceived in the bubble of common sense and the conventional laws of physics, where linearity, objectivity, space, time and separation are accepted postulates. Reality is formatted and the consciousness does not take part in it, coexisting with it without interferences.
What if reality was our opportunity to express the natural creativity that we have and since we have at our disposal a field of unlimited possibilities?
Then we have to consider the miracle as an opportunity that is always lurking and already inserted in the possibility that life is constantly and always being renovated systematically. In effect, life is a possibility and a miracle in itself. Nothing is out of it and the possibilities are unlimited.
Physics and quantum mechanics state it and prove it. Everything that exists came from a state of probabilities that has updated itself and the quantum soup, the kingdom of possibilities, is inexhaustible.
The field of unified consciousness is the field of the endless possibilities that move within it; they are in an undefined state, fit to be crystallized by a creative act, be it by the field or a human being, generating reality.
The quantum leap consists in each one of us choosing another possibility besides that which conventional reality shows us and focusing this in a conscientious and united manner, bringing it to life. It could be admitting that it is possible to heal yourself even when conventional medicine denies it; it could be persisting down the path to scientific creativity, even if teachers dismissed your intelligence; or assuming that it is still possible to participate in the Olympic Games in spite of being chosen as a substitute athlete on the official team.
This perceptual action of coverage and connection is the detonator of the miracle, and the miracle in itself, because we are its creator, the creature experiencing it and the observer of that same reality in the world. And everything started by choosing another possible result.
Maria dos Anjos (whose testimonial will be shared a few pages ahead) had a malignant disease and accepted another possibility that cured her cancer. The scientist Albert Einstein, considered inept and dumb by some of his teachers, chose another version of reality and invented the theory of relativity, revolutionizing physics. The athlete Raj Bhavsar, a substitute on the U.S. Olympic team for Beijing, maintained his intention, confidence and training until the night before the athletes boarded and chose another possibility. He managed to be selected the night before and won a bronze medal at the Olympic Games in Beijing.[2]
It is always possible for another miracle, another possibility, or another opportunity of life to show up with the contours, colors, feelings, resources and dimensions that we

---

[2] Summarized from an Interview of Marcia Wieder with RajBhavsar—Dream University 2010/2011, please see www.dreamuniversity.com.

human beings placed there through intention.

Intention in Health

"Miracles do not happen in contradiction to nature, but only in contradiction to that which is known to us of nature."
Saint Augustine

"Miracles are natural. When they do not occur something has gone wrong."
Anon

"Evil does not exist, it is only disorder (…) and good exists only…"
Saint Augustine

In 1987, when I was eighteen years old, I read a book by Heinz Konsalik which awakened my soul and set my heart jumping. The story talked about a girl that was able to cure people by laying her hands on others in an inexplicable manner. I was so impressed that I devoured the book and did not sleep that night. Somewhere inside me, a voice echoed saying that this was not a story—it was real. I found myself thinking of how and when would I do this. I felt so alive in the story that I continued thinking about it for days.
I come from a family with a long connection to the healing arts. My grandparents were experts in teas and one of them was often consulted for back straightening procedures, which also solves delicate gastrointestinal issues. My grandfather Francisco straightened "stickleback" and my mother is an expert with the "turned craw" and other herbs. Still today at the age of eighty-eight my mother helps neighborhood babies and children, or whoever asks, when they have a "turned craw": normally the symptoms are vomiting and diarrhea without an apparent cause. What is important is that it works and has no indications to the contrary whatsoever.
As I have always interacted with conventional medicine in parallel to popular knowledge, in reading the story of Konsalik I admitted that what the character was doing was possible, although I did not quite know how. Who would have dreamt that my life would change so much from that intention: from working as hemodialysis practitioner and then a lawyer and finally a return to healing? At that time, only my soul knew this.
For me, health comes first. I understand health as wellbeing at all levels, from physical, emotional, mental and spiritual. That is, natural harmony and integrity working perfectly for us. We all use intentions regarding health every day and those impact our lives that's why our focus is going now in that direction.

Does an act of intention affect our health and the health of other people?
I believe it does. In fact, we all know or intuit naturally that good intentions, thoughts on health, well wishes, a prayer, meditation, or a connection with a higher power, heal. Most probably, we have felt it and practiced it. We live with it daily.
We have always been formulating intentions about health. When a baby is conceived, the first wish of the mother and father is that he will be healthy; we say "perfect". After the birth, family and friends wish the baby to be very healthy, and have a long life, full of happiness.

All through our existence, if there is an illness, we think of getting better and this is also intention. Friends and people who we relate with send get well wishes, hope for a cure, pray for us or "send" energy. These actions are also intentions. It is even possible to cure ourselves, even instantly, as a result of a clear intention of a cure, united with a feeling of "it being done," connecting internally with the field of unified consciousness and letting it be. As it happens, besides this knowledge, or natural experience, there is scientific proof that the power of intention has an impact on health.

It is scientifically proven that focused intention can cause a change in the enzyme function, the viral development, the blood pressure and muscular activity, interfere with bacteria and cell preparations, namely blood cells, amongst other things.[3]

We will show one of the various experiments already carried out in this field. The scientific experiment carried out by Dr. William Braud, described in his article "Consciousness interactions with remote biological systems: anomalous intentionality effects," whose aim was to find out if human intention could affect red blood cells, keeping them alive in hostile conditions. It was proven to be true.

The objective of the experiment consisted in having "red blood cells in test tubes where the salt concentration of the blood plasma was ideal and adding salt, which is fatal for the life of the blood cells, understanding if the human intention of protecting the blood cells would permit them to live a longer life. What was proved was that the blood cells resisted much longer to the changes in the salt concentration, as a result of the intentions of the participants in the experiment."[4]

Other scientific experiments show that it is also possible to positively affect the rhythm of the heart or brain waves through intention.

♥ Stop, Breathe, Love

It is also possible for intention to take the form of prayer, through one or various prayers with the purpose of positively affecting health, with gradual improvements in health or even immediate healing ... Who has not already done this for ourselves, for a parent in hospital or a friend? And what are the effects of our prayers for the health of those we love?

The effects are real and measurable and directly affect those for whom we pray; they can be healed totally.

As an example, we will mention a scientific experiment that proves the impact of prayer on health. It was carried out in the American Heart Institute and it came to the conclusion that the heart patients in the hospital who were the object of prayers had fewer complications. *"Remote, intercessory prayer was associated with lower CCU course scores. This result suggests that prayer may be an effective adjunct to standard medical care"*.[5]

Prayer is intention felt and focused on greater wellness: a state of openness to other possibilities, in union with the All, or a higher power (superior entity), to which we

---

[3] Braud, W.G., Distant Mental influence: Its Contribution to Science, Healing, and Human Interactions. Hampton Roads Publishing, December 2003.
[4] Braud, W.G., Schlitz, M.J. "Consciousness Interactions with Remote Biological Systems: Anomalous Intentionality Effects." Subtle Energies, Vol. 2, 1991, pg. 28.
[5] Harris, W.S., "A Randomized, Controlled Trial of the Effects of Remote, Intercessory Prayer on Outcomes in Patients Admitted to the Coronary Care Unit," Archives of Internal Medicine, 1999; 159(19), 22738.

trust and put that being in His hands. It is a triple force of communion and deliverance that reorganizes the information, the brilliant vibration and the personal energetic field, actualizing health.

Through intention we influence health, more precisely we create it in tune with the field of unified consciousness. In fact, each one of us takes part in the creation of reality through the information that each intention contains, which is shaping, and manifesting health, expressing life.

❤ Stop, Breathe, Love

Reality is a dynamic relationship between us, the field of unified consciousness and the planet, allowing us to imprint, through our attention and intention health in our lives.

An intention can be formulated for us or for our loved ones, relatives or friends and it is not limited by space or time. It works **both in person and at a "distance." The moment we formulate, and feel inside us, the whole universe becomes actualized and you could experience your manifestation immediately.**

Effectively, from the quantum point of view, all possibilities exist simultaneously and our intention is a point of infinite possibilities, defining a particular state for what, up to that moment in time, had no form (inform). There is no time or distance for something that was in an undetermined state and takes on a form, because it has always been linked, potentially, to it. It simply happens. It is.

Intention is an active force linked to the Force. We are always in communication with the Force simply by using the language that it knows to get answers.

Intention is, simultaneously, the information and the language that the Force recognizes, manifesting any reality evoked. It is not important who evokes it, where and when it is going to happen, seeing that the Force knows who the target is, what the easiest form is and what the quickest and most efficient way of achieving it is. What is important is the manifestation, and that is already happening.

I will leave an example of one of the possibilities of intention affecting another being, even if he is on another point of the universe, in another city.

A very dear friend telephoned me at 23:30, telling me that she was in the hospital. Knowing that she was pregnant, I thought she was going to give birth to her baby. But no. Although she was not due yet, the doctor decided to admit her into the hospital because she was losing amniotic fluid, and this could bring on labor.

She asked for my help, because she wanted to have a natural birth, for which her husband could be present and she could not understand what was happening.

I told her I would help her. I used the language of creation of intention, in the sense that the womb with the amniotic fluid be maintained cohesive and that the birth of her daughter would be in the best possible manner and at the right time for the baby, and I called upon the angels of birth. Then I went to sleep. In the morning, my dear friend telephoned me, radiant, saying that the doctor had sent her home and that everything was fine with the baby.

Here is her testimonial:

Testimonial

Susana had helped me prepare for giving birth to my first daughter and everything went very well: a natural birth. Perfect. With my second pregnancy, three years later, my wish was to repeat the experience.

Without knowing why, I was a little anxious regarding giving birth. One day, unexpectedly, I felt a little loss of amniotic fluid. I went to the hospital and was admitted and there was a great possibility of inducing labor, due to amniotic sac rupture.

I did not accept the diagnosis, because what I really wanted was my daughter to have a natural birth. I telephoned Susana and asked her for help so that my situation would be reversed, although I did not quite know how this would happen. I was sure that it was possible to return home and carry out the pregnancy. From a distance, Susana formulated her intention of a cure, and the following day, the doctor who observed me in the morning assured me that there was nothing wrong with my amniotic sac, everything was perfect and sent me home. The baby was born a week later, a natural birth, just like I had envisioned.

Rita Pinheiro, teacher

♥ Stop, Breathe, Love

On another level, intention can be linked to meditation or certain spiritual practices, the use of an energy or information system that facilitates a person's improvement or the healing.

The inner purpose of reestablishing health is simultaneously the fuse and the gunpowder that triggers the change in the quantum world in the energetic state, and shares the information and light, allowing the return to order, that is, to equilibrium and the perfection that is immanent to nature.

It is relatively frequent for people to cure themselves, normally by spontaneous remission of the disease, with the medical world not able to find a normal cause for the disappearance of the symptoms; there is even a medical publication that refers to this type of cases.

The book *Spontaneous Remission,* by Caryle Hirschberg and Brendan O'Regan, refers to these types of situations and describes the "case of a sixty-four year old man, who was advised to have surgery and chemotherapy when a malignant cancer in the rectum was detected. The man did not accept this approach. He resorted to the practice of intensive meditation, two hours in the morning and one hour at night and the tumor disappeared in the space of a year, without any medical treatment."[6]

It is also possible for symptoms to disappear in an unexpected manner, sometimes immediately, without the patient being submitted to any type of treatment or surgery, using energy or another spiritual practice. In cases of cancer, I personally know some people to whom this has happened. Here is the testimonial of one of them.

Testimonial

My name is Maria dos Anjos. I was diagnosed with a tumor on my breast and I did not want to have neither surgery nor chemotherapy. They told me that it was possible to heal diseases through energy and intention. I have always considered myself as a

---

[6] Summarized from Hirschberg, C. & O'Regan, B., Spontaneous Remission: An Annotated Bibliography, Institute of Noetic Sciences, 1993.

woman of faith and saw this as a sign.
We came together at a meeting where the curing energy was going to be shared and the intention was my healing. I felt that the Divine Holy Spirit was with me. I felt a warmth rise up my legs and settled in my breast like a fire. It was like it was consuming me and I felt the peace and the presence of the Divine Holy Spirit looking after me. This lasted for about ten minutes. In the end I felt cured and I told the group with all confidence. The following month, when I did a breast exam and blood analysis, the doctor concluded that I was well. For me this was a divine cure.

Maria dos Anjos, retired teacher

When formulating an intention we give an instruction in the sense of order and the order underlying all life responds, synchronizing the subatomic rearrangements for natural health to manifest itself. Since we are always connected to health it is easy.
It is a conscious click of opening to the infinite possibilities. This click can be done personally or with other people or a group of people. **What is important is the internal availability, the "blank space" so that the underlying unity of all life completes it in the intended sense.**

♥ Stop, Breathe, Love

Intention is a language that both we and the field of unified consciousness are fluent in, allowing us to communicate and still construct reality. This quantum dialogue is realized at each moment, such as in the sharing of information and the manifestation of the construction of life.
Regarding health, we are systematically recreating it in the image of our communications, observations and intentions, imprinting it within the organic substrate that we call a body. A formulated intention at a given moment can constitute a crucial turning point in health.
In effect, the action of intending a given possibility regarding a medical diagnosis, the result of a test, or the acceptance or rejection of a treatment or surgery, can make all the difference. The decision we make is going to influence decisively which path can be taken from the energetic point of view, neurally or molecularly affecting all of the biology of the individual.
In the case of the diagnosis of a serious disease, it is totally different to think that it may not be so and get a second opinion from another specialist, repeat the tests or look for other alternatives, rather than being automatically conditioned and stuck to one possibility, which from the quantum point of view, coexists with so many other, certainly healthier, possibilities. We can accept that there is at least a fifty percent chance of it being so, and the other fifty percent has the probability of being different. When we mentally consider other possibilities, the brain, as a quantum processor in communication with the field of unified consciousness, links other possibilities and updates other types of neuron connections, secreting other type of chemicals and differentiated hormones resulting in distinct nervous and muscular movements.
This dynamic, evoked by a distinct thought, a desire or a wish, could be the drop that causes the overflow in the ocean of infinite possibilities, a chain of events and phenomena completely different than what was indicated, because other information

was actualized and became available for the manifestation.

Who knows if it is possible that from this turning point, the disease disappears or the most dangerous aspects become dormant, namely because the immune system has become balanced. In these cases, intention is the most sophisticated laser technology and it is ready to be used by any human being at any time, modifying the probabilities of disease and transforming them into opportunities for health.

Here is a testimonial of a decision/intention that constituted the turning point, changing the personal universe of the person in question.

Testimonial

I went to a consultation with Susana Cor de Rosa because at that moment in my life I was very scared. My medical tests were completely altered and the diagnosis pointed to lupus. I felt like I was on the edge of a cliff and did not know what to do. I decided to follow the advice of a friend that had suggested the work of Susana. During the consultation, Susana pointed out the diagnosis, telling me that I did not have to validate it. It was merely a hypothesis. I could choose (decide something else) to give myself the possibility of being healthy. I accepted that idea, although I did not know how it was going to work. We worked together during the session and at the end I felt happy, brilliant and at the same time, I felt I had power over my own life.

I went back to the lupus specialist (who is well known internationally) for testing. After consulting me, he congratulated me. He said, "I do not know what you did, but a barrier prevented the disease from manifesting itself. I have no scientific explanation for it. Whatever you were doing, continue with it, be happy and have fun."

After hearing this, I laughed and smiled continuously. My life changed in the blink of an eye. A simple intention. The decision to accept that it was possible to choose something else, to be healthy, had worked. Bless the hour that I went to the consultation on unified quantum healing; I believed in being healthy and, with Susana, I changed my energy.

Margarida Reis, economist

It is really impressive how intention interferes with health, challenging the established logic and the laws of conventional physics. After all, how is it that something like a thought, a desire or a focused purpose can affect matter, change how health progresses, or eradicate disease, or even make our organisms healthy?

This is possible because intention is an active force of nature, linked with life and in constant interaction with it. It is not separated from the field of unified consciousness, the seat of all manifested and unmanifested reality. It is entwined in the All and in everything. From the moment it is evoked, it updates information and reality emerges immediately organized.

Our natural state is influencing life and being influenced by it in creative dance together. The subatomic particles that we are made of are connected to the particles that make up the trees, the sun, or the stethoscopes with which the doctors listen. Furthermore, they are constantly communicating amongst each other, they speak a common language, sharing information and affecting each other, mutually manifesting life. As a result of our essential connection, when one of us is cured, experiencing health, all of humanity is healed and expands healthily, in a growth of wellbeing.

Health is a construction *made instant by instant by our observation and intention. It is in us and in everything, always available to be actualized. We have to be attentive and use it appropriately.*

Multifunctional Intention

"What we discovered on a fundamental level of the universe is that there is a universal field where all forces and particles are united, they are one (...)."
Dr. John Hagelin

"Intention allow us to create the apples of the tree of life, and give them to those who we love."
Maria Costa

Story
A very ancient fable tells that magic exists in the man that thinks, wishes and purposely moves in the direction that he envisions.
One day, a traveler passing through paradise desired to eat apples. Immediately, the apples appeared and he picked and ate them. Because he was alone, he idealized a mate. She appeared in his dreams. In that dream state, he touched her hair and she materialized. After that, he thought of a family. The whole of humanity appeared. Enthusiastically, he began to hug them.
We are that travelers in paradise and now have the possibility of enjoying it.

 Let's do an exercise to practice:
- For a few moments, imagine that you are the character of the story: a traveler in paradise. Feel awed by that grandiose sensation of being in paradise and able to touch, move, smell, hear, write, eat, love, give, win...
- Write 2 intentions you have manifested out of the blue.
- Write down 2 intentions you materialized that were extended in time.
- Now write this sentence: I made this I can do it always.
- Close your eyes and notice your brain, heart and all your body feeling that you are capable. You are a powerful manifestor.

Intention is the language of creation and it is inside you to use in your life, with your family, colleagues, with the planet and all in tune with the field of unified consciousness. As we have mentioned, you have limitless possibilities to intend and exercise your quantum creativity, bringing to life unlimited manifestations. Actually, you are doing it at this very moment, even if it is creating and recreating the same as always, making it appear that you are not creating anything. *THAT IS PURE ILLUSION.* You are always creating. That is your and our fate (fado). The great news is that we can always create new and different things, if we decide to do so.
The things, people, and events that we experience individually or as a group, are the results of the focus of our observation and intention kept present in our consciousness. They are the translation of the internal environment with external representation, mirrored in the field of unified consciousness, so that we can continue creating them

or modifying them.
The applicability of intention is total. It is an instrument of the All that the totality has made available to us to actualize reality together. It can appear as finding a teaching position near our home, finding roller skates for your son in the first shop you go to or meditating at Santiago of Compostela. It all depends on the choices you are making.
Is it clear now that intentionality affects reality? I will reiterate: any reality is affected by it, because from a fundamental point of view, reality is one.
Intentionality affects, creates reality.

The issue here has to do with the "material part of things."
Does intention also interfere with objects? Conceptual and perceptual normality tells us that things are solid; they are already determined and set and are not susceptible to being changed by something so insubstantial as a thought, a desire or a purposeful and focused will.
Wake up to the fact that both objects and intentions are particles of energy, light waves and information fields, vibrating in the quantum ocean of unlimited probabilities. Reality is only one and it is interpenetrated and actualized by the direct participation of man in the field of unified consciousness, in a gigantic and interdependent web. An act of human will make it possible and intercrosses with the will of the All, bringing that same purpose to life.
Let us think of a simple thing. Have you ever wished that the gas in the car could last until you reached the gas station and that it happened? Or that your mobile phone rang with a call from your love and it happened? These are small experiences where we already use intention to affect objects and many others could be reported here, to prove that such is possible.
One of the things that challenged my beliefs and capacities the most was being able to affect matter with my intention. Being more precise, bending metal spoons and forks, using only intention. My small hands, not used to physical force (and above all, the mental conditioning I received and accepted as truth) did not permit this. However, I was told in a seminar that it was possible to do this; I accepted, and I could not resist, bending metal. For a long time, I have said that what one human being can do, another can too. The truth is that through voluntary and conscientious intention, the opening of the heart chakra, feeling detached from our suffering and connected to the earth, I realized that it is perfectly possible that I could bend metal spoons and forks. When I connected with them, with my firm and loving intention, the objects (spoons and forks) become hot, malleable and able to be bent. This experiment freed me from a number of preconceptions and limitations. I expanded consciously and felt how much I was connected to All that existed and how life is available to work in a team with me.
But there is more. It is very probable that the reader has experienced focusing intention and was able to materialize things. It could be a nice car with a special price, a pay raise, or anything else. You used The Code of Creation— intention—to make real that which is meaningful for you and will continue to make it because it is your nature to create.

♥ Stop, Breathe, Love

Is it possible for intention to affect animals and plants? The answer is Yes. It is very probable that we have experienced the impact that we have on houseplants and also on our pets, when we wish for something to happen.

Whenever my mother picks a plant to plant, she has the intention that it will take immediately. It is certain that with her, plants grow and live. Also, whenever she buys flowers, she makes the intention that these should last long, and it works.

It is scientifically proven that plants are affected by intentions and react to them. Dr. Cleve Backster proved, with his studies using a polygraph, that plants reacted to his thoughts and intentions, changing the delineation of the polygraph both in his presence and at a distance. In one of his experiments, he came close to a plant (*Dracaena Massangeana*) "with a match and the intention of burning it, the graph skyrocketed in relation to that plant, as if it had gone mad (...) as well as with all the other connected plants. They all reacted in unison with a strong disorganized delineation." [7]

In another experiment, Dr. Backster sent a thought to his plants, "telling them that he was coming home—he was many kilometers away—when he arrived he found that the plants had reacted when he sent the thought, as shown in the intensive change in the polygraph." [8]

Intentionality also works with animals. They listen to us on a very deep level and recognize immediately the vibration we are irradiating through the thought or desire we emit. For those who have pets, the language of intention is extremely useful in the day to day. For example, to call them home when they are lost and to find the way.

I have already been able to communicate with the cat of a friend of mine, Tico, formulating the intention that he should come home by the end of the day, since he had been away for three days, and he returned.

From a scientific point of view, it has been proven that intention interferes with animals. A study made by Gerald Solfvin proved "that the desire/ intention that mice infected with malaria should recover faster positively influenced their recuperation." [9]

How is this possible? Everything is linked and reality is built and updates itself each moment, and we as human beings, are active builders of that same construction.

Our nature and the underlying unity of all creation allows us at each communication to inform and enform (give form) life, and due to the fundamental interdependence between everything, it is possible that the energetic effect occurs immediately or throughout time.

Intention is a language that the whole field understands. It is urgent to use it in a positive manner, creating harmony between us and the ecosystem on which we depend. We can intend, for example, that dolphins return to the Tagus river and collectively create the conditions of life for that to occur.

Is human intention also suitable to affect the collective, the planetary consciousness?

The concept of the collective consciousness can be understood as a collective force that emerges as a result of the intentions, images, words, feelings and behaviors of all people in a community or society and that it affects that said society and the globe.

---

[7] Please read more about the author and the experiments Backster, Cleve, "Evidence of a Primary Perception in Plant Life," International Journal of Parapsychology, Vol 10, Winter, 1968, N° 4.
[8] Tompkins, P. & Bird, C., The Secret Life of Plants, 1973, Harper & Row.
[9] Solfvin, G. F., "PSI expectancy effects in psychic healing studies with malarial mice," European Journal of Parapsychology, 1982 N° 4, pp 160-97.

Each person contributes to the collective with their energy, light and information and the sum of this builds a dynamic field of energy and of interference with the elements that constitute it and with all the entities with which they relate (animals, plants, minerals, etc.), as well as, with the fields of planetary and unified consciousness.

Is it possible for a group or groups of individuals to modify aspects of society and even of the planet? Does this group have any power? And is there a minimum number needed to create a critical mass to achieve measurable results?

Effectively, it is possible for the focus of attention and intention to be directed to positively affect the collective. With effect, one percent of the population (more appropriately the square root of one percent) produces measurable effects in its community and produces a turning point in the collective consciousness.

There are scientific studies confirming it. Experiments carried out in the United States, in the scope of the practice of transcendental meditation (Maharishi Mahesh Yogi) with the objective of proving that through the focused intention of a group in a meditative state, it is possible to achieve peace, had surprising results. In fact, a group of 7.000 meditators, 1% of the world population, came together at the University of Maharishi Mahesh Yogi, in Iowa, with the purpose of creating peace in Lebanon, during the civil war. The practitioners of transcendental meditation, meditated according to specific techniques (TMSidhi) and with their intention focused on internal peace. And by achieving internal peace, they created a network effect, measurable in Lebanon. *"The effects were the following: 71% less deaths on the warfront, 68% decrease in the assaults/ violence, 48% decrease in the accidents of war and an increase in 66% of efforts in the sense of cooperation to end the civil war. These results were analyzed and external factors such as, cycles, season changes, etc. were completely eliminated as being the cause of these crucial changes in the war of Lebanon."*[10]

This study is in fact disconcerting and also fascinating. This leads us to think seriously of our role in creating peace in the world. It takes us out of the concepts of separation and of impotence, very often generalized regarding the power that we have.

After all, the focused intention and the internal peace acquired and felt by the group, generate powerful waves of form with real impact in the worst scenarios of violence, the civil war. What happens inside us has implications on what surrounds us, reorganizing it in the direction of coherence and of harmony. We are a conscious hologram and a change on a point, or in various points, has implications in the whole hologram. When one of us becomes pacified, many are pacified. We can effectively create peace on the planet on a global scale.

Many authors have written and we confirm that the collective consciousness can be infected by distorted emotions, such as fear, hate, anger, intolerance, authoritarianism, insecurity and stress generated by individuals that vibrate on this level of the dysfunctional consciousness, infecting the community and the whole planet with a general discomfort. But we have an alternative, as a community and as individuals. Be united in a common purpose and create a field of interference affecting the community with love, peace, happiness, tolerance, richness, security and serenity. With effect, an intentional experience of peace or of love is a field of information and of highly coherent energy, which informs and gives form to reality that is in an intimate

---

[10] Maharishi Effect, published in Scientific Research on Maharishi's Transcendental Meditation and TMSidhi Program: Increased Progress towards Peaceful Resolution of Conflict; Collected Papers, Vol. 4: 335, Lebanon; 337.

connection with it. And such is possible because we are all linked in a dynamic web that communicates, interrelates and interacts at each moment, that is, the field of unified consciousness, of which all human beings, planets and the universe are part of and are one.

It is probable that the words of Christ *"when two or more gather in my name, there am I with them"* is a wake up call, inviting us to work together, introducing the values that make sense to be reflected in reality.[11]

Also, that each man is a sovereign decider of peace in the world. Who knows if 1% (specifically, the square root of 1%) of the population shown by the studies is a parallel that was already started by the apostles, creating a critical mass of people who want to implement changes in the world?

Independently of each one's religious beliefs, it is confirmed that this percentage of the population of one community, or even a number of people at work or in the family, with the focused intention and in an energetic state of coherence, produce waves of energies and light irradiating order. That same order generates harmony and more coherence in the energy systems with which they are in communication and interaction.

For example, consider the resident population of Portugal: in 2013, approximately 10,427,301 people, 1% of this number is 104,273.01 people, and the square root of this 1% is approximately 323 people. This is the number (323) needed to leverage change in Portugal and create the turning point of consciousness.[12]

It is not important if the people or the situations on which we are focused are next to us or on another continent. The information is shared and the consciousness is changed at any point of space or time.

Actually, we can choose to turn the community and the whole planet into a place of peace, solidarity, respect for biodiversity and of love, focusing collectively and purposefully in what we want to create. Can we do it or be it, now? For example, we can create food for Africa, or the cleaning up of the estuary of the Tagus river. The *"subtle technology"* of intention is present to allow miracles that have always been destined to be created/created, in unity with the field of unified consciousness and for the good of all beings.

Coherent Intention

"Doubt moves away the good that already exists."
Jean Paul

"Intention, good or bad, influences our life directly."
Buddha

We have been showing the nature of intention, its power and applicability to life, and I am sure that at this time it is clear that it is, simultaneously, a subtle force of nature, as well as the language of creation of reality that human beings use in partnership with the field of unified consciousness to communicate and participate in life.

As this topic is vast, it is more than probable that many questions arise and, because of this, I am going to list some of them, which I believe are important to clarify.

---

[11] The Bible Matthew 18:20
[12] Data collected from Portuguese statistical office IP Portugal (Resident Population 2013)

Are all intentions the same and affect or influence reality in the same way?
First, it should be understood that intention is one and all of it affects reality.
We, as human beings, are fated to take part in life and create with the field of unified consciousness. When we formulate an intention, we are communicating with the field of unified consciousness and it with us and with the planet, reorganizing life. Therefore, any intention affects reality. Now that this point is made clear, let us continue.

A different issue is understanding whether intentions can be different and affect reality in distinct ways.

Yes. It is possible, depending on whether the intention is "positive or negative," voluntary or involuntary, coherent or incoherent, of being conscious of being a creator united to the field or not, amongst others....

Regarding intention being "positive" or "negative," we can confirm that both produce effects.

Using a linear language an **intention is "positive"** *when its effects are what we want or are in accordance with our purpose and we perceive it as such.*
An **intention is "negative"** *when its effects are opposed to the ones we want, those we desired or purposely focused and we perceive it as such.*

Any intention produces results, always. These can be "positive", indifferent or "negative as long as they agree or not with the expected results and their respective perception.
People that use the **language of creation of intention** and have "positive" or "negative" intentions in respect to themselves, or others, manifest in their energy field, in events, situations, objects or persons with who they get along, the subatomic rearrangements of their intentions.
Remember that when focusing your consciousness on things that are "positive," in the first place, it is you that all the energy dynamics positively affects and also the people or community that you belong to. Inversely, if you focus on the "negative" you are already creating patterns of energy interference to experience that immediately for yourself, and also for the person that is receptive to your "negative" vibration.

On the other hand, as we are all connected to each other, when emitting a distorted pattern (negative) you are generating distorted waves for the people surrounding you, and to the community you belong to, causing a drop in the vibrational level of the cosmos. Therefore, be careful with what you are intending, because you are responsible for both yourself and for the All.
In case you have the perception that you are having or capturing an intention that is considered to be nonpositive, you can always alter it, changing your intention and perception. *We are all powerful and the same in the light of the field of unified consciousness and no one has more power than the other. Only limiting beliefs can separate us. The power you have is the power of unity and it is able to transform everything.*

One of the possibilities is thinking and feeling that you are secure; that love illuminates you, or that peace is here at this moment. You can also consciously irradiated light. One of the most efficient ways that I know to neutralize any type of less than positive intention is for the person to enclose himself in a cylinder of pink energy that irradiates out packets of pink waves and enclose himself in a cocoon of silver fluorescent light. That cocoon pulsates with the vital energy "I am at the service of good, divinely protected and I send light waves to the All, neutralizing any vibration different than this intention."

♥ Stop, Breathe, Love

Another aspect regarding intention has to do with the way it is formulated.
It may be involuntary or voluntary.
The involuntary or automatic intention can be understood as that thought, wish or unconscious will for something that emerges from thought on autopilot and that, as a general rule, is unconscious and tendentiously negative.
What is the level of "efficiency" of these types of intentions? What do they construct? In cases where you intend in an unconscious or automatic manner, normally as a result of the excess of external stimuli or by involuntary negative thoughts (which we have interiorized since we were small and that are vibrating in the collective consciousness), the result is probably "negative." The tendency is towards the occurrence of a "negative" manifestation and the person not assuming what he constructed, rejecting the reality that is emerging as an event, experience, situation or person, denying responsibility for the events. It is the others, the time, the economic environment, etc... but he has nothing to do with it.
For example, you want to rest and your boss sends you home to rest, and you become furious. Or, you wish for a quieter boyfriend because the previous one was very talkative and then complain that this one hardly speaks. That is why the frog in the story says "be careful with what you desire."
In involuntary intention there is still the probability that the concretization of the intention occurs in a diffuse and dispersed manner, or does not occur at all, because the person has meanwhile focused on resistances or has problematized and cancelled the intention.

The voluntary conscious intention can be understood as a focused thought, desire or purpose for something that makes sense for the person at that moment. It is a conscious decision directed at an objective. Generally, it is directed towards the "positive" and towards the personal and common wellbeing. It is the natural tendency to be "better" as a person, doing a certain activity "better" and or having something "better." In other words, it is our being that gives the impulse of progress, with that state of being having implications in doing and in having.

An intention can be moving houses, getting a promotion at work, having the desire to take a sabbatical leave to care for family, or work in another country. It can also be for the purpose of ending social exclusion and poverty or being kind to a brother.
Guided by that conscious intention, our field of information and energy cooperates in tune with the field of unified consciousness and the planet. In that sense, multiple

possible scenarios emerge, and specific events are particularized in accordance with the intention. Contexts, situations, and events are formatted and also people appear synchronized temporally and spatially to align with the intention. These all serve the decision of personal sovereignty, allied to the cosmic sovereignty and the manifestation occurs.

It is very important that in this decision process coherence is maintained; *that is, the alignment with what has been decided, from the decision to the thought, the speaking, the imagining, the feeling and the action. Furthermore, being the embodiment of what we intended.*

On the level of voluntary intention, it is fundamental that once an objective is delineated, the course is maintained. If perhaps we formulate an intention and then we problematize it or we become confused, the tendency is that it does not manifest itself or that it is manifested in a distorted manner.

For example, we decide to change jobs and the opportunity emerges, but we do not go to the interview. It is obvious that we are not being coherent with the decision that was made. Or if we decide to be kind to our neighbor and we see her loaded with shopping bags and we do not help her, we are also out of alignment.

The lack of coherence has to do with the fact that the conscious intention can clash with limiting beliefs that were hidden, or the lack of attention or even the absence of assumption that all the universe is already united to bring to life what we intentioned.

Speaking once again of coherence, from a quantum point of view, when we emit an intention that is completely coherent with that which we emit, it enters in phase and interferes with other waves in the same frequency, cooperating and affecting each other, manifesting. On the other hand, if there is incoherence, the waves will be out of phase, they will not interfere amongst themselves or they could only interfere to a minor degree, they may not cooperate or co-operate very little, they could even mutually cancel themselves out, there could be no manifestation or the manifestation could be much later or scattered.

One of the situations that destabilizes voluntary intention with great frequency is the creation of doubts and problematizing things, and it is also the question of "How?". Because of the "How" a person could even possibly be giving up on what he had evoked and preventing the manifestation of the intention. As a general rule, "How?" is associated with limitation, fear and tension. "How" am I going to achieve if I do not have the means, the knowledge, the experience, the physical robustness, the qualifications, the money, the thinness, the recommendation or the intelligence? Or "How" am I going to be able to if my cholesterol is high, I am over forty, I have flat feet, three children, am under or over-qualified or anything else? The "How?" has to do with linear thought, with the laws of conventional physics, with the perception of separation, with fear, limitations, namely of space and time, means, resources or the conditions.

Actually, the truth is that human intention is a wave of quantum possibilities interacting and communicating with the energy of the field of unified consciousness, behaving in a nonlinear way, being in superposition in various places at the same time, transcending space and time, manifesting physically and instantly with full abundance. The field of unified consciousness is complete in itself and limitless, and what we evoke is possible of being manifested, from the smallest detail to the most gigantic event. Therefore, when using the energy of creation of intention, forget the "How?" because it is possible to bring to life what you want.

In voluntary intention, once the decision is made, attention is focused on the purpose. There is verticality in the whole process, until the manifestation. The thoughts and the mental images are maintained clear and directed to our resolution. The words and the silences are in tune with our intentions. The feelings and emotions are harmonious, peaceful, happy, connected to what we proposed ourselves and, naturally, our actions are coherent with what we previously decided. The manifestation is inevitable.

Voluntary and conscious intention faces us with clarity and asks us:
"Are you ready to continue to be united with your purpose?" "Are you open to be what you proposed to be?" "Is your will clear, firm and detached?"
This being firm, i.e., is internally clear, then it purely and simply happens. When dealing with intention, which is energy informing and enforming and also giving sense to the purpose expressed, the probabilities of manifestation, in the here and constant now, are endless. As a rule, what happens is that unexpectedly an idea emerges that until then had not been pondered, or we find someone who directs us to the next step, or something happens that is directly related to the intention meanwhile formulated. The entire universe is synchronized to work in our favor.

♥ Stop, Breathe, Love

Besides the internal clarity needed for a manifestation to occur, it is also important to be in a state of openness. Normally it is sufficient to be neutral, without any resistance for the intention to occur. If we are in a state of fluidity, open to the infinite possibilities, then it is magnificent.
The doubt, the mistrust or the "how," is pure resistance. If there is fear, it closes the infinite possibilities and builds more fear and limitation.
The clarity, neutrality and openness which I mention can be just a nanosecond, or minutes, or days and even months continuously in this vibration. When in a state of openness, any impulse, any information that is placed by us in the field of unified consciousness, is fit to materialize immediately, and it is only necessary to be receptive to receiving it. Any person can do it and normally it has to do with returning to be a child, to be innocent, playing happily and flowing in life. We are no longer in control of the situation. We do not know how it is done or what is going to happen and in what way. We stand back to see the goodness of what we evoked, and that can be even greater than we have ever imagined.

On another level, is intention also affected by the "level" of consciousness of the subject who has formulated it? That is, **does a person who has full consciousness that he or she is the creator of reality in connection with the field of unified consciousness, manifest reality faster or more consistently, and accept it?**
The human consciousness that is aware that in the act of making an intention is

communicating, sharing information and shaping reality, in unity with the field of unified consciousness, knows that he or she is an unlimited being and that everything is possible. In this sense, he or she is aware that whatever is purposely intentioned can emerge instantly, that time and space can be transcended and that any form, object, person or state is available in the present.

On the other hand, even if the manifestation extends over time, the consistency, that is, the perception/ attention on that which has been evoked, is already done, it maintains it. The connection persists and is actually producing results. Furthermore, the perception of unity, which is the underlying coherence of all reality, and the person who experiences it, be it for a nano second, thirty continuous days, or a whole lifetime, accepts responsibility for what is created. He is one with it and knows that he can always recreate again.

All the masters, from Krishna to Christ, used intention in a conscious manner to create. Their attention/perception was focused on the totality of possibilities, and they actualized the reality to be manifested. As it happens, each one of us is also his own master, and already has with him the intention, as well as the state of unity. We only need to be what we are, *complete* and having attention/perception connected, communicating and participating happily in life in the present.

Intention is a force of creativity connected to possibility, and from a quantum point of view, creativity is plentiful and is present in both a potential and as manifested state in life. We can create everything. Because the possibilities are unlimited and the opportunities are too.

Here are two testimonials about intentional creativity.

Testimonial

After a divorce, I had serious financial problems, and I did not know how to get enough money to meet my household expenses, the cost of food, and my child's education as well as feeling lonely and without the support of my family who was in Angola. I was a bursary student completing a master's degree at the university (sometimes the bursary money was not paid) and I wanted to find a job in my field of chemical engineering and return to Angola to be closer to my family.

During a seminar with Susana, I became aware that it was possible to be completely successful and reorganize my life.

I formulated the intention to have a well-paid job, to earn over €3,000 per month, and that all issues related with money and my return to Angola would be solved. Let me tell you: the week after the seminar, I received the overdue bursary money and I saw an advertisement in the Expresso newspaper for a position in an oil company in Angola. I applied for the position. During the two months, I had left to complete the Masters', I received the bursary in time and was able to pay all the bills. I was successful in getting the position as a chemical engineer. And you know what? I began working in Angola after completing the bursary, and they even paid my travel expenses.

It was my clear intention that unleashed this whole process. I am grateful to life, which has led me masterfully to the right people and events.

Joana Bernardo, chemical engineer

Testimonial

Since childhood, I had the dream of dating and getting married. However, that was not easy for me. I did not like my image, I felt less for having more... (you know what I mean)... then it seemed that men of the marrying type did not exist. Those things referred to as colorful relationships, were not my cup of tea. The years went by without the right man for me coming along.

At work, everything was going right and with my family too. One day a friend spoke to me about Susana and I decided to try a seminar. And I loved it.

When I realized that I could create my reality, the time has come for me to materialize the relationship. That very delicate subject, that I had not been able to deal with, was now open, and I was prepared to be freed of all resistance regarding it.

I wanted to experience the love and have my partner/husband with me. My intention materialized in an unexpected manner. Who would have said it would have been so fast; it was already available for me? Yes. I already knew him, just like he knew me. He was my brother's friend, but we had hardly ever spoken. After the seminar, we came across each other at dad's house and we had a long conversation. This had never happened before. From that moment on, we never left each other and today we are together and have a beautiful son.

Ana Silva, manager

In the Footprint of Intention

"It is the intention, and not the donation, that makes the donor."
Gotthold Lessing

"The intention is the start of the action."
Jewish Texts

Intending is an act of personal creativity allowing us to express beliefs, dreams, hopes, visions and objectives, both personally and collectively, every day and which becomes linked to the creativity of the field of unified consciousness and the planet. Any intention can come to life. It can be finding a life partner, the vaccination against herpes, getting good service at the tax office, but it also could be confusion, suffering or failure.

A very important point regarding intention is the sense of internal realization. The internal sensation that what we intend is already present. This feeling can occur naturally, especially if we are in a state of openness and unity, and it can also be important to stimulate it so that it happens.

One of the best ways to experience this feeling of realization when intending is by using the senses. Sense the smell, the taste, the movement, the color, the shape, the equilibrium, the temperature, the sounds and even the empathy. Feel in a clear and perceptible manner the result of the intention—the realization—in a way that the body, the emotions and the mind experiences it at that exact moment. And this energetic state, this amplified sensorial information directed towards a purpose, is so strong that it actualizes in tune with the field of unified consciousness the manifestation of the intention.

For the person using the senses and experiencing the sensations, the intention is already materialized at that moment. Be it only for an instant, he becomes one with what he was observing—creating—in the reality of that moment. Even if it is just for a fraction of a second, a point of the matrix has been changed as a result of the process of sensing the intention. That point is the turning point for an entire universe perceiving and recreating itself at each moment.

Therefore, feel intensively that your intention has already materialized. See the colors, the shapes; feel the movement, the temperature, the taste. Touch, hear the sounds, feel the equilibrium, the vitality, empathize and communicate, even telepathically if you so decide in your intention. In parallel, feel the beauty, the joy, the happiness and the love for the realization. These feelings attract even more energy, more information and light promoting the realization. Feel intensively, because the field of unified consciousness feels with you and actualizes with you the scenarios that you formulate and manifests that experience.

Because the act of intending is a process of communication and interaction between us and the field of unified consciousness, it is possible to receive messages informing us of what is happening.

These are postcards from the universe giving us news, the so-called "signs" that we can follow. They can emerge through intuition or clairvoyance, but also through the sense of movement. For example, the intuition to phone someone or dress in specific clothes; having a premonitory dream in which the image of a place emerges. It can also be noticing the accelerated movement of the molecules when you are walking to a set place. The senses can also use the feelings, the sensations and the body to perceive the messages. It can be a sensation of warmth on the face, an undulation in the body, a sensation of pleasure in the chest, serenity or even sudden joy. But also, if we are steering away from the intention, then an ill feeling can emerge, tightness of the chest, fatigue or spent energy etc. Other times the feeling comes with great intensity; it can be seeing beauty in everything, intense love, a sensation of power, strength or vitality, confidence and a lot of joy. What matters most is being attentive.

♥ Stop, Breathe, Love

The moment to formulate an intention is always in the present and from that moment on, the immanent forces of life communicate and interact between themselves, so that what has been intentioned happens. Entwined as we are in one another, in events and in life, we cause the emergence of events in a team with the field of unified consciousness. It can be people crossing our way, having time, or resources and objects emerging.

Sometimes it happens that the results appear instantaneously, as if they came from nowhere; sometimes they occur in a set time that can vary between a few minutes, weeks, months and sometimes years. It is still possible that when we formulate the intention we have to take steps, and act in its materialization and other times, it is enough to accept it. Depending on the intention.

For example, the intention to find the best hairdresser, at the best price, in an unknown place and in five minutes, the manifestation occurs, because we bumped into a friend whom we had not seen in three years and she owns a hairdressing salon.

I will now refer to another example, where the manifestation is extended in time. The intention to create an association for the protection of abandoned animals can be materialized in stages, with actions linked in the sense of the intention. Namely, in the legal constitution of an association, attracting funds, and choosing a place to keep the animals, canvassing for volunteers, having a veterinarian, etc. In any case, the intention is the star that guides the whole chain to materialization.

🚀 Exercise: be aware of your power with intention
- Write 2 intentions you have manifested out of the blue.
- Write down 2 intentions you materialized that were extended in time.
- Now write this sentence: I made this I can do it always.
- Close your eyes and notice your brain, heart and all your body feeling that you are capable. You are a powerful manifestor.

Does intention need action to realization?
Yes, they are two cheeks of the same face.

Intention is complete in itself and, when formulated, it already has the power of materialization, just because the events are intertwined with themselves, the subsequent action is what materializes the intention. In this sense, intentional acts reflect the confidence that what we have intentioned is already happening, as well as actualizing the following events that allow the realization.

Intending without acting as a consequence of that same intention is to sabotage yourself by going against the quantum movement started for the realization, and therefore not receiving what has been created. In parallel, self-confidence decreases, and also delays, confusions or tensions can emerge, preventing other processes connected with the intention to appear.
Following an intention with an action resulting from it, is being coherent and open to other outcomes, sometimes unimaginable, which come from the result of intending. When formulating the intention, a variety of possibilities, of scenarios, of meetings and situations become available and we only need to follow up with the linked action so that the realization occurs. Or until a better or greater possibility emerges.
Paraphrasing Henry Stapp *"By virtue of the quantum laws of movement a strong intention, shown in the great fastness of similar intention acts, tends to maintain the model associated to the action."*[13]
Intention and action are, in this case, two sides of the same coin, that actualize themselves mutually, causing the desired result to happen. It can be a small action; going to the supermarket, taking the dog to the vet, speaking to the teacher, accepting an unexpected invitation, attending a dance class, etc.
Besides the action required by the intention, at a more fundamental level We Are What We Intend, and this state of being is the most important vibration to the materialization. For example, for the intention of having abundance, the state of being that is linked to this is being abundant. This could imply sharing the abundance, however small the action is, or buying something.
In the intention of having success, the state that is connected to it, is being successful.

---

[13] Stapp, Henry P, *Mind, Matter, and Quantum Mechanics*, Springer Verlag, New York, 1993.

We can do something with success for us or for others, as a result of that internal state of success. For example, speaking in public. Being what we intentioned is the fastest way to the manifestation. Because being is complete in itself and is united.

♥ Stop, Breathe, Love

Another fundamental point of intention is the focus of attention.
Every day, through attentive intentionality, we are expanding our personal and collective universe, affecting other universes. So, it is essential to be aware of what we are intending and paying attention to, because what we focus on, we manifest.
Therefore, we have to select both the intention as well as the attention to create *"the best of all possible worlds."*[14]
What is important to remember in relation to attention and is also applicable to intention is:

The What, When and How of attention.
1) **What** will we focus on? **What intention do we choose to focus on?**
2) **When** are we going to focus our intention? **In the past, in the present or in the future?**
3) **How** are we going to focus? **Do we focus on intention in a concentrated or distributed manner?**
The intention that we focus on, the moment in which we focus and how we give attention to the intention, interferes with it, namely with the concretization of it.
For example, we intend to complete an architectural project within fifteen days and we focus on that. We give concentrated attention to the project; we work on it and complete it by the target date.
Another example: we intend to make peace with a colleague at work. However, we continue to systematically focus our attention on what "she/he did wrong" (from the beginning of the relationship) and the next day we do not even speak to her/him. We boycott the intention.
What is important is understanding that as we continue to feed intention with the focus of attention, the intention is manifested. That on which we concentrate (be it good or less than good), we materialize.
When using intention and attention, we are imprinting in our life, and in the field of unified consciousness, vital instructions regarding the experiences that we want to experience. We have a choice, always. We can change both the intention and the attention and create a better world and for the good of all beings.
Just one intention can be the radical turning point for a better life. Be a deliberate creator, choosing and daring to broaden your horizons. Feel connected to the intention and let this connection, which is the reality underlying life, be it in a potential or manifest state, be with you in any steps or leaps that you may take. Your life, family, community, world, universe will be different because you intentioned it.

---

[14] Gottfried Leibniz, "Essays on the Goodness of God, the Freedom of Man and the Origin of Evil".

Intention Practical Guide:

To make it easier to use intention, I leave a step by step guide:

1) Formulate an intention.
Formulating an intention depends on you. What do you wish or want? What is the purpose? Open yourself for your own good and the good of all. **Always think of the end result as an intention.**

2) What is the "plan" for the intention?
When formulating an intention, it is important to use **the best image, idea, or perspective of the situation, the person, the things or the events and declare to yourself that it manifests itself in the physical plane**, in current earthly reality and in the present. You can even imagine the place, the date, see the radiant face of the person, what he/ she is wearing, his or her feelings, the people with them, the positive changes that will happen in their lives, etc... and place it now in the current context. State it in first person and in the present tense, leaving out the word no.

3) Statement of intention.
An intention is a statement of the principles of the infinite possibilities. Accept that it is **possible** and that it is real for you.

4) Feel the realization of the intention.
Feel the sensations, be aware of the smells, tastes, what you are listening to, what you are touching, what colors you see, the movement, the temperature, the vitality, the position of the body and which positive feelings you have (for example, joy, satisfaction, realization, etc. Make the experience vivid in your body, mind and emotions. Put your cells processing the multidimensional experience, now).
The feeling or the emotion of the materialization of your wish or intent—**experienced currently**—make the materialization of your intention possible. Also note the intuition, telepathy or clairvoyance which can emerge.

5) Keep the focus.
Instead of evoking one thing and then changing to another, or to another, and to another, **the best is to maintain the focus of what you want to achieve (focusing on the final result)** and relax. Keep focused on the heart, with the feet well anchored on earth and the head in the stars.

6) Detach yourself.
You should free yourself from the issue; its purpose is delivered. Relax, all is well. Keep yourself innocent like a child. It is already finished.

7) Keep yourself attentive and act.
It is very important to be attentive and be receptive to information. You may receive messages both internally (dreams, visions, intuitions, feelings) as well as externally (billboards, news, conversations, telephone calls, or a white feather) that emerge in

the course of the intention. **Pay attention to what reaches you. Which people, which situations, what opportunities and act.** For example, if your intention is finding a job and suddenly you walk past a shop and perceive that it is there that you wish to work, do your share: go in and tell them you wish to work there, ask if they need employees, leave your curriculum vitae, ask for an interview, etc.

8) Moment.
The moment of the materialization of the intention that has been formulated **is always in the present.** It is in the constant now, in the continuous present that life is happening, and the intention and its respective materialization as well. The intention can materialize immediately or not in the physical plane, depending on the perception of what is possible for the subject. For many people, things need time. It is useful to change the perception for the possibility that it happens instantaneously in the physical reality. For those that wish to accept the idea that the manifestation happens in the correct and perfect timing, everything is alright too.

9) Result of the Intention.
Accepting that as the result of creation there is the **possibility of the manifestation being even better and greater than what was formulated.** Something unexpected can be manifested, different, strange, and even greater and better than you thought possible. Keep the perception that only the best is happening.

10) Crystallized reality.
Intention is already materialized in your life; you have already embodied what you evoked. **State that it is real and that what is happening is good for you and for everyone.**

11) Thanking.
Gratitude keeps you linked to the blessing of your creation as well as to the flow of infinite abundance, recreating more for yourself and for the world. Place what you have created in an open manner and intend the wellbeing for all beings, from the depth of your heart.

It is always possible for one more possibility, one more miracle, which is another opportunity for life to appear with the contour, the color, the sense and the dimension that we human beings have placed through the focus of the intention. Focus intentionally on the "positive" changes that represent you and that simultaneously are for your wellbeing and for the wellbeing of all beings. In that action, you cause the rise of the whole of humanity and positively change the face of the universe.

Key points:
- Intention is a consciousness tool to create reality.
- It is a universal language we were born with to communicate with each other, with the field of unified consciousness and the planet.
- Our thoughts wishes and most intimate purposes are intentions.
- Intentions are an active force that human beings have to imprint their mark in

- the world.
- The power of intention is in each one of us, and we can use this advanced *"subtle technology"* for human realization;
- It is available twenty-four hours per day, 365 days per year, during all our existence, and it can be applied and change deeply and positively our lives.
- With intention, you can affect "cells, enzymes, ocular and brain movements". Also, it is possible to interrupt the manifestation of diseases and even be cured.
- An intention can heal us, create health in the people we love, even if we are kilometers apart.
- It is true that a thought, a wish, a focused purpose does affect animals and plants and make us understand that we share a bond with all living beings.
- It is effectively possible to affect objects with our intentions, bending the notions of material reality, solidity, and relationships of extreme objectivity that we held since we started studying and applied them to facilitate our lives.
- Focused intention coherently affects the collective consciousness and it creates conditions for extreme transformations on the globe, even at a distance and even in a scenario of devastation like a civil war.
- We are being of limitless possibilities and our intentions are acts of creation to create reality instant by instant.
- What are we going to create now consciously through intention is the most important question that we can ask ourselves?
- It can be: to be healthy, to have relationships full of meaning, earn more, have a new house, to go to the theatre with our family, that all children in the process of being adopted get a new family, or reforesting and returning animals to the jungle.
- The field of unified consciousness knows the fastest, the shortest, the easiest way to bring to life your intention
- The field will synchronize people, events, circumstances, objects, situations in order to each one of us experience the results of our intention.
- In a state of openness, detachment and coherence it is possible to receive even better and greater what we have intended.
- Just one intention can be the radical turning point for humanity and it depends on you to start. Use your intentions wisely.

Self-reflection:
❶ What intentions have you already materialized in your life? Describe three of them.
❷ What scientific experiments shown here made more sense to you and why?
❸ What beneficial intention for yourself and for the community will you put into practice?

Exercises:
❶ Establish three or four simple intentions for things that are unusual in your life; for example, the attendant at the dry cleaners who is normally serious smiles at you; your husband says thank you, or take the groceries of the car; or someone who you have not spoken to for a long time phones you today.

❷ In the morning, when you wake up, or when you go to bed, formulate your intentions for your day. What makes sense for your day to be? Focus on the materialization, observing the steps formulated above. Remember the feeling. The more it is felt and experienced the better. Make a note on paper if you wish. In the evening, confirm all the chain of steps that allowed the concretization of your intention. What you thought, the image you had, what you feel, how you acted, etc. Write in a notebook or diary. Repeat the exercise for three weeks.

❸ Intending materializing something that has significance for you. It can be changing jobs, going on a trip, etc. Follow the steps I mentioned above and focus on the materialized event. Remember to feel; smell, hear, taste, touch, the temperature, the vitality, the movement, the position of the body, the intuition you have, etc. The more it is felt and experienced, the better. And live the joy, the love, the satisfaction of the realization of the intention.

❹ Focus on internal joy every day, have the intention to expand it throughout your city and wherever you go. Be and spread joy.

6 Thought

Story
A long time ago, in Greece, there lived a very wise old woman whom they called Flowering Oracle. One day, Flowering Oracle was pouring water in a glass when a very serious man, spoke to her in a rough voice: "Are you the one who people go to with their questions?" The old woman said yes. The man told her that he had walked five days to visit her because he needed answers. Flowering Oracle sat on the floor and the man sat in front of her saying: "I do not understand my thoughts. Some overwhelm my head so much that it seems like it will explode and I am so harsh on myself. At moments like these, the whole family runs away from me, as if I was a lightning storm and my life goes awry. At other times, thoughts fill my mind and are friendly to me. I see life in color; I become happy and notice that everything goes well; even the neighbors ask me for advice. What is more intriguing, there are times when I am free like the wind and a gust of ideas come to me, and I don't even know where they come from—it is not me thinking—it appears that I am being thought. How is it possible for one single head to have so much activity and produce so many things?"

Flowering Oracle smiled. She also knew what the man was talking about. Then she told him, "When the head is full, empty it; when you see colors in the world color it, and move yourself with the wind." After saying this, she looked at the man in the eyes and stood.

"Everything we are is the result of what we have thought. The mind is everything. What we think, we become"
Buddha

In your day-to-day life, which character are you? The Flowering Oracle or the troubled man? It is probable that you are both. The truth is that thoughts exist and learning to deal with them is extremely useful. Thoughts produce reality: yours, mine, the collective, global and even universal reality.
We are going to discuss them in detail.
In a wider sense, thought is information, energy in movement (discontinuous/continuous) and light vibrating in the field of unified consciousness.

Thought is an instrument placed at the service of the human consciousness so that she can create reality. It is still **a language** through which the field of unified consciousness communicates with us and us with it.
The field of unified consciousness is the source of every being and naturally, of thought as well. To better understand and organize the explanation, we will confirm that thought has three "origins":
❶ Unified consciousness
❷ Individual consciousness
❸ Planetary consciousness
However, the energy of thought is one. Let us now address the three origins of thought.

❶ Thought from the unified consciousness

Infinite information exists in the field of unified consciousness. Any piece of information—regardless of its place in time or space—is vibrating in the field of unified consciousness. It is the database of eternity, with multidimensional information, even working beyond the speed of light.

When we are consciously in resonance (communication and interaction in the same wave frequency) with the field of unified consciousness—the field of information—the consciousness/brain matrix captures the information and mirrors it instantly.

According to Karl Pribram, our brain functions by structuring vision, hearing, taste and other functions, holographically. The information is distributed through the whole system, wherein each fragment reproduces the whole. The brain and the memories that it has are organized, functioning as holograms in movement; they are images of a greater image that are being actualized and in constant communication between the brain and the field of unified consciousness.

Pribram admits, through the holographic model of brain functioning, that the brain is communicating with the field of unified consciousness at each moment, permitting experiences that transcend space and time and instantly receiving information from the field. According to him, we have direct access to any possibility, to any piece of information in real time, immediately and "alocally." Any solution is available to us, be it the cure for a disease, a new architectural form, a new spatial technology invention, or an ecological cleanup. Human beings accesses and receives information from the field of unified consciousness and makes it theirs, through the focus of the consciousness and the acceptance of the information.[1]

❷ Thought from the individual consciousness

Our consciousness produces thoughts, because human beings were endowed with the faculties of thinking, reasoning, reflecting, judging, comparing, etc. The brain is a processor and a capacitor of energy, as well as a biotranslator. Thoughts are self-produced energy waves in the consciousness/brain matrix permitting us to make decisions (I am going to the dentist; I am going to make a tortilla for dinner; I am moving houses), establish comparisons and perform logical, deductive reasoning (recognize that today is colder than yesterday, the resolution of an equation, study, analyze concepts, present a paper, etc.), foresee situations that we are mentally occupied with (if I do this, the consequence is this, or if I say this to my mother, she will reply that), make judgments (what we think is right or wrong, admire a work of art), and so many other functions that are not mentioned here.

When we think, we send out energy that is manifested in our energy field and also in the field of unified consciousness, which mirrors it in the reality around us, and thus, we can understand the type of creation we are performing.

❸ Thought from the planetary consciousness

Earth is also an energy field with specific energies, continuously sending them out to

---

[1] Pribram, K.H., Brain and Perception: Holonomy and Structure in Figural Processing, Hillsdale, NJ, Lawrence Eribaum, 1991.

the entire community of beings living on it and also to the field of unified consciousness. It also receives information from the human community and the field of unified consciousness.

Earth's energy field receives all human thoughts and retransmits them in the same vibrational frequency to the human community and field. Each person or group of people then have the capacity of accepting, changing or rejecting the thoughts that have meanwhile been formulated, feeding back into the planetary consciousness.

Thought in Process

"A particular train of thought persisted in, be it good or bad, cannot fail to produce its results on the character and circumstances."
James Allen

Thought is a dynamic process that occurs in the consciousness/brain matrix at an incredible speed. From a quantum point of view, it is a subatomic dance where there is sharing of information and interaction between waves of energy, bits of information and light, in a gigantic and colorful intertwine.

In this universe where information is plentiful, the consciousness/brain matrix captures the information through the senses and processes it internally, linking them to each other, giving them meaning, associating the information and storing it in the memory. A thought is an energy input, a frequency of energy which the quantum processor, the brain, emits and processes internally and to which it also gives significance, linking itself to other data, and other energy frequencies. For example, images, feelings, or words.

Thinking is communicating in a broader sense; in the act of thinking, we share information. A bit of information vibrates in our energy field and simultaneously in the field of unified consciousness and the planet. The information then updates on the level of the information field as a result of the fundamental interconnectedness of all reality.

Each thought is linked to the All on a network. The field of unified consciousness listens to our communications, understands the language that is thought and answers us: reorganizing life, and manifesting reality.

Thought is a "subtle technology of consciousness" that allows us to communicate, interact and reorganize the quantum world in accordance with our own subjectivity, and in a team with the field of unified and planetary consciousness. Thinking is shaping reality.

When we think of a situation, event or person, we automatically vibrate and the field of consciousness vibrates with us, representing reality to us with the quality, dimension and color of our thoughtful impression.

♥ Stop, Breathe, Love

Imagine that your five-year-old child asks you, "Mom/Dad, what are thoughts for?" What would your reply be?

I am going to give you the simplest reply. They serve to create life. *It is exactly that. In the language of creation, thought has the function of building reality. Each thought is an energetic instruction, an order for that which is in potential to take form, have*

meaning or dimension and manifest in reality.
Thinking is a powerful act. It is bringing to life what you have thought. In each moment of our lives, we are informing and giving form to life through our thoughts. From health, entrepreneurial success, good family communication, to misfortunes, criticisms, revolts and also pleasures or anything else. The human consciousness is there, bringing to life scenarios, experiences, people and circumstances, through our act of thinking with the field of unified consciousness.

Thought is an instrument of human consciousness that creates reality in partnership with the field of unified consciousness. Before emitting a thought, the subatomic particles are moving and exist in a state of indetermination within our field of energy and in the field of unified consciousness. When emitting a thought, our consciousness concentrates it on a point of information, a point of vastness and actualizes it, causing the subatomic particles to become particularized, gaining a set form, in tune with the field of unified consciousness.

The question that could be asked is as follows: **what reality can we build with thought? What can we manifest in life?** The answer is that any reality can be manifested by us through thought. From entrance to a university, to good customer service at the supermarket, to getting rid of stress or healing chickenpox. Each thought, in itself, is capable of crystallizing life.

Thought is a subtle force: an energy interacting with the energy of the totality. When we think, we imprint our view of the world in the wave of possibilities of quantum reality and that vision is intertwined with the vision of the totality and emerges physically manifested.

It does not matter what we are imprinting, or what we are focusing on, the field of unified consciousness simply actualizes it and places it "online" in the cosmic internet of our creations.

Independent of size, quality, context, people, resources or events involved and even space-time, any reality is possible. Thought functions in the scope of the infinite possibilities that the field of unified consciousness has in itself and that is also in us. We can create limitlessly, because the probabilities that we have available are infinite.

Directed Thought

"There is nothing either good or bad but thinking makes it so."
William Shakespeare Hamlet

Thinking is a subtle force of the manifestation of reality that we have. At the same time, it is a creative language that we speak, which the field knows and replies to, bringing to life that which we have communicated. In this constant dialogue between us and the field of unified consciousness, we are free to choose what we manifest at each second; the field of unified consciousness reflects our joint creations like a magnificent mirror.
The truth is that we are always thinking; could it be that any thoughts we emit can affect reality?

Any thought affects reality; more appropriately, it is reality interfering with the infinite possibilities of reality. The nature of reality is one and so is thought.

Therefore, it is only possible for thought to affect reality because that is its role, its immanent nature.

A different question is knowing if thoughts can be different and if they influence reality in the same way?

Yes, of course. It depends if the thoughts are "positive" or "negative," voluntary or involuntary, coherent or incoherent, and if in the act of formulating them, we are conscious of their creative power and united with the field of unified consciousness or not, amongst others.

Regarding thoughts being "positive" or "negative," let us make the following clear now: thoughts are what they are—reality. "Positive" or "negative" is an energy charge that subatomic particles may have.

Considering a thought as "positive" or "negative" has to do with the mental constructions associated with the rules, values and cultural, philosophical, political, social and religious aspects that we give significance to. "Positive" and "negative" are perceptual and behavioral references through which we govern ourselves in a given moment, as individuals and as a community.

As it happens, these constructions are subject to the natural changes of human beings, the respective community and its environment. And what was positive at a given moment, can cease to be and vice versa. A negative for one particular human being can be positive for another person. Therefore, the issue is not set, and has to be seen in the light of the "level" of consciousness of each one.

For example, the thought of leaving a job can be negative for one person; another person in the same physical, familiar or financial situation can consider this to be a good idea. It is the old story of one person seeing the glass "half empty" and another person looking at the same glass and seeing it "half full."

Now that this point is clear, let us look at the possibility of what can be "positive" or "negative."

A thought that is considered positive is one that manifests the results we want and makes sense for us at the time, and we perceive it as positive. For example, passing an exam, having a day off, flirting at lunchtime. **A thought can be considered negative** if its effects are the opposite of what we wanted, of what we have focused on, and also if it reflects what we perceive as negative. For example, being late for a meeting, a problem with our mother in law, or a tummy ache.

Using the **language of thought creation,** thinking "positively" or "negatively" about ourselves, about others or about situations, we manifest in our field of energy, in the events, situations, objects or people with whom we deal with, the subatomic rearrangements of those thoughts.

It is extremely important to understand and practice that, each time we focus our consciousness on positive things, we are automatically benefitted. The energy rises to the first place in our field and affects us, as well as those close to us and the planet.

Inversely, if we focus on the negative, our energy drops, we create dysfunctional waves for our life, and we also affect the person who is (are) receptive to the "negative" vibration on an individual or planetary scale, causing a drop in the collective and cosmic, seeing that we are all interlinked.

Therefore, we should be careful with what we think, because we are responsible for ourselves and the planet, and it is important to respect our wellbeing and that of all other beings.

Each one of us, when creating thoughts, can use a formula that allows us to expand our consciousness level. This formula is, **"That it should be for my good and the good of all beings."**

When coming in tune—personal and global good—we are using a multidimensional trampoline which opens infinite possibilities and brings us peace. Therefore, when emitting a given thought, for example, being promoted at work, we can add: "that my promotion is for my good and the good of all beings." This means that we are using the highest criterion, a broader level of consciousness so that the actual wellbeing is compatible with the wellbeing of others.

However, if we have the perception that we are having or capturing a thought that we consider negative, we can always change it. For example, we can always change it to the opposite or even neutralize it. Choosing another thought is an act of personal sovereignty. It is us that choose to change and reorganize our energy field, because we are the creators of our reality.

From the point of view of the field of unified consciousness, *we are all equally powerful* and it is easy to neutralize any type of thought. *The power of unity is at our service and it is possible to transform any reality.* You may think, for example, "I choose peace" or "that only love exists and this converts in love," and then carry on with life.

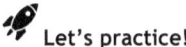 Let's practice!
- Stand up, breathe deeply three times.
- Ask yourself. *What am I thinking now?* Notice if your thoughts are sensible and reflect your intentions. If so, reinforce them. If not guide your thoughts to another idea and sensation.
- Then place your hand on your heart and think: All is well, life is on my side.

♥ Stop, Breathe, Love

Thoughts can be voluntary or involuntary. We consider voluntary the thoughts that we choose conscientiously and involuntary those that are on autopilot and are unconscious and emerge normally as a habit. Involuntary thoughts, as a rule, are assimilated in an unconscious manner and we reproduce them mechanically. They translate beliefs, suggestions and the experiences of others that we accept as valid in a given moment and the majority of times, they are negative. They can be prejudices about your father, a friend, a teacher or the government.

The thoughts that confirm beliefs and negative suggestions, namely, limitations, impossibilities and fears, in a clear or surreptitious manner, which we accept unconsciously and we repeat mechanically, we call **negative involuntary thoughts**.

For example, "I cannot," "working with family is worse than working with strangers," or "there is no money" or "it is difficult to achieve goals in this country." These vibrations, which we have never confirmed as valid, continue to work in our field of energy, creating results in line with what they convey.

What do these involuntary thoughts construct in our reality and in the community? Normally the results are perceived as negative because the energy is directed to what we do not want, to the dysfunction, to the limitation or fear. The "complicator" is turned on and the probability that problems, confusions and difficulties will emergence is great. The tendency is for this to be repeated systematically, until the automated cycle is interrupted.

It is also probable that the person who is unaware that he is creating that reality (the problems) will project it out to other people and circumstances. This lack of responsibility reaches a peak when the individual feels like a victim of his own reality. In the last instance, the world is like it is because we built it like this. *But we can change our way of thinking, the manner in which we think, and how we perceive the world and inclusively effect that world.* **We are powerful creators of reality and this is changeable.**

For example, repeating mentally that there is no employment and focusing attention on that does not help in any way to find employment. On the contrary, thinking that it is possible to find employment and focusing on that, stimulates mentally and gives hope to the person, evoking other possibilities on the level of the field of unified consciousness.

The field is going to actualize itself according to the communication issued, sub-atomically rearranging events, situations and people that are in tune with this vibration.

When you feel that your head is full and in a negative automatic pilot, stop. Breathe deeply and think. **Is this what I want to construct in my life?** This question interrupts the distorted thought. Then, think about what you want and focus on it as intensely as possible. Relax, breathe deeply once again and nurture the current thought.

In parallel, there are also **voluntary positive thoughts.** As the name indicates, these are conscious and purposeful choices. The act of thinking is focused on the objective or wish that is considered positive for the person, for others and even for the community. *We make the decision on what to think about, when to think, and how to think about ideas, people, events, or life situations and we are present in that act.*

The focus of our consciousness is clear and we communicate that same clarity to the field of unified consciousness and Earth. As a result of this communication, a great number of possible scenarios that are available are defined and specific events emerge. Space-time is synchronized and the resources, objects, events and people needed to manifest what was decided by the thought appear in a rich and dynamic interlace. Reality is created according to the quality, color and dimension imprinted by the author. For example, the decision to write an article for *Time* magazine and sending the article the next week, the thought of donating winter clothes, or that hoping the surgery of a friend is successful. These thoughts are aligning the subatomic rearrangements that make the concretization of these events possible.

♥ Stop, Breathe, Love

Thought is an act of quantum creativity that is entwined to the quantum reality underlying life and with it, we can bring to life any reality. Independently of the form, dimension, speed or the "how," *everything is possible*. The intelligence that the field of unified consciousness is, knows the direct route, the people, the easiest and the most efficient way, the perfect result and even the immediate manifestation.

The more open we are, detached and in a state of receptivity without resisting, the better. At the speed of a smile, life jumps, actualizes itself and transforms itself into

our biggest creative adventure.
Below is a testimonial of that creativity.

Testimonial

Since Susana entered into my life, it has changed completely. When I met her, "I was inside-out," especially professionally, without any objectives and with a clear dependence of everything that was a problem and nearing a big depression.
With her, I learned with her in an alternative way, concentrating on solutions, and discovered that we all have a great internal strength. When I discovered my power, all became different. A year and a half later, after many seminars and appointments, I found myself, and that made all the difference. My professional life is continually improving, and everything is practically solved. My self-esteem, which at the time was destroyed and without strength, is now strong. I started to believe in myself once again, and I am able to create EVERYTHING for the best in my life. I feel healthy, joyful and well with my family. Thank you, you are a blessing to my family.

Richard Rocha, therapist

Each thought is a communication, loading an energetic instruction so that what has no form assumes a form and manifests it. We always have the possibility to choose what we are thinking and manifesting it in unity with the field of unified consciousness. If we do not like the manifested reality or it does not make sense, we can reorganize it, transfiguring it, changing the information and also the enformation underlying the thought.
Instead of wanting others to change, and that circumstances or events be different, we have the role of changing the creation that we are realizing. We have the lead role in the life we have, and only we can participate in it and give it the desired form. In this process, we are connected to all the life that supports us unconditionally and mirrors any construction that we realize.

♥ Stop, Breathe, Love

Regarding the probabilities of the manifestation of thoughts in reality, *coherence* is an extremely important aspect: coherence means *integrity*, the complete alignment with what we are thinking. When thinking, we are cohesive, without leaking information in other directions. This "entirety" makes the immediate manifestation possible. It can be an issue at work, in a relationship, or with health.
For example, when I decided to go to England to study in the field of Waldorf Pedagogy, it was very clear that this was what I wanted to do. Instead of questioning how the man I loved would cope without me during the time away, I decided that we would both be very well. I was so focused on this idea that everything went very well. Even in moments when nostalgia flourished or I heard something different to my decision, I remained firm. The thoughts, the words, the feelings and behaviors were in unison with the decision taken. Upon returning I noticed everything was peaceful, and this was a very gratifying for me.
Coherence requires us to live what we are thinking, keeping the course of a decision. Because the field of unified consciousness is united with us and mirrors the creations

that we have realized, the results reflect our internal coherence.

The delays, difficulties and tensions, the diversions and incoherencies that are very often unconscious, have to do with limiting thoughts, fears and the lack of attention in relation to the objective being pursued. *They can also be the result of being unaware that from the moment we emit a thought the whole universe unites to manifest it.*

The need to control, the need to know "how?" or not knowing "how," are normally mental and emotional obstacles that viciously jeopardize the behavior, even prevent it. For example: how am I going to manage if the country is in crisis? On the other hand, how am I going to love again because...has already happened? Or I do not know how it is possible to do...seeing that I only have two hours?

Thinking about "how" a situation will be resolved could be a stage and can often be problematic. What I want to highlight is that the "how?" is not your main task. What is important **is what you focused on with your thought**. Keep focus on the thought that has been emitted and accept/believe that the solution is possible, for the wellbeing of everyone, leaving space for the movement of the consciousness to "fill in the blank spaces."

From a quantum point of view, when we emit a thought that is completely coherent with what we emitted, it enters in phase and interferes with other waves on the same frequency, cooperating and affecting each other, manifesting itself. On the other hand, if there is incoherence, the waves are out of phase, and do not interfere with each other or interfere to a minor degree; they either do not cooperate or cooperate very little; they can cancel each other mutually and do not result in a manifestation, or the manifestation comes later or is scattered.

The "how?" originates in linear thought, in the laws of conventional physics, in the perception of separation, in the fear of space, time, means, resources or the conditions—the supposed obstacles of the conditioned mind. **Change the perception**. Accept that you are linked to infinite intelligence, unlimited resources, endless possibilities and opportunities, because that is the truth from a fundamental point of view. That is the reality underlying the whole of life. In effect, thought is a wave of quantum possibilities interacting and communicating with the energy of the field of unified consciousness, behaving in a nonlinear manner, able to be superimposed in a number of places at the same time, transcending space and time and manifesting itself physically and instantaneously in total abundance.

Thought is made of the same material that everything is made of and it interacts with totality, manifesting each possibility that we focus on. The field of unified consciousness is complete in itself and unlimited, and whatever we evoke in our communication and interaction with it, is possible to manifest. From the smallest detail to the most grandiose event, the probabilities are unlimited. Therefore, let us leave the "how" aside when using the energy of creation of thought, because the concretization of what we want is possible.

It is important to be clear, detached and in a state of openness for what can happen, because it can be even better and greater than we had idealized. Remember that the field of unified consciousness is intelligent, sensitive and is totally at our service, manifesting perfectly in every instant, united with the thought we have. We can relax and be innocent, because life is on our side.

♥ Stop, Breathe, Love

Does a person who is conscious of the creative power of thought and its union with the field of unified consciousness manifest a thought "faster"?

From a quantum point of view, any thought has the possibility of immediate manifestation because it already exists in the field of unified consciousness. *Thought is reality linked to all of reality. It is only our perception and lack of attention that disconnects and distances us from the manifestation.*
A human being who, in the act of thinking, is clearly aware that he is communicating and giving form to reality in unity with the field of unified consciousness, and the planet, knows that everything is possible and that the realization has already taken place. He is in an internal state of unity and experiences the totality immediately, and the totality replies. Time-space is collapsed in that instant along with any form, object, person or instant that is before it, in it and in the All: because it and the All are one. He perceives himself already realized.
On the other hand, even if the manifestation extends over space-time, the cohesion with the produced result is maintained. One behaves as if it has already been accomplished and continues life under that assumption.
One can experience that state for a fraction of a second and manifest the thought immediately, or it can take minutes, days, weeks, months or even years. He has the potential for the manifestation, and he knows that he can always create and recreate. The assumption of responsibility for the result of the concretization is done in totality because he knows that he is the creator of his reality and of the community.
All the wise people of this planet, the reader included (although at the moment you may not perceive this) use focused thought and purposely decide reality. Thought is a force of creation tied to the cosmic creation. We have a field of unlimited opportunities at our disposal, and humanity is counting on us, just as the field of unified consciousness and planet are, to participate in life, imprinting our decisions on it. The state of unity is already in us, and thoughts as well. All we need to do is think, focus and open ourselves to the good for us, and for all beings.

♥ Stop, Breathe, Love

Another fundamental point on thought is attention. We mentioned it in the fourth chapter, but it is so important that we are going to refer to it again here.
Both thought and attention are tools for constructing reality. They are both the language that we use to speak to the field of unified consciousness and the language it replies to us in. Both are necessary in the process of constructing reality. Attention is presence; it is directed consciousness and consciousness manifests what it is attentive to.

Attention feeds thought and structures manifestation.

When we focus our attention on a thought, even just for a moment, we are selectively choosing that specific information and giving it relevance, and this act, from a quantum point of view, crystalizes the information, which represents the idea and

makes it current, that is, fit for manifestation.
Attention and thought are a wave of possibilities determined by the decision of a conscious entity that participates in life and reorganizes it, giving it form, context, color or dimension according to the choice that was made.

Attention and thought affect the manifestation. A focused thought is a manifested thought. At each instant, we are recreating our world through the focus of our attention on specific thoughts and the field of consciousness also focuses and mirrors them, making them visible in reality so that we can consolidate them or change them. The reality that we perceive is the simultaneous result of the thought and the attention that concentrates reality and makes it real.
So be careful with the attention that we give to our thoughts—focused thoughts—because they form reality.

In summary, let us remember some of the concepts of attention here.

1) **What** thought are we focusing on? We choose to pay attention to a thought about a person, an object, situation, event, etc. amongst so many other possible thoughts.
2) **When** do we focus on a thought? We decide to give attention to thoughts which we placed temporally in the past, the present or that we project for the future and bring to life events related to them. For example, when we focus on a negative thought from the past, it continues to be present from the point of view of its manifestation in our current life.
3) **How** do we focus on thoughts? In a concentrated or distributed manner?
If you take one or the other route, it is going to interfere with the manifestation of reality. Attention and thought are two sides of the same face and show us beauty or ugliness in accordance with the information that is being moved by the human consciousness in tune with the field of unified consciousness. It is up to us to be selective and use the greatness that we own, which is common to all of humanity, as well as all beings.

🚀 **Exercise to clear your attention and focus:**
- Breathe deeply 3 times and shake your body, releasing any tension you may have.
- Inhale as you count to 6 and then exhale, counting to 10, releasing all the air.
- Now close your eyes and place your attention at the tip of your nose until the only thing that exists is your nose.
- Think deliberately about something positive or meaningful for you. Stay present.
- When you feel ready, you may open your eyes and move on.

The System of Beliefs

"Whenever you find yourself on the side of the majority, it is time to pause and reflect."
Mark Twain

"Avoid the crowd. Do your own thinking independently. Be the chess player, not the chess piece."
Ralph Charell

Each one of us is bombarded with information; our senses continuously capture over ten million bits per second and transmit them to be processed internally and filtered on the level of the brain, namely by the limbic system, neo cortex, thalamus, and visual cortex, amongst others, to a processing level of between 2 and 40 bits per second. That is, a very small part of the information actually reaches us, and this happens so that we are not overloaded with data. In this process of the selection of information, our internal filters enable us to accept information as valid or reject it, giving it a sense of adequacy and or internal coherence and making associations on the level of the associative memory by generalization. Underlying these filters are, namely, values, rules, beliefs, emotions and behaviors that will be used so that the information that is set in movement within the energy system can be coherent with that to which value is given. It is also in coherence with what is perceived as right or wrong, what is believed as possible or impossible, what is felt (happiness, wellbeing or pain) and, still, with what you consider yourself able to do or not. The information is presented in a congruent manner to the person, to what she is or was.

In this process, **attention** is present because it is what will activate, in synergy with the consciousness/brain matrix, what information will be selected and actualized. That is, what is going to be accepted, what is going to be put in evidence and what is adequate. And, also what memories we have on a theoretical, emotional and/or behavioral level that are in line with what the attention is focusing on, feeding back the system successively.

For example, when we want to buy a new computer from brand X, we naturally focus our attention on the many existing computers of that same brand. Or when we fall in love, we systematically focus on couples in love. Or if we like to wear red, we notice other people wearing the same color. In the film *The Father of the Bride* there is a perfect image of what I am stating. The female character—who is over forty—knows that she is pregnant and is happy, while the husband is not. They are in a car, on their way home and she sees positive relationships with children on her side of the road; he, on the other hand, only sees problems and annoying events associated with children on his side of the road. *What we focus on becomes evident in our reality, recreating itself constantly. Therefore, it is important to focus our consciousness on what we want, instead of on what we do not want so that reality appears with the desired contours and contexts.*

Regarding the thoughts (and the images, words, emotions, sensations and actions), that which we emit reproduces the system of beliefs by which we are governed.

A belief is simply information, something we believe in. We may believe a lot, very little, a little or "so, so" in an idea, sensation or experience. The belief—the acceptance that it is so—can be done in a conscious or unconscious manner, as we receive the information during our life.

Very often, we are not even aware of the beliefs that we have, because we have accepted them in an automatic manner from our parents, teachers, colleagues or media and we simply process them systematically. The truth is that although we have believed in an idea, emotion or experience between 0.1% and 100%, we can change any belief that we wish. *We have the choice and the power regarding what we decide to believe in. This change makes all the difference.*

♥ Stop, Breathe, Love

We understand a system of beliefs as a set of ideas, concepts, rules, suggestions, sensations and experiences. That is, the world vision that we have acquired throughout life (even inside the womb) in a direct or indirect manner, through imitation or through creation and in which we believe with a variable degree of certainty or conviction.

Whether we are dealing with "negative", neutral or "positive" thoughts, the system of beliefs (that which we believe—minimally or totally) is present; therefore, it is indispensable that we understand what type of beliefs exist.
In a binary language of 0 or 1, we consider there to be two types of beliefs.
There are constricting beliefs (0) and expanding beliefs (1). All the possible combinations of beliefs are based on this binary language.
For example, if we received, accepted and assimilated, even if unconsciously, a negative suggestion made by a nursery schoolteacher that "men don't cry," this belief became active with a degree between 0. 00001% and 100%. The child, who assimilated this belief 100% as an adult, may have difficulty in expressing the emotions of crying, because he grew up believing that he had to behave that way, from the moment this was transmitted to him.
In cases where we have received, accepted and assimilated information, even from inside the womb, for example "the world is a peaceful place," this became a positive belief on a scale of 0.1% to 100%. And throughout life, the perception that we have of the world is affected by this belief, interfering in our relationship with the world from people, events, or experiences, etc. If we receive the information, accept it and assimilate it during our life experience that there is "sufficient abundance for all" and we believe in that experience, it is natural to see mirrored in our daily life that same belief in various forms and in the most varied contexts.
The truth is that we are successively feeding—through our attention, in the consciousness/brain matrix—the emission of that same scenario or experience, which is by then in resonance with the energy systems in the same energetic frequency.
The beliefs we have are references used in the filtering of information that is received by the sensory channels. That is, a belief can inhibit or allow the entry of information through the senses and the respective treatment and assimilation of information. As such, it is indispensable to actualize the system of beliefs and activate only those beliefs that are beneficial to us, leaving the others to perish by themselves, as a result of their disuse.
For example, if you believe that "angels do not exist," even though the angelical information is being captured by your higher senses and trying to reveal themselves, there is the probability that such data will be rejected automatically by the system processing the information, because it goes against a predefined and neurally structured idea. Even if an angel passes by, and even if the angel is in your presence,

you may not see him, because your belief does not permit it. The belief can become an obstacle or a trampoline for the construction of your reality in accordance with your vibration if it is constricting or expanding.

We consider beliefs to be constricting when they bind directly or indirectly, namely, ideas of impossibility and limitation or impressions/emotions of fear, loss, or guilt, and that convey behaviors of impotence and irresponsibility.

We consider beliefs to be expansionary when they convey, directly or indirectly, ideas of possibilities and opportunities, emotions and sentiments of confidence, security and motivation, conveying behaviors of responsibility and realization.

To understand what type of belief is underlying that thought, suggestion, sensation, or experience that we are intimately witnessing or that is communicated to us directly or indirectly, it is useful to ask ourselves **"does this belief constrict/limit?"** or **"does this belief expand/enable?"** Depending on the reply we get, we will change it, keep it or even stop believing in it, removing its power. *It could be that we think of the opposite of that belief, we create a point of equilibrium for a new belief or stop thinking about it completely, because we decided so. In this act, we reformulate the perception we have of the world and the world appears to be changed; actually, it will never be the same, because we are different.*

In cases where we are, interacting with others and the belief conveyed is constricting, we can think, even without saying it, the following: **"That is your belief. I will choose a better one!"** and concentrate on a positive belief. For example, my friend Ana was training in sales and the trainer said, "Businesses do not hire in the summer." That is his belief because businesses will hire employees any time of the year. When they want and need, they recruit employees, full stop. Ana immediately thought, "That is your belief. I will choose a better one for me; there are opportunities for employment any time of the year." In this way, she created an expansive belief that would allow her to link with employment at any time of year.

Evidently, choosing a belief that constricts or a belief that expands has implications in our field of energy, in the field of unified consciousness and the planet, because they are linked to persons, situations or experiences in the same vibrational coordinates as the beliefs that are meanwhile nurtured.

In reality, what we are communicating with the field of consciousness through our beliefs is an instruction so that the quantum world takes on the form of our communication and is actualized. Due to the fundamental entwining of all things, events, occurrences, objects and persons are synchronized, allowing the manifestation, mirroring what we are thinking or feeling as true. Furthermore, vibrationally, we constrict or expand our life, that of the collective and even the universe, as a result of this participation in life.

At my "Mental Vitamin" workshop, we worked on changing beliefs with advanced and very simple techniques and the results were surprising.
Here is a testimonial:

Testimonial

I attended the Mental Vitamin workshop in February and I can only say that in two months, my life changed in a way that I could never believe possible! Indeed, it was me who changed. It is true! I registered to attend without knowing what it would be like, as I had never done anything of the sort. This workshop, as the name suggests, gives vitamins to our mind. In my case, I am a mother, I work and study in the evening; I was at a stage in my life where I needed help: the pressure at home, at work and all the commitment that a higher education course requires, leaves a person "on all fours." Not to mention my low self-esteem, always being scared to speak, scared of what others may have thought of me, and the frequent pessimism. In addition, I had few dreams, because I thought I would never be able to achieve them, anyway, all nonsense, as I saw later. At the workshop, I really learned how I could change my way of thinking; my mind left the comfort zone, to become aware of what is happening currently. Today, I can easily abandon the pessimism and believe that everything is better, thinking positively, changing perspectives that appeared to me to be bad into something that can be solved.

It was possible for me, after this experience in the Mental Vitamin workshop to pass two subjects of my course, which I had thought I would not be able to do so fast. I am also doing an academic project that I showed at work, so that they could assist me in obtaining information regarding the care for patients of Alzheimer's. Surprisingly, the idea was considered important at work, and may give me the opportunity, who knows, of implementing it in reality, helping other people. I changed; I am confident in who I am. I now talk to anyone without feeling embarrassed or not knowing what to say. And it is not only me saying that I have changed; my husband thinks the same, he is surprised with some of the plans I want to carry out. After seeing my change, he wants to attend the workshop too. With this work, Susana is able to help people to change their mentalities and wake up for life, which has such good and positive things. I love living, love feelings, and love being happy! A big hug, Susana, it was great attending the Mental Vitamin workshop.

Marta Esteves, secretary

♥ Stop, Breathe, Love

It is not others that have to change their beliefs. It is us. We are the universe. We are a point and the totality. Everything is in us. We are not separated from others, objects or nature. We live in a holographic universe where any communication, relationship and action is integrated in the whole, happens simultaneously and functions in a network, multidimensionally. Any alteration, however small, affects and modifies the face of the whole universe. Yes, of your life, of your family, friends, work colleagues, the lady at the fish shop, Portuguese or Greek debt crisis, the police in Japan, peace in the Middle East, the planetary ecosystem and the cosmos.

It is up to us to choose which beliefs we are going to manifest into reality and furthermore, how much attention we are going to give them. *When we focus our attention on a belief/thought (constricting/expanding—negative/ positive), be it for a nanosecond, three hours or five days, what we are doing is highlighting them, giving them substance, because whatever our consciousness gives attention to, it constructs.*

In fact, we select, through attention, from a great number of thoughts or possible beliefs, the one that we want to give form to, and materialized in reality, knowing that the field of unified consciousness is in tune with our decision.

People who achieve what we consider extraordinary have beliefs supporting this.

Intimately, they accept that it is possible and are united with that conviction. For example, people who levitate show how it is possible to levitate and are united with the belief that the body can rise and contradict the law of gravity. People who admit the possibility of doing million-dollar contracts, every day and maintain themselves united to that belief and put it into practice, are multibillionaires. Human beings diagnosed as "incurable" by traditional medicine admit the possibility of being healed and, united in that belief, they find healing. The world is full of people whose beliefs about themselves and the reality in which they exist are expansive, and they give us living examples that there is more for us to experience.

We live in a universe of infinite possibilities were the opportunities are endless. Believe in this thought, in this belief, because it is real; put it into practice, expand into yourself and into the cosmos. RESTART TO DARE AND FEEL GOOD. NOW.

 Exercise:
- Write 5 beliefs you think that an inspiring or successful person may have.
- Write 5 bold beliefs that you already have.
- Propose yourself to incorporate the other 5 successful beliefs and write down how you will make them your own.
- What kind of thoughts and actions are aligned with these new goals? Act immediately.

Reconnecting Thought to Health

"The only worship that pleases God consists of sacrificing the evil thoughts, words and actions in the altar of consciousness."
Nietzsche, *Thus Spoke Zarathustra*

"You become what you think."
Earl Nightingale

From the beginning of human civilization, the sacred scriptures of the Bible, the Upanishads or the Koran, have warned us about the creative power of thought. The message is common and prompts us to look after our thoughts, and to be aware of what we are thinking about and to think in a careful manner because of the impact that each thought necessarily has on the person and the whole. The sacred scriptures still allude, sometimes in a more metaphorical manner, sometimes in a more literal manner, to the fact that thoughts can be assistants in the construction of health or can be the agents of disease.

Medicine has already become aware of the significance of thought in the formation of disease, namely the classic psychosomatic diseases, such as nervous ulcers or psoriasis. Currently this perception is extending in the sense that it is possible that all diseases are considered psychosomatic (the psyche interfering in the body—somatic) and that, as we change our manner of thinking, we are affecting, cooperating and reconstructing the body, moment by moment.

Effectively, our thoughts influence health; actually, they construct it. A thought is made of the same thing that constitutes a muscle, bone, an organ or blood cell— subatomic particles, energy in movement, information vibrating and luminous frequencies. In the act of us emitting a thought, it communicates and interacts with the energy underlying all the reality that exists inside the human being who emitted it, and with the field of unified consciousness, changing it in accordance with the information that it contains.

Although a thought could be considered as a very small energy, for example the size of pinhead, its impact is tremendous because it is a point of the All and is capable of changing the totality.

A thought is reality and is linked with any reality, be it in a potential or manifest state. From the moment when it is formulated, it provokes and particularizes a precise status, affecting the entire personal, planetary and macro cosmic universe. **Thinking is giving life to what is thought.**

A thought is capable of changing the human energy field and as a result of its information, a set of instructions are sent in a chain, affecting the hormonal and enzymatic components, the emission or impediment of releasing white blood cells, the blood pressure, amongst others, that could trigger processes of disease or healthy recovery.

We have probably become aware that when we brood over worries, problems or negative opinions, disagreements and feelings of guilt, fear or hurt, the tendency for illness is great. So just for the simple fact of recycling those ideas or emotions, we are weakening our energy system. In fact, we are using the language of creation thought in disorganization and chaos which communicates to the organism, causing it to become destabilized and unbalanced, creating the conditions for disease. In effect, disease is nothing more than the disorder in our energy system and thoughts affect it constantly.

Our thoughts can be constructors of health or of disease, depending on the information that it has and the forms they represent. Dysfunctional information makes possible subatomic rearrangements of dysfunctional forms. Orderly in formation makes orderly subatomic rearrangements possible. It is us who are choosing at every moment what we want to bring to life in unity with the field of unified consciousness, through our thoughts and what we communicate.

"Negative" thoughts influence cell organization and organic functional dynamics become distorted due to the information and impression contained in the thought, boosting disease. Inversely, "positive" thoughts that translate balanced information, wellbeing and impulses of life, are health boosters, both for the cells as well as for the organs, functions and energy systems existing in human beings.

It is amazing to think about the power that we have to disorganize and cause death based on the idea that we no longer wish to live. The decision, even if unconscious, to die potentiates chaos and disorder on an energetic level, making it possible to trigger suicidal behaviors on the level of brain cells, namely through the releasing of proapoptotic cells that will generate brain destruction.

On the other hand, **the decision to live,** is a very powerful command that opens doors and permits powerful links of vitality that trigger real miracles in health. That is, the decision to live is like a rocket that causes the explosion of numerous possibilities of health, actualizing the one that is in tune with what was thought or desired.

Thoughts are energy in movement in a set frequency that comes into resonance with other energy systems, as in the case of cells or organs, creating force fields that aggregate and manifest themselves in accordance with the vibration/instruction contained in the thought. Changing the thought towards health, harmony is reestablished.

The truth is that we are changeable, and the human organism is constantly changing, adapting and reconstructing itself from the blood cells, the enzymes, the fluids, the muscles, hair etc. and thoughts affect the system in a consistent manner creating woven links in the existing life.

In the act of thinking of health, we instruct the quantum world towards order and the order underlying all of life answers us, synchronizing the subatomic rearrangements so that natural health is manifested. From a quantum point of view, we are always connected to health. It is abundant and easy to experience it. It is a conscious click of openness to the infinite possibilities and it manifests itself in our existence.

This click can be done personally or with another person or group of people. Face to face or even at another point of the planet. What is important is the internal availability, the "blank space" so that the unity underlying all of life fills it in the sense of the intentioned thought.

Here is a testimonial of a click that can change the vision of the world.

Testimonial

After a caesarean section to give birth to my daughter, I suffered from pain in my hip, my left leg was misaligned, and I had the sensation that my pelvis was out of place. The pain and discomfort increased each day. I saw a doctor but there was no improvement.

In conversation on the telephone with Susana, I mentioned it and she told me that in the evening she would work with me energetically and that I should call her next morning to let her know how I felt. The next morning when I woke up, I was well. My pelvis was fine; I could move my left leg naturally and felt that everything was in the right place. I immediately commented to my husband about how well I felt and I could only laugh.

I have learned that it does not matter how it happens, what matters is it happens and it is great.

It is fantastic what we can experience when we open ourselves to the possibilities. Even 300 km away, life is our friend!

For all this and much more that I could share with you, thank you Susana for all the good you brought into my life and my family.

Inês Medeiros, coach and psychologist

♥ Stop, Breathe, Love

We understand that the thoughts we emit our health. **Are the ideas, beliefs or suggestions of others also capable of interfering with it? Do we have to accept, or validate these ideas/suggestions for them to have an effect on us?**

I believe the answer to both questions is yes. The thoughts, opinions, suggestions or beliefs of others can interfere with our health. We only need to accept, even unconsciously, the information transmitted for it to be installed in the field of energy to be able to produce results. For example, has it ever happened to you that a friend told you that one of his family members had a bad flu and then you also got the flu? It is very likely that through that suggestion, which you accepted unconsciously, you prepared a "good bed for the flu to lie down."

From the moment a person accepts the idea that information is emitted to his field of energy and simultaneously to the field of unified consciousness and is available to be concretized. The field merely reflects the choice.

On a conscious level, the **negative suggestion** given by another and accepted by the person, causes physical symptoms. It is enough for the person to just accept the possibility, for the manifestation to occur. In a scientific experiment, mentioned in the book *Seven Experiments that could Change the World* by Rupert Sheldrake, *"electrodes were placed on the heads of persons (who were the objects of the experiment) and the researchers suggested to them that they were linked to an electric current capable of causing headaches. It was later confirmed that two thirds of the subjects developed the symptoms, although there was no electric current."*

The fact of accepting and validating the information as being true creates the connection between the thought and the development of the physical symptom.[2]

Therefore, be very careful with suggestions that convey illness, pain, or discomfort. The best thing to do is to reject them internally, thinking in the format of a litany: *"Maybe it is so... but for me I choose health and joy."*

When positive suggestions are given, does the organism also react in harmony with that energetic instruction? Yes. If we accept and validate them, even automatically, the suggestion is processed on a mental level interacting in cascade with the different functions and systems creating a new scenario for the organism.

Have you ever felt a little apathetic and a friend tells you that you are looking good and immediately you feel better? He gave you a suggestion in the format of compliment and you reacted? One of the most blatant aspects corroborating that a positive suggestion or information affects health directly, is the so called placebo effect, in which, for example, a flour pill is given to the patient and the latter believing in the therapeutic properties of the pill feels better. I remember when I worked as a hemodialysis technician there were patients who during the hemodialysis no longer reacted to the normal medication for pain. At that time, the doctor would tell them that he would give them a strong injection of PS (Physiological Serum, which is innocuous). What was found was that patients got better or were pain-free. There are a great number of scientific experiments showing that the placebo effect provokes positive effects in patients, with a success rate of over 40% improvement in their health condition. What was also found was that the beneficial effects for the patients are greater when the doctors or the nurses do not know that a placebo is being administered.

How is this possible? *From the moment when a thought is internalized and validated, the human energy field, in tune with the field of unified consciousness actualizes that information internally and materializes it. From a quantum point of view, one bit of information communicates and interacts with any existing information, actualizing the totality of the information, because on a fundamental level there is no separation between the bit of information and the global information. It is united.*

On another level the positive belief in a specific medicine or surgery, even though it is merely palliative, can produce health improvement effects and there are scientific

---

[2] Sheldrake, Rupert, *Seven Experiments that Could Change the World*, Riverhead Books, 1995, Summarized from pg. 272 of the Portuguese edition. (Editora Sinais de Fogo, March 2002)

experiments proving this. One of them is described in Rupert Sheldrake´s book mentioned above. For example, in the surgery connecting the mammary arteries to treat the pain in angina, it was found that "even those patients who had not done the surgery to connect the arteries, but had only an incision on the breast, showed the same improvement regarding the pain relief of angina, just like the patients who were subjected to the complete surgery (connection of the mammary arteries). All patients showed a reduction of the T wave in the electrocardiogram and the respective inversion of this wave and other physical changes."[3]

The power of a thought or a belief is fascinating in a particular therapy, surgery or medicine. This acceptance causes improvements or healing of the symptoms. Even when the physical part of the treatment is not done (not doing the linkage of the mammary arteries) the impact is the same: relief of pain and physical changes (reduction and inversion of the T wave). Perhaps the primary health care is that of the mind? Caring for the mind first, making it receptive to the correct information to get even better results in health?

From a quantum point of view, a change in the health paradigm can be caused by only a thought, a belief. That drop in the quantum ocean of infinite possibilities can cause the formation of gigantic waves and these break up on the energy beach which is our bodies. We should pay attention to health and promote it systematically.

♥ Stop, Breathe, Love

The power of a thought that we believe in, the belief in a certain medicine or therapy, are decisive elements for their success. In parallel, it is extremely important to trust in the doctor or the healthcare personnel, as well as the credibility they have and which we accept. They are considered the owners of knowledge and our "saviors." All these aspects together make a great difference. However, it should be understood what thoughts or beliefs are being passed on to us by the healthcare professionals, with all due respect and gratitude for the medical profession and all healthcare professionals of allopathic medicine and so-called alternative medicine. They are certainly doing their best and in accordance with studied and tested principles. They are worthy of trust.

However, every moment things change, and how often does a different opinion change the life of a person? A belief or an opinion can make the difference for the "good" or "bad." Since the information given by a healthcare professional and the acceptance of it is going to decisively influence which paths can be followed from an energetic, neural or molecular point of view, affecting all the biology of the individual. This opinion can constitute a turning point, very often without return.

For example, when a doctor prescribing chemotherapy speaks of the side effects and lists them, is he not conditioning the patient, negatively predisposing him to experience that reality? Since it is normal to accept that message from the doctor, whom we trust, and who is an authority on the matter. However, being subjected to chemotherapy and having side effects is not automatic, and the adverse side effects may even never happen. According to the surgeon Dr. Bernie Siegel, *"people subjected to chemotherapy and to whom the side effects were never mentioned, found that*

---

[3] Sheldrake, R., *Seven Experiments...*, summarized from pgs. 268 of the Portuguese edition.

they did not experience them." A great number of people cared for by Dr. Siegel, are subjected to chemotherapy and have vitality, feel well and carry on with their daily lives; to a great extent they are being mentally prepared to take advantage of the benefits that this therapy can give them.[4]

The same can be said in relation to the side effects of medicines. Does mentioning these or reading about the side effects not predispose the patient to experience the symptoms mentioned?

What about those people taking antibiotics or undergoing physiotherapy, who at the same time think or say that it does nothing for them? Aren't they sabotaging the treatment and themselves?

Being open to a positive result that can happen and the strengthening of the therapeutic properties, in the improvement of health or cure, can be an excellent alternative.

Information transmitted positively, with confidence and authority of someone the patient values and recognizes knowledge (while the patient believes the best regarding the medication and or physiotherapy), allows new life connections that may even have surprising results.

On the other hand, the opinion regarding the persons cared for is also decisive and the ideal is that these are aligned with health. A thought is an energy wave that is captured and interferes with other energy waves. When a thought is emitted, it is automatically shared on the quantum field and interrelates with all existing thoughts. Therefore, a thought emitted is not innocuous; it is always information capable of conforming and manifesting itself in reality.

It makes all the difference if before surgery, the doctor thinks "This patient has no chance" or "I am going to do my best and "miracles" are always happening, even if I don't quite know how." The consciousness of the doctor is working in harmony with that of the "patient" and with the field of unified consciousness.

From a quantum point of view, they communicate, interrelate and interact. A limiting thought of impossibility constricts the energy field where the intervention is happening, creating a resistance to the flow of life. On the contrary, a thought of possibility expands the energy field where the doctor is intervening, facilitating the realignment process with the life forces. A thought, or a belief, can construct a turning point and decide on life or death. When mentally equating another possibility, the brain as a quantum processor in communication with the field of unified consciousness, co links other probabilities and actualizes other types of neural connections, secreting other type of chemicals and differentiated hormones and performs distinct nervous and muscle movements. These dynamics are triggered by a thought, a wish or belief, and can be the drop that causes the overflow in the ocean of infinite possibilities, a chain of events and phenomena completely different from those indicated, because other information was actualized and became available for manifestation.

♥ Stop, Breathe, Love

Health is a construction, or rather a creation in which we participate actively, in a team with the field of unified consciousness and the planet. The ideas and beliefs that

---

[4] Siegel, *Love*....Summarized from pg. 191 of the Portuguese edition.

we have regarding illness and health affects us individually and also interfere with the collective. Let us remember the concept of collective consciousness as a force that emerges because of the thoughts, images, words, sentiments and behaviors of the human totality that affects the human community, as well as all the entities they relate with (animals, plants, the planet and the field of unified consciousness).

Systematic thought on illnesses creates a *"morphic field"*[5] which is linked to the field of unified consciousness, stressing and recreating more disease. For example, the avian flu has a great *"morphic field"* not only because many people died, but because the information was transmitted from a global point of view, since the news was alarming and was repeated incessantly and mentally, causing millions of human beings to think about these and validate them. The mental contamination of the avian flu was greater than the physical contamination and generated a distorted field of information, able to produce more disease. Any thought of avian flu is energetically charged with a million other thoughts in harmony and can potentially trigger its manifestation. Therefore, be careful what you are thinking about, choose something else to focus attention on and feed the collective consciousness with other information, namely healthy information. It is fundamental to use thought in health clearly.

Pay attention to what is healthy and organized so that the collective consciousness regarding health is strengthened.

To summarize
- Health is a creation that we nourish throughout the days, weeks, months or years through ideas, feelings and behaviors.
- Instead of giving and/or receiving beliefs, suggestions or opinions that convey illness and disequilibrium, it is essential to focus our attention on ideas of vitality, wellbeing, pleasure and the will to live.
- From a fundamental point of view, we are all connected and we are one.
- Each time we think and accept health, when one of us gets better or is healed, humanity, the planet and the field rejoice in health and in order.
- The decision begins in us. One makes all the difference; one is the All.

Exercise:

Breathe deeply three times and as you exhale loosen your body. Then open your mouth as wide as possible and make the sound AAAAHHHHHH. Prolong it for as long as possible. Breathe deeply again and make the sound AAAAHHHHHH again. The aim is to make the sound five times consecutively. When you finish, think for a few minutes "I love my health." Observe the sensations you are feeling in your body and beyond it.

Genetic Thought

"The Portuguese soul sees 'fado' as the expression of a wish; that D. Sebastião returns and saves us."
Maria Costa

---

[5] Morphic field, concept created by Rupert Sheldrake. "Morphic Field is a vital model of organization" a field that transports information on a number of levels, for example. "Mental, social or behavioral and coexists with the electromagnetic, gravitational and quantum material fields": the information of the morphic field can transcend space and time. This field is based on an informational affinity. For more information please see www.sheldrake.org/ research/glossary.

"Whether you think you can or you think you can't; you are right."
Henry Ford

"In every culture and in every medical tradition before ours, healing was accomplished by moving energy."
Albert Szent-Györgyi, Winner of the Nobel Prize for Medicine, 1937

We have been talking about thought and viewing it as an informational reality that is present in life and is able to affect life in its numerous stages and manifestations.
Is it possible for thoughts to be present in us, despite the "passage of time"? Can thoughts be ours, our ancestor's or even from the whole universe? Is it possible that they are still able to affect us?
We consider a thought to be one bit of information vibrating simultaneously in the conscious/brain matrix and in the field of unified consciousness—the information field. From a formative point of view, we have a highly concentrated informational code underlying human life that contains data about the dynamics of the human organism—the genetic code, DNA.
Genes are small particles of the chromosomes, which contain coded instructions so that the necessary proteins for the construction of all the cells of the human organism are produced, in accordance with a set sequence. The genes convey hereditary data at all levels, from the capacities or incapacities of the motor, sensorial and intellectual sectors, and can also transmit the information on an emotional level, namely the likes, the sensibility, the affections, the temperament and character traits or behavioral habits.
During the decoding of the human genetic code at the beginning of the 21st century, scientists found that from the three million pairs of genes, only 3% of these, that is 30 000 genes, had a function in human beings; the remaining 97% was considered as waste DNA. Subsequently, the scientists found that the waste DNA also had a function: to convey the code of the evolution of life, in the last 2.5 million years.[6]
Based on the idea that human DNA has the genetic memory not only of a human being as an individual, but also of the evolution of all humanity, the planet, and even the cosmos, it is acceptable that data in the form of thoughts, emotions or attitudes are transmitted to us genetically life after life, and we reproduce them, even if we are not aware of their origin.
We can reproduce the ideas of our mother, the sensitivity for music of our father, the genius of our grandfather, the vice of a more distant relative, and still nurture behaviors from our ancestors from the caves, and remember planetary living conditions or even moments from the creation of the universe.
We genetically mirror individuality, the parental component, social, educational, and philosophical aspects, amongst others, of the community, the nation, the globe and the cosmos in a perfect manner during our existence, through DNA.
Is DNA the time machine of the genesis of life which we already have and which we were not even aware? It probably is. And after all, are we and do we have, the multidimensional, multigenerational and universal information inside us? Effectively, yes.

---

[6] In *Diário de Notícias* (Portuguese main newspaper), April 16, 2002, pg. 24.

The human being can be envisaged as a microcosm inside the macro cosmos—a field of information connected to the quantum ocean of information— and DNA is the concentrated and particularized representation of a specific human being and the whole universe in one. We are an information point of the universe with a human form and we are linked to each point of existence, from the star, the dinosaur, the plankton, the pen, the tree or the fire. The totality is inside us in real time, available to be actualized by the human consciousness. the star, the dinosaur, the plankton, the pen, the tree or the fire. The totality is inside us in real time, available to be actualized by the human consciousness.

In respect to thoughts as bits of information/energy, they are also connected with the bits of information, the energy that DNA is, and simultaneously linked to the field of unified consciousness in constant communication and interaction, making it possible to access this information, naturally because it already exists—we call this "genetic" thinking.

Let us now give examples of what can be considered as being in harmony with genetic thought: when we look at a work of art of a Renaissance artist, whose work we had never seen before, a type of thought arises, "I have always enjoyed working with this guy" and an emotion of nostalgia missing that person and that activity, emerges. It is probable that we are in harmony with a "genetic" thought.

We decide to visit an exhibition of the torture instruments used in The Inquisition and our thoughts are normal. Unexpectedly, our thoughts become intensively mixed, mental images arise like "flashes," also emotions and bodily reactions such as feeling cold in the stomach or trembling. There is a great probability of being in harmony with "genetic" thought.

♥ Stop, Breathe, Love

Genes carry data from all stages of human evolution and life itself and that information can be affecting us in a positive manner or not in the present moment, making it necessary to screen information so that we can release it and assimilate it consciously. For example: in spite of having grown up, having had all our daily needs in abundance, and having good financial conditions, every time you see the pantry half full, you think, "There should always be a large quantity of food stored here because something could happen," and you are scared of going hungry. You do not know where this thought of "need" and fear of going hungry comes from. In your present life, there is nothing that could have caused this; you always ate what you wanted, you had a happy childhood, neither your mother nor your father thought this way or had identical behaviors to yours. One day, when your grandmother comes to visit you and sees your pantry full, she says you are like your late grandfather who stored a lot of food because he thought it might run out at any moment, and feared he may suffer for the lack of it. You inherited your way of thinking and acting from your grandfather.

This "genetic" thought was transmitted to you and you have been using it as if it was the truth for you. Is this perception that you want to have in your life, now? This thought of need and fear of going hungry and the behavior of stocking food, how is it serving you? It is merely more of the same. And for what?

It is time to actualize that information—**dissolve the thought in the field of unified consciousness,** changing simultaneously the thought and the DNA, in a movement of the consciousness on itself, in communication and interrelation with the field of unified consciousness. It will probably feel like emptiness, or strangeness, but the change has already happened. Then we substitute the "blank space" with information. Or we leave that task for the field of unified consciousness or we imprint a new thought, actualizing a new link. It can be for example: "I have natural abundance daily." For a moment, feel it intensively, and act: keep the pantry with free space.

♥ Stop, Breathe, Love

We understand that genes are information, energy in movement, linked to the field of unified consciousness that is its seat. The issue we face is: **"Is it possible to change genes through thought?"**
Yes, we confirm it. In effect, from the quantum point of view the nature of a thought or a gene is the same: information, subatomic particles in movement in our energy field and in the field of unified consciousness, who can both communicate in an instantaneous manner and affect each other immediately.
DNA is a codified representation of the life structure and of the universe; a tiny point that contains the totality of information. It is a vital hologram inside the human organism, linked to the universal hologram—the field of unified consciousness—in a relationship of functional interdependence. Thought and DNA are one; they are not disconnected from the consciousness of the person that emitted them, or from the field of unified consciousness. From the moment that one is changed, the other resonates, and moves itself too.
DNA works in a quantum manner and communicates in a nonlocal way and instantaneously. In effect, we have trillions of cells in the human body and all of them have DNA. From the moment an instruction is changed, the sequence of DNA is modified and is automatically communicated to all the cells of the organism. It is the "domino effect" on the level of DNA: the change of a portion of DNA causes all the pieces to fall, instantaneously changing everything.
It takes "no time" for the trillion of cells to know what is happening and change themselves because this communication works in a network and is actualized in real time, simultaneously in the energy field of the individual and in the field of unified consciousness in a constant dialogue.
Now imagine the possibilities each one of us has when communicating in an authentic manner and in the language that the organism recognizes— that of health and order.
We merely need to reconnect to the order underlying all of life, vibrating in the frequency of light and correct information, and get out of the way so that the infinite intelligence does the work. It is already operating in us.

To summarize:
- Each one of us has the power to change our field of energy and change our biology, even at a genetic level.
- The human consciousness can access past data from thirty seconds ago or from thirty thousand years ago with the same simplicity in the wink of an eye.
- Our innate capacity to access information and process it in a unique manner has an impact on a quantum level, affecting also that which the DNA is made up of: energy, light and information, vibrating.

- We can deliberately change ourselves from the inside out and change our consciousness.

I also facilitate a seminar on DNA—Subtle Activation of the DNA—which uses ideas and energy tools, allowing the change of the state of consciousness and enabling the change of DNA.

Thoughts Entwined in the World

"We are seeking the simplest possible scheme of thought that will bind together the observed facts."
Albert Einstein

"This integral universe registers and feeds all we do and think, we are not only immersed in it, we are part of it."
Dr. David Lloye

For the majority, matter is still perceived as something solid, lifeless and separated from the subject. For any change to occur in the material component there has to be a physical action, local, and preferably visible and measurable. Very few people still admit that their thoughts are able to affect matter, interfere with it and can place it in their energy field in harmony with the energy field of any material reality, making everyday life easier.
The issue that we face is this: **"Is it possible for our thoughts to affect material reality?"**
We say yes; however, before answering further, we have to make it clear that the vision of matter as something substantial and consistent is fragmentary, and eighteen years ago, when I first heard these ideas in a seminar by Christiane Águas I was shocked and amazed at the same time.
I have also experienced the connection between thought and material reality in my own life and sometimes with strange results: One time after a big discussion with my boyfriend, my car broke down and the radiator was exploding. I remember thinking and feeling "I am stuck in this relationship." The car was showing me exactly my thoughts and feelings! Nevertheless, there are also positive events that I have experienced over so many years, for example, thinking about a white jacket and finding it in the most unpredictable place.
From the point of view of quantum physics, matter can be perceived as a point of energy vibrating in the field of unified consciousness and in cooperation with innumerous other fields of energy. That which we know as matter (table, dog, pencil, tree) has mass and has physical properties (inertia and gravitation), but actually, it is energy. It is the product of a subtle dialogue where subatomic units are configured and organized, are inseparable in themselves, and interact with their respective quantum fields and the field of unified consciousness.
Then instead of thinking of matter as something static in the matrix of space-time, we can consider it as a point—energy/wave—intricate piece of information in movement in the field of unified consciousness, linked to everything existing in it.
Returning to the issue of knowing whether our thoughts interfere with material reality—if we think of the process of thinking as a set of chemical and electrical

reactions produced locally in the brain, it does not appear possible that our thoughts can affect other living beings as well as non-living matter. However, if we consider that:

a) There is a field of unified consciousness, a field of information, where everything is potentially connected at the same time and on various levels, extending infinitely.

b) We understand the brain as a quantum energy system in correlation and communication with the field of unified consciousness and with what exists in it, namely, the objects/machines or other living beings, which are energy waves, coagulated in the field of unified consciousness.

c) It is possible to have communication, transference and sharing of information even at a distance, non-locally, and interference between energy systems, able to generate new energy coherence patterns, with "material" results.

Dr. Helmut Schmidt did one of the most fascinating experiments that corroborates, in my understanding, what we have stated above. He wanted to discover if a thought could affect the behavior of a machine (a kind of version of the flip of a coin), its random movements. This machine functioned in accordance with the binary system, yes or no, 0 to 1, carrying out random movements clockwise (heads) and counterclockwise (tails) shown by a circular movement through a lighting sequence of nine light bulbs arranged in a circle. When "heads" were chosen, the bulbs would light up in the direction of the hands of the clock (clockwise). When "tails" came up, the bulbs light up in a counterclockwise direction.

For the test, two participants were chosen (a man and a woman) to purposefully affect the machine to produce more "heads" than "tails." The result "was that the woman was able to affect the movement by producing heads
52.5% of the time. The man produced tails and the counterclockwise movement, although he was thinking of heads, the results being 47.75%".[7]

It is unbelievable how, one thought, one bit of information, is able to interfere with other points of information, entering with them in communication and interaction and causing movements that are different to the usual.

Have you imagined the possibilities of being able to take advantage of placing this force, for example, at the service of your work? Or even in those unexpected situations, for example, with your car or cell phone? What a great help it is to use the resources that we already must simplify our lives.

On the other hand, when we ruminate on hassles, on problems or illnesses it is also possible to interfere with objects around us, but in a negative manner. In those situations of bad mood, of anxiety, unloading on everybody else, it is possible to have the tendency for situations of breakdown or misunderstanding regarding what is happening with our cell phones, computers, toaster, washing machine, car, etc. The human energy field comes into communication with the energy fields of the objects and interacts with it.

When the vibrational quality of the waves of thought are dysfunctional, emitting-disorganized patterns, the field of the machine receives them, and they interact between themselves, creating a vibrational interference of disorder. This causes a drop in the frequency, emitting a sign of dysfunction, and the object showing a breakdown—that is, incoherence in its energy field.

---

[7] McTaggart, L., *The Field; The Quest for the Secret Force of The Universe*, Element, HarperCollins Publishers 2003, pg. 138, and Schmidt, H., *Mental Influence*.

When the field of energy returns to a vibrational frequency of order, namely because the thoughts are of simplicity, possibility, realization and flexibility, the exchange of information between energy systems occurs.

In this exchange, a pattern of interference of symmetry and of the flow of energy between the human energy fields, the machine and the field of unified consciousness (automatically emitting the information of functionality that is the energy of coherence), allows the normal functioning of the object.

My friend had an experience that, in my understanding, confirms what we have been explaining regarding the possibility of affecting the energy of machines.

Here is the testimonial:

Testimonial

I had a problem with my washing machine; it was not emptying the water, and systematically flooded the kitchen. An expert was called and he could not understand what was happening, because he did not find any anomaly. When speaking on the phone with Susana I told her about this situation. Later, I became aware that "my head was spinning," very tense, and brooding over the past. A few days after this conversation, I went to a seminar. On the first day, I released a lot of emotions and my head became empty. When I arrived home, after the seminar Saturday night, I decided to try the washing machine and I found it was working normally.

I must confess I was surprised but at the same time, something told me that from the moment I solved my internal issues, outside things would change. It was not only just the washing machine that began to function well. My family and I now communicate openly, are united, and find each other's company pleasurable.

Anabela Couto, beautician

The truth is, we are always communicating and interacting in the quantum world.
The field of unified consciousness and what exists in it also share the information we emit. Objects and things are made of the same matter as thoughts and when we have a thought, a subatomic particle is changed, communicates and interacts with that which the objects are made of, subatomic particles, also enabling changes in these.

If, each one of us accepts the possibility that our energy field interferes with the energy field of household appliances, the car, the computer, the cell phone and, in all strictness, with all the existing energy systems in the field of unified consciousness, we may become aware, with greater ease, when we are irradiating good energy or not, and change the quality of our energy frequency, simplifying our daily life.

♥ Stop, Breathe, Love

Now we have another issue. **Are we able to influence other living beings with our thoughts, for example plants or animals, even at a distance?** Yes, we confirm it. You have probably been through an experience of it. For example, having the thought that your plant should flower fast and it happened. Or thinking, "where is the dog?" and he suddenly appears. The thought waves produced are information from the field of unified consciousness vibrating like the plant or the animal. They are information coagulated in a space-time matrix, vibrating in the field of unified consciousness, and what they do with each other is exchange information. When expressing a certain signal (thought) with a set energy frequency, it enters into communication with other existing energy frequencies, informing and enforming the field of energy that it is in resonance with, creating a new modulation in the energy field that it is interacting with, that is, a new energy pattern emerges, showing an actualized energy "face."

One of the scientific experiments we know that proves that it is possible for our thoughts to affect other living beings, specifically, plants at a distance, is described in the book *Vibrational Medicine: New Choices for Healing Ourselves* by Dr. Richard Gerber. This experiment was done in the USA, by Dr. Robert Miller. Dr. Miller asked a couple who lived 900 km from his laboratory, to focus their thoughts on plants (rye grass) at 21:00 hours. To carry out the experiment, the rate of growth of the plants was monitored in the laboratory and this was measured at 6.25% thousandths of an inch per hour. At 21:00 hours the *"registered growth rate was 52.5% thousandths of an inch, 840% more" (...)*, and that was corresponding with the sending of thoughts in the form of prayer and visualization of plants full of light, by the couple".[8]

What shall we say of the possibility of affecting other human beings with our thoughts, even at a distance?

That is possible; and it is very probable that we have lived situations where our thoughts interfered in the quality of life of the people we love. For example, when my mother did a biopsy, she was very nervous. I was outside focused on her wellbeing and internally I was thinking of calmness and how friendly, competent and committed the doctor was and how concerned he was with her wellbeing. My mother became much calmer, and everything went well. It is also possible for a thought to lead a person to a certain place even though she may not know the way and be without a cell phone: a sort of telepathic GPS. Or even a thought to help when someone is needing our help and when we think of that person, we think of the person happy and joyful, and subsequently, in a telephone conversation, that person reports exactly that.

Scientific research done by the psychologist William Braud proved that it is possible to affect the mental and emotional state of a person at a distance sending her thoughts of calmness or concentration.[9]

How is this possible? Our unique nature and the unity underlying the whole of creation, allow that with every communication we inform life and are able to give it form. Because of the fundamental interdependence between all things, it is possible that the energetic affectation happens immediately and even at a "distance."

The thought, to affect another person, can be something simple, for example, the wish that all is well, or that the person relaxes.

Indeed, the mental attitude of thinking that all is well is highly recommended for others and for you also. The first time I heard that was in a conference by Christiane Águas in 1997. She was always reinforcing the idea that "all is well," and "how you need to think/say it to yourself and to others, especially when you or the other person(s) are "observing" things and want to stay open (maintain a positive focus) to receive the best." In effect, a study was done at a university in the United States of

---

[8] Gerber, R., *Vibrational Medicine: New Choices for Healing Ourselves*, Bear and Company, 1996, summarized from pg. 257 of the Portuguese edition (Editora Cultrix)

[9] Braud, W., Mental Influence Research, Hampton Road Publishing. Also see, Braud, W. et al, "Attention focusing facilitated through remote mental interaction," Journal of the American Society for Psychic Research, 89, 1995, pgs 103-115.

America, by Rex Stanford, and was published in the *Journal of the American Society for Psychical Research* "proving that people can positively influence events in their life (and in the lives of others, I add) through hoping and wishing that all goes well, even if they did not quite know what, or how."[10]

Thought is information that is connected from a fundamental point of view to any existing information. From the moment it is emitted, it communicates and interacts with another point of information, actualizing the field of unified consciousness and simultaneously the field of the person that we are focusing our thoughts on.

There is no distance for thought; it is reality, even if in a potential state. Thought does not need to travel anywhere because it already is in the field of unified consciousness; for the effect to appear, it suffices that a conscious entity actualizes it through the focus of his attention.

Therefore, from now on, if we or anyone of our relationships are/is faced with a situation that is seen as a problem, a change in the perception, changing the mental attitude, will establish a connection with the solution.

We can always focus our consciousness on **"everything is well"** or **"now the solutions are on the way"** or even **"I am open to the best and will accept whatever comes in the next ten minutes"** to allow, in fact, new possibilities. That is, energy organizations of order and flow, in harmony with our decision, expediting the resolution of the situation in question. We can apply this focus when we are going to pick up the children from school, writing an article, catching the bus, solving a family issue, assisting a friend, etc. Focusing the consciousness on the solution or on "all is well" is the accelerator of particles that allows to experience the resolution of situations, facilitating our daily lives.

The influence of thoughts, even at a "distance" is due to the quantum nature of our brains and thoughts, which function and cooperate with each other linked to field of unified consciousness, allowing the sharing of information is done in a way that is non local and automatic, manifesting a new state of energy coherence.

"Who Are We" then? We are thinkers in a multifaceted universe that is concerned with us, giving us the power of affecting life profoundly and recreating ourselves, at each nanosecond, through what we think and are integrally. It is time to think big and be whole.

 Key points:
- Thought is a tool to create reality. All things started as ideas before they appear on our lives.
- Thinking is communicating in a broader sense; in the act of thinking, we share information with others and with the world.
- Negative and positive thoughts impact our lives distinctly.
- The delays, difficulties and tensions have to do with limiting thoughts, fears and the lack of attention in relation to the objective being pursued.
- It is essential to understand that from the moment we emit a thought the whole universe unites to manifest it.

---

[10] Stanford, R., "Associative activation of the unconscious," and "visualization" as a method for influencing the PK target" Journal of the American Society for Psychical Research, 1969; 63: summarized from pg. 33851. See also, McTaggart, L., "The Field; The Quest for the Secret Force of The Universe", Element, HarperCollins Publishers 2003, pg. 242.

- Clear your mind with the attention exercise as much as you can and focus.
- A belief is information something you believe in and can be changed.
- When we are interacting with others and the beliefs they express are negative we can think: *"That is your belief. I will choose a better one!"* and concentrate on a positive one.
- Health is built day by day through our thoughts, feelings and behaviors.
- Negative suggestion given by another and accepted by the other person, can cause physical symptoms. Don't allow your health to be affected. Say *stop. I choose Health.*
- Positive and healing suggestions affect your body and build health.
- Placebo effect is real and works. How can you implement it in your life now?
- Focus your consciousness on these three open and general thoughts : *"everything is well"* , *"now the solutions are on the way"*, *"I am open to the best and will accept whatever comes in the next ten minutes"* to allow, in fact, new possibilities.
- Your thinking mind is shaping reality constantly. Be Bold.

Self-reflection:
❶ What made most sense in the scientific experiments described?
❷ Describe three situations in which you noticed the influence of your thoughts.
❸ Formulate a thought that you are going to use over a week and be attentive to the results.

Exercise:
Constructing Beliefs
❶ Write five ideas that are new, open and positive for you.
❷ During the following eight days, fall in love with these ideas, nurture them any way you see fit, for example, researching the topic, thinking, drawing what comes to mind as a result of these ideas, speaking about them with enthusiasm, etc.
❸ In the following eight days, plant a bush or a plant in a pot and associate it with those ideas. Take care of the plant. Place it in the sunlight. Water it, give it music. You can also buy a plant in a pot and bury in a paper with these ideas. The important thing is taking care and maintaining the beliefs.
❹ Over the following eight days, visualize the plant growing. On the last day (the 24th day) give the plant to someone and give this person the message of the positive belief and what it means for you.
❺ Inform the person about the purpose of passing on positive beliefs to someone in twenty-four days, for her to create a new cycle.

7 Image

Story
A long time ago, a very talented weaver lived in a village; she made the most beautiful quilts in the kingdom. She was also a woman that searched for knowledge and wanted to know more about the essence of life.
One day, on her way to the market, where she was going to sell a quilt, she came across an elderly tradesman who had fallen; she helped him get up and picked up some of the things that had fallen on the ground. He was so touched by the weaver's curiosity that he decided to present her with a box. The weaver thanked him and on opening the box, she saw her own image, and that of an old man whom she did not know. Surprised, the weaver widened her eyes and asked the tradesman: "What magic is this, dear soul?" The tradesman smiled and told her that this was a mirror that he had received when he had helped an old tradesman who had fallen.
The weaver smiled, thanked him for the present again, embraced the old tradesman and said goodbye. That day when she returned home with a big smile on her face, her husband and daughters asked her: "Was business good today?" The weaver answered, "Something much better happened. I saw a part of me and of the whole in a mirror." Touched by the possibility of seeing themselves more deeply and the All, they hugged her and opened the box with the mirror. They all wanted to experiment. So the weaver handed over the box with the mirror.

"And God created man in his own image."
The Bible

"Imagination is more important than knowledge."
Albert Einstein

It is possible that, like the weaver, we also wish to know ourselves better? Life can provide us the encounters to attain that knowledge. It can be done in an unusual manner: through other people we are given mirrors with which to see ourselves, others and the intricate cosmic tapestry. Such moments are available to us in any instant, and can make all the difference in our lives.
To better understand the images that the mirror of life can show us, we will investigate the **language of image creation**. This will allow us to work small and big changes into our lives.
In a wider sense, images are information, energy in movement and light vibrating in the field of unified consciousness. Images are also **a language** through which we communicate with the field of unified consciousness. **Images are also an instrument placed at the service of human consciousness so that it can construct reality.**
As we have mentioned, the field of unified consciousness is the basis of life and naturally, by extension, of images.
As a matter of organization, we will state that there are three "origins" of images:
❶ Unified consciousness
❷ Individual consciousness
❸ Planetary consciousness

❶ Images from the unified consciousness

These images are the representation of pure information existing in the field. It is the legacy of perfect forms that are manifested in existence, from a solar system to a galaxy, mountain, animal or atom. The human consciousness accesses these images when it is resonating in frequency with the field of unified consciousness, capturing information through the "superior" senses —which we mentioned in the second chapter: namely clairvoyance, intuition or inspiration—since the brain, as a quantum system of energy, receives information and makes it accessible biodynamically in a frequency understood by human beings.

The information from an image obtained directly from the field of unified consciousness is nonlinear; it merely appears as if it came from nowhere, can be transmitted at the speed of light (or even faster), and transcends all limits of space and time; that is, it can be information, for example, from this solar system or from another, and the information is instantaneously communicated to the brain´s quantum system. This system functions on a network that reflects the received holographic information like a mirror.

One of the most fascinating scientific experiments and that seems to corroborate the information here was conducted at the Stanford Research Institute, USA, by Hall Puthoff and Russel Targ in the scope of researching clairvoyance with Ingo Swann. The objective of the experiment was to know whether it was possible to see at a distance, without being physically in that distant place. Would it be possible for Ingo Swann to pre-view images of the planet Jupiter before the NASA sonar got them? During the experiment, he entered into an altered state of consciousness and continually gave information on what he was seeing on Jupiter; he even drew a ring around the planet. In disbelief, the scientists rejected this information; but later the NASA sonar confirmed the ring around Jupiter. The vision of Ingo Swann was real.[1]

The imagetic information from the field of unified consciousness is multidimensional, timeless and nonlocal. It is available to be accessed by any human being at any time, if he focuses his consciousness and changes vibrationally into a state of communication with the field of unified consciousness, permitting him to access data about any plane of existence. It is up to us whether to accept or reject this information. When we accept it, we are enlightened and we reach a higher level of consciousness.

❷ Images from the individual consciousness

Consciousness builds mental images through the information that comes via the senses, reproduces images from memory and has the capacity of producing images from others. Via imagination, consciousness can also create them anew.

A few simple example: we are seeing a tree in our garden. The sense of vision captures the information of a tree in our garden and sends it to the information processing systems of the brain, namely the visual cortex, which will internally show the image of the tree,—thus, we see a tree.

When the image of our first kiss emerges, the memory centers are activated, and

---

[1] Puthoff, H., "CIA-Initiated Remote Viewing at Stanford Research Institute" paper, 1996, and Targ, R. and Puthoff, H., Mind-Reach: Scientists Look at Psychic Abilities (Studies in Consciousness), Delacorte Press, 1977.

mentally reproduces that image for remembering. When we observe an object, develop an image and create new functions for it, like a cell phone—which was first for calls and now plays music—we are using abstraction and imagination together.
And when a new image emerges for a picture we are painting, or for something we wish to find or invent, we are using the creative process that is the imagination or visioning. These capacities that human beings have associated with images, namely representation, memory, abstraction and imagination, are just one in itself, and they are processed internally and communicated both to the field of unified consciousness, who receives them and mirrors them automatically, placing us in resonance with the information transmitted and to Earth's energy field, which receives it and retransmits them as well.

❸ Images from the planetary consciousness

Earth is a living entity and is full of imagetic information in various forms, sending this energy to all beings and to the field of unified consciousness. Earth's energy field receives the images that human beings, individually and collectively produce, retransmitting them in the same vibrational frequency to the human community and the field of unified consciousness.
Every individual or community has the capacity to accept or reject the images that have been formulated, feeding back into the planetary consciousness.

Now that we have explained the origins of images (the field of unified consciousness), we will look especially at the images of the field of human consciousness.

❤ Stop, Breathe, Love

In our universe, we are constantly surrounded by images—whether in nature or within our minds. We are systematically capturing information through the senses, perceiving the world and images are plentiful.
Images are aggregated energy, formatted in accordance with certain patterns and accepted by our consciousness and also produced in it. In fact it is information existing in the field of unified consciousness, in the field of human consciousness and also in the field of planetary consciousness that we perceive and give significance to.
The function of an image is to build reality. Any reality. From the meal we share with a friend, to the clothes we wear, or the kiss we give to our newborn child.

Images in Process
"We all live under the same sky, but we don't all have the same horizon."
Konrad Adenauer

The images we have of life are waves undulating in the field of unified consciousness with the purpose of expressing creativity at the highest level.
Images are the language of the field of unified consciousness and that simultaneously communicate information and manifest the creation of that same field. The human form is the result of the creation of a primordial idea molded in the genetic code (spiritual and physical), visibly represented in the physical plane. All other

manifestations of the field of unified consciousness (from a comet, a mouse, a proton) are also images of an original idea linked to each other in a luminous network that reflects and aligns itself constantly.

Images are also a tool of the human consciousness, since we have the capacity of creating them. It is simultaneously information and "enformation" because it molds life.

Each time we use the language of the creation of images, we are informing our energy field and it acquires and manifests form, as well as automatically transmitting coagulated data to the field of unified consciousness and simultaneously to Earth. This information is automatically placed "online" since the field of consciousness works holographically, mirroring each piece of information added and connecting it to all energy systems existing in it, or that may exist in the future.

♥ Stop, Breathe, Love

At this stage, we may ask ourselves: how important are images for our daily life?

The significance of images in life is enormous because an image is formatted light and coded information. Light is a universal phenomenon that affects all existence. In effect, the images we access or produce are luminous pieces of information that are present in all of creation, from atoms, to objects, circumstances or events.

By using images, we are creating probabilities of interconnections and of manifestations in harmony with the vibration transmitted in the image.

Human beings are systematically interacting with light and when receiving or emitting images, are processing meaningful luminous signals which move rapidly. These signals will also be in tune with the luminous information that is vibrating in its energy field, the field of unified consciousness and Earth's energy field, materializing existence.

When we work with an image, we are interacting with light that contains patterns in a subtle form, which cooperate, and interrelate with existing luminous patterns (from photons to cells and much more) and that are present in the energetic reality of any type of manifestation.

Using an image is giving it life, bringing light to that which we are focusing on.

Think of what you wish to bring to life. A romantic weekend, a different set of earrings, or a warm conversation with your mother. These can all be created through images.

Since we are frequently processing images (observing, imagining, remembering), could it be that any image that we emit or receive can affect reality?

Any image can affect reality; more accurately, it is reality interfering with the infinite possibilities of reality.

The nature of reality is one and so it is with images. Therefore, it is *only* possible for an image to interfere with reality because that is its function; that is its immanent nature.

Can images be different and still manifest reality in the same way?

We confirm that yes, they can. Depending if the images are organized or disorganized, considered positive or negative, and if we are conscious of their being creative and being connected to the field, amongst other things....

Regarding images being organized or disorganized, and what is possible to achieve:

We consider images to be organized when they convey structured information in an integrated and symmetric manner, and when expressed, make cohesion probable. They are coherent in form and structure and have an elevated vibration. For example, and image of love between father and child allows subatomic rearrangements of coherence and aggregates both internal and external forms of beauty, interacting and communicating with other energy fields in this pattern of form.

We consider images to be disorganized when the information conveyed is disorganized and confused and when expressed, makes destruction and distortion probable. Their shape is incoherent and has a low vibration. For example, an image of violence between father and son makes possible in coherent subatomic rearrangements, and the forms that emerge both internally and externally are destructive and disorganized, interacting and communicating with other energy fields in this same shape pattern.

A scientific experiment regarding the power of images in life that corroborates what we have said above is mentioned in the book *The Miracle of Water* written by Masaru Emoto. In his book, Mr. Emoto clearly shows the potential of images to affect water molecules. The images placed in the energy field of the water affect the molecular structure of the water crystals. When photos of natural landscapes are placed under a jar of water, the water molecules are symmetric and very beautiful. On the contrary, images of confusion create deformity.[2]

Regarding images being "positive" or "negative," we are going to explain the following: images are what they are—reality. Positive and negative are energy charges that subatomic particles may have. It is not good or bad; it is what it is.

*From a simple perspective, we can state that we are emitting or receiving images considered **positive** when they bring order to our lives, build the results we want, which make sense to us at the time and we perceive as positive (for example, the image of receiving a present).*

On the contrary, images emitted or received can be considered negative when they bring disorder or dysfunction to our lives, whose effects are the opposite of what we want, those we have focused on, and are perceived as negative (for example, the image of an accident).

When we emit images that we consider as "positive" or "negative" for us, for others and for the world, we are automatically vibrating in that energy, and the effects of that image are felt first by us, because we are the epicenter of that information and internal formatting. We manifest in our energy field, and in the events, situations, objects or persons we encounter, the subatomic rearrangements of the images that we are processing. Therefore, it is best that we choose carefully what we bring to life. This being so, when an image emerges, we should ask: **"Does this image bring order to my life? Is it beneficial for me?** If the answer is **positive, we should keep the image,** if the answer is negative, then we replace the image.

On a more advanced scale: **"Is this image good for me and for Earth?"** In the case that the image is for my good and bestows good on all beings, I will focus on it and feed it, if not, I will change the image. The images emerging from the field of unified consciousness are always organized and "positive"; the self-produced ones may be so or not, according to the patterns imprinted on them and the perception we have of them.

---

[2] Emoto, M., *The Hidden Messages in Water*, Portuguese edition (Editora Estrela Polar), pg. 124 and following

♥ Stop, Breathe, Love

Another issue regarding the manifestation of images in our reality **has to do with the type of images that we observe, imagine or remember and are being focused voluntarily or involuntarily.**

We consider images voluntary when we choose them consciously and involuntary those that are on autopilot, which are unconscious and result normally from routine.

Involuntary images generally emerge in an unconscious manner and are on autopilot, producing content that we consider "negative," namely by excess of distorted information that we can capture from the exterior (television, internet, etc.,) or by many internal images that have emerged from moments of discomfort, personal pain or frustration and that emerge simply by habit in the mental screen.

Examples for both situations: we voluntarily choose to focus on images of beauty wherever we are and notice, for example, a flower on a balcony or a gesture of goodwill. We are fixed involuntarily on an image from a dramatic film we saw yesterday.

What do involuntary images construct in our reality or that of the community? Normally results perceived as "negative." The drama that we feed mentally and which we project externally is directed at what we do not want, to the dysfunction, the limitation or fear. It is a black and white film in which the characters and dialogue are distorted. The "complicator" is connected and the probability of problems, confusions and difficulties arising is great. The tendency is for these to repeat themselves systematically, until the automatic cycle of the old film is interrupted.

It is possible that the individual is not even aware that he is creating that reality, and projecting externally, to circumstances, and to others that which is not going well for him. He is taking no responsibility for what he is creating and what is happening. The problems, the confusion or the pain are because of his mother-in-law, the weather, his children, taxes; attributing responsibility to everyone but himself.

However, we have the power to change the images that we focus on and those we have been fixed on. We can perceive the world in a different way, modifying the images we focus on and necessarily the field of unified consciousness will reply to us with other images of life.

We affect the world with our presence and reality is changeable, changing with the alteration of the images that we are observing, remembering or imagining. For example, facing an image of financial disruption that causes even more tension, we can focus on an image of everyone paying at businesses. This image stimulates other neural connections, it causes the secretion of other types of molecules and muscular movements and simultaneously raises other possibilities from the energetic point of view that the field of consciousness will rearrange in a team with us, making available and synchronizing the means, resources and solutions.

It is probably necessary to practice very often until the process is interiorized. If an image of tension appears, breathe deeply and exhale with force. Repeat the breath three times and then place an image that makes sense.

Voluntary images are conscious and purposeful choices. The act of observation, imagining or remembering is focused on an objective or desire considered "positive" for you, for another and even for the community. We make the decision of **what to observe**, imagine, and remember, and **when to observe**, imagine, and remember and

how to observe, imagine, and remember ideas, persons, events or life situations and we are present in that action. We make our life easy.

The focus of our consciousness is clear, and we communicate that same clarity to the field of unified consciousness. As a result of this clear communication, various scenarios are possible, because they are available, and defined and specific events emerge. Space-time is synchronized and the resources, objects, events and people needed to manifest what was decided by the image that was observed, imagined or remembered previously, appear in a colorful and dynamic entwine. The reality is created in accordance with the quality, the color and dimension the author has attributed to it.

For example, the decision to observe the way our tennis coach plays, imagining the success of that public presentation, or a lively conversation with a friend. These images are aligning the subatomic rearrangements that make the achievement of these events possible.

🚀 Exercise:
- Visualize an image of something positive and important for you and breathe seven times.
- Then imagine that image between your eyebrows, becoming bigger, clearer and full of energy.
- Release the image to the universe and feel alive, full of love.
- Repeat the process 3 times a day and notice the outcomes.

❤ Stop, Breathe, Love

The factors that generally interfere with the manifestation of the voluntary image that we are observing, imagining or remembering are: the lack of attention, attachment, desire for control, incoherence and not being aware that you are the creator of reality.

⊛The lack of attention is the lack of focus on the image that we have meanwhile decided to focus on, focusing on other things that have nothing to do with it. For example, focusing on an image of being healthy and then looking at images of illnesses. It is necessary to persist with our attention, focusing consistently on what we wish to manifest. One of the best ways is to fall in love with the images and feed them; have them with you in your bag, or the fridge door, see them frequently. Maintain them present in your energy field.

⊛Another aspect is attachment, the need for something to happen. Attachment has the underlying state of need, limitation or fear. That vibration interferes with the image, and instead of making the concretization probable, it delays or prevents it. The field of consciousness is abundant and has no attachment or any need; it simply is. We are and have (although in a potential state) that which we observe or imagine. The more relaxed we are and allow creativity to occur, the better. We can consider the tendency to control the process as a type of attachment. For example, an image of a job had to coincide exactly with what we imagined. It could be even better, bigger and easier, therefore, why limit what has no limits?

⊛On the other hand, there is also the tendency to control, wanting to know the "how":

"How am I going to manage if I have no money, I do not speak English, I have never worked in that area, or I do not have the figure of a model?" or, *"How am I going to achieve anything if I am 5'5" and live in the country"*; *" My children need me; My husband will not let me,"* or anything else. When we are observing or imagining images, we very often do not even allow ourselves to dare or broaden our horizons.

The "how" is the "blablabla" that makes it impossible, scares or close doors that can actually be opened from the moment we are focused and in harmony with the decisions we take. Changing our perception is urgent. The field of unified consciousness is limitless and the human being is too. We should not waste our internal resources on that which is false. *The truth about us is that we are inevitably linked to abundance, wealth and unlimited possibilities and that opportunities are never ending. Our fundamental nature is one with what is manifested and with what is possible to manifest. It is complete therefore, it has everything and is connected with the field of unified consciousness at each moment, breathing together.*

⊛Incoherence also interferes in this process in which we are observing or imagining. For example, it is incoherent when focusing on an image of flowers and suddenly, faced with the possibility of receiving them we reject them. Or focusing on an image of love and communication and instead of giving and communicating it, we have the old attitude of keeping quiet. There was no verticality between the focusing of attention on the image, the feeling, and the respective behavior. The coherence requires clarity, openness and integrity from the act of observing or imagining until the assumption of the responsibility for what we have created. *The conditions are always there to exercise the decision we have made when we observed or imagined. The universe is ready for us and the more we embody the images we focus, the clearer and more immediate the realization.*

Does a person who is aware of the creative power of an image and her union to the field of unified consciousness manifest what she evokes?
First, it should be explained that, from the quantum point of view, any image has the potential for immediate manifestation; that is because it is in the field of unified consciousness. *The image is reality (even if just virtual) linked to all reality. Only our perception and absence of attention disconnects us and distances us from the manifestation.*

A human being, who in the act of observing or imagining, is aware that he is communicating and shaping reality in unity with the field of unified consciousness and the planet, knows that all is possible and that the realization has already happened. He is completely receptive and sure of the manifestation. The person may be experiencing this state in a fraction of a second and manifest immediately what he observes or imagines. In a state of unity, space-time is collapsed in that instant and any shape, object, person or instant is before him, in him and in all; he is the presence witnessing the omnipresent and omnipotent.

On the other hand, even if the manifestation is spread over space-time, the cohesion with the result produced is maintained. The person behaves as if it is already achieved and continues with life in that assumption. The assumption of responsibility for the result of achievement is done totally, because he knows that he is the creator of reality and the collective.

♥ Stop, Breathe, Love

Another fundamental aspect of images is attention. We discussed it in chapter four, but its great importance justifies returning to it here as well.

Both image and attention are tools for the construction of reality. They are both the language of creation, which we use to communicate with the field of unified consciousness and which it recognizes, and answers us in. They are both connected with the process of constructing reality. Attention is directed consciousness, present and in presence. And whatever consciousness observes, it manifests.

Attention feeds the image and brings to life the manifestation. When we pay attention to an image, even if for just a minute, we are selectively choosing that specific information and giving it priority, and this act, from a quantum point of view, crystallizes the information represented by the image and actualizes it, that is, makes it ready for concretization.

We participate in life and reorganize it, selecting actively and simultaneously the attention and the images that we focus on. *What we observe or imagine through our attention is permeated with our presence and is present, passing from a state of infinite possibilities to something particular and with shape, color, taste or any quality we wish to give it. Attention affects the concretization.* **A focused image is a concretized image.**

Remember some of the concepts of attention summarized here:

1) What *image are we focusing on?* We select, giving attention to images of people, objects, events, nature, etc., amongst many other possible images.

2) When *do we focus on an image?* We pay attention to images we place temporarily in the past, in the present or that we project in the future, and that the focus of attention brings to life events related with it. For example, when we pay attention to an image of past success it continues to feed the results in the present.

3) How *are we focusing on images? In a concentrated or a distributed manner?* When we choose to pay total attention to an image or share the attention with various images, it interferes with the probability of the image being manifested in reality.

At each moment we are recreating our world by focusing attention on selected images, which the field of consciousness also focuses and mirrors, making them visible in reality so that we can continue creating them or changing them.

So be careful with which images we pay attention to, because they become reality. Attention and image are intimately linked and reveal the information that is being edited by the human consciousness in harmony with the field of unified consciousness, and which will be magnified in the cosmic screen and particularized in events, people or objects. The possibilities are numerous and we can bring to life the most beautiful scenarios that can be enjoyed by humanity together with the planet and the field of unified consciousness.

Imagetic Multifunctionality

"Who looks outside, dreams; who looks inside, awakes."
Carl Jung

"Logic will take you from A to B. Imagination will take you everywhere."
Albert Einstein

Images are energy, information and light at our disposal to create reality. Images can create the reality that makes sense to us, which makes us happy and in tune with life, but also the one we consider boring, difficult or hard. It can be a meeting with our godmother, going to our favorite restaurant or visiting a church in Venice. We can also create the lineup at the supermarket, a disagreement between lovers, or tension in the shoulders. The variety is enormous, and there are always more choices for us. In effect, what we are always doing is creating and recreating, even when we think we are not, because what we have before us is similar or the same as what we have had, and we do not like it, giving us the sensation that there are others, or many others leading our life.

There is no illusion; the helm is in our hands because we are the only being that can live, carry out, feel and organize our lives. That prerogative, the right to creation, is with us for eternity. The question that opens doors to creativity is this: **What can I create at this moment?** From this point on, we have the universe at our disposal. Through the images we choose, we rearrange the possible tendencies of reality and new forms, content, persons and events emerge.

Images are the "laser technology of the consciousness" used to imprint that which we observe, imagine or remember. Each time that we focus on an image we are co-linked internally with the biophotons that we emit and with those vibrating in the planet and the field of unified consciousness, and in that luminous dialogue, we shine and cause reality to sparkle. From a subatomic point of view, it is possible for subatomic particles (including photons) to communicate and interact in a nonlocal way and the manifestation by image can possibly occur instantaneously.

We ask once more: what can I create this instant? Whatever you decide, because the possibilities are unlimited.

Be it through observation, remembrance, abstraction, visioning or imagination, images are giving life to the information they have—whatever the image or form—and manifest the reality. The applicability of the *"subtle technology of the image"* is absolute. From relationships, to health, work, finances, or physical activities or studying, we can be fulfilled as human beings using this language that the field of consciousness has given us. It is ready to be used; in fact, we have been using it for many years.

The aim is to become a purposeful creator instead of a disorientated creator and to use images for your good and for the good of all other beings. We can visualize, imagine, observe or remember to bring to light the achievements that make sense; in this act of imagetic selection, the film we bring to life is viewed and processed immediately in the field of unified consciousness, which edits it completely and mirrors it back to us.

There are many scientific studies that prove that the brain reacts to real or clear imaginary situations in similar ways as if it was living a physical experience. The brain makes itself available in the same manner, activating the same brain areas, sending neurotransmitters to stimulate the production of molecules, reconstructing cells and even functions.

Based on this knowledge, there are many doctors who use images to cure or improve health with positive effects. Here are some examples:

A study carried out in 2008 at the William Beaumont Hospital in Royal Oak, USA with thirty women and a duration of eight weeks, confirmed the efficiency of visualization in the treatment of interstitial cystitis: *"For twenty five minutes per day, a group of fifteen women visualized a cure for the bladder, the relaxation of the pelvic muscles and the nerves of the surrounding area. The remaining fifteen women of the control group rested, without doing anything. After eight weeks the fifteen women who used visualization had a significant reduction of the symptoms and pain in comparison with those who did not visualize."*[3]

On the other hand, a mental image of anger, associated with the respective experience of anger, is capable of destabilizing the "pH of the blood" and creates the conditions for infections. On the contrary, the use of images associated with states of physical and mental relaxation and feelings of peace and hope are highly recommended in the stabilization of "pH" and the recovery of health.

In respect to wounds and the healing of sutures, visualization also has positive effects. A study made in 2007 at the Nursing School of Southeast Louisiana, with twenty four patients who had surgery to remove their gallbladder, found that visualization had a double effect: *"reducing levels of anxiety and hormonal stress in the patients subjected to the surgery, as well as reducing the levels of erythema on the sutures (redness around the suture indicating infection or inflammation). The study found that visualization accelerated the healing of the sutures and wounds."*[4]

At the same time, visualization has been utilized successfully in the case of cancer; the work of Dr. Carl Simonton is one of the best documented and includes cancer curing results. Patients carry out visualizations to strengthen their immune system, eliminate diseased cells, recovering functions, and successfully reconstructing health and also self-esteem. These people have better results with visualizations when they choose clear mental images, as if they were seeing these for real, and feel free to create the desired result. Many of them imagine the sun melting the diseased cells, or the white blood cells eating the diseased cells, and do so in a state of physical and mental relaxation focused on these images and living them in the present, feeling peaceful and confident.[5]

Besides assisting in the cure, visualization also reduces the risk of re-incidence of breast cancer. A study in 2008, involving thirty-four women in an eight week program of visualizations (published in the *Journal for the Society of Integrative Oncology*), showed that *"women who had visualized reduced their stress, improving their quality of life, decreasing the rate of cortisol which is the indicator of the probability of cancer, and reducing the probability of the re-incidence of cancer."*[6]

Other scientific studies done with terminally ill patients who were subjected, on a daily basis, to a therapy with images that stimulated laughter, confirm that the patients experienced significant improvement and some of them even had spontaneous remission of the disease.

It is impressive what we can do internally with an image and what we experience as a

---

[3] Dr. David Hamilton, Digital Magazine, Whole Science, August 21, 2009. See also, Dr. David Hamilton website: http://drdavidhamilton.com/category/visualization2/page/2/.
[4] Dr. David Hamilton, Digital Magazine, Whole Science, August 21, 2009. See also, Dr. David Hamilton website: http://drdavidhamilton.com/category/visualization2/page/2/.
[5] For more information about the work of Dr. Carl Simonton please visit www.simontoncenter.com and read Getting Well Again by O. Carl Simonton, M.D., James Creighton, Ph.D. and Stephanie Matthews Simonton. Bantam, April 01, 1992.
[6] Dr. David Hamilton, Digital Magazine, Whole Science, August 21, 2009.

result of paying attention to it attention. From a neural point of view, the imagetic information is recognized and the whole energy system is activated from the neurotransmitters, stimulating the production of specific substances for the recuperation of organs or the decrease of pain. We reconnect ourselves internally with health. The images speak a language that the brain, as a quantum processor, recognizes, and this adapts and reconfigures itself and the body in accordance with the vital instructions that are transmitted to it.

The power we have to recuperate health or improve ourselves through the practice of visualization is incredible. This technology of the conscious ness is available to be used, has no side effects and allows us to contact and update internal medicine, the self-cure that we are born with. The studies mentioned here make us think and free us from limiting beliefs, opening the possibility of internal self- transformation, expanding ourselves.

The images we observe, imagine or visualize are in the field of unified consciousness, and the brain, as a quantum processor of that information, works in tune with the field of unified consciousness. The instant this information is processed, numerous possibilities are open and these are particularized and defined, in accordance with the information and form shown by the image. *It is us that instruct the field: we limit or expand it, in accordance with the imagery imprinted, the imagery's significance and our underlying beliefs. It is in our hands to communicate and use this technology of the consciousness with confidence.*

Reflect now:
- Have you ever felt that your own thoughts or visualizations have improved your health?
- With whom can you be in harmony today? See it, feel it, and be happy.

♥ Stop, Breathe, Love

We reiterate from a neural point of view, the act of observing, imagining, envisioning or visualizing triggers intelligent answers. Even without physical movement, they activate the different sections of the brain, which is sending neurotransmitters, producing molecules, and also giving life to the functions, muscles, nerves and cells that may be damaged.

In this respect, let us look at the function of the mirror cells that were discovered by the neuroscientists Giacomo Rizzolatti, Leonardo Fogassi and Vittorio Gallese, at the University of Parma in Italy in 1994. The neuroscientists found that *"the simple observation of unrelated/outside actions activated the same regions of the observer's brain that is normally stimulated by the person performing the action herself. Everything seems to indicate our visual perception starts a type of internal simulation or duplication of the acts of others."* In another study, *"using functional magnetic resonance (FMRI), the researchers mentioned above measured the brain activity of volunteers while they watched a video that showed a sequence of movements with the mouth, hands and feet. Depending on the part of the body that appeared on the screen, the motor cortex of the observers became activated with greater intensity in the region that corresponded to the body part in question, even though they remained motionless. The brain seems to associate the vision of outside movements to the planning of its own movements."*[7]

One of the most enthusiastic cases that has been brought to my attention when hearing an interview—that is in line with what I have just described— is the case of an Olympic athlete from the United States, Marilyn King, who won two Olympic medals in the pentathlon in the Olympic games of Munich and Montreal. *"In 1979, Marilyn King had the goal of classifying in the top three places of national athletics so she could go to the Olympic games in Moscow in 1981. In that same year, before the start of winter training, she was involved in a car accident, causing an injury to a disc in her spine, which was not immediately diagnosed. This undiagnosed injury caused further damage and resulted in the athlete being completely unable to carry out any physical training. She was ordered to bed rest, where she remained for months.*

Internally, she maintained her passion and her goal to qualify in the top three places as a national athlete in order to go to the Moscow Olympics. She achieved this. In hospital, for seven consecutive months, unable to step out of bed, Marilyn proceeded with her mental training. To that effect, she visualized films of the Olympic games she had participated in and of world champions; she would watch these four hours per day. Besides this, she mentally trained the pentathlon for four hours per day. And, without any type of physical training after the hospital stay, when she did the qualification trials for the team that would go to the Moscow Olympics, she came second in the national team for the United States of America."[8] It is scientifically proven that mental images can develop physical resistance, agility, speed, performance and attention, because they trigger neurophysiological procedures that affect the heart activity, breathing, muscle movement, physical resistance and concentration.

Top athletes in sports from golf to football, use visualizations to improve their physical performance, to have better muscle tone and firmness, more attention and flexibility and are able to achieve the success that they intended. These athletes understand that it is on a mental level that we build the body and any physical reality; they use images to their benefit. Besides the effects in adults, visualization also improves performance in children. *"A study done with children aged seven to ten years, in the scope of table tennis, showed a significant improvement in the group that used visualization in their training, as compared to the group of children who only trained normally. There were significant results in the concentration level, the movement and the placing of the ball on the side of the opponent."*[9]

Other scientific studies confirm the positive effects of visualization in public speaking, in preparation for childbirth, or even to improve sexual performance, and achieve significant results. What these studies prove is that reality is mutable and that we are able to affect it and change it in a significant manner. We have within us the most advanced tools for human realization. It is so easy to gain quality of life, be healthy or

---

[7] Binkofski, F. and Buccino, G., Scientific American magazine Mente e Cérebro, Brazilian Edition 171, April 2007, Duetto Editorial. If you would like to read the original article in English, please see, Binkofski, F. and Buccino, G., "Therapeutic Reflection," Scientific American Magazine -Mind, Edition 171, June/July 2007.

[8] From Marcia Wieder's interview with Marylin King, Dream University, 2010/2011; To know more about Marcia Wieder's work please visit www.dreamuniversity.com and www.WayBeyondSports.com by Marylin King.

[9] Plessinger, A., "The Effects of Mental Imagery on Athletic Performance," published by the Psychology Department of Vanderbilt University

recover it, experience success and have family harmony, by making images work for us reorganizing the world and bringing order and joy. We are a point in the universe with a human form, linked to totality in a gigantic cosmic hologram. Any image we observe connects virtual points and transforms them into real points on our hologram and in the field of unified consciousness.

Who knows if the existence of mirror cells is simply another way of the universe speaking to us intelligently about its nature? A quantum mirror that sees and reviews itself and through the human being, an active participant in life?

The image is an instrument of creation of reality and also a language that we know and which the field recognizes when we use it, giving us answers.

In the quantum processor that is the brain, there **are mirror cells** that reflect the image information and the quantum enformation that we perform in tune with the field of unified consciousness.

The intelligence underlying life when facing images knows what synapse to link, which molecule to segregate, or which endocrine gland to activate and in what measure, what nerves, muscles, functions or capacities to activate, develop or suppress in a perfect relational web.

The field of unified consciousness, to which we are linked in the presence of images that we communicate, implodes and explodes life so that we experience it.

In the act of observing, imagining or visualizing, we are mirroring and being mirrored, informing and being informed, giving form and being en formed in an interdependent and dynamic web where everything affects and is simultaneously affected in a subatomic dance.

Observing, imagining or visualizing attentively, means living what is observed, imagined or focused. The possibilities are unlimited for what we can bring to life, with this cocreation language and subtle technology of the image.

Impression by Image

"We don't see things as they are, we see them as we are."
Anais Nin

Images are aggregated pieces of luminous information that we capture with the senses. The conscious/brain matrix is organized and structured in a holographic form, processing the images at an incredible speed. The brain, our quantum processor, selects, stacks and makes the images intelligible in a way that they make sense according to our ideas of what's possible, along with our values, beliefs, education, etc.

The art of seeing is in direct correlation with who we are at a given time, as the subjectivity of our observation of the world is present all the time.

Strictly, we see life dyed with our peculiar way of thinking, talking, feeling and acting, and that world vision is able to change us internally and also to transform the world that we live in.

There is a Zen story that illustrates well the issue of the perception of the world and the respective effects of that perception.

Story
A peasant decided to leave his village, taking his family with him, to find a better place to live in. At a given stage on his way, he met a Zen master and asked him: "Do you know if the village that is a two day walk from here has people who welcome outsiders? As I have heard they are inhospitable." The master answered, "It is possible." The peasant arrived at the village two days later and was not welcomed at all, so he decided to leave again. At another stage of his journey he saw the Zen master and told him: "In fact, they were nasty to us in that village. We have now decided to travel to another village that is three days away to the East. Do you in your wisdom know if they will welcome us?" The master answered: "It is possible." Months later, the peasant had already settled in the village, when the Zen master passed again. When the peasant saw him, he thanked him because in that village they had welcomed them.

It was the perception of the peasant, his belief and his world vision that built his reality, and all of us, with greater or less awareness, are constructing our reality daily; regarding images, we interpret them in accordance with the perceptual filters we have.

When observing an image, it is us who give it meaning through the interpretation we make of it and place it in context. Then strictly speaking, in spite of wanting to see reality objectively, reality is always riddled with something of "me" that is placed in that observation, and that is very important for us to understand the role of quantum observation.

Quantum physics, when admitting the role of the observer in the creation of reality, does it because it has understood the connection between what is observed and who is observing it, the human consciousness. It understood that the observation, the intention, the feeling or even the method used, affect the characteristic or the form in which reality will be presented. The fundamental reality, before the moment of being observed, was pure potential, and as a result of the observation will show itself as a particle (small "points" of energy in movement) or as a wave in movement. The observation is essential to create reality. As far as images are concerned, the way we see the information contained in an image, depends also on who we are, what we think and how we feel. In effect, that perception has consequences in our energetic system, because we activate that vibration internally as well as emit that vibration simultaneously to the field of unified consciousness and to Earth, affecting reality and bringing it to manifestation.[10]

♥ Stop, Breathe, Love

Now that we are admitting that what we perceive is something unique, even though it is seen by thousands of people at the same time and in the same circumstances, we can use images in a focused manner towards happiness.
How do we do this?
Exposing ourselves internally and externally to the input of image information that we consider valid for us. Images that are: ordered/positive/ voluntary/coherent and perceiving the positive side of any situation has, re-signifying the situation. Also

---

[10] This story was found on several sites on the internet

neutralizing the image. This is the key to the quantum success of an image.

Through observation, imagination/visualization or remembrance, we can create reality: any reality that we decide and focus on. From an 18 out of 20 in our chemistry exam, to the preparation of an architectural project, the concession of a municipal license, attracting a partner for a business, to our son riding a bicycle. We can also construct a headache, a problematic trip or failure. It is all a question of choice and focusing attention on images.

And is there a technique that is more efficient than others in the creation of reality through images? Many studies have been done, namely in the area of sports, which show more efficient ways of achieving results, namely the "visual motor behavior rehearsal (VMBR)." Besides the visual aspects, this technique uses the auditory, touch, emotional and kinesthetic aspects of the process of visualization, obtaining scientifically proven results. However, the beliefs underlying the techniques influence the results and it is also important to consider what I mentioned previously in the sub chapter on images in process. *We point out that images always affect reality, because reality is made of them.*

I am speaking of imagination/visualization as a process that is beyond visualizing ourselves mentally doing something; to have a goal, to live in a state where we do not need to perform any physical movement.

Effectively, imagination/visualization is beyond the visual model and we use **the rest of the senses (sixteen) and the sensation component (emotion/feeling), reintegrating the experience totally in us, in interaction with the world, in the present.** The moment we are visualizing, we are interacting with the image as if we were in the real world.

The aim is to have a multidimensional involvement in what we are imagining and **notice the neurophysiological reactions as a result of the image.**

For example, we become aware of the heat or the acceleration of our heartbeat, or the peacefulness, or intuitions that may emerge.

Besides this, and because we are on a perceptual field, each image has a different meaning for each person. Each person interprets the images in a different and distinct manner. **Therefore, when visualizing each person should choose those images that are meaningful to himself/herself.**

After the visualization process we continue to be connected to the present, and we follow **our intuition or inspiration, and act accordingly. We are what we imagine or visualize.** All these steps unite the process. Do what you feel is right for you. When we process the meaningful images, living the sensations and interacting internally with the physical world, we trigger images, sensations and meanings holographically in the quantum processor that is the brain and that hologram is simultaneously being communicated to the field of unified consciousness, which actualizes it and makes it available to be seen on the cosmic and planetary screen.

Visioning is also another possibility to create reality. You could have a vision for your life, overall, and that imagetic information could be intensified, through feeling it more deeply, and adding each time you feel it more details, colors, sensations, people, etc., creating more connections and possibilities to emerge in your reality. Visioning can also be a process where you are receptive to information from the field of unified consciousness, for example by clairvoyance, intuition, empathy, or telepathy and you receive this data, feel it and integrate it in your energetic field. This imagetic information and other data are unpredictable and can change the way you perceive yourself and the world by improving your results.

Be it through imagination, visualization or visioning, we are quantumly speaking to ourselves and to the field of unified consciousness. Inwardly, this quantum communication and interaction is neurally connecting pathways, multidimensional information and chemical substances, nervous and muscular reactions, states of humor or affection and cognitive aspects, for example intelligence, creativity or concentration.

At the same time, due to the fundamental interdependence of our quantum and every day worlds, subatomic rearrangements occur, and people, events, situations and objects are aligned vibrationally for manifestations to occur, in a common dance of the consciousness.

♥ Stop, Breathe, Love

For example, the imagining/visualization of a new job: regarding what it is, what you do, whether you will travel, etc... You have a great number of images to decide. Choose the ones you like most and that have more significance and impact for you. Make the film as meaningful as possible. Make the image real, by being aware of the **smells, tastes, of what you are hearing or who you speak with, what you are touching, what colors do you see, the movement, the temperature, the vitality, the position of the body or the empathy.**

Feel the positive sentiments (for example, happiness, satisfaction, fulfillment, etc. Make the experience intense in your body, your mind and your emotions. Let your cells process the experience multidimensionally, now). The feeling or the emotion of the concretization of your desire or intention—**experienced in the present**—makes the concretization possible. Let your body send you messages and give you feedback.

Pay attention to detail while at the same time being relaxed. It is possible to receive messages during and after the visualization of intuition or telepathy that can guide you to success. Follow them because you can manifest what you visualize or something even better.

The objective is to totally embody what you are visualizing and then bring it to your life. For example, if you are a nurse and you wish to work in the health center near your area, wake up in time for work, put on your uniform, and feel pleased to go to work, speak to the people at the health center. Feel employed. *Furthermore, allow intuition, inspiration or empathy to drive you, because they are all working in partnership with the field of unified consciousness.*

We are all using our inborn creativity to construct daily reality. We chose to give life to this reality through the images that we are feeding. And the truth is that there is an abundance of images and plenty of reality that we can create with them. It is a question of choice. It can be something very simple, but it can make all the difference. Here is an example of creativity with imagination/visualization.

Testimonial

I am very pleased for having used visualization. It is easy and always works so well, that it seems to be magic. I am a teacher and I was working in Alentejo, far from where I live, in Lisbon. Besides the fuel costs and being far from my husband and small daughters, I felt unhappy. I did not want to go to work with this sensation. After learning from Susana that I can build my reality, I decided to use visualization and my thoughts to get placed nearer to home.

Before the application period for the next academic year, I often focused my attention during the day on the following thought: "Now I have been placed nearer to home and my timetable leaves me free time for myself and my family." I began to imagine, and see myself placed at a new school, with different colleagues, a good work environment and able to spend various afternoons with my daughters playing, hugging them and hearing them saying: "It is so nice mom! You are now with us and at a new school near home," and I felt that I was at a new school already, enthusiastically working, I felt the warmth of the hugs, heard the laughter. It was real. The sensations were of happiness, vitality and at the same time peace. Internally I knew it was so and relaxed. When I went to look at the placement results in September, I was delighted. I had been placed in the South Bank area, thirty kilometers away from home and had three afternoons free. Yipee, yipee! Thank you, Universe.

Ana Rita, teacher

♥ Stop, Breathe, Love

An additional way of manifesting is through observation: to observe is to focus attention on the image. It is being present in the image and allowing it to be present in yourself in a clear communication. Insofar as you have it with you (internally or externally) you are always activating that information and enformation in you and in the field of unified consciousness and that it can be materialized instantaneously or "requires" time.

Depending on the clarity, the perception that we have about being possible or not, of the "how?" amongst other things which we have previously spoken about.

One of the most efficient ways for me is surrounding myself with images; I have them in my handbag, in exercise books, on the dashboard of the car and make them as visible as possible to communicate with them and them with me or that I see them in my mind, for example every hour.

Remembering is one more way of manifesting reality through an image. When we remember things that have happened to us, we are automatically experiencing it internally. It is a known reality, neuronally we know the way, the sensations, the movements and the behavior. In an act of remembering, we strengthen the neuronal links, the sensations and the behavior that this particular image arouses. We are activating that information and enformation in our field of energy and in the field of unified consciousness, and the probability of manifestation will be increased ("positively" or "negatively").

Still, regarding the imagination/visualization process (that besides the imaginative part) the sharpness of the image (shape and detail), the color, (light and brilliant), the movement and the size of the image, associated with the emotion or sensation and the significance that the images have for you are fundamental.

For example, let us imagine that we want to change our self-image as mothers, because the old standard was the "overprotective mother." We define a "good mother," what type of thoughts she has, feels or does, which are her characteristics, and then we bring the image to life with emotion. The joy of being a good mother, the enthusiasm in doing new things with the children, the movements that they do, the love felt by seeing them growing, the loving comments given and received from the children and the sensation of gratitude for having them. Let us live the image intensively, the sounds, the movements, the emotions, the feelings, the significance of the interaction and being open to what intuition or empathy communicates to us during and after the process and embodying it, **we are what we imagined in the small and big gestures with our children.**

Our energy field will resonate and be in communication with the field of unified consciousness and the planet, drawing to us all that is being created through imagination/visualization.

♥ Stop, Breathe, Love

Are there certain times when images have a greater impact?
Images are always in communication and interaction with reality (they are it), therefore, they always have an effect on it. There are times when we are internally more aware. We are clear, aware, relaxed, and happy, in love, in a good mood or energized, full of vitality and when we focus on an image these rapidly format reality. We may focus just for an instant or have a process, lasting for four minutes, twenty minutes or an hour. Personally, I like alternating fast things with slower ones.
For example:
- You are dancing and you feel full of energy and that is an ideal moment to visualize the desired objective (be it thirty seconds, two minutes, etc.).
- Or in the middle of sharing laughter with friends you will see in your mind the realization of your project.
- You meditate for twenty minutes and at the end of it, imagine/visualize in detail.
- After an exercise class, imagine/visualize what you wish.
- It can also be a great moment of love and peace and in that state you feel the realization totally (it can be one minute, thirty, one or two hours or even all day).
- Doing this just after waking up or just before going to sleep is excellent.

Any of these procedures work. You may even establish a rhythm, (morning and evening, or every hour). *The objective is to be present and the more we do and experiment, the more connected we feel. The connection is all.*

On the other hand, in the process of imagining/visualizing it is important to have fun and enjoy it. The master of transcendental meditation Maharishi Mahesh Yogi states that "enjoyment is the great secret of life" and I absolutely agree with him. In the act of imagining, we are playing the game of infinite possibilities. Enjoy yourself: imagine more, move your body, speak loudly and act for the pleasure of doing so.

From the neuronal point of view, pleasure, play and fun cause you to explode in a sensorial way and the field of unified consciousness bursts joyfully with you as well as the entire planet.

♥ Stop, Breathe, Love

Another issue that arises regarding images is knowing when they affect the energy field, that is, when we observe, or imagine/visualize or remember an image, when do they have an impact in our life? I have the conviction that the image has an impact in the present, even if it is an image that comes from the past, or an image projected to the future.

How many of us have remembered a scene from our life where, for example, we were rejected, and when we see that image on our mental television, we experience bodily changes, mood and behavioral alterations? The body contracts, we feel listless, unwilling to take any action. I am also sure we have all remembered a time when we were happy, full of energy and self-confident, and that image brought vitality to our body; we felt happy and our attitudes were more self-confident and everything went well in the situation we were in.

What happened was the consciousness/brain matrix, when processing the imagetic information through the memory, reconfigures the neuronal links biochemically, the endocrine segregations, the muscular movements and the cell component in the same manner as it was registered and organized mentally, emotionally and on a behavioral level for this image event.

From a quantum point of view, what we did was select the known information and enformation and the subatomic particles acquired forms conditioned by the previous perception manifesting in reality what we placed there.

The image, although from the past, affects us now because it is in the present that the focus of consciousness edits the chosen scenario and communicates it to the field of unified consciousness that accepts it and replies, there being communication and interaction regarding the information that is "online" at the moment, so that it is manifested.

And now, how often do we visualize situations for the future in which the images were confused, or we predicted the worst and the body feels it, we feel indisposed and without motivation for action. Probably, countless times. It is also true that we have had moments when we imagined the best for the future, be it a loving relationship, to employment and the corporal posture changed, the emotions were clear, and we felt good and acted with confidence.

From a quantum point of view, that information/image, from the moment it is focused, is immediately communicated to the field of unified consciousness and ceases to be in a state of indetermination and assumes a form, manifesting reality.

On the level of the quantum processor, which is the brain, from the moment we imagine and project the image, the electrical chemical information is automatically triggered, affecting namely, neurons, hormonal secretions, blood pumping and the muscle movements that are structured for this new image scenario.

Although from a mental point of view, the projection being for the future, the impact in the energy field is felt in the present, because it is in the now that the instructions regarding the event are being read, understood and processed, stimulating the energy contained in the image.

However, as the instruction for the manifestation is for the future, that is, it was what we thought, imagined or felt would happen in the future, we cocreated a different moment from the present, there being "expansion" between what we see mentally and what we manifest physically from the linear point of view. And the tendency is for the information contained in the image possibly being manifested, or not, in that time apparently delayed, in the future.

Actually, if those images of the so called "future" are felt intensely and persistently experienced as real in the present, such a "future" event is manifested, because the person is merging and integrating the information and embodying it, the event which was imagined to be living and BEING IT, it has to manifest.

What to say of the images that we feed in the present?

Those images have an impact in our energy field immediately, creating order or disorder in our lives from the moment they are perceived. For example, if as soon as we wake up, we begin to see on our mental television that the day is going to go wrong, we are going to get upset in the traffic or at work, that is, if we focus on what we do not wish to happen, the probability of it happening is high, because we are inviting disorder to our day, via the emission of the information through an image, which is suitable for fast materialization. In fact, when launching these images, even on autopilot, we simultaneously send this energy to our energy system, predisposing ourselves mentally, emotionally and also on a behavioral level to have a "dreadful day," as well as sending the information to the field of unified consciousness and to Earth, being in line with other energy fields, such as people, objects, animals, events, etc., that are in the same wave frequency of a "dreadful day."

On the other hand, if when we wake up, we imagine the film of a "perfect day," with good quality images, we are sending that vibration to our energy field in the sense of the order, which will generate waves of mental, and emotional symmetry, as well as on a behavioral level. We also emit image information to the field of unified consciousness and to the whole planet, being in resonance with the energy fields (people, objects and situations) and that move in the frequency of the order, making possible the manifestation of events which during the day are in the same energy frequency. For example, green traffic lights, good customer service at the municipality or a pleasant phone call. And day to day on our mental screen, automatically or voluntarily, we recreate reality through images in unity with the field of unified consciousness.

At each moment, we are creating and recreating the next moment and the days, weeks, months and years reflect the images we are giving life to. A change, however small, in the present, has a real impact in our life because it foresees other results, many of them inconceivable because we are faced with other possibilities.

Using images is both a choice as well as an act of quantum creativity. In this selective act, infinite possibilities already existing become intertwined and become available for us to bring to life any reality. We are connected to the universal creativity and everything possible of being created.

Independently of the form, the dimension, the speed or the how, the concretization is possible. The intelligence which the field of unified consciousness is, knows the direct way, the people, the easiest and most efficient manner, the perfect result and even the immediate manifestation.

The clarity of the image on the objective, the state of openness and receptivity to best are like multidimensional trampolines that the field of unified consciousness accepts. The world and our lives can be actualized in a heartbeat, ultimately transforming into an adventure of creative plenitude.

Self-image

"From my village I see as much as from earth one can see of the Universe... Therefore, my village is as big as any other land... Because I am the size of what I see, and not the size of my own height..."
Fernando Pessoa

We now know that images are a "consciousness technology" that allow us to create reality in a team with the field of unified consciousness. We also understand that it is a language we communicate with, we use to relate and interact with one another and with the field of unified consciousness, affecting each other mutually.

And what do we say of our self-image? Does it also interfere with reality? Is it possible to change it, in case we decide to do so?

Self-image is the vision we have about ourselves. It is what we believe we are as a person; our self-image is being constructed like a puzzle from childhood until we leave this world, based on the perceptions and experiences that we accumulate and attribute significance to. We create energy links, neural links and a personality based on the information that we receive both internally and externally, and what makes sense for us in the light of our values, beliefs, emotions and learned behaviors on our level of consciousness. From birth until about three years of age, the perception that we have of ourselves is totally united to the universe, to our parents and the environment surrounding us; although the child becomes aware of herself through the development of the senses and the respective perception of the body, the people, the objects and the surrounding atmosphere are part of her because the child does not dissociate herself from the world but rather, she encompasses it. Only when the child reaches the stage of individuation, using the first person instead of the third, is when she defines roles and separates from her environment. This differentiation between the child, the parents, the animals, the plants and the objects, in summary, from the world, will bring the first features of self-image. That is who I am and how I see myself. As children, we are dependent on our parents for sustenance, affection and security, and our perceptual tools are in development. The norm is to accept the information from our parents, grandparents, nursery schoolteacher or the catechism teacher, and assimilate it, thinking it is the truth about us.

We receive verbal or emotional messages and behavioral ones that become part of us. Try to remember if you were ever told "You are ugly," when you were contradicting someone in the family. Or if your mother expresses her sadness one day by saying, "You will be my end." Or your father has "jerked" you when he saw you picking your nose. Your teacher may also have said, "You will never get anywhere."

It is very likely that something like this or other has happened to you and you have kept this internally. After childhood, during adolescence and adulthood, there are still people, ideas or circumstances that we have empowered to affect us in the way we see ourselves "positively or negatively." It could be a model who incites us to be thin so that we will like our body; the leader of a school group who tells us that we must boycott the work of the school assistants in order to be cool; the university professor who praises our final assignment; the rock singer who prompts us to take control of our life; the supervisor at work who says we are barely productive because we do not stay at work from 09:00 to 21:00 and that he is going to replace us, undermining our self-confidence, or a divorce that we are facing as a new phase or as very upsetting.

It is possible for our self-image to change this way or in many other ways.

Despite the concept of self-image having to do with personal image, little of that image is genuinely personal in the sense of questioning who am I and how do I see myself, and how do I see what is happening to me.

Normally, the processing of mental, verbal, emotional and behavioral information is done automatically, without any type of reflection, being at the mercy of the opinion of others and what we call circumstances. *The issue is that it is normal that there may have been less than favorable opinions from others and we have all had or have circumstances like these in life.* But, the way we choose to look at life and act defines us as people and necessarily affects our self-image and that gives us work to do; we have to emerge from the past, let go of old beliefs, change the way we feel, create new references and act accordingly. Many people prefer to keep the old scenarios, comments, emotions and attitudes that are familiar, even if they are dysfunctional, because it is the only image they have. They have not understood, or wanted to accept, that it is possible to build a new image, reformulating themselves.

Returning to the issue of knowing if the image we have of ourselves also interferes with reality? Evidently, yes.

We are reality; we are part of it, and we create and alter it. Just due to the fact that we exist, the planet and the universe are different, because they contain our face, observing it and mirroring it.

Self-image is the information that we emit continually, from the moment we climb out of bed to the time we go back to sleep, and it is always giving us information and transmitting data to others, and also giving form to reality in a dynamic web of multidimensional faces that we interpret. It is our fate to create realities, and the image we have of ourselves is a link that the cosmic internet recognizes and authorizes the manifestation of, at "a known internet address," in the form of a human, and equipped with a consciousness, participating in all phases and moments of life.

We can now stop using our consciousness to observe a certain event and cease creating subatomic, neural, emotional and physical rearrangements in accordance with that limited image. The way we observe life, and the perceptions we have create reality, modeling it in accordance with what we imprint in our energy field, the field of unified consciousness and in the planet. The probability of attracting events, people and circumstances in our lives that are in line with that limited image, pain or suffering, is real, perpetuating the same level of consciousness we already have. This will happen until we decide to look at ourselves, editing a new image of Who We Are.

The real issue is: **Who would we be without this self-image?** Certainly, very different. Happier, clear and free for a life of plenitude.

♥ Stop, Breathe, Love

The image we have of ourselves is a hologram that we call personal reality, within the hologram of our family, our community, our planet and the universe, which is affected and mutually mirrored in a gigantic web.

What we see in ourselves and irradiate in our energy field, the field of unified consciousness, in a team with us, accepts and responds, rearranging itself sub-atomically. In the quantum mirror that is life, the people, events, objects or situations that are in resonance with the communicated message, show themselves. We become vibrationally in tune and aware of **seeing what we see within us, in others, in things or in situations.** Our personal reality is intertwined in the personal reality of others, and the collective.

In parallel, **what others see in us is also theirs:** reflections of their beliefs and images and the collective images that we edit together for the field of unified consciousness and the planet.

Effectively, we change reality by changing the way we see ourselves. We are the face of the field of unified consciousness individualized. We are connected to the field, we are a field and we make up the field of unified consciousness. We are one. And a light, an angle, a color, or a detail changed in the face, changes the subject's entire face, as well as the totality.

The only people that "need to change" their self-image is you and me. We are the sovereigns of the creations that we realize. The "others" only change if they want to. Our change is powerful. It affects the All, because we, the others and the All are one. A change in us is contagious for others, the planet and for the field of unified consciousness. We choose to change our self-image and feel good about it and it makes all the difference. *To achieve it, we are open to seeing ourselves and the world in an alternative way and allowing ourselves to be seen in another manner by others and by the world. We can also see the world through the eyes of others, in case that reality makes sense and we change our self-image.* In this informational and formative symbiosis, we actualized other possibilities that are then particularized in personal, collective and cosmic images.

What can we change in our self-image? Whatever we decide. Each one of us is free to choose what makes sense for us/you. What we can state is that there are numerous possibilities for doing so. At each moment, we can free what no longer makes sense and construct a new vision of Who We Are and share it. *The language of the creation of images* and the respective "subtle technology" for the manifestation of reality *is with us wherever we are, with whomever we are, and is always operational.*

From a quantum point of view, it is possible for an image to be actualized immediately as well as changing definitively. Numerous people have already radically changed their self-image and the way they see the world, in the wink of an eye. That is what they are doing at this moment. It could be realizing a dream, feeling a great love, the birth of a child, or simply deciding to live. And, from that moment of truth, they interiorize and are the change they decided to be, and consciousness guides them.

This happens because a decision, an image or a state of being, is a wave of possibilities linked to the "quantum soup" from which life emerges, and from the moment the decision, the image or the state of being are experienced, possibilities are immediately particularized and manifest themselves in reality in the defined dimension.

I leave here a testimonial of that creativity.

Testimonial

A few years ago, I experienced a quantum leap in my life.
I opened myself to the freedom and the capacity to be the creator of my own reality. I had just turned thirty and I felt lost and tied to a job that did not make me happy where I was for many years, limited by "comfort" due to old beliefs and the notion of "security."

During a seminar of unified quantum healing with our dear author, "I shouted out" what was at the time my dream job... a flight attendant; this came back to me a few weeks later in the form of an advertisement. I applied, facing all criticisms, opposition, disbelief and past insecurities. I saw myself with different eyes and life too. I decided that this time it would be different. Internally I thought it was possible.

I managed to realize my dream. Today, I am happy and grateful for this new "vision" of being the creator of my reality. I am convinced that the way begins with us and that we are our best masters. It is enough to be open and receptive to receiving great blessings, and always believing that the best is possible. I received the gift of finding myself and believed that miracles happen in our life everyday... Believe!

I am now a very different person, always progressing and growing. Thank you for reading my words and sharing this testimonial that marked my life in such a unique way.

Cátia Antunes, flight attendant

Reformulated Image

"Who am I to be brilliant, gorgeous, talented, fabulous? Actually, who are you not to be? You are a child of God. Your playing small does not serve the world."
Marianne Williamson

In childhood stories, there is always someone that speaks about self- image. Normally, there is a pretty girl looking in a mirror, unsure of the image that she has of herself and asking the mirror if there is anyone in the kingdom more beautiful than her. Naturally, as long as the character perceives herself as being in competition or believing that there can only be one model of beauty, or that there is no place for variety, her self-image is in danger.

How do we change our self-image? Changing the images, beliefs, sensations and the experiences underlying them, bringing to the fore new images. This can **be done by using internal or external references, real or imagined images.**

1 - We can change our self-image if we use **internal images** where the perceptions that we have of ourselves are clear and coherent with Who We Are. For example, being able to say no serenely to someone. Or honoring a wish to become a veterinarian that appeared to us in an image from nowhere, and we following that path by studying for the exam.

2 - It is possible to change our self-image based on **external images,** which our perceptions are leveraged on to catapult us to the "next level." How many of us, when seeing someone carry out a task, get the notion that we are able to do it too. Be it a top athlete, a guru, a friend or a work colleague giving the example, that image is the model we follow. Many years ago, I remember using the attitude of a neighbor who had applied to study at a university as an example for me to apply too and also be accepted. What I told myself at the time was: "If she can, so can I." The image of success that she transmitted to me, and which I accepted, was the trampoline to a new state of consciousness, also changing my self-image as a successful woman.

3 - It is also possible to change self- image by **reusing real images** that served a certain purpose to which we gave a positive meaning. That is, we recycle images of power,

success, joy, love, acceptance or any other situation in which the impression of the image brought us a state of consciousness of openness and development and that is beneficial for us. For example, we can focus on an image of the completion of a higher education course, or the birth of our first child where the delivery was fantastic and you feel that you are a superwoman, or that heartfelt embrace. We clearly make the film, with emotion, with sound, with motion, with significance and we are attentive to the answers.

4-We are also able to change self-image through the **imagination**, representing situations or events in which we intervene in an ideal manner and with beneficial results. Or on which other people participate of our world, positively also. The aim is to feel and give meaning. For example, imagine ourselves winning the Nobel Peace Prize to motivate ourselves further to be peaceful in the community, and feel it. Another example: we wish to change our self-image regarding the self-confidence it takes to speak in public. What is the body posture of self-confidence? How do we speak? How do we look at things? What do we hear? Do we have a smile on our face? How do we feel? What meaning does it have for us?

Regarding to make love with our beloved. We can also imagine our husband saying, "You are very sensual today," and we smile and feel warm. The idea is that it makes sense and that preferably, it should be fun.

♥ Stop, Breathe, Love

For some of us, the change of self- image needs external references; that is, external images that make sense to be copied. This is **the change of the self-image by imitation;** the general rule is that this is the easiest one because it is the most entrenched, due to the fact that human learning in the early stages of life and during it, are done through imitation. The imitation of a behavior, an idea or an external image is an association with something that is already consolidated and transmits known information to us. It is also triggering to the vision of "what a human being achieves, anyone following his footsteps also achieves," and you can even do better, since the capacity we have to transcend ourselves is inborn. We can also change our self-image based on internal references, imitating ourselves in those moments when we thought we were well, and we reproduced them. We are remembering, replicating, "copying" an energetic pattern and there is the probability of us feeling comfortable and familiar with a situation. It was already in our "morphic field"[11] and in the field of unified consciousness. After all, we had already dealt with that energy and our neurons, the mental maps, the emotional and behavioral component, emerge reinforced from that image; we are in the field of the known because we know that this does us good and those moments are a trampoline for an improved version of ourselves.

In addition, we can also **change our self-image by creation.** Yes, we can invent new ways of being and living that are in tune with Who We Are on an essential level. Intimately, we know that we are being guided on the highest level and we see ourselves distinctly and with clarity. In this case, our interpretation of Who We Are and what life is, is original. We simply are and we are ok with that. We are in the unknown and

---

[11] This concept was created by Rupert Sheldrake: please see his work at www.sheldrake.org for a full description.

creativity abounds, each moment is unique and mirrors being. We transcend ourselves naturally in every gesture, sensation or look. We are open; we can be different in every instant and flow with life. We jump and do pirouettes in the unknown, which is welcoming and renews our strengths. We understand that we are more than a personality. We are being—a creative entity and one—linked to the unity of all life.

Wanting to change our self-image, we can use all these tools or others that makes sense for us.

In this universe of infinite possibilities, where images are abundant, animating personal images with the inborn splendor we have, is our mission. To be Who We Are is to use our talents, our gifts, the specificities that characterize us and that make us unique beings. A clear, brilliant, loving and powerful self-image is an act of creativity connected to creation.

The ego and the personality may want to tempt us with false modesty, limitations, fears or vicissitudes, disconnecting us from the happiness that is always present. **Who We Are** shines anywhere, is tuned in any circumstances, reinventing itself purposely and has the power to create, to manifest any reality.

The spotlights of the cosmos are always pointing at us and on all human beings, at the same time, allowing us to participate in life and recreate it in every instant, affecting the planet. The question we are asked in every instant of our lives is, "What are you going to create this very instant?" And in the next moment?, and so forth *"ad eternum."* The self-image that we have, how we perceive ourselves, others and life, interferes in the quantum lake, creating waves that spread in all directions and bring to light those same images, beliefs, feelings and experiences.

Albert Einstein stated that: *"The most important decision we ever make is whether we believe we live in a friendly universe or a hostile universe."* The image we had of that same universe would give us completely distinct versions of reality. This is possible because we are partners and not mere spectators of life, interfering with it. We are linked to it in a moving web of presence.

Why should we see small when the universe is gigantic? Why should we imagine difficulties in us and in life, atrophying paths, when the highways of information and communication are always open? Why shade the smiles that the whole of creation gives us freely? What is the sense of that? We do not serve ourselves or others with scenarios of limitations, fear or exclusion. Moreover, we repeat in our personal and planetary televisions old images that feed what we say we do not want. Enough. **Who Are We** then? We are unlimited, grandiose beings, gifted with intelligence and sensibility, and more, we are creators, great communicators and actors on the quantum stage, giving life to what we represent, connected to existence.

Now is the moment of actualization. Having a self-image focused on the infinite possibilities, the unlimited opportunities and on recreating ourselves, the planet and the universe. *Only a small change is necessary. A point, a different vision, a detail of the self and a global image—"we live in a friendly universe"—that we are focusing our attention on, so that the impact is intense. In that act of differentiated observation, which is a small drop in the ocean of probabilities, waves undulate and are converted immediately into reality, showing a new quantum photograph of the person, the family, the community, Earth and the Universe in the vital hologram. This is the end of one paradigm and the beginning of another that will be for the good of all beings.*

💡 Key points:
- Images are light in movement
- Image is a language through which we communicate with the world and the field.
- When we observe, remember or visualize something, we give it life.
- Focusing on positive, coherent and organized images produces results.
- We have the power to change the images that we focus on and those we have been fixed on. This will change our energy and point of creation.
- Mirror cells do a great job helping us rebuilding our bodies.
- The brain makes itself available in the same manner, activating the same brain areas, sending neurotransmitters to stimulate the production of molecules, reconstructing cells and even functions.
- Pay attention to the images you feed regularly. You are the film director of your life.
- Playing small doesn't serve you, nor your family or community. Raise your standards.
- The aim is to become a purposeful creator instead of a disorientated creator and to use images for your good and for the good of all other beings
- Self-Image is the vision we have about ourselves. It is what we believe we are as a person.
- The only people that "need to change" their self-image is you and me.

🚀 Exercises:
❶ Look into the mirror and discover something you appreciate about yourself. Every time you pass in front of a mirror repeat that same appreciation.

❷ Focus on a goal or a vision of yourself or your life with passion; it could be for 3 minutes or 20. Remembered what was mention on page 137.

❸ Today walk confidently and see yourself as a wise person.

💬 Self-reflection:
❶ Have you ever thought that images can originate in different places?

❷ An image is luminous information. Based on this perspective, what do you want to illuminate in your life right now?

❸ What images should you see before going to sleep to make yourself happy?

❹ Have you noticed if any image from the present, which you have been feeding, has manifested itself subsequently? For example, after one day, three weeks, or a year, after seeing the
m?

❺ Were you enthusiastic about the above-mentioned scientific experiments regarding the power of the images? If yes, which ones?

❻ Who was the person or people that gave you the most positive role model in life? Describe some of them.

❼ Has it been made clear to you that the responsibility for changing your self-image is totally yours, and that such change can be beneficial to all beings? You can do it!

8 Word

Story
"A long time ago, a wandering wiseman lived in a European city. He walked all day and whenever he was questioned, he answered wisely, in few words.
One day, the wandering wiseman was walking through town, when a maestro, on his way to the theatre, bumped into the wiseman. The maestro fell and dropped all his music sheets on the wet ground. The wiseman helped him stand up and pick up all the music sheets, however, most of them were ruined.
Witnessing the maestro´s despair, the wiseman immediately said, "The good is happening!"
The maestro could not contain his fury and shouting, with arms in the air, said, "The good is happening! How can you possibly say that, you fool? All my work of years, months, days and nights, destroyed, lost because you bumped into me. How? How can good be happening?" He stormed away from the wiseman, fuming with rage, towards the theatre, which was still far away. He was crossing a square when he suddenly saw what seemed to be his wife on the ground. Very frightened he ran towards her, fearing the worst, since she was in late pregnancy. His wife had gone into labor at that moment and it was by mere chance that he was there by her. At that instant he remembered the words of the wiseman, "The good is happening," and was grateful for the incident.

"For clearly the gods call things by the names that are naturally right. Do you not think so?"
Plato, *Cratylus ([391e])*

"Words are the most serious energy that we emit. With the words said or withheld by our mouth, incredible worlds are coagulated."
Teachings of the Navajo Indians

This story has taught me a lot. I frequently use the saying of the wandering wiseman, *"The good is happening"* especially when I cannot understand the reason for something happening. These words have the power of opening other possibilities for me and to calm me down until the information reaches me. This can follow immediately or later. Is there a word or a saying that you use that places you on another vibration or state? It could be a phrase that someone dear has said to you in a special moment, or that you have learnt and made sense for you. Be aware of it and then let it go.
We have meanwhile begun to use the **language of the word.** We will explain better: What is a word? In a broader sense, a word is energy in movement, in formation and light vibrating in the field of unified consciousness. **A word is a tool placed at the service of the human consciousness so that it can build reality.**
As we have been saying, the field of unified consciousness is the essence of life, and naturally, of the word as well.
As a matter of organization and to make it easier to understand what we are saying, we say that there are three "origins" of the word, even though the energy of the word is a whole:

❶ Unified consciousness
❷ Individual consciousness
❸ Planetary consciousness
Let us look at each of them.

❶ The word from the unified consciousness

The field of unified consciousness is the seat of endless information. It is here that we find pure ideas, original concepts, values, and also the primordial sounds and archetypal forms of words.
All languages or dialects with their respective sounds and original characters have their source in the field of unified consciousness which transmits these to the human consciousness, taking into account the developmental process of humanity, so that they can exchange information amongst themselves and also with the information field.
The field of unified consciousness is the cosmic database that we can communicate with and access the multidimensional information vibrating in it. In order to receive pure information on a sound or symbolic level via the energy of words, we have to be consciously in resonance (communication and interaction in the same wave frequency) with the field of unified consciousness—the information field; the brain, as a quantum system of energy, captures the information and mirrors it instantly.
The brain is the quantum interface that when receiving the sound in formation or the characters representing the words from the field of unified consciousness, accepts them and makes them intelligible. That is, it places the information on our mental screen to be "read" with the software that we have.
 We can receive sounds that represent a known or an unknown language that will complement or innovate the information we have, and whose origin is not limited by space or time. They can originate on the planet Earth, or other solar systems or universes; they can be ancient, present or future information and the nature of this information can be subtle.
Sound information or information in the form of characters can be transmitted instantaneously and the consciousness/brain matrix reflects it automatically, actualizing our electromagnetic field which contains information that is always vibrating. We can hear the sounds of the celestial spheres, compose a piece of music or a symphony, access an innovative concept in the field of communications, speak to beings from other dimensions, receive symbols for a new architecture, or healing geometries "supra-electromagnetic," etc.
The possibilities are infinite.

❷ The word from the individual consciousness

The consciousness/brain matrix produces words. It entwines thoughts, memories, learning, language, the phonetic apparatus, images and even feelings in a perfect manner so that what we convey through words makes sense, and we can communicate with ourselves and the world in an intelligible manner and consequently, act.
Words are energy waves that are self-produced in the consciousness/brain matrix that we express through both internal and external dialogue. The expression of words

enables us to share information, make decisions, reveal states of spirit, change behaviors and even heal. When we use words, either verbally or written, we are emitting energy waves which are in communication with the field of unified consciousness and with the field of planetary consciousness. Our energy field immediately becomes in resonance with the words that we emit, and becomes in tune with other energy fields which reflect the quality of what we are emitting, helping us to understand the type of reality that we are evoking.

❸ The word from the planetary consciousness

The energy field of the planet Earth is systematically emitting energy waves to all beings living on it and also to the field of unified consciousness.
Earth's energy field receives the words that human beings produce individually or collectively and retransmits them in the same vibrational frequency to human beings and the field of unified consciousness. Each individual and collective has the capacity to accept, change or reject the words formulated, refeeding the planetary consciousness.

We have explained the origins of the word, which strictly speaking are just one—the field of unified consciousness. Therefore, we will now especially incline ourselves to the word from the field of human consciousness.

❤ Stop, Breathe, Love

There is a question that emerges immediately when we think about the word, and that is, "What is it for?"
The word has a double function and is processed simultaneously: expressing information and creating reality. Through the word, we transmit data and command energy, giving it form and sense in concretization. The act of using words brings what is in potential into manifestation in accordance with a set constructive intention, making this energy visible with a determined dimension, content and meaning.
Words are in themselves coded concepts and with meaning that when actioned, turn potential into a creative act.
Putting it simply: **when expressing ourselves through words, we are indicating how it would be sensible for the world to show itself to us—** we may say that we want peace, a happy love relationship, a good job, sexual satisfaction, the best holidays or anything else.
Words are vital information and have the power of manifesting themselves in accordance with the laws underlying the creation of the universe, from neutrinos, galaxies to worlds. **Each time we express ourselves** verbally or in writing, to ourselves or to others, be it a person, animal or plant and even God (for those who believe), **we are inviting what we are transmitting to emerge in our lives;** we are saying "I accept that this materializes itself." "I choose this for my life."
Words are power. Simultaneously, power of expression and of manifestation, enabling us to build reality in accordance with the choices we make in our vocabulary.
In case we decide that it makes sense to alter the way we communicate and to transform our lives, our words have to follow that decision and follow the movement

of change. Here, the principle of coherence is applied; that is, the link between the decision and the attitude so that there is a correspondence. When we change how we express ourselves, selecting the "correct" vocabulary that is consistent with our real intentions, we actualize the energetic manifestation of what we are emitting through the words and the field of unified consciousness will multidimensionally mirror what we evoked through them. It is simple. We just need to practice.

On the Path of Words

"And now, as we are looking, you and I, we already see one thing we did not know before, that names do possess a certain natural correctness, and that not every man knows how to give a name well to anything whatsoever. Is not that true?
Plato, *Cratylus* ([391b])

"He who asks is a fool for five minutes, but he who does not ask remains a fool forever."
Confucius

The word is the language of creation that we and the field of unified consciousness use. It's also an instrument of the field of unified consciousness to distribute and order information in an intelligible manner and create the reality—that human beings also use.
We use words to communicate with other human beings and the field, transmitting information in an organized and coherent manner, with a specific sense and they construct reality through the energy they contain.
Besides being symbols representing ideas or states of the soul, words are also sounds with meaning that can be expressed by the phonetic apparatus (vocal chords, mouth and nose) and are propagated infinitely in waves.
The quality of the sounds of words is completely distinct in the case of pronouncing vowels or consonants. In fact, vowels are more associated with primary sounds, to the communication of states of being. It is impressive when something touches us internally or amazes us, we say "AhAhAhAhAh." When we hurt ourselves, we say "Ouch!" It is also interesting to see that when we think we are ascending, we say "eeeeeiiiiii." The expression is immediate, short and concise.
Regarding consonants, their sounds are more linked to the objective part; the mental component interferes more actively, describing life in a linear manner; they are more elaborate and longer sounds.
When we use words, we are using energy, dealing with power fields that are present in a reality that is already manifested, as well as with what is in potential, giving them sense and context in our life. In fact, we are simultaneously actualizing the power fields, as well as giving them a set organizational frequency and structure, in accordance with what we say, which will become reality. This is the multifunctionality of a word because it is, simultaneously, information and enformation which should be considered when using them. **It is the language, the *"technology"* of reality,** and its applicability to our life is total.
We can manifest healing through words for various situations: a loved one, enter a public position, sing on a famous stage, buy the best Christmas present for mommy, have a productive business meeting, get the attention of the whole class, or create

national or planetary abundance. The possibilities are vast and all depend on our choices. We will now give you some coordinates to use language and the *"technology of creation of words"* in a functional manner for the good of all.

You can find more detailed information about this matter at my workshops entitled "Unified Quantum Healing" and "Mental Vitamin," as well as in my next book.

In the act of using words (written or spoken), we select specific words that make sense for what we want to transmit, the subject and the verb tense. Besides this, it is possible that we may want to portray the image of what we are thinking or feeling and what we aim to do or want to be realized. All these factors together are linked naturally to words and produce an effective impact on reality, on an individual, community, global and cosmic level.

The first issue that can possibly arise after being aware that the function of a word is to express and build reality, is as follows: **"Which words are adequate for our life? Or, are there "correct" or "positive" words to create reality?"**

The answer to these issues is delicate, since right and wrong are concepts associated with values, namely "the good" (its absence being the bad), "truth" (its absence being a lie) and "justice" (its absence being injustice). These values are permeated with cultural and social beliefs, in a defined space and time, and continue to evolve.

What we can do is indicate a possibility that in our opinion, makes sense. In conformity with this, we say that **"right" words are those that express, with ownership, what we want to transmit and make probable in the construction of reality that makes sense for us to experience.**

From a linear perspective, **words considered "positive"** are those that convey what makes sense and bring to reality the results we perceive as positive (for example, arriving at work on time).

Words considered "negative" are those that communicate what does not make sense and bring to reality the opposite of what was intended, and that we perceive as negative (for example, not having time for anything).

Then, when we speak, write or read we can immediately pose the following question:

"Does this make sense to express and live in my reality?"

This is because *by communicating through words we are not only saying what we think, what we feel or the experiences we have been through.*

Effectively, we are using energetic resources, codified information that organizes itself on a subatomic level and has the tendency to manifest itself in our reality, with a visible face such as an event, thing or even the people we meet, or family situations, amongst others.

Summary:

☺ If what we say or write makes sense and is perceived as "correct" or "positive," then we maintain the words.

☹ In case what we say or write does not make sense and is perceived as less or not at all beneficial, then we can change the words to facilitate new connections.

☺ *When we emit words that we consider as "positive" or "negative," it is important* to be aware that in the first place, they automatically affect our energy field. The words that we speak or write for ourselves, for others, or about life, use the technology of creation/ of the word, in unity with the field of unified consciousness. They make probable events, situations, objects or people that we deal with, because we are the center of the information that is rearranging life in that way. Therefore, pay attention to what we say or write about ourselves or others, because we experience that energy inside us first- hand.

☻ *For example, if we criticize our neighbor, we are necessarily criticizing ourselves and making ourselves available for the criticism of others, familiar or unfamiliar, because that information is "online" in the information system.*

❤ Stop, Breathe, Love

One of the biggest issues related to words **has to do with their use being voluntary or "involuntary."**
*We consider words to be **voluntary** when we choose them consciously and know what they manifest; these imply a clear choice targeting the concretization of what is expressed. We consider words to be **involuntary** when they are on autopilot, when they are unconscious and inconsistent, when they emerge normally out of routine and when we do not even realize what they can bring to reality.*
Most of us were raised and conditioned to use words that deny what we want and tend to construct difficulties, confusions or fears.
Involuntary words are normally set in an unconscious manner, reproducing, generally, for the "negative" the beliefs of others (mother, television, father, supervisor, etc.) or words that left a mark on us in times of tension or limitation.
This vocabulary is reductive because it is systematically reproduced, gaining importance, reappearing in numerous scenarios, despite it being inadequate. It is like we go around in circles, gravitating around a nucleus. We recycle ideas, feelings and acts using the same type of words with the same underlying limited beliefs.
A common bad habit in expression is using the word "not" in a random manner. We say or write what we do not want, what does not make sense, instead of communicating what we really decided or are choosing for our life. For example, a few years ago, I was thinking about what I would like to receive from Quim as a birthday present and I verbalized to myself, "I do not want a watch; I already have five: three swatches and two classic ones. Anything but a watch. " Quim was travelling just before my birthday and I had never spoken to him about a present. I wanted him to surprise me. Imagine what he gave me: a red watch. Another example: In a seminar that I was running, I was explaining this inadequate use of the word "not" and a participant raised his hand immediately and asked to speak, saying enthusiastically "now I know why I fell off my bicycle when I go for a ride. I am always telling myself softly, "you are not going to fall off, you are not going to fall off, and I always fall." At that moment all the participants started laughing and we all learned to ride a bicycle without falling. Instead of saying or writing: "I do not want my mother to shout at me,", "I do not want to lose my job", "I do not want a possessive boyfriend/ girlfriend," we should verbalize or say "I prefer that my mother speaks quietly to me" or "I am going to keep my job" or "It makes sense in my life to have a boyfriend/girlfriend that is serene and trusting."
The crux of the matter regarding the word "not" is when concentrating our attention

on what we say we do not want (instead of concentrating on what makes sense or what we wish to manifest in our life), we are evoking, the manifestation of events or situations in line with our focus of attention.

As I became aware of the power of words, I often decided to change what I was saying or was going to say, because I know that the expression was unfavorable. For example, I used to say, "There is not enough time for anything," or "the day should have forty-eight hours." This statement evoked what I did not like; it created tension for me and increasingly, I seemed to have less time. I began to use the following expression: "**I have enough time for what I need and now it is organized in my favor**" and now I can see a difference in the experience of it and live more simply and in harmony with the time issue. After all, we all have twenty-four hours per day and this act of using words in a coherent manner helps the community function better with time.

I used to say this while driving: "I am sick of seeing people wasting time on the road"; I was evoking what I found unpleasant with words and channeling my attention to what I was tired of, causing the materialization of what I did not want. I decided to play with the idea that "I only find people on the road who drive at a good pace" and I verbalized that joyfully, while driving, to evoke that beneficial possibility in my daily life. Invariably, I have found that there are faster people on the road.

Another example: one of the sentences I often hear from mothers is "this child only causes me headaches." This statement is dysfunctional, because each time it is repeated you are giving an instruction on a neuronal level to internally produced chemicals and organize the muscle movements predisposed for pain. What that person is doing, without being aware of the power of the words used, is using her energy field linked with the field of unified consciousness to rearrange pain. These mothers can use a different command, for example: "This child brings me joy" or "this child is special" in order to facilitate new tendencies in life.

Regarding words, it is urgent to select them in a conscious manner, so that they correspond to our real intention, bringing to manifestation the results we want for our benefit and the benefit of all.

♥ Stop, Breathe, Love

Considering involuntary words that are common for people to adopt is calling themselves stupid, boring, dumb, fat, stupid or lazy and then complaining that in certain situations, they hear those insults and do not like them. That is, they invest energy, attention and emotion in a certain event that they named, and which evokes threads on a subatomic level capable of setting up realities, and then they believe they are not responsible for anything. One of the most common situations that illustrates this, is parents calling their children dumb and then being "furious" and "having a fit" when the neighbors or other parents verbalize the same type of words. Parents were the ones who opened the doors and invited in those in the same wave frequency.

Evidently, offending other people, both on a molecular and subatomic level, alterations in the energy field, in the quality of the information and the structure of the body of those emitting these names and those receiving them and giving them significance. Therefore, it is important saying to others and to ourselves, different things such as: intelligent, competent, useful, productive, different, or kind, which trigger new life organizations.

Here are some examples of words that are considered involuntary and how we can change them to voluntary, "positive":
- ➢ This gets worse by the day: **From now on it can only get better.**
- ➢ I will never find the solution for this in my lifetime: **The solution exists, I will find it.**
- ➢ Misfortunes are always happening to me: **I am open to seeing something positive in this situation.**
- ➢ My mother only criticizes me: **I am prepared to understand and be understood.**
- ➢ My boss is overbearing: **There are fantastic bosses and I want to find them.**
- ➢ Men/women are boring: **I accept that there are interesting men/women in this world. Who knows, today I will meet one.**
- ➢ I will not be able to achieve anything without higher education: **I will achieve whatever I wish. Look at the number of successful people without a higher education degree.**
- ➢ I cannot find work because I do not know anyone with influence: **I am able to find a job on my own merit. There are job opportunities which I will accept.**
- ➢ If she/he changed, I would be happy: **My happiness depends on me. I can change and make new choices for me.**
- ➢ It is because of my wife/husband that I am like this: **It is because of me and not of others that I am like I am. When I want, I can be different.**
- ➢ You cannot trust anybody: **I am trustworthy, and I know there are many people we can trust.**
- ➢ I am fat; no one is going to like me: **I like myself, and if I allow it, I will notice that there are a great number of people who like me as I am.**
- ➢ Life is a battle: **Life is a pathway that I walk in gratitude.**
- ➢ I am tired of suffering: **I now choose happiness and harmony.**

To change the way we express ourselves, we need to train our attention, focus it on the process of understanding if what we say or write is in accordance with what we feel and if we would effectively like to see it manifested in our reality or not, and use our creativity to change our discourse, selecting words that are more adequate to that moment and situation.

♥ Stop, Breathe, Love

Another aspect regarding words is the choice of subject. This indicates to us who is the protagonist or the receiver of a certain action. That is, the subject is the active or passive agent of a set behavior. When we express ourselves, we very often indicate subjects that are not the adequate ones, permitting errors in the interpretation and irresponsibility for our action.

For example, when we state: "You make me feel bad when we argue," we are saying that the other is responsible for our bad feelings. It appears that we have no choice. However, there are alternatives. The other person may have triggered the stimulus, but there is the possibility of rejecting the idea, the sensation or the behavior. **I am sure that some time in our life we have had this experience, irrespective of what the other was telling us, we decided to feel good and that happened.** Then it is more correct to affirm, "I feel bad when we argue," because we admit that we are playing a role in the process and it is possible to choose: another position.

An additional example that is relatively frequent is to use another subject in a question directed to us. The question is then: "So are you feeling better?" and we reply as follows: "my wife/husband thinks so." In this type of expression, the subject has removed himself totally. For those who have the tendency not to reply for themselves, there are two questions: "What information do you think you are giving yourself, to the field of unified consciousness and to the planet by not assuming that you are the subject of your life?" "What consequences can it have in your life, in case you continue to be unaccountable for what you are, feel or do?"

♥ Stop, Breathe, Love

The use of the verb tense is another important aspect of what we say or write. The notions that we have of time are linear, that is, we imagine time as something that occurs in a line *__*_* where the past is behind, the present is in the middle and the future is at the front of the line. This is a mental representation of time that has its limitations and repercussions in the way we face life and express ourselves. When using tenses, we communicate the time when the action is taking place and we also indicate the time when that behavior or action is manifested. Let us use these types of references in a linear manner, so that the impact of the words is experienced according to our choices.

Present—In order to manifest in reality, the experiences that make sense in daily living, we use the indicative present tense: I have, I like, I do, I choose, I want, I request, I state, I am open to, I see, I accept, I allow, etc. When using the present tense, the information and energy are anchored in that moment, ready for concretization.

Past—For what no longer makes sense to build, that is information and energy that we decided to detach ourselves from, we use the past tense—the simple past: I did, I said, I imagined, I experienced that, etc. In this manner, we can put in second place the importance of a certain issue, as well as the energetic impact (the concretization) is moved from the present (to the past). The abstention of speaking or writing about past issues, not giving them any attention, can be beneficial because we will have more energy for the present.

Imperfect tense—For those situations that are not yet properly defined within us, or are in transition, we can use the imperfect tense or another compound verbal tense. (I have been stubborn, I was confrontational, I have been reluctant, I have messed up, etc.). Here the indication we are giving ourselves and the field of unified consciousness is that we need to become more mature, and that the information and the energy of the situation, as a rule is not "positive," continues to be absent from the present.

Future—If we use words in the future tense, it is there that the energy is set (in the future) placing events, situations or characters at a distance. The events have a tendency not to happen, because the information and the energy, are not expressed, oriented and formatted for the present moment, which is where everything is happening. For example, instead of saying "I will be happy," we say: "I am going to be happy," because it is a choice directed to a closer moment that allows subatomic rearrangements for a current experience.

Conditional—When we use this tense, we are setting the conditions for something to happen. That is, we are giving space for the uncertainty and/or for alternative scenarios, for the materialization or manifestation of a result.
The tendency is the uncertainty regarding the action and the result, leaving it open to other possibilities.
When we move our attention together with the verb tense to a set time, we are organizing ideas, feelings or attitudes expressed in our words, as well as putting in memory what we wish to remember, and release what we want to forget, allowing us to experience more and new information, because we are receptive and in flow with space-time, having more light and energy to use in the present which is where reality is always happening.

♥ Stop, Breathe, Love

Regarding words, it is also useful to understand our emotions or feelings when we speak or write; what images are associated with them and what behaviors do they trigger. The words we use neurally activate connections and create life links at various levels, causing the organism to present itself and acquire form in consonance with what we say, write or even read. For example, we place the image of "being as light as a feather," or "We are feeling like we have our head in the clouds" and that is imprinted internally and brings us sensations.
We also speak with love or bitterness and that causes us and others to have that sensation or emotion. And it is still possible, because of one word, to be motivated to finish that task, or apologize. In this case, a word can trigger one or more behaviors and even to its omission (for example stop smoking).
In deciding to alter our lives, modifying our words is essential for changes to occur, both on a psychic, emotional and behavioral level, contributing to the crystallization of that change in our organism. The act of naming is the ignition for creating/ and evokes subatomic rearrangements in consonance with what we state, aligning events, situations, objects, and people that are vibrating in the field of unified consciousness and planetary consciousness.
We are the creators of reality and we use creativity on the level of words to experience the manifestation of what the words provided. We can use them in an intelligent manner and directed to any area of our life, bringing good to our lives and the lives of others. It can be in our family, work, finances, or our internal growth because their applicability is total.
Here is a testimonial of that creativity.

Testimonial

I met Susana through a friend who spoke to me about the wonders of her work. As I am very curious, I decided to meet her and take part in a seminar to find out what it was about.
I tell you it was one of the best things I did (and do) in my life. With her, I have learnt and put into practice small and great tools that make all the difference (for the best)

and have given me foundations for growth and wings to fly. The most important thing I have learned with Susana was to think and use words correctly and coherently. As a salesperson I work with the public and I must have an intelligent and objective discourse so that the client understands the product, is impressed and becomes loyal. Instead of just selling, my objective is to give quality to everything I do, and I am an expert at that, because my thoughts, words and attitudes are positive, clear and properly focused. The clients understand the difference and know what is good.

I understood how the hierarchy had a discourse that was less motivating, negative and forced, and had the opposing effect to the one they intended. Now I select what makes sense and use only what favors me and the results, which are for the good of all. Also, what I have learned is reflected in my relationships with my colleagues, because as I correct my vocabulary, I have a more peaceful relationship; I focus on their positive side, and I express myself in a clear organized manner, being understood and acknowledged. My relationship with them is friendlier and pleasant and we have a good work environment. The way I apply the positivity, clarity and mental, emotional and behavioral coherence, causes my brain to work better, that I have more energy and achieve more in less time and always with good humor. And this is learnt and practiced. Internally, I am aware and I increasingly filter with greater ease if what I am being told has the quality that I need, and if it does not, I reject it. This mental attitude frees me from unnecessary noise and tension that distorted thoughts cause.

My colleagues, bosses and clients are interested in what I think and say and are motivated to listen to me, want me to teach them to function better and I explain the advantages in practicing positivity and coherence.

On an emotional level, I am more balanced because I ceased to feed the negativity of the thoughts of tension, discomfort and frustration that caused negative emotions and my words are pleasant and in consonance with my values. Things ceased to have the load of a problem because I do not see it there anymore, and I know how to resolve emerging situations. I find solutions naturally. I believe life is full of opportunities and that everything is easy if we allow ourselves to work in harmony with our internal strengths.

I discovered my strengths and talents and now I am a much happier, satisfied and more loving than I was.

The work with Susana Cor de Rosa is an investment for life that I recommend because we discover ourselves and feel totally at ease in our skin, to do, have and be whatever we wish. Thank you for allowing me to share a little bit of my life story with you.

Elisa Serra, sales

♥ Stop, Breathe, Love

Still in relation to words, it is crucial to approach the issue of coherence, and this means that in the act of expressing ourselves, we must honor what we say or write. Coherence requires verticality, openness and clarity. We simply assume what we say, and we are working in tune with the field of unified consciousness. For example, for some time we have been saying that we want to take part in a training event and faced with that possibility, we register, attend, are open, motivated and apply what we have learned.

It is also coherent to embody what we say; that is, be what we state or write. For example, if we verbalize that we are a fun person, we can choose each moment to have fun. When we state that we are increasingly more confident, it is good to exercise that confidence in small and great things. For example, leaving our small child in the care of a family member for a weekend, can be a great step, just as accepting a project and completing it.

Being what we expressed is a quantum "boom," since we are united and aware of our connection with the field of unified consciousness and able to achieve the ventures we take on and which are beneficial to all beings.

Words are paths that we tread internally. They are at the same time the language and the code of creation that the brain quantum system acknowledges and shares with the field of unified consciousness and that it recognizes and communicates with us, manifesting multiple realities.

Words bring to life what we express: the argument with the cleaning lady, the bad service at a restaurant, the ease of parking, the perfect baptism or the clarity of reasoning. They are destined to create reality. Any reality we choose.

The 5 factors that normally interfere in the manifestation of words are: the excess of information/confusion, lack of attention, attachment, doubt, and incoherence.

⊛The excess of information means that we have not adequately selected what we wanted to manifest or there is confusion. The clearer and more concise the words are, the easier the process of manifestation becomes.

⊛The lack of attention consists in defocusing the words we have decided to choose, focusing on other ideas or sayings that have nothing to do with the subject. For example, we decided to focus on the word "success" and then feed conversations about failure or complain about what we did wrong. It is necessary to persist in the attention; focus consistently on what is to be manifested: the success. One of the best ways I know to do this is to fall in love with the words and then feed them; have them with you in your bag, write them on your computer, see them frequently. Keep them present in the energy field.

⊛Another aspect is attachment; the need that what we said or wrote, happens. Attachment has the underlying emotions of fear and beliefs of lack. These vibrations interfere, delay and sometimes prevent the materialization of what is verbalized or written. The objective is to be clear, open and relaxed because the reality we are writing or saying already exists in the field of unified consciousness. Otherwise, it would not even be possible for us to think it, or state it. It is already in us (although still in potential state) and as we accept it as a present, it manifests itself.

⊛On the other hand, questioning ourselves how a given thought is going to be manifested, also delays or prevents the manifestation. The "how?" is the doubt of a limited intellect and that can only see small or defective.

In fact, we live in a universe of infinite possibilities, intelligent and perfect, to which we are connected, and which is abundant in resources, in synchrony, in communications and in everything we evoke. Why should we want to control and guess the next steps, if there are steps that are unknown and are present in the unlimited? Leaving space for creativity and natural abundance is an intelligent act, because we are linked to it at each instant. Therefore, let us leave the how and get out of the way so that the manifestation can occur in unity with the field of unified consciousness. The field knows the easiest way, the easiest method, quickest and most efficient way of working, and the words we use and the acceptance that all is possible is the password enabling us to realize what we evoke.

⊗Incoherence also interferes in the manifestation. For example, it is incoherent to focus on the word peace, and facing the opportunity of pacifying the environment where we are, in a conversation and we incite disagreement. There was no verticality between what we affirmed and the behavior we had.

The field of unified consciousness already has what we have invoked through words, we only need to embody all we affirmed to experience its manifestation.

We can state simply that to speak or write, our consciousness/brain concurrently activates the language and memory centers and can also activate the centers of emotion and image in an informational cocktail that organizes itself with form and sense to translate ideas, feelings, images and also experiences. We mobilize energy, information, light and organization simultaneously to express ourselves both internally and externally, and in that dance, the body follows both on the soul level and also on a neural, emotional and physical level, acquiring movement, form, position and structure in accordance with the words we use.

The word is productive and always have an impact on reality. It is reality, affecting any reality, from the biology of our bodies, the mind, the emotions, the behaviors, the soul or any other reality such as objects or plants and animals. The words live in us and in the All; they are the language we know and that the field recognizes in the dance of life to manifest existence.

♥ Stop, Breathe, Love

Another fundamental point about words is attention, as was gone over in the fourth chapter.

Both words and attention are instruments that build reality. They are both the language and the technology that we use to communicate with the field of unified consciousness which it recognizes and responds to.

Attention is present consciousness and linked to the field of unified consciousness. It is the presence that focuses and whatever it focuses, the consciousness that is aware manifests.

Attention on words increases the manifestation.

Fixing the attention on words, even if just for a tenth of a second, we are choosing that information in particular, giving it importance, and this act of paying attention is capable of coagulating the information that the word shows and represents, updating it for manifestation.

Our participation in life runs simultaneously as a result of the acts of attention and the words we select, and on which we are set at a given time or situation. What we say is present and interacts with the field of infinite possibilities, which become available to manifest what we set and expressed in words, giving them quality, form or color in accordance with our specific instructions.

A refresher of some of the concepts of attention here:
1) What words are we focusing on? We choose to give attention to words/ sentences

that express ideas about people, objects, events, nature, etc. from a great number of possible words.

2) When do we focus our words? We pay attention to the words/phrases that are temporarily set in the past, in the present or that we project to the future and that focus of attention brings to life events related to these. For example, when we give attention to a word of richness in the present, it nurtures results in the present, and they can also be entwined in the future.

3) How do we focus on words? In a concentrated or distributed manner?
When deciding to give total attention to a word or phrase or distributing the attention on various words or phrases, this interferes with the probability of manifestation of the word into reality.

At each instant, the field of unified consciousness reflects the reality created by us in partnership with it. It results from the focus of attention on the words we choose and decided to give life to in the vastness of endless probabilities. We can decide to give life to whatever we want through the natural creativity we have and the whole universe assists us in that act. So be careful with the attention that we give to words, because they inform and give form to reality.

Declarations of Life

"Everything was done first with words. If I want to be someone else, I have to change the way I name myself."
Teachings of the Navajo Indians

"I want for myself the spirit of this phrase, transforming its form so as to marry it with what I am."
Fernando Pessoa

Story
A very long time ago in a remote village in Croatia, lived a wise old man who was visited by those who wanted to become "a new person." Each one of the visitors would tell the wise man what type of person they intended to become, and he would listen attentively. Then the wise man would go to the field, and bring back with him a stone which he would give to the visitor saying: "Name this stone in accordance with your intention, and from this moment on, keep it with you so that you remember who you are. In naming the stone, you are naming yourself and you are allowing nature to know what you brought to life."
The visitor would leave the route to his destination. The change was done.

How many of us have faced situations where we wanted to be someone else, from the type of ideas we have, to the way we permit ourselves to be affected emotionally by others? Who knows, we may even wish to change our character and have distinct attitudes then the ones we have normally?
It is likely that, at least once in a lifetime, we have been through this situation, and most probably expressed the desire to merely change into our innermost self or had written it or verbalized it. When we make the decision to be different from what we

were, the written or spoken words should also be changed. **This is because words are forces of the I and these reveal the identity of the one who speaks them.** If we want to change the person we are, the way we name ourselves and name life, we must be changed so that the interior and exterior are in tune and reflect the same vibration.

The truth is words bring to life what they name or indicate, since they have a soul and uplift the soul in accordance with the information, energy and light that they contain in themselves.
When we call ourselves or give names to other people, situations, objects or events, we are using our soul and the soul of everything else to live, therefore, it is of utmost importance to use words consciously.

All sacred scriptures mention the creative power of words metaphorically or objectively. Through words, we call upon God or Gods, doorways are opened to the invisible and we invoke the forms for the earthly plan. In the metaphors used in the Bible about the creation of the world, God gives life to plants, animals and even to a woman when He allocates her a name: "This is Eve," and this act of naming is a giver of life. Another biblical reference to the creative power of words to bring to life what is named is embodied in the expression, *"The Word became flesh,"* this means that the words transform into matter what they express, bringing to life situations, things, events, people or circumstances, aligned with its vibration.

We can admit that when we speak, or write, God speaks through our mouth and writes with our hand, because we are his creatures and also intelligent creators, gifted with free will and with the ability to affect the reality that we are integrated in.

When we decide to be someone else, a different entity to what we have been—that is, be a new person—the words we use to define who we are, who others are and what the world is are also an expression of this newness and change. The metamorphosis of the being is in resonance with the metamorphosis of the words in a profound dialectic. As a human being, I transfigure myself, that is, I change my image, and my words feed and substantiate my transfiguration and that of the world in an innovative and coherent manner, in a dance between the invisible and the visible.
When naming the qualities, values, ideas, feelings, and behaviors that make sense for us to experience while "new people," we pay attention to them, give affection, importance and experience them from morning till night, one day after another and we find that the transformations occur in and outside of us, in a myriad of possibilities. **When we change the words, we bring to life a new life—our life—and entwined as it is with so many other lives and beings, it unleashes changes, sometimes subtle, or profound transformations** *in the family, friends or in the community in which we live, in the country, the planet, and the cosmos. It is a phenomenon in a network, with endless and unimaginable repercussions when we trigger it. The change of words is an act of quantum creativity, and each one does it at his own pace and at the cosmic pace, in a joyful song of life.*

Words with Impact

"In the same way that the loom is the instrument used by the weaver to weave, so we also use names to name. With it, we indicate the reality of things."
Plato, *Cratylus*

"In the beginning was the Word, and the Word was with God, and the Word was God. (...) The Word became flesh."
The Bible

"Never say it is impossible. Say I still have not done it."
Japanese Proverb

Story
A traditional story[1] tells us of a curious boy from a remote village in Greece; he was very interested in acquiring knowledge. One day he approached his master because he wanted to tell him something. The master looked at him and said: "Has whatever you are going to tell me been through the three sieves?"
The boy asked: "What are the three sieves?"
The master answered: "They are the filters through which we should strain whatever we want to say. The first sieve is Truth. What you are going to say to me, is it true? Have you checked its origin? Have you heard someone saying it or are you just saying it for the sake of saying it, without knowing or feeling if it is true?
The second sieve is Kindness. Is what you are going to say good? Will it help to build the way for anyone?
The third sieve is Usefulness. Is what you are going to tell me useful? Who does it benefit? An individual or a whole community?"
The master then looked deep into the eyes of the boy and said: "If whatever you were going to tell me goes through the three sieves, then tell me. If not, bury it forever so that there is more light in the world."

Each time I read this story I always find it can be applied to something in my life. It brings to my attention the function of the word, of its impact on reality and the way we should be respectful of its nature. The issue is applying this knowledge to our lives, all the time, and seeing results.
Words are powerful, because they are aggregating and multiplying forces of what we name, bringing to life what we express. The simple act of naming things causes them to emerge in reality, with a face, and features in accordance with what we named.
Researchers think this is so because words are linked to primary geometric shapes existing in the field of unified consciousness, and are implicit in the energy fields of quarks, planets or human cells, and these forms, when triggered, have the tendency to manifest themselves as entities, things, or events in life.

---

[1] This story was found on several sites on the internet. It seems to be attributed to Socrates, but may be part of the work "Lives and Opinions of Eminent Philosophers" by Diogenes Laertius.

Words create reality, bringing to us what we have named, whether we are aware of it or not. They purely and simply construct dynamic networks of life.

The issue is then, knowing what we are giving life to through words. Are we bringing to life disease, discontentment, problems, dissatisfaction, and scarcity or are we bringing to life health, understanding, solutions, satisfaction and abundance through our choice of words?

Of the countless words that we know, we select them in a conscious manner or automatically in order to express ourselves. In fact, any word necessarily moves force fields and interferes with other energy fields and information, potentially capable of manifesting and creating reality. **They are the language and the "technology of consciousness" in unity with the field of unified consciousness.**

The words we use are energy in movement, that is, vibrations with a given wave frequency that, when going into resonance with other vibrations, cooperate with each other, causing subatomic rearrangements in tune with the instructions that the words convey, and make possible the materialization of events, moods or any other situation raised.

 Exercise:
1. Today write two sentences about your positive traits of personality.
2. Write the most important praise you have received and have given unto others.
3. Describe in detail three things that bring you happiness and why.

♥ Stop, Breathe, Love

The applicability of words is vast. We can build reality with them, such as the recovery of health, family harmony, the fast completion of a task, the birthday party of our children, whatever we want. Words are there, bringing to life what we evoke with them.

The impact of words is real in the world. They imprint form, give substance and affect reality. Better still, they are reality interacting with the reality of what everything is made of: particles/subatomic waves in communication and interaction in the field of unified consciousness, molding life. Using words is changing the world.

Experiments done with the aim to know what the impact of words on water molecules was, showed that in accordance to whether the words were appreciative or offensive, the geometric forms were altered. In fact, Dr. Masaru Emoto proved that water crystals became distorted when something offensive was said, for example, "moron" and when the words "angel" or "you are beautiful" were said, the water crystals showed neat and intricate forms.[2]

Do we really understand the power that words have on our biology and to affect our health? In accordance with the experiment, the water molecules are distorted with words like "stupid," "I hate you," "You are worthless," amongst others. Well, our body is made up of 70% water and billions of water molecules are in movement and become distorted as a result of the vibration of offensive words, imagine what we are doing to our health and to the health of the others, when we use these types of words or speak

---

[2] Emoto, M., *The Hidden Messages in Water*, Portuguese edition (Estrela Polar, 2006), pg. 32

of diseases or problems. We are telling our bodies to become unbalanced and create the conditions for disease.

We use words in the internal dialogue we have with ourselves, in what we say and hear from others and we communicate that to the field of unified consciousness regarding our health or lack of it, as well as regarding all aspects of our life.

These subtle or evident communications that we emit or receive, very often, hour upon hour, over many weeks, months or years, gain dysfunctional forms because we are telling the organism to remain without vitality, tense or broken. And the intelligence inherent to life responds in harmony.

Illness or health is built up and it is up to us to decide what we want to bring to life. We can become happier with other words and experience health.

For example, instead of telling ourselves and others, "This is going from bad to worse," "The disease has taken me over," or "You are worthless," or "No one likes me," we should choose to bring to life another internal or external dialogue, so that from a subatomic, molecular and cellular point of view, other healthy rearrangements emerge. For example, "From now on this can only get better," or "Health is the truth about me," or "I am valuable for life," or "I like myself and life loves me just as I am" are only a few of the possibilities.

Using words is an act of creativity and we can use it to create a joyful, satisfied, healthy and happy life for ourselves and the community. Here is a testimonial of that creativity.

Testimonial

I began by consulting Susana at a stage in my life when I faced many difficult challenges. I must confess I did not quite know what Unified Quantum Healing was, or what was awaiting me. I was surprised because everything I solved in the consultation never worried me again; this is really healing. It is not a therapy that temporarily diminishes pain or a health issue that then returns, not with Unified Quantum Healing; healing is the keyword. It goes from the core of the issues, to the causes and eliminates them and that is in fact a miracle, a relief, and brings priceless internal peace. By the hand of Susana, I was able, for the first time, to see myself in the mirror, dive into my eyes and see the real me. After this I did a seminar on Unified Quantum Healing.

What changed? Everything! My vision of the world as a set of independent elements was transformed into a vision of the world as a whole. I understood the purpose of life, what we were doing here, and how we are all connected. It was also transforming to understand and integrate the power of words; while at the same time it was challenging to begin to take care of my discourse, analyzing the words that I choose for me and for my world.

As a teacher, I noticed a great difference in the articulation, clarity and interaction with students. The true power is learning to heal yourself and your family and friends. It is one of those experiences that are difficult to explain; you need to experience it, with commitment and confidence... and everything changes!

Mónica Loureiro, teacher

Words are a "subtle technology" in unity with the field of unified consciousness and manifesting reality. They are able to change the human energy field and as a result of the information, a group of instructions sent in a chain, affecting the entire organism (namely the hormonal, enzyme component, the emission or prevention of sending white blood cells, blood pressure, amongst others), they can trigger processes of disease or the recovery of health.

We have probably understood that, when we say or listen to things that hurt us, we focus on problems, on negative opinions, conflicts and emotions of guilt or fear, the tendency for disease is great. Just for the simple fact of recycling the underlying words or emotions, we are "causing a deficit" to our energy system. In fact, we are using the **language of words** in disorganization and chaos, which communicates to the field of unified consciousness, with it being unsettled and unbalanced, creating the conditions for illnesses.

The words that we emit can construct health or illness, depending on the information they contain and the forms they represent.

Dysfunctional information enables subatomic rearrangements with dysfunctional forms. Organized information enables organized subatomic re arrangements. We are the ones choosing, all the time, what we want to bring to life, in unity with the field of unified consciousness, through the words that we communicate.

Words are energy, light in movement, and on a set frequency they enter into resonance with other energy systems, as is the case of cells or organs, creating force fields that join and manifest in accordance with the vibration/instruction contained in the word. Change the words towards health and harmony is reestablished.

When we use words, verbally or written, in connection with health, such information is already present in the quantum world, as order and harmony underlying life and is actualized as a result of our act and is automatically communicated to our organism in harmony with the field of unified consciousness.

From a quantum point of view, we are connected to health; that is, we are healthy. We only need to be open to that probability so that it is manifested.

We can personally experience this state of order, of health or wellbeing, personally or be lead to it by another person or people, in their presence or not, united with the field of unified consciousness.

♥ Stop, Breathe, Love

Can the words of others and their respective beliefs and suggestions affect our health? And do we have to accept or validate these words, so that they influence us? The answer to both questions is yes.

The words, opinions and suggestions of others can interfere with our health if we allow them to. We only need to accept, even if unconsciously, the transmitted information for it to be lodged in our energy field and be able to produce effects. For example, have you ever been told that you were full of energy and you immediately noticed that your vitality increased? You probably did this in autopilot. Or when a child falls and begins to cry, we say, "It's fine," and she gets up and is fine? Or when chatting, we say that drinking water makes you lose weight, or a particular food is good, and we notice it? These are opinions, beliefs or suggestions which we consider positive.

But it is also common for people to speak of illness daily, from the news in the media, small talk on public transportation, or even between family and friends. We can be influenced, or not, depending on the acceptance and attention we are giving these issues.

For example, there is someone complaining of a disease next to us at a restaurant and we think "This could also happen to me." We are not only paying attention to the conversation as well as accepting as possible the disease in us, that is, we are predisposing our energy field and organizing information in harmony with that probability. Another very well-known example is the "old competition of illnesses," to see who has the worst illness, who suffers more, or is worse off, seeking attention and achieving it in the name of suffering. The type: "I twisted my ankle and had to have surgery" and someone else says, "That was nothing compared with the five surgical interventions, the issues with the anesthesia, etc..." and we enter this wave of self-pity or "Life is like that" or "We have to accept it," and we are accepting this information.

From the moment we accept the idea, we emit this information in the energy field and simultaneously to the field of unified consciousness and that information becomes available for materialization. The field simply reflects the choice. Therefore, be careful about what you are choosing, even if unconsciously.

On a conscious level, the negative suggestion made by another that is accepted by the individual, causes physical symptoms. The person only needs to accept that possibility for the manifestation to take place. There are scientific studies that prove the impact of a negative suggestion accepted as valid. The book *Love, Medicine, and Miracles* by Dr. Bernie Siegel, reports a scientific experiment *were a group of men were told verbally that the pill they were taking was oral chemotherapy, when in fact what they were being administered was a laxative; it was concluded that as a result of this verbal suggestion 30% of the men lost their hair.*[3]

It is therefore imperative to ask: "How can I remain neutral to what is suggested or experienced by others as illness?" They are normally full of good intentions and just want to tell me about it.

Maintaining attention focused on health and not accepting that it has to be like that. While listening or reading, keep the perception that there are other realities, and for you it can be different and better. Because that is in fact the truth. There is always another probability in this universe of infinite possibilities where we live. One of the things that works well is, while you listen or read, think in the form of a litany: *"For you it was like that, for me I want equilibrium, or then, I choose a different reality, an alternative one where health is expressed."*

This attitude, selecting another type of data, is reprogramming our minds for health and can be done by each one of us. When we do it, we are imprinting clear and healthy information in our energy field, as well as transmitting to our interlocutor these "positive" vibrations, which are in interaction with the field of unified consciousness and with the planetary field, increasing the number of people on Earth vibrating and transmitting healthy information, increasing the vibrational quality of the planet also expanding to the field of unified consciousness, in a conscious, harmonious dance.

♥ Stop, Breathe, Love

---

[3] Siegel, B.,"Love, Medicine and Miracles", Harper & Row, 1986, Summarized from pg. 191 of the Portuguese edition.

Measuring the energetic field of a person before the person hears words that are considered offensive, violent or morbid, and again after hearing these, the changes are evident. After hearing these words, the energy field decreases, changes color and form, and can even show breaches in some parts of the body or organs with changes.

Children that are subjected to depreciative comments by their parents, like, "You are stupid" or "You are good for nothing," immediately show in their body language a contraction and a closed look, but also a decrease in vitality in their energy field: a dark grey color and deformed geometric forms, in their auric field and some energy knots and this can also be the case with adults when receiving something they consider to be critical or offensive.

In relation to what we have been mentioning, I remember a five-year-old girl I assisted and who was about to have a surgical intervention, because her ears were full of pus; she suffered continually from otitis and could not hear well. Once I understood internally how difficult it was for her to hear her father shouting, and the aggressiveness that he could not control; I permitted her to express herself freely. I then energetically removed the pus from her inner ear, healing the eardrum. At the end she herself told me that she was healed; she was not going into surgery and jumped with joy. Two weeks after our meeting, the mother took her to the ear specialist, and he cancelled the surgery because the medical tests showed that the ear and the hearing were normal.

Here is a testimonial from the girl.

Testimonial

I am very happy. I hear well, my ear is not sore, and is dry. I will not be operated on. Let's go play mommy.

Joana, five years old

Every word is a set instruction for what is in a potential form to assume a definite form. When we use words, we write in the book of life, and biologically we see the representation of the forms that we animate through words. We have a choice in relation to the words we use.

Words are the language of creation and the "subtle technology" that allows us to manifest reality. The issue here is using this high technology that every human being has, in the service of health instead of disequilibrium. Because its effect is, in fact, real.

A word spoken with sense at the right moment in a "positive" manner can save a life. Who knows, someone we love? On the contrary, words considered "negative" and or with a strong emotional charge, have the probability for dysfunction. In this case, these should be neutralized and a new order created so that the body returns to health, which is its natural state.

Do words in the form of prayer have effects on health?

Effectively yes. Words said in the form of prayer supported by the belief that healing or improvement happens through divine intercession or another type of power, are one of the oldest methods of cure. Thousands of people daily see their prayers answered, when evoking verbally with conviction that the healing is manifested and this occurs in sanctuaries like Fatima or Lourdes, Tokyo or Jerusalem, and Mecca but also in hospitals or in residences, on the road, in schools, basically in a myriad of places, with all kinds of people and various creeds.

There are people who do their prayers saying exactly what they want, for example the healing of the left hip or kidney, and there are those who simply offer their prayer saying that the person (Amelia) needs help, and that the best may happen. In one way or another specifying the result or leaving it open to divine providence to do whichever is best, what is seen is that improvement or healing happens.

I am sure you know someone who has been the object of prayer to get better and got better or was healed completely. Prayer works on such a profound level while at the same time so subtle, leaving us stunned. I remember the mother of a friend of mine, who lived in Venezuela, receiving the news that her son was involved in a serious road accident where the expectation to survive was minimal. This mother would not accept the idea of losing her son and went to the chapel of the hospital and prayed continually. The next day the son was out of danger.

The energy of words together with faith in divine power is coherent and organized light that is communicated to the energy field of unified consciousness, and it responds immediately making the manifestation also immediate.

Prayer is a conscious technology that has a real impact on health and has been the subject of scientific studies that prove its efficiency. I mention one carried out by Dr. Randolph Byrd, at the Coronary Unit of the General Hospital of San Francisco, which involved 393 patients admitted to the CCU over ten months. While Hospitalized 192 patients received intercessory prayers from people outside the hospital (Christians praying) and 201 patients did not receive prayers (the control group). At entry to the unit both groups where in the same medical conditions. *"Analysis of events after entry into the study showed the prayer group had less congestive heart failure, required less diuretic and antibiotic therapy, had fewer episodes of pneumonia, had fewer cardiac arrests, and were less frequently intubated and ventilated."*[4]

What this study indicates is that prayer works. It has a beneficial therapeutic effect in patients admitted to a CCU.

♥ Stop, Breathe, Love

It is urgent to change our verbal or written language, using supportive words that allow the situations that we are involved in to heal, because the function of words is to embody, give substance to what we name in a coherent manner.

Be it in an internal dialogue, in what we say to others or listen to, words are informing us and giving form to reality, namely to illness or health. Speaking about illnesses brings us more disease, predisposes us to it and lowers the vibration of our organism. We are using the language of creation for disorder. We are focusing our attention on disease instead of on health, focusing and observing what is already consolidated, instead of opening the window to another possibility.

But we can change the situation and create health. Move the point of creation, writing, speaking, focusing attention on everything that is healthy, within and around us. Focusing on the new state of vitality instead of on what happened before, on the

---

[4] Byrd, R., "Positive Therapeutic Effects of Intercessory Prayer in a Coronary Care Unit Population," Summarized from Southern Medical Journal, July 1988, Vol. 81:826-828.

symptom, we focus on the freedom of movement, the equilibrium, on what is better or different. At each instant this conscious choice that we are giving our attention to, develops into health. The construction of health, from improvement to improvement, or in a quantum leap, requires simultaneously that attention is focused on health and the words spoken follow that trend, so that on a subatomic level, there is the possibility of creating coherent rearrangements with health.

It depends on each one of us choosing to focus on the words that we want to be manifested in the individual and collective reality regarding health. We can start by perceiving that *health is extremely abundant* and that the natural state of the human being is being healthy. When we focus our consciousness on that reality, we are individually and globally actualizing a health plan accessible to all, as well as, creating information fields laden with order that become available energetically to mold our DNA and change the genes. The changes are profound and the results beneficial for the human family. We then use words as a high potency healer and we honor the sublime result for which it was created, molding harmony. This is because from a fundamental point of view we are linked and are only one; each time we accept and health, in each instance, one of us feels well, gets better or is healed, a quantum leap occurs. Humanity, the planet and the field of consciousness, at that moment also resonate in health, in order. *The decision starts with us. One makes all the difference; one is the all. Now choose healthy words.*

Besides the impact that words have on our health, they also affect the behavior of humans, animals, plants and water molecules. As a result of spoken words, we can generate feelings and move masses into action, influence our pet to sit, to eat or have more energy and we can also affect the growth of plants and are able to affect the molecular format of water.

Tomato plants that are subjected to words of incentive and care grow faster, produce more and bigger tomatoes than those who merely get the traditional care (soil, water and sun exposure). The same happens with pumpkins and houseplants.

The technology of words is informing and giving form to these fields of energy and information, communicating with them and simultaneously with the field of unified consciousness, bringing to life the manifestation.

Words are powerful and have a real impact on this planet and universe: both on our existence and in that of other beings coexisting with us. The scientific experiments reported, as well as the testimonies given here lead us to think and dare to transcend the beliefs and limits that we may have. Words have the power to create improvement or healing in the case of health, and encourage positive results at work, in relationships and even affect animals and plants. The impact is real and it is happening at each moment, simply using for the effect the language and the technology for the creation of words.

Beyond Linear Words

"You know the name you were given; you do not know the name you have."
José Saramago

"We weave life with the words we say and the threads with which the tapestry is woven can be changed."
Maria Costa

"Nothing is impossible, the word itself says 'I'm possible!"
Audrey Hepburn

We have been writing about words to understand their function, their attributes and their mission of creating reality. This topic of words is so vast that we have not yet pondered the importance of words beyond the linear. It is a fascinating topic for me, causing me to open my eyes in awe and feel profoundly connected with life.
We are used to facing reality in a conventional manner, especially regarding the dimension of time and space, that is, things need time to occur and happen in a set place and one at a time. This is the vision of sequential reality, logic, oriented in a straight line and to which our conscious/brain matrix is accustomed, formatted, with hundreds of years of knowledge and the conventional scientific vision. Therefore, when we use words written or verbally, somewhere we think that this is going to take a while to happen. Well, this linear and sequential vision of reality, of space and time is limited. It is only one face of the coin. Reality is in fact much vaster; things can happen instantaneously, everywhere, simultaneously. What we verbalize or write is immediately available, temporally and spatially for us, for all and for the entire existence—because we are one—we sing in unison the same song that is sung by the field of unified consciousness.
Words are information and **information is** — **pure and simply IS**— vibrating in the field of unified consciousness or the informational field, being in communication with any information independent of its form or context and not separated from anything—it simply happens.
Words are energy. Potential energy and expressed in act—**and energy simply IS**— vibrating in the field of unified consciousness and communicating and interacting with any energy field independent of time, space, form or dimension assumed. It is connected to the whole and reproduces the whole.
Words are light—luminous irradiation in a spectrum visible to the naked eye or not. **And light simply IS.** Vibrating in the field of unified consciousness, communicating and interacting in the field, affecting and being affected by the light of the field. And being light—it is light independent of dimension, form or assumed context, connected to all and manifesting all.
It is our perception of being separated from things, others, life and also the perception that time and space are linear that also causes events, and situations to occur in a linear manner and take time or appear in a set sequence. Already Einstein in the twentieth century had unified space and time in the dimension space-time, and quantum physics has been admitting that it is possible that there are dimensional encasements and that events and time and space references can be piled up, overlapping profoundly and circulating; this probably results in the phenomena happening simultaneously. We can then admit that the other face of the space-time coin is that things can happen immediately and they "do not need any time" because they are *It*. And that, when we use words, they are automatically manifested and what they name or indicate, is immediately created in the field of unified consciousness and our life.
The dimension of space-time is also consciousness in the field of unified consciousness—a face of the vast number of existing faces, linked inevitably to the

matrix and linked to what is in potential and has already manifested by the consciousness in the endless network of life. A human being is also consciousness, and when emitting words is in a network linked to any other consciousness in the field and to the field of unified consciousness, communicating and interacting immediately from micro to macro.

That is, whatever comes out of our mouths, our pens or computers is a "focal point of consciousness" that is immediately served by it, and it multiplies and manifests itself at the exact instant that it is evoked, because it is one with the field of unified consciousness. What we speak or write is destined to live, and embodies, from the moment our consciousness raises it, in the quantum soup.

As it happens, most people have probably never admitted that words "took no time" to be manifested and so we have waited and convinced ourselves that it is so and naturally, we created that reality repeatedly. Why? Because our creative consciousness intervenes in the process of life also creates the reality that way through beliefs, feelings and experiences. Or that is, we have the perception of separation in relation to words, time, and things, and they appear disconnected from us.

A human being, that is aware of the nature of words and feels connected to them and to everything, is so complete that the result of his conscious integrity can only automatically reproduce his connection with everything.

From a quantum point of view, any word is potentially capable of immediate manifestation because it is in the field of unified consciousness. The word is reality (even if virtual), manifesting the infinite possibilities of reality. We bring to life the messages that we communicate with our mouth, pens, computers or iPads, in unison with the field of unified consciousness.

It is therefore necessary that we have the perception of being one, that words are also one and are connected to all beings and things, that the field of consciousness understands our communication, and that in partnership with it, we manifest them. The immediate and instant realization of what the words provided is natural. It is in their essence to create worlds and forms. The immediate manifestation of what we say or write is possible.

With this perception of unity, we have total trust that whatever we say or write is powerful, has substance, and materializes. In a state of unity, we know internally that whatever we formulated, verbally or in writing, is done. It is given to life and is already life.

In this state, what we call miracles, happen. Water in lakes can become unpolluted, as in the case of Lake Biwa, in Japan, according to the words spoken, illnesses can be cured and responses obtained, amongst others.[5]

In a state of unity, we are all in the kingdom of infinite possibilities and we materialize whatever we invoke through words, instantaneously, with a conscious click.

Words are life and support us in bringing to life whatever we in tend, think or feel. Independently of the size, quality, context, people, resources or events involved, and even space-time, reality is manifested through them. Any reality is possible. Words function on the level of infinite possibilities that the field of unified consciousness has in itself, and so do we. We can create without limits because the probabilities that we have available are endless.

---

[5] Emoto, M., *The Hidden Messages in Water*, Portuguese edition (Estrela Polar, 2006).

♥ Stop, Breathe, Love

Who Are We now in possession of the wealth of words? We are the sovereign deciders of life and we have, in words, the power to transform, naming the existence and bringing it to life with the contours, colors and the dimension we wish. We can incarnate the words with affection and with gestures full of meaning in a giant symphony where we can hear ourselves, we are heard and understand ourselves perfectly.

It is essential to understand that both faces of the coin exist: time and "no time," space and "no space," particle and "antiparticle," matter and ""antimatter," and how we observe the world, the way our consciousness pays attention, have an intention or wishes, it is capable of affecting and consolidating it. Regarding words, it is also our perception about them that is going to actualize and allowing what we say or write to take time or happen immediately.

It is our perception that is going to define if there is only one way for that situation to manifest, or if there are various possibilities for that particular situation. It is still our perception about reality that gives us the illusion that nothing is happening when we use the words, that these are sterile, when in truth they are creators of reality, immediately. Everything is a choice of our consciousness.

A human being that, in the act of speaking or writing, is aware that he is communicating and giving form to reality in unity with the field of unified consciousness and planetary consciousness, knows that everything is possible, and that the concretization has already happened. He is totally receptive, sure of the manifestation and will accept total responsibility for the creation. He embodies what he expresses, feels, acts accordingly and IS what was stated or written.

We can choose to be one with the words that we speak and use them with profound wisdom because we know their function, power and magnificence in the endless now. This is a task we all have, and especially those of us reading this book because we already know how powerful and capable we are in transforming reality. We can start with one or various words—saying them, writing them, feeling them, and acting.

Just as in the story of the three sieves, at each moment our inner wisdom warns us to understand which words we are expressing and what we are building. They affect us individually, but also collectively. The words we use are shared in the collective consciousness and are the quantum switch for the people in our family, work, community, our parents, the world and even the universe. Independent of the distance or the timing, words are there, animating life, and only one consciousness is needed (ours) for the vital hologram that is the universe, for the changes to occur and being mirrored, and communicated automatically and in a network with the entirety of beings.

It is so simple to choose words that are coherent for us, that facilitate our daily life and give us quality of life and to the community, the planet and the cosmos.

It is urgent to leave aside the illusion of fear, separation or lack because just as in the story, we know internally what is real, what is good and what is useful for the All and we animate it purposely, with words, creating a world where we are united, in peace in a meaningful existence.

Key points:

- A word is a tool placed at the service of human consciousness so that it can build reality.
- Words support us, bringing to life whatever we intend, think or feel.
- You can choose your words and through them select different outcomes.
- Different words change your brain and your level of energy and coherence.
- When you speak the whole universe is listening and paying attention to you.
- Speaking about doubts, fear, limitations, and tensions lowers your vibration.
- Ask yourself "Does this make sense to express and live in my reality?"
- Change your focus, there is more for you.
- Size, quality, context, people, resources or events are easy for the field to organize. Let the analytical mind go.
- Your health can be increased by your words. Embody health and it will follow.
- Words matter and affect matter.

Exercises:

❶ Write a sentence that you want to share with the world and that is for the good of everyone.

❷ Note the involuntary words that you have written or said and change them to voluntary words.

❸ Have you considered the idea that you want to be a "new" person? If yes, what words emerge to describe that person? Write it in detail and then be it.

❹ Write a letter to a person dear to you, mentioning every wonderful quality that she has and how important she is to you.

❺ Have you ever noticed that as soon as you spoke or wrote a sentence, it was immediately manifested? Describe it in detail using "positive" words.

Self-reflection:

❶ What made most sense to you in the chapter about words?

❷ Is it understood that if you pay attention to disease you are making it possible? Is that what you wish for yourself and others?

❸ What healthy words can you write or say, from now on, to yourself and to those you come in contact with?

❹ Today, who are you going to pray for, for better health or healing? It can be for the first person that comes to mind, or someone you meet on the street.

❺ See in what situation in your life you can apply the story of the "three sieves."

9 Emotion

Story
A shared traditional story[1] tells us how a long time ago, in a beautiful village there lived a shaman whose name was Blue Eagle. Blue Eagle's knowledge had been passed down from his ancestors, which he used to speak to the divine, practice the art of healing, and reconcile conflicts within the community. One day he was called urgently because two youngsters were ferociously fighting with each other for the love of a woman.
When Blue Eagle saw them, he shouted and placed his staff between both men, interrupting the fight. Then, showing his authority, he took both youths to the forest where they walked a full day in silence. During their trek, they witnessed a fight between two bears and hid behind some shrubs to watch. Blue Eagle then said:
"Observe the fight between the beasts and see what each one has been. A bear of jealousy, hate, rage and sadness who wants to be in control at all costs... and inside you both there is also a bear of compassion, of joy, friendliness and happiness. Who do you want to be? What are you going to choose when faced with the truth? Because the bear that wins is the one you feed internally..."
At that time, the young boys looked at each other, saw eternity in that instant, hugged and were deeply moved.

"Everyone knows what an emotion is, until asked to give a definition. Then, it seems that no one knows."
B. Fehr and J. A. Russell

"There are beautiful wild forces within us. Let them turn the mills inside and fill sacks that feed even heaven."
St. Francis of Assisi

Have you ever noticed that you were in an internal struggle? Emotionally divided and feeding the strength of the "bad bear"? Do we give it so much strength that we feel devoured by it? Did we strengthen the "good bear," experiencing joy or happiness very often? It is more than possible that all this has happened. And who knows, maybe there were times when there was no bear...
It is indisputable that emotions are part of life; they give it color and meaning; it is without question that our emotional states are able to make a perfect day or the opposite. This being so, we understand what emotions are, what they are for and how they function, amongst other issues. It is crucial to have a richer emotional life. We will reply to these and other issues in the course of this chapter with enthusiasm, which is one of the most beautiful emotions in life.
What is emotion? In a wider sense, emotion is conscious information in movement in the field of unified consciousness. It is also energy, a wave vibrating in the cosmic

---

[1] Adaptation from variations of a popular story. There is some reference to "The Holy Spirit: Activating God's Power in Your Life" by Billy Graham, page 92

ocean, interacting with other energy waves. Emotion is also light irradiating in scintillating frequency which affects life. **It is the language of creation placed at the service of human consciousness, so that it constructs reality.**

As mentioned in the first chapters, the field of unified consciousness is the basis of life and, naturally of emotion as well; there are three sources of emotions:

❶ Unified consciousness
❷ Individual consciousness
❸ Planetary consciousness

Let us look at them.

❶ Emotion from the field of unified consciousness

Emotion from the field of unified consciousness is pure, perfect information. It is also potential and manifested energy that pulsates in the absolute and distributes itself to other energy vortices. It is pure light and it irradiates to existing centers of light.

The human consciousness, in resonance with the field of unified consciousness, accesses this information (energy and light) captured through the higher senses—namely empathy, intuition, clairvoyance and inspiration—and the brain, as a quantum system of energy, receives this information (energy and luminosity), and makes it biodynamically accessible in an intelligible frequency and language.

Emotion originating in the field of unified consciousness is alocal; that is, it transcends space; **it is atemporal,** or, it transcends time; **it is nonlinear,** it can be in superposition and emerge at a given point in an unprecedented way and **it can vibrate at the speed of light.**

Emotion originating in the field of unified consciousness can transcend space and it is possible to receive this information/emotion wherever we are, as well as at any point of the All.

Emotion can also go beyond time and we can receive this energy/emotion from any moment in time (past, present, future) and still experience the energy of the whole of life in one unique moment.

Emotion from the field of unified consciousness can also enable us to simultaneously perceive a multidimensional reality in a single focal point. It is still possible to receive the information/emotion as if it had emerged from "nowhere" and vanishes itself in "emptiness."

It depends on us accepting or rejecting the emotion from the field of unified consciousness. When we accept it, we experience states of unity and transcendence that give sense to life.

❷ Emotion from the individual consciousness

Our consciousness/brain matrix constructs emotions through the information that is received through the senses, processing it, giving it sense and context and then expressing it in the human energetic system. This process of emotional experience has an impact in the body, giving us the sensation of the emotion; we perceive that something is affecting our body, and it can also affect the mind and the soul.

In the production of emotion, the consciousness/ brain matrix intertwines thoughts, images, feelings, experiences and memories giving them context and connection. The emotion is the response to this information cocktail, a "boom" of energy that runs through the body giving it the indication of a certain emotional, mental and anemic state.

Each one of us can choose the type of emotions we want to experience. These can include sadness, frustration, enthusiasm or happiness. The range is greatly varied and it is susceptible to being changed according to the decision and the attitude we choose at each moment.

Emotion from the field of human consciousness is information, energy waves and self-produced light that is automatically available in the field of unified consciousness and in the field of planetary consciousness, affecting the field of personal energy and also global energy.

❸ Emotion from the planetary consciousness

Earth is consciousness in movement and is emitting information and energy to all beings living on it, as well as to the field of unified consciousness.

The planet receives emotions that are produced by men individually or collectively and retransmits them in the same vibrational frequency to human beings and the field of unified consciousness. Each individual and the collective have the capacity to accept or reject the emotions already emitted, refeeding the planetary consciousness.

We have already made explicit the origins of emotion that, strictly speaking, are only one—the field of unified consciousness. In the following, we will look especially at emotion emerging from the field of human consciousness.

The Discovery of Emotions

"I feel curious about emotions. About facts, whatever they might be, I feel no curiosity whatsoever."
Fernando Pessoa

"The emotion is a starting point with the arrival set by fate."
Maria Santos

Emotion is a grandiose internal event; it is like a party with guests, music and fireworks. It is a dynamic process, occurring simultaneously in the consciousness/brain matrix and the field of unified consciousness, being brought about based on information. Emotion is a language that we speak in common with the field of unified consciousness and the field of planetary consciousness. It is energy, information and light, moving inside us and in the All, affecting and being affected by reality.

We can state that in the process of triggering emotion, information is captured through the senses and is processed internally connecting itself to the data we already have. Energetic links will be made, namely neural, internally going through information highways and on that path, contact points at the associative level are searched via our thoughts, images, words, emotions and feelings, or behaviors that we have experienced. In case the information from the perceptual view has significance and is considered capable of causing an emotion, we respond emotionally. Emotion is produced as the appropriate reaction to the information that was processed and understood as "valid" in the emotional framework that we have.

From the beginning of our existence, we have developed "emotional hardware and software," that is, data that is being saved in our energy field, more appropriately on the level of our emotional body—which is a field of subtle forces vibrating in specific frequencies—and in the deepest areas of the brain, the reptilian brain, namely the amygdala. This emotional data is common to humanity, and the reason why they were created was to allow human survival and evolution. Emotion was developed and refined in the consciousness/brain matrix and is a self-regulating instrument adapted to life conditions, permitting us to react, progress and understand life in all its aspects, in harmony with the field of unified consciousness.

Although we may think that emotion exists only in the brain, it is in the whole body and the cell, as consciousness, vibrates with the emotion and has a register in its memory of the past emotional experiences.

Every human being comes equipped with the basic emotional "hardware/software," that is, with the emotions that are common to all and in parallel, each one of us also builds his own emotions based on the experiences that we have throughout life. That is, in our basic kit, there are the emotions of fear, anger, sadness, contempt, joy, acceptance, and surprise, amongst others. Scientific experiments have proven that there are a minimum of six different basic emotions: anger, fear, sadness, disgust, surprise or joy. And regardless of geographic area, culture, customs or level of education, we facially express these in the same way.[2]

A native of a tribe from Guinea, as well as a man in Germany will both show the same facial expression and characteristics when faced with the emotion of anger; that is, the same type of muscles are moved. They show similar facial expressions, mannerisms and looks displaying the emotion of anger.

Besides the emotional similarities, there are also differences because it is possible that the information and the perception of information can arouse emotions (or not) in a person, or even arouse different emotional responses, and that can be due to cultural, or geographical conditions as well as personality. For example, a sexual initiation ritual in an African tribe is seen as a natural thing, causing an emotion of pride and self-confidence for the native experiencing it and the respective tribe. For a westerner, this can cause an emotion of disgust or repugnance. Another example, there are certain individuals that when faced with a first setback get angry with rage and explode, and others, when faced with the same circumstance, event or person, react calmly. We are the same on a basic emotional level, and different on the level of perception, learning and emotional response to a particular situation, and that is the great human wealth.

From a quantum point of view, emotion is a subatomic waltz, where there is sharing of information and interaction between energy waves, information bits and light in a gigantic and colorful intertwine.

Emotion is the subtle language and technology of consciousness that allows us to communicate, interact and reorder the quantum world in accordance with the

---

[2] Ekman, P. "Facial Expressions of Emotion: New Findings, New Questions" Psychological Science, Vol. 3, No. 1, 1992, pg. 3438.

subjectivity of each one of us, in a team with the field of unified consciousness and the planetary consciousness. **"Emotionalizing" is moving and shaping reality.**

Each time we have an emotion, we are energetically instructing life so that it shows itself with a face that makes sense to us and it responds in harmony. Emotion is an instrument of human consciousness that creates reality, in a team with the field of unified consciousness.

Before experiencing the emotion, subatomic particles were moving and existed in an undetermined state in our energy field and in the field of unified consciousness.

When emitting an emotion, the human consciousness concentrates on a point of information, a point in the vastness, and actualizes it, causing the subatomic particles to become specific, gaining a certain form, in harmony with the field of unified consciousness.

The issue we may face then is **"What can we manifest in life with emotion?"** The answer is that any reality can be manifested by us through emotion. From going to a rock concert, a financial savings, doing the shopping, the enthusiasm in doing a talk, buying a new house, healing a tumor or a fever.

♥ Stop, breathe, love

Every emotion can create reality. Any reality. It is creative power in action that is inside us and in interaction with the field of unified consciousness. It is the language that we use and the field recognizes, manifesting reality, in accordance with the emotions we emit and it is also the "laser technology" of the manifestation.

Emotion is an energy that interacts with the energy of the totality. In the act of having an emotion, we imprint on the wave of possibilities of quantum reality, our sensibility and our vision of the world, and it connects to the sensibility and the vision of the totality, appearing manifested in reality.

It does not matter what we are imprinting on an emotional level; what we are focusing on and feeling, the field of unified consciousness simply actualizes and places in the cosmic internet, "online," our creations, independent of the size, the quality, the context, the people, the resources or events involved and even of space-time. Any reality is possible. Emotion works in the scope of infinite possibilities that the field of unified consciousness has in itself, and we have in ourselves as well. We can create without limits, because the probabilities that we have are endless.

In the Steps of Emotion

"Emotions are like a thermometer that gives us information about temperature, and helps us decide what to wear."
Margot Phaneuf

"Pleasure is a force creating bonds, connections with the world and with others (...)."
António Alçada Batista

"If you are not good company for yourself, you cannot be good company to others."
Popular proverb

Emotions are common to all human beings and to the field of unified consciousness, and is being used constantly, weaving the daily tapestry that we call reality.

Emotion is built in the consciousness/brain matrix that captures information through the senses—namely through the senses of vision, auditory, movement, intuition or empathy—and processes this data, responding with an emotion.

For example, we are listening to a symphony by Mozart with pleasure, and we notice that our heart beats slowly and we feel more relaxed. Or we have information through intuition, that we should not cross the road yet, we notice palpitations and we stand still: suddenly, a car appears and we could have been run over.

Emotion can also be perceived as a response to an internal or external stimulus; that is, emotion is a reaction to certain circumstances, events, thoughts, images, feelings or behaviors that have a meaning for us and that cause an impression. In response, we trigger an emotion. For example, we remember a disagreement with our best friend and can still hear the unpleasant words that she said. At that time, we experience anger and our head is throbbing. This emotion has an internal cause as it was triggered as a result of us remembering an episode that for us has a negative connotation. Another example: we walk in the street and see an adolescent couple courting and it evokes tenderness and nostalgia of our adolescence and we smile. In this case, the stimulus or cause of the emotion has an external nature, causing a set reaction.

We know we are facing an emotion, because something has changed inside us in a sharp or subtle manner. There was a change from one energy state to another, and both body and mind, as well as the spiritual component, show signs of that change.

Emotion is a bioenergetic response that translates the inner work of confrontation with a given reality. The organism reports in an active manner that something is happening and requires our attention. Emotion is then the signal that warns us that the internal or external conditions of life have changed and we have to be present.

Our energetic system, besides sending signals through the emotions about changes in life conditions, also creates adaptation mechanisms to preserve life. For example, we capture information via the sense of smell (a bad smell), and we have a response of nausea or vomiting so that we abstain from eating that particular food.

♥ **Stop, Breathe, Love**

Linearly speaking, emotions can be organized as primary or secondary emotions, positive and negative. They are all information and enformation of reality. *They transmit messages and simultaneously affect the human energy field, and the fields of unified and planetary consciousness: they are the "technology of creation" of reality.*

Any type of emotion, be it primary or secondary, "positive" or "negative", manifests life because they are life in themselves, linked to the whole of life.

The **primary emotions,** such as fear, anger, sadness, joy, surprise, disgust, and happiness are part of the basic emotional tool kit that is common to all human beings and independent of geographic position or culture. These are experienced and expressed facially in an identical manner. Scientific studies have proven that from a neural point of view, these emotions are inborn and independent. An Asian or European person, married or single, graduate or illiterate, rich or poor, facially expresses sadness or happiness in the same manner.

The **secondary emotions,** such as anxiety, anguish, indignation, heartbreak, enthusiasm, care, astonishment are emotions derived from primary emotions but have a learning task where the cognitive component is more present. That is, these are more elaborate emotions that can be experienced or expressed in a differentiated manner by each human being.

The information that the emotion wants to give us is different when facing a primary or secondary emotion, namely because the basic emotions are stronger and directly related with the instinctive component of the human being, al lowing the satisfaction of our fundamental needs, such as security or freedom.

One of the possible messages that fear may want to transmit to us, is that we are in danger and have to protect ourselves. With this information, the aim is to assure the survival and the satisfaction of the need for protection. Anxiety is a byproduct of fear, and one of the possible messages that is transmitted to us is based on the fact that we should take control of the situations, events, or people. On a certain level, we admit that something is escaping our control. Anxiety can also be a warning sign indicating that things are not what they seem.

For example, I was once walking in the mountains, and I began running down a steep slope. I gained a lot of speed and was scared of falling, because I knew that if it happened, I may not even survive. What fear was informing me was that I was putting my life in danger and should slow down as fast as possible. Another example tells another experience: my mother has the tendency to become anxious when I do not phone her regularly. She needs to know that things in her world are in order, and naturally confirm that I am well. The anxiety message for my mother means that she needs to be sure, to control, and to know that the people she loves are well.

Regarding "positive" and "negative" emotions, these are what they are: energy, light and information vibrating, that is reality; "positive" and "negative" are energy charges that particles can assume.

They transmit messages and simultaneously affect the human energy field, and the fields of unified and planetary consciousness: they are the "technology of creation" of reality.

Any type of emotion, be it primary or secondary, "positive" or "negative," manifests life because they are life in themselves, linked to the whole of life.

On the other hand, positive and negative are perceptual and behavioral references by which we are guided at a given moment as a person and as a community and to which we assign meaning and continue to develop.

Normally we consider positive whatever we interpret as such, within a given context and that gives us results or consequences that we consider beneficial. And negative is the opposite of this. If we think of a vertical line, at the top of the pole we have emotions such as joy, happiness, sympathy, enthusiasm or satisfaction which are associated with pleasure. At the bottom of the pole, we have emotions such as fear, guilt, shame, sadness or anger which are associated with displeasure or pain. In this polarized perspective, the two opposing emotions are love and fear. And we are always vibrating in one or another.

We can consider the emotions associated with the top of the pole/pleasure as being "positive" emotions, and the emotions associated with the bottom of the pole/pain as being "negative" emotions.

However, they should be framed and understood so that the label is not limiting. For example, the flight reaction can be good when faced with a wild animal, because they trigger the instinct for survival, but being systematically in a state of fear in survival mode, namely when someone strange approaches us, is more than likely to be harmful for us, it causes an imbalance and is "negative."

In this perspective, we consider as **"positive"** (bringing results perceived as favorable) the emotions of joy, happiness, empathy, enthusiasm or satisfaction, which are associated with pleasure.

We consider as **"negative"** emotions of fear, guilt, shame, sadness or anger, which are associated with displeasure and bring results to our life that we perceive as harmful.

♥ Stop, Breathe, Love

The issue that we may face is knowing if emotions considered "positive" or "negative" can both manifest reality? The answer is affirmative.

When using the language of creation of emotion with **"positive"** or **"negative"** emotions about ourselves or others, we manifest in our energy field, in the events, situations, and people we interact with, the subatomic rearrangements of the experienced emotions.

That is because the nature of emotion is to create reality. It is both the language as well as the force of creativity in action. It is a force united to the larger Force, moving in our energy field and in the field of unified consciousness and planetary consciousness, united in the manifestation. Independent of the polarity positive or negative, the materialization of what we sensed emotion ally happens.

What is important to hold is focusing our consciousness on "positive" emotions; we are automatically affected by them because we are their emitter.

It is good for us and for the people we direct them to or for those near us, as well as the collective and the cosmos.

On the contrary, if we focus consciousness on something "negative," emotionally we are immediately creating patterns of energy interference, to experience it internally and externally. It is not good for us, and it also affects the people who are receptive to the "negative" vibrations, as well as the community in which we are integrated, the planet and the universe.

In order to better understand the issue of manifesting emotion, both "positive" and "negative," we are going to use a metaphoric and binary language, highlighting what we have already stated. The "positive" emotion is high speed vibrations, "fine" energy in ascending waves, with the potential to materialize immediately, being the context of energetic expansion. The "negative" emotion sends out low speed vibrations, "dense" energy and in descending waves, with the potential of immediate materialization occurring in a context of energy contraction.

When we experience a positive emotion, we vibrate better and we are open to life. When we experience a negative emotion we do not vibrate so well and we are in tension with life. The positive emotions trigger symmetric and ordered states of flow, in which all systems of energy concentrate and cooperate, in union and for the common good, and internal and external synergies are created so that all the players in the process benefit. On the other hand, the negative emotions have underlying internal states of limitation and disorganization, being that the energetic systems are in effort, become contracted and isolate themselves, creating synergies of loss/gain and separation from what is considered threatening or dangerous.

The emotional environment from the point of view of health, in the case of positive emotions, is conducive to wellbeing at all levels, seeing that there is free flow and order that generates equilibrium. In the case of negative emotions, the internal environment is of contraction and effort, with the organs, systems and cells working much more to compensate for the disorganization. In case the negative emotion is felt with high intensity or the duration of the emotion is excessive, the organism triggers bioenergetic imbalances that could be conducive to illnesses.

Summary:

⊗ The emotions associated with the bottom of the pole, for example, fear, anger, shame or guilt. are in the key of pain and their vibrational frequency is low.

⊗ The energy that will be crystallized in the human energetic system and the individual experiences that will be aligned in resonance with those emotions tend to become dense and cause friction, confusion and disorganization.

⊗ In the wave of these negative emotions, which we focus consciously or on automatic pilot, we permit the emergence or permanence in our lives of people, events, or contexts where emotions are reproduced electromagnetically.

⊗ If we persist in the same type of thoughts, mental images, words, feelings and dysfunctional attitudes, we can feel that we are victims of the circumstances or of others, which is not true.

⊗ We create problems and confusion; we promote disorder which facilitates disease and we feel down; until we change the information that will cause a change of vibration and new results in our life.

⊗ We will also be aligned vibrationally with all the people on our planet that are emitting the same type of negative emotions, increasing the ranks of fear, guilt and anger amongst others.

⊗ We cause the vibration of Earth to decrease, who has meanwhile resonated in those dense emotions and retransmitted them to the human community and the field of unified consciousness.

🚀 Exercise to clear your emotions:⊗

1. Close your eyes. Breathe deeply three times.
2. Notice your emotions, they are like waves in an ocean. No matter how tall they may be or seem, you know they will always break towards the shore.
3. Focus on the shore now. Let go.
4. Look at the ocean, it is blue, so blue. You can move freely. You can breathe freely.
5. When you feel ready you may open your eyes.☺

♥ Stop, Breathe, Love

The emotions associated with the top of the pole, for example, happiness, joy, satisfaction and sympathy, are in the key of pleasure, wellbeing and their vibrational frequency is high, moving at a great speed, and the energy rapidly coagulates in the energy system.

And this is what we can experience:

☺ The individual experiences that will be aligned and in resonance with those emotions lead to lightness, easiness, simplicity and organization.
☺ In the wave of these emotions, we attract and are attracted, electromagnetically, to people, situations, environments and experiences where the emotions we have been experiencing are mirrored (happiness, joy, sympathy, etc.) We are refeeding the system whether we are conscious of it or not.
☺ If we persist in the same type of thoughts, images, words, feelings and functional attitudes, we can feel that life is on our side, that there are opportunities and resources for us;
☺ We create easy features and good communication; partnerships of common gain and we foster the natural flow which promotes health. In summary, we optimize all frequencies of life.
☺ These waves of wellbeing and sensations of being in luck and full of energy will be maintained or changed according to the quality of the information that we are processing.
☺ We will also be vibrationally aligned with all people on the planet who are emitting the same type of positive emotions, increasing happiness, joy or sympathy in humanity and we cause a rise in the vibration of Earth.
☺ Earth resonated in those emotions and in turn retransmitted them to human beings and the field of unified consciousness, in a constant movement.

So when we have the perception of emotion, we can immediately ask the following:
Does it make sense to let this live in reality?

Because when we communicate through the emotions we are expressing what we are thinking, what we are feeling or the experiences we have lived or want to experience; we are also using the energetic resources and coded information that on a subatomic level organizes itself and is manifested in our reality with a visible face such as an event, thing, opportunity or person, altering our universe: personal, planetary and the totality.
Choosing emotions is our mission at each moment, because **to emotionalize is to realize.**

More than Emotion

"A change of interpretation changes the meaning of a situation, and as such, changes the emotion experienced."
E. Lazarus

"We all have emotions. What we do with them is the great secret."
Maria Santos

Emotions are part of our daily life and occur when facing the most varied situations, informing us of what is happening, as well as activating mechanisms of adaptation/reaction, responding in relation to the internal or external event that is being experienced. Although emotions occur at great speed and in an almost automatic manner, the issue here is to know if we are able to control its expression or not. That is, is it possible to live an emotion and still channel it or use it in a different manner than the one we are being shown? For example, is it possible when facing an emotion of anguish, to change it, expressing it in a different way, or even make it disappear?

The possibility is there and is totally applicable to our lives, since internally, we have functions to approach the emotional reality we are faced with, and we can change it. Let us explain better. For an emotion to be triggered, first there has to be information that is considered as valid for triggering an emotional response. That is without perceptually catalogued data fit to cause emotion, there is no emotion. This recording of data is stored in our energy field and especially in the reptilian brain, namely in the amygdala or the cingulate cortex. Faced with data considered perceptually useful to trigger an emotion, the proper emotion mechanisms are triggered. In effect, the information that aroused the emotion is **represented** perceptually, and it is in this **process of immediate emotional reevaluation** (and that is processed by the brain, namely the frontal areas, the neocortex) **that we can relativize the emotion, intensifying it or even taking it out of context, expressing it or not. That is, the emotional data is represented internally and perceptually, we give it significance or not, devaluing it or giving it meaning and expressing the emotion or not.**

The moment the stimulus is perceived as valid to evoke an emotion, representing the information so that it can continue its course takes a fraction of a second. The great majority of us are barely aware that it exists. But it is only in this minute space-time of representing the information again (and it always exists), that we have a choice and can decide what to do with the emotion. It is here that we are aware of the emotion, reevaluating her, without being in automatic pilot, what is happening, and we are free to transcend the emotion. It was triggered but can be transformed and channeled according to our decision. This is the moment when we observe the emotion and perceive if it is good for us or not, if it makes sense or not for our life at that moment. It is because of the existence of the process of **representation** of the emotional information that we can take a position regarding the emotion and decide what to do with it. This is a moment of awareness where we can be different from the emotion, changing it or even behaving differently from it. When we do this, we are more than the emotion.

Therefore, it is possible (faced with the same emotional situation, for example, of rejection) for a person to shy away, isolate herself and avoid a person or event, and another person faced with the same situation and in the same context, faces the situation or person, looks for friends and learns with what the emotion is teaching.

I have been through the experience of rejection when I was not invited to some birthday parties. The first "shock" when that happened was experiencing the rejection, but in the next moment there was a thought or a voice that told me: "There is another party for you, where you will be welcomed" and I would find myself doing things that I liked, with people I liked. Quickly, I began to understand who my friends were and saying yes or no assertively.

♥ Stop, Breathe, Love

Having emotions means necessarily being confronted with them, and this confrontation starts immediately as soon as the emotion emerges through the process of representing the emotion.

It is when the emotions are perceptually representing that we see internally the scenario that the emotions are causing. And here we can take out the batteries and devalue the episode, or stress even more what we are feeling, intensifying the emotion, being "shaken" by it or still make a completely different choice than we have ever made before.

Inside us, we have the capacity to observe, choose and learn with the information that the emotion brings. It is true. This is why there are people that in the most varied circumstances, many of them extreme, who can be more than what their emotions tell them.

This was why in spite of the injuries, the suffering and the fear of death that a young man was able to save a friend in a car accident. Or that Buddhist monks, even when being tortured and in suffering, remained praying to show themselves as compassionate instead of hating their enemies. Only if they rose above what the emotion in a first instance was transmitting and causing on a psychophysiological level, could they surpass it.

Our emotions are useful tools on a day-to-day basis, allowing us, namely, to know, assess and interact with ourselves and with the world. But this does not mean that we are at the mercy of emotions, reacting to the stimulus without any type of consideration or maturity.

We are more than emotion. We are the ones who are aware of emotion; who observe emotions and who can change the perception and behavior in relation to emotion. The truth is, we can use emotions in a "positive" manner and grow with them. Using their strength and power to increase our capacities, activities, connections and still communicate even better with ourselves and with others, manifesting reality according to our wildest dreams.

We have all had moments when we felt sadness, and as soon as the sadness was perceptually represented, we thought or felt that it was not worth being sad and relativized whatever was the stimulus for sadness. Or who knows, we may even have made sadness disappear immediately because we decided "not now."

It is necessary to understand that emotions move in the plane of the known, of what is perceptually understood as valid to trigger emotion. For the change of an emotion to be possible, we have to respond in a differentiated manner, that is, enter the unknown in relation to the emotion that we are experiencing. As a general rule, it is in the unknown, that is, outside of the emotional context before us, that we find solutions for emotional experiences that we are living, and that requires us to observe in alternative way, think differently, experience a distinct emotion and, especially, change our behavior.

Here is a testimonial of an act of emotional creativity.

Testimonial

I was brought up in a family where everyone spoke very loudly, even shouting just to state their position in a household issue. Even when I was living in my own home, whenever I visited my family the same scheme was repeated. That was very tiring and made me feel bad because I was always doing what I did not believe was correct and felt angry without knowing why. I noticed that in the relationships with my friends, sometimes the same situation emerged, and I wanted to solve this bad feeling.

After being with Susana, things changed. I understood that I am the sovereign of my universe, and I can change what I feel, what I think and what I do. On one occasion, I went to a café to meet some friends and one of them was talking too loud for my liking and even abruptly. I automatically remembered what I had discussed with Susana. Interpret differently and act differently. I spoke to him softly, serenely and with clarity. He quieted down immediately and for the rest of the evening was always correct with me. From that moment on, our friendship changed and now I am always well treated and respected by this man and friend. This experience had such an enormous impact on me that I decided to apply this also to the case of my family. Now I am not part of the game of shouting or anger, because I am in peace. I choose to say things in another manner, feeling internally firm, and quickly detach from situations instead of ruminating on them. I feel good, and my family appreciates my new way of being, and asks me for advice, which would never occur previously. It was me who chose to understand a different way of being and be the owner of myself and of my emotions, as well as acting in a different way. Thank you, Susana, for your precious help.

Maria Susana, lawyer

Emotional Impact

"Sadness is but a wall between two gardens."
Kahlil Gibran

"Find a place inside where there's joy, and the joy will burn out the pain."
Joseph Campbell

"Only unhappy people can become slaves. A happy person is free: she conquered her independence."
Osho

"When humanity is making love, the conflicts decrease."
Philippe

Emotions are present in our daily lives from the moment we wake up to the time we fall asleep, and they often inhabit our dreams as well. Being alive implies being emotional with ideas, people, events, an animal or works of art. We are systematically choosing what causes us sensations and simultaneously we mark our energetic territory emotionally, as well as that of those who we live with, leaving our emotional fingerprint on the planet and in the cosmos. Emotion is an expressive language and also an impressive one, highlighting what moves us while also showing consistently what makes sense to experience in reality.

Emotion is powerful because it is a communication about what moves us and touches us internally; it is also the mold that crystallizes the energy underlying the emotion, making our energy field, in union with the fields of unified and planetary consciousness, manifest reality.

Becoming emotional is moving from one state to another, moving naturally, the entire universe with us on a path of endless probabilities for realization.

Of the vast number of emotions known to us, those we choose as adequate for a given situation build reality, whether we are aware of it or not, because they are a creational force united with the field of unified consciousness which is the seat of manifested life and life that is to be manifested.

We are fated to create in the act of having an emotion because emotion is the language that the field speaks with us and us with it. Emotion is also the "subtle technology" that imprints form, giving substance and quality to what we observe in reality and that the field of unified consciousness observes in it and through our participation in the world.

The issue that we are really faced with at each moment is not whether emotion creates reality, because that is its nature. **The issue is what reality will we animate through the emotions?**

The practical applicability of emotion is extensive. Any area of our life, situation or moment, has emotions. With emotion, we can build happiness in our home, sadness or satisfaction at work, be slim or accept the body we have, recover our self-esteem, create the depression or the cure for our stomach, and get enough enthusiasm to complete our thesis, or hug our best friend. The emotions are there bringing to life what we evoke with them.

The impact of emotions is real in the world. Better still, they are reality interacting with the reality that everything is made of: subatomic particles in movement, consciousness communicating in a relationship and in interaction with the field of unified consciousness, sculpting life.

Emotionalizing is moving and changing the world as we know it, so that it shows itself to us just like our emotions, in unity with the field of unified consciousness that places "online" what we experience emotionally as individuals, and as a human community, in a gigantic and intricate mirror of life.

♥ Stop, Breathe, Love

Since ancient times, the medical community has been aware that there were emotions that caused disease and made recuperation difficult, such as anger or melancholy, and that other emotions were synonymous of health and promotes healing, for example, joy and satisfaction.

Alongside this, popular and even religious knowledge also urged people to feel better, trust and share love as a form of prevention and release from illnesses. The popular proverb "Happiness is the cure for the bones" or the biblical phrase *"Be happy with the kingdom of heaven"* are examples of this.

We have probably become aware that when we show or keep the feeling of anger, sadness, victimization or grief, the tendency for disease is greater. We become more seriously ill as a result of repeatedly feeding those emotional states, because we are exposed intensely to those emotionally distorted vibrations. For example, heartbreak, grief, loss and the recycling of those thoughts, images or sensations that feed the "negative" emotions, provoke more imbalance and reinforce disease.

In truth, emotions build health or illnesses, and the fact of us recycling what makes us feel ill, causes a deficit in our energy system. On the other hand, stimulating what makes us feel good, revitalizes us.

The "negative" emotions place the organism in stress, overloading the vital functions, and can create dysfunctions on a cellular level, causing disease or limiting the recovery of the same. For example, a person who is systematically angry, who becomes stressed at the smallest stimulus, who is highly competitive and who wants to control everything around, has a greater predisposition for a heart attack, than another who faces all situations calmly, managing the stimuli received in a balanced manner, who is able to delegate and create synergies with partners who he trusts.

Scientific studies carried out to assess hostility and anger and its consequences on a cardiovascular level showed surprising conclusions. "Experiments done on males proved that *men who are hostile, that shout, get cross and direct anger to the exterior at the smallest sign of annoyance, namely when they have to wait, are at a bigger risk of having heart attacks as well as suffering from cardiovascular diseases.* In another scientific experiment, also carried out with men, where they were asked not to express anger—contrary to what we thought—blood pressure dropped, and the homeostatic recuperation was much faster.[3] Although women have, as a general rule, lower blood pressure, the expression of anger is susceptible to having the same reaction as in the case of men."

We use emotions in the internal dialogues in the attitudes that we have with ourselves, in what we express to others, and what we feel from others and we communicate that to the field of unified consciousness regarding health and the absence of it. These subtle or evident communications that we emit or very often receive—every hour, over weeks, months or years—gain dysfunctional forms because what we have been communicating to the organism was to become tense, painful, without strength or broken. The intelligence inherent to life responds accordingly. Illness or health is constructed, and it is up to us to decide what we want to bring to life. We can animate ourselves with other emotions and experience health.

It is scientifically proven that "negative" emotions can cause changes to the level of neural receptors, which become distorted, preventing cells from receiving the necessary quality and quantity of nutrients, affecting cell division. People who experience emotions such as shame, guilt or sadness repeatedly or experience peaks of great intensity of those emotions, are susceptible to inflammatory processes, the alteration of blood pH and develop viral infections that could cause more serious

---

[3] Chesney, M.A. and Rosenman, R.H. (eds), Anger and Hostility in Cardiovascular and Behavioural Disorders, Hemisphere/ McGraw Hill, London, 1985.

diseases, namely cancer. The alteration of the emotional state of guilt or shame for liberation and forgiveness is capable of healing and allows the natural resources to return to equilibrium. There are numerous cases of remission of cancer associated with the freeing from grudges and guilt that has been kept for years, which at a given moment, the person allowed to leave. Regarding this, I remember a lady that consulted me about a health issue around the vaginal area. After telling me about an episode in her life, for which she felt guilty, and having forgiven what had happened, she recovered her health and the gynecologist congratulated her.

In summary:

- The emotions that we emit can be constructors of health or disease, depending on the information contained and the way they are susceptible to being coagulated.
- Dysfunctional information allows the possibility of subatomic rearrangements with dysfunctional forms.
- Ordered information permits the possibility of ordered subatomic rearrangements. It is up to us to choose, moment by moment, what we want to bring to life in unity with the field of unified consciousness, through the emotions that we are communicating and the achievements underlying these.
- To emotionalize is to materialize, and our organism responds in consonance with the emotions we have because it is always listening.
- So be careful with the emotions that you are feeding, because they are powerful forces in the upkeep of health.

♥ Stop, Breathe, Love

Another emotion that has an impact on health and affects the immune system, positively or negatively, is expectation. Positive expectations activate the immune system and negative expectations depress it.
The book *Love, Medicine and Miracles* by Dr. Bernie Siegel describes an experiment done by the psychologist Shlomo Breznitz in Jerusalem, where he intended to establish the relationship between positive and negative expectations and the immune system. This study showed that expectations are able to cause hormonal alterations in the levels of cortisol and prolactin in the bloodstream which affect the immune system.
"The experiment consisted of giving various groups of soldiers different information regarding the number of kilometers they would have to walk in adverse conditions. It was found that the hormonal levels were altered according to the positive or negative perspective of the effort the soldiers would have to put in, with the route in itself being the least important factor."[4]
"It is not only expectation that affects the immune system, emotions of frustration, anger and compassion also affect it. Scientific experiments show that there is a direct correlation between negative and positive emotions and the levels of segregation of salivary immunoglobulin A (SIgA) which is a primary antibody in the defense of the organism and the variation in the amount of salivary immunoglobulin A is an indicator

---

[4] Siegel, B.,"Love, Medicine and Miracles", Harper & Row, 1986, Summarized from pg. 53 of the Portuguese edition.

of the response of the immune system to infections."

Dr. Glen Rein, Dr. Mike Atkinson and Dr. Rollin McCarthy, of the Institute of HeartMath carried out an experiment to discover the effects of anger, frustration and compassion on human beings, and if it was possible to establish a correlation between these emotions and the levels of salivary immunoglobulin A (SIgA) and if there were any effects, for how long would the emotions affect the salivary immunoglobulin A (SIgA) and the respective immune system.

During the experiment, the individuals experienced the specific emotional states of frustration and anger intensely as well as of compassion and care (through the self-induction of those emotions or watching films that caused those emotions) for about five minutes. Saliva was collected for tests before and after experiencing these emotions. *"It was found that the negative emotions of frustration and anger caused a decrease in the concentration levels of salivary immunoglobulin A (SIgA) during five hours. On the other hand, with the positive emotions of compassion and care, there was an increase in the concentration levels of salivary immunoglobulin A (SIgA) during the next six hours after experiencing these emotions."*[5]

This experiment makes us think. Actually, five to six hours of effects in our immune system as a result of experiencing an emotion (negative or positive) wakes us up to the fact that if we wish to be healthy, we have to choose "positive" emotions instead of "negative."

The truth is that because it is us who receive the information and give it emotional significance, we can decide how to react to the stimulus and act in a differentiated manner, expressing the emotion or not, channeling the emotion or not, and neutralizing the emotion or even intensifying it.

Let us stop saying that it is because of others that events or external things that make us irritated, frustrated, or angry or embittered. It is because of us, we decided to react in that manner, either consciously or automatically, to the stimulus provided to us. The same applies to the "positive" emotions such as joy, satisfaction or care. The events, the things or other people were only the energetic impulse we accepted and interpreted as valid, to respond with joy and happiness.

Understanding this and practicing it is having emotional maturity and being responsible for what we feel and see in the world. Now we know that if we have one of those days when we are having a tantrum and frustration, we are telling our immune system to become fragile, inviting viruses and bacteria to enter our bodies. On the other hand, if we have compassion for ourselves and others, or care for others, we are communicating to the immune system to become more active, which means that the antivirus and antibacterial system of the person is high, and that the other systems, organs and functions can perform with greater vitality.

Emotions are energy, light in movement in a determined frequency that enter into resonance with other systems of energy as in the case of cells or organs, creating force fields that come together and manifest according to the vibration/instruction

---

[5] "Physiological and Psychological Effects of Compassion and Anger," Rein, Glen., Atkinson, Mike., and McCraty, Rollin HearthMath Institute, Journal of Advancement in Medicine, 1995; 8 (2) 87105. Summarized from text

contained in the emotion. In changing the emotions towards health, harmony re-establishes itself in the organism.

♥ Stop, Breathe, Love

We have a choice in relation to the emotions that we nurture and the decision to opt for a certain interpretation of situations, framing them, intensifying them or relativizing them, depends on us. The emotional quality of our days, the experience of positive emotions instead of negative, is decisive for our wellbeing.
In the field of unified consciousness there are endless possibilities for creating health. That is, health is plentiful and is always available to be actualized by an act of consciousness from the human being who chooses it.
Health is an act of quantum creativity and each one of us can exercise it at any moment, in any circumstances, creating the reality of vitality and of wellbeing, aligning it vibrationally with health on an emotional level (joy, satisfaction, happiness, acceptance, compassion). In effect, our energy field listens and understands the messages and the forms that each emotion has, and the field of unified consciousness listens and immediately formats that reality inside us, the planet and within it.

A human being is a luminous quantum composite emitting light at each moment. Biophotons in movement communicate amongst themselves and with the field of unified consciousness, in a conscious conversation, formatting light and information fields that are reality on a fundamental level.
Emotions are subatomic particles and when we express ourselves through them, we emit biophotons that carry luminous information, affecting our cells, organs and functions which emit luminous signs and information in harmony with the emotion. The light in the body in a state of coherence is aligned with positive and organized emotions that communicate and revitalize health.

At each instant we are choosing to feed one emotion in detriment of another; for example, instead of choosing fear, choose love and that choice changes the course of our lives, very often in a way that was unimaginable to us. A small change can make all the difference: for example, deciding to live instead of becoming ill, or even dying. Here is a testimonial of creativity, where it was decided to live, leaving the loss and the pain, opting for nurturing love.

Testimonial

Before attending the seminar on unified quantum healing, I was a very depressed person. Nothing in my life made sense; I had lost my mother nine months before and I simply had no will to live. Internally I believed I would not be able to carry on with my life. I was always dressed in black and my face reflected pain, grief and despair. I complained of everything and everyone. I could not get along with anyone and my excuse, month after month, was having gone through the death of my mother. But the truth was that I already felt this way even before experiencing that loss; I was not living or valuing the life I had. I was a person with a hard face, too hard for my age. With the mourning, this gained bigger proportions. I thought of dying very often. At the time of the seminar, I thought that I wanted to get divorced; I wanted to end seven years of marriage, because nothing was going right. I even had the thought that if I had lived through the loss of my mother, I could also live through a divorce. At the seminar, I understood that I had to carry on with my life, victimizing myself for what had not happened made no sense. I understood that I had a lot of Good things to live. I stopped wearing black.

The mourning was over. Now I have to continue. I have a great will to live. I smile a lot. I sing a lot. I live with a lot of joy. I value everything I have. I love everything I see and everything surrounding me. I love being with people, talking and laughing. I understood that it makes no sense to speak of the past, because there is nothing, I can do to change it; it is important to speak of the present and ensure that it is what we intend. My relationships with the people around me improved, and consequently my marriage did too. I breathe better; I am more calm and serene.

I live with a heart full of love. Love for myself and for life. I have a smile tattooed on my face. I am happy.

Mónica Alves, administrative assistant

To emotionalize is to illuminate and it is up to us to bring light to health by having emotions of joy, love, happiness and satisfaction.

 Exercise to revitalize yourself:

1. Stand up, staying still, and close your eyes.
2. Say to yourself *I am alive*.
3. Inhale deeply from your belly until you can't take in any more air.
4. Exhale until all air has been emptied from your belly area while still contracting this zone.
5. Keep your eyes closed! Now, inhale again while picturing a pink balloon of energy.
6. Keep the air in your belly for a few seconds, then let it all out and feel the energy spreading throughout your body.
7. Inhale again while picturing a green balloon of energy.
8. Hold your breath while counting silently to three, then let it all out again, and feel the energy spreading throughout your body.
9. Repeat these steps until you've reached seven. Feel free to count higher if you feel comfortable, alternating the colors (pink and green).

♥ Stop, Breathe, Love

Can the emotions of others affect our health? And do we have to accept them or validate them so that they have an effect on us? In effect, yes.
Other people's emotions **can** interfere with our health **if we allow it**. We just need to accept (even if unconsciously) the information transmitted, for it to be installed in our energy field and be able to produce effects. For example, someone irritated at work, full of stress, screaming and shouting. Those emotions can influence the health of our colleague, transmitting irritation or stress, if one allows it.

It is also possible to positively affect the health of another. For example, we visited a friend in hospital and we are full of joy and love and he feels much better in your presence. Or a friend who is frustrated with a pain in the stomach and our happiness and satisfaction affects him, causing him to feel well, without pain. Besides these possible situations, we can also be affected by emotions associated with illness (facilitating it or building it in public places), as a result of the information disseminated by social media. Another example: the exposure to disease, or the emotion of pity or repugnance for a person who is begging because he is blind, handicapped or has a tumor on his face which causes repugnance. This tendency to expose suffering, or the "poor thing" and even compete in terms of suffering, is a program culturally installed in Judeo-Christian societies, and the absurd paradox is that we are convinced that the one who suffers the most is the "best" person. Emotional expressions of misfortune are exploited and faced with this, we can be programmed for the suffering, pity, "the poor things," and the excluded.

If we so choose, we can be compassionate and caring instead of feeling pity or "the pain of others." Besides improving our immune system and moving us into action, these emotions also influence the well-being of the person we focus our attention on. In this way, we make the difference and a great one. In fact, where we focus our attention, we move the creation point and in this case to health.

On the other hand, the focus that social media gives to disease is greater than the focus it gives to health (a pathology is talked about and explained a million times more than the numerous health cases that are the norm and not the exception). The fear of disease and of suffering and sometimes panic can be installed this way. For example, the fear of avian flu.

Obviously the role of warning society and preventing disease is being taken care of and that is the aim; the issue is inundating the population with the same type of information and with "negative" emotions, predisposing them for disease (in case it is inadvertently accepted).

In parallel, the emotions expressed by friends and family can also influence us (if we allow it, obviously). For example, a grandmother who is scared of catching a disease, is always tense, cowers and cringes and will not be touched, and is washing her hands constantly, can pass the fear of disease to a child or an adult who she interacts with.

How do we validate or accept emotions?

Focusing our attention on them, identifying ourselves with them and with the people who experience them, believing that these are real, and it can only be like that. From the moment we accept the emotion, although unconsciously, identifying ourselves with the person and their environment, we send that information to our energy field and simultaneously to the field of unified consciousness, making the information available for materialization. That is more emotions and situations aligned with that vibration. In that case, we are potentiating disease instead of health.

The next question is this: **How can I stay neutral in relation to the emotions of others (when they are very often, full of good intentions), sharing their experiences of illness with me?**

Keep your attention focused on health, and do not accept that it has to be so. Staying emotionally neutral or then, in a state of emotional positivity. Not identifying with the situations or people that experience it, because there are other choices, there

are other emotional realities.
One of the things that you can do faced with an emotion that you consider "negative" is to cocoon yourself in a sphere of pink light and think automatically:
"I choose to see love in this situation" or "open up yourself to health on all levels" or "There is an alternative reality for you and me now."
With this attitude, leave aside the emotional roller coaster of others and keep your **emotional soberness**. Each one of us who has that behavior, is doing the emotional reprogramming for you, for the family, friends and the community, raising the vibrational level of the planet and the cosmos.
We are responsible both individually as well as collectively for health, and each emotion in harmony with wellbeing and happiness is a valuable contribution. We can do it today, now, with us, with family, friends, strangers, work colleagues, or the internet. We keep ourselves in a state of emotional soberness affecting life positively. This information and enformation which we give through emotional soberness creates health in unity with the field of unified consciousness, for us and for humanity, in a harmonious movement of wellbeing and joy. It is necessary to persist at each moment to see concrete results in our lives and in the All.

♥ Stop, Breathe, Love

Emotions are the "technology of creation" and have the power of multidimensional affectation. That is, they affect the human being from a physical, mental, emotional and spiritual point of view, as well as, interfering with reality on all levels, namely with water, plants, animals, objects and with the collective consciousness.
How is this possible? That is what we are going to address next.

The impact of emotions on water. Water molecules are affected by human emotions, organizing themselves according to the specific information that the emotion carries, creating forms in harmony with that information. "Negative" emotions molecularly distort water, which shows patterns without form and "positive" emotions molecularly organized water to show patterns of symmetric forms. These form patterns are transmitted to the energy fields that water is communicating and interacting with, modifying them.
One of the scientific experiments about the power of emotions to affect water and plants that impressed me the most, was done by Dr. Bernard Grad, professor at the University of Montreal, Canada, who did various experiments with water and the energy that could be transmitted to it. Glass bottles filled with water from the tap were placed for fifteen minutes between the hands of someone who has a gift for looking after plants; others were placed in the hands of a person suffering from depression and then the water was used to water plants in the same stage of development and of the same species.
"What was found was that the water charged with the energy of a person who had the gift of looking after plants caused a significant increase in the growth of the plants and, on the contrary, the water charged with the energy of a depressed person, promoted a regression on the level of development of the plants, considering the

growth pattern for that species."[6]

In fact, the influential power of the energy of emotion is impressive.

This experiment proves that the depressed patient affected the development of the plants. A person in that state of depression experiences emotions of sadness, pain, hopelessness and even possibly the loss of the will to live. These emotions influenced the water and the plants in such a way that the plants regressed in their growth, that is, "involved." The "negative" emotions were incorporated in the energy field of the water and the plants and deformed the normal developmental rhythm of the plant, delaying it.

On the other hand, the person with the gift for looking after plants who was experiencing the emotion of care (and possibly of satisfaction, contentment and joy in caring for the plants), passed these emotions to the energy field of the water and the plants, promoting their growth.

We are 70% water; imagine then the number of times that when drinking water you are emotionally vibrating in sadness or depression, and what does that do to your body? Evidently, nothing good. Or how is it possible to drink water and selectively choose to be joyful and happy, embedding those emotions in our body and having vitality and wellbeing?

We can consider, as a result of the above experiment, and also accept as possible, that what is growing in our life is affected by the emotions that we emit, namely to our children.

Children need "positive" emotions to have healthy "emotional" food for their development, namely the emotion of caring and joy. Negative emotions are weeds that could decrease or put in effort on their beneficial development. As such, are we open to living in emotional positivity, also for the wellbeing of our children?

Caring for emotions is an act of intelligence and sensibility benefitting us and those we love and what surrounds us. Returning to the plants and the possibility of human emotions affecting them, what happens when we are experiencing an emotion is that the plants capture the emotional information in their energy field, process it and then mirror it in a clear manner. We are always in communication and interaction with the quantum world, and the plants, just like us, as subatomic entities equipped with consciousness, mirror the fundamental link underlying reality, and simultaneously share it with us, with the field of unified and planetary consciousness.

♥ Stop, Breathe, Love

Emotions also affect animals. The truth is animals capture our emotions; they feel them and respond. How many times have we been through the experience of being happy and the dog kept jumping and barking with joy? Very often. And also when we go through loss or moments of great loneliness, the cat or dog affectionately went to sleep with us, even if that was not the norm; he would be around us and licking is affectionately. My dog was an expert in knowing my emotional state and took care of me perfectly. I am sure that anyone who has a pet knows that the animal is aware of the emotions that the "owner" is experiencing. My friend Salomé says when she is sad,

---

[6] Grad, B., The Biological Effects of the "Laying On Of Hands" on Animals and Plants: Implications for Biology. In Schmeider, G, ed.; Parapsychology: Its Relation to Physics, Biology, and Psychiatry, Metuchen, NJ: Scarecrow Press, 1976: 7589.

her cat "purrs" a lot and licks her tears. Another friend, Natasha, gets extra doses of playfulness from her dogs that jump on her shoulders and practically overthrow her when she is happy. It is also common for dogs to sense the fear in someone, and attack at that moment or bark. We may not know how our pets' sense what is going on with us, but it is evident that they know.

A scientific study in Britain led by Dr. Kin Guo of the University of Lincoln, suggests that dogs can detect human emotions and that they look at the face of the owners to sense signs of anger, happiness or sadness, just like human beings do and react to these emotions.[7]

If we consider animals as beings separate from us, as not being connected to a fundamental intelligence and having a material nature, the probability of accepting that they receive and retransmit our emotions is practically null. This objective and materialist vision of life is limited, and strictly speaking, is not real. But now if we broaden our perception of life, and admit that animals, just like us, are information vibrating in the field of unified consciousness, and that emotions are also a subtle information that moves in this field which we all share, and to which we are connected and in constant communication, it is possible to accept that the sharing of information occurs and that animals capture the information and respond in harmony with it.

♥ Stop, Breathe, Love

Is it possible for emotions to affect objects as well? Obviously, yes. And we all know how great or weird this could be. Eighteen years ago. when I heard Christianne Águas speak about this, I thought it was too much, too freaky for my conventional mind. But when I started associating the times when I was out of alignment, I experienced, for example, not having a connection to the mobile phone, or the water heater didn't work in the middle of the shower. In that time, I realized how I was affecting my life/objects with my vibrations. Has something similar happened to you? It seems that everything is conspiring against us or that we have a dark cloud on top of us. The sensation is uncomfortable and internally we know something is amiss.

The truth is that objects are in harmony with our vibrations and respond according to the information we emit, which was a disorder of the energy system. My friend Sofia, who works with computers, very often tells her work colleagues: "The problem with the computer has more to do with you than with the hardware"; she states this because she knows the language of creation. When we are entangled, perturbed, or upside down, the information passes to the objects and interferes with them. Of course, when I am radiating joy, love, or freedom, the messages that I receive from the objects are different, for example from cars, to different devices and you probably experience this too. When we are happy, we emit ordered information and the objects tend to follow order, in tune with the information that we are emitting.

If we think of objects as material things, lifeless, without any relationship with life, it does not appear possible that they are in communication and interaction with us in relation to our emotions. However, objects are energy vibrating, subatomic units and "empty" space in movement, just like our bodies are. We are fields of light interacting

---

[7] Eatherley, D., "How Pet Dogs face up to your moods," New Scientist, 29, October, 2008, based on the work of Guo, K., "Left gaze bias in humans, rhesus monkeys and domestic dogs," Animal Cognition, May 2009, Vol. 12 Issue 3, pp 409418.

with other light fields, and with the field of unified consciousness, which is the field of all fields, and we are not separated from anything, nor absent from communication and interaction with what exists. Just emitting information (and that is happening all the time) to get a response from whatever is able to communicate, and objects, especially our own—which we have a more conscious connection with—communicate and interact with us, responding in harmony with the information emitted, based on the principle of resonance and interconnectivity, assuming vibratory states that materialize.

In case our emotions are negative, the vibration is of tension, the information is disorganized, and it is very probable that the objects behave in a disorganized way, for example, lack of communication, breakdown, deprogrammed, etc. When living positive emotions, the vibration is of fluidity, the information is ordered, and it is very likely that the objects behave in an organized way, for example, there being a better network, more battery, faster actualizations or with better performance.

It should be remembered that emotions inform and simultaneously enform reality. They are the **language and the technology of creation** in movement in our lives and in the All. It is now essential to take care of our emotions, because they interfere with the objects (that are abundant) in our daily lives so that we can have a day to day life that is simpler, functional and with improved performance.

♥ Stop, Breathe, Love

Emotions, besides affecting our health, also interfere with interpersonal relationships (be it with family, friends, work colleagues, or any other person) affecting the collective consciousness.

When we are cross, sad or fearful, relationships with others tend to lead to conflict, isolation, competition, denial or lack of communication. The strategies that we invent to deal with the people around us are based on threats, tensions, deficiencies and losses and, obviously, we are closed to go beyond our own belly button. We become heavy, and the tendency is not to create synergies and we do not cooperate with one another for the greater good. We are vibrating in a pattern of separation and separation only builds more alienation and exclusion. And that is not going to make us happier. In fact, it will crystallize in our energy field and on that of those who are in resonance with it: more contradictions and difficulties, when in fact, what we want is a better life. The field of unified consciousness expands what we are emotionally emitting and reality is shown to us as events, issues or people who feed the vibration of fear, sadness or guilt, until we decide to change the emotions.

Changing the emotion, we emit different information that promotes new possibilities in the field of unified consciousness, and simultaneously with our energy fields and the energy fields of others. We can do it, for example, by deciding to smile at everyone today, or take a run to relieve tensions, or neutralizing emotional states with a meditation, or vibrating in light.

Positive emotions give us different signs in relationships and affect us in a different manner. When experiencing positive emotions, we can talk to the boss or a client and get a positive response or even relativize a no; we feel it is a good moment to make the decision to buy a house or sell a business.

When we experience emotions like contentment, satisfaction, joy or sympathy, we are a positive wave for ourselves and for those surrounding us at home, at work, at our voluntary work, at the supermarket and in the world. The relationships we establish are cordial, flexible, of acceptance and the communication flows naturally. We invent ways of dealing with people and situations in which we permit ourselves to trust, assume responsibilities and delegate, as well as share the existing resources. We expand ourselves and include others, cooperating for a general wellbeing where we all profit. We feel light, open to life and concentrate on creating more opportunities for ourselves and other beings. The sensation we have is that good things happen naturally, and we feel good. We spontaneously find the people, the answers, the solutions and life becomes simpler. The field of unified consciousness actualizes the information which we are emitting and people, events or things emerge, in tune with the vibration of happiness, affection and satisfaction, and we build a wave of good things for the whole planet.

Creating good relationships is possible, experiencing predominantly positive emotional states throughout the day. The issue is taking the initiative and maintaining the resolution of doing so systematically, until it becomes a healthy habit.

As it happens, there are a great number of people who, when faced with delicate emotional situations, what they do is state that they are correct and that the others have to change their emotions. Well, since the others only change when they want and how they want, the tendency is that the emotional situations become worse rather than being solved. This attitude is another form of being irresponsible, because we transfer the power of what we are feeling (the emotions we are experiencing, and how we act) towards others, and that will not make us reach where we say we want to go. In effect, we are competent in changing the way we respond to emotional stimuli, and a small change has an enormous impact on us and on others. Instead of thinking "What can I do with my positive emotion if I am only one and in the office we are twenty?" or "I am not so powerful as to affect or change others," we can think and feel that each emotion we raise is a very powerful vibration that changes the face of the whole universe, because we are that universe linked to the universe.

The truth is that we are one person (amongst twenty) made of the same substance that everything is made of—vibrating energy—and this energy affects and is affected by energy. **Who We Are changes everything.**

In addition, emotion is energy in movement, subatomic particles in a dance in our field in unison with the field of unified consciousness. An alteration in the vibrational quality of the field is reflected in the All and enables change on the emission point of the All that emits it and in the fields that are in communication and interaction with it. One is all, and we all are one.

On a fundamental level, the exchange of energetic information and interaction is happening at each moment, and the materialization is the result of that constant dialogue. *In accordance with this, a drop of emotion causes the overflow of an ocean of possibilities, and waves of form are manifested as a result of a single drop united to one ocean.*

And further, our issue is not knowing if we are powerful in relation to others and if we are able to affect or change them. Because effectively we are the power, and the reality is that we affect each other, at each moment of our lives and changes are always happening.

The issue involves the assumption that the power is within us, and in everyone,

and that our intention, emotion and action of internal and external change will cause the collapse of the new possibilities in the multidimensional hologram that is life, affects all human beings and the planet in unison with the field of unified consciousness.

The power assigned to us, which is immanent to the human condition, is that we are the creators of reality and not mere spectators of the world.

We are those that observe reality and take part in it, selecting one amongst endless quantum possibilities at our disposal at each moment. When selecting the emotion of joy, peace or happiness, we are activating waves of form that come into resonance with other waves, building quantum scenarios that are materialized and raising more well-being for the world in unity with the field of unified consciousness.

Each one of us is the epicenter of the universe and we have the power to affect the community. Even a small number can cause a great impact, and it depends also on the quality of our emotions. Emotions of peace and joy create energetic coherence and are powerfully affecting reality. Scientific experiments done in the scope of transcendental meditation, where people meditated, in accordance with advanced techniques, to create peace internally, affecting the cities where they lived. The studies revealed that the coherent emotions caused a decrease in the violent crime index: *"In the city of Manila, during the time when the meditators were focused and lived in internal peace, the violent crimes decreased 23% and the meditators represented only 1% of the city's population."*[8]

We can start by being those who vibrate in joy and in peace constructing a better world, be part of the 1% that contributed to the emotional coherence and soberness that benefits us and that is for the good of all beings.

♥ Stop, Breathe, Love

At this stage, we have understood that to emotionalize is creating, bringing to life what we feel in unity with the field of unified conscious ness and the planet. Emotion is an act of personal creativity allowing us to express dreams, hopes, visions, beliefs and objectives, both individually and collectively, in everyday life, and that is linked to the creativity of the field of unified consciousness and the planet.

Through it, we can manifest any reality. From a plane ticket to a tropical paradise, dancing entwined under the stars, frustration at work, disease or the recovery of health. Everything is possible. That is because emotion is a wave of possibilities vibrating in the field of unified consciousness and has the potential of materializing immediately, not being limited by space nor by time, it is simply reality, united to the reality that is always present.

The moment to have an emotion is always in the present and from that decision, immanent forces of life itself communicate and interact with each other so that the emotion occurs. Entwined as we are in each other, in events and in life, we cause the emergence of events, in a team with the field of unified consciousness. It can be people crossing our path, special sensations, objects emerging, or having the means for what we desire. Very often it happens that the results appear instantly, as if coming from nowhere, sometimes they take time, which can vary between minutes, hours, weeks

---

[8] "Consciousness as a field: The Transcendental Meditation and TMSidhi program and changes in social indicators," Journal of Mind and Behavior, 8(1), 67104, 1987.

or months. The more coherent we are with the emotion that we are feeling, the greater the probability of immediate manifestation.

Emotions are the raw material of creation and are available to materialize what we desire. *They are the force united to the Force that feels and moves infinite possibilities, of which we are one of them and with which we cooperate and participate in the dance of life.*

Taking care of our emotions and being in a state of openness, soberness and emotional coherency is the way that enables us to have quality of life and manifesting the reality that makes us happy and it is for the good of all.

Who Are We? We are the ones who emotionalize, moving heaven and Earth in a resounding encounter with our will to mold the world.

The choice and the power of this "consciousness technology" is already with us, available 24 hours per day, 365 days per year, being exercised in accordance with our freedom of choice. Let us remember that the human family is counting on us to live in a world of peace, joy and unity, and that this step of happiness exists in us, and is dependent on us, always.

Every day, at each instant, we persist in the emotions that elevate us, which make us feel connected, loving, powerful, capable and with enthusiasm. Life thanks us.

 Key points:

- Emotion is energy in movement.
- Emotion is the language that the field speaks with us and us with it.
- Emotions influence human beings from a physical, mental, emotional and spiritual point of view and create reality.
- Each emotion has an impact in our life, others' lives and in the material world as we know it.
- The field is like a mirror showing our emotions, our creations and we can change them as often as we like.
- Emotionalizing is moving and changing reality as we see it. We can manifest what we want: a new job, our passions, connection with the divine, the car, a gift, the trip, or good friends.
- Our emotions can affect people near us and even at a distance. Stay aware.
- Emotions expressed by friends and family can influence us if we allow it. Say No to negative vibes and direct your focus and emotions on love, joy, freedom and exhilaration.
- Emotions matter and create matter.
- Positive and negative emotions effectively affect our health.
- Recycling what makes us feel ill causes a deficit in our energy system. On the other hand, stimulating positive emotions, what makes us feel good, revitalizes us.
- Children need positive emotions to have healthy "emotional" food for their development.
- Animals are connected to the field, sense our emotions and respond in harmony.
- Emotions interfere with the objects in our daily lives. Negative ones create blockages, malfunctions and disorganization. Be aware of your vibes today.

- The collective consciousness is affected by our emotions—peace, safety on the streets, and famine extinction is in our hands.

Self-reflection:

① What is emotion for you?

② What emotions have you experienced when reading this chapter?

③ This week, have you had any emotion that was triggered by an external stimulus? How did you react?

④ What emotions did you cause in yourself with your thoughts, your images or behaviors?

⑤ Remember a situation in which you emotionally responded to the same person, idea or event in a distinct manner. Write about it.

⑥ Is it clear to you, that you are constructing disease or health with your emotions? What are you choosing at this moment?

⑦ Which scientific experiments referenced in the chapter had an impact on you and what will you do with the information they provide?

⑧ What objectives do you want to achieve and what positive emotions can you feel to materialize them?

⑨ Describe an experience where you felt connected emotionally to a group (for example, at a concert, a football game, in a meditation, etc.). What "positive" emotions will you feed in a conscious manner to the collective from now on?

An exercise to access the messages that the emotions want to transmit to you.

Find a place where you can be quiet and without interruptions and turn off any telephones. Sit or lay down. Breathe deeply, slowly, five times, and allow yourself to consciously feel your breathing and your body. Now center your attention on your chest, more appropriately on your heart, and imagine yourself breathing through the heart. Relax even more and observe. If you could give a color to this emotion, what color would occur to you? If this emotion had a shape what would it be? Is there any part of the body that emerges linked to this emotion? Be aware of what emerges. Relax even more and continue breathing through the heart, feeling it.

Now ask yourself internally, what does this emotion want to tell me? And see what appears: it can be a sound, a voice, and image, a memory, a dream, etc. and accept whatever comes as the possibility of an answer. Then allow that information/sensation to rise towards the sun, go in and dissolve it in the light and spread light throughout your body and life. Breathe deeply various times, and only when you are ready, you should get up. Meanwhile I suggest you carry out another activity, preferably manual, to allow that more information comes to you. If the message that the emotion transmitted to you contains an action, and as long as it is beneficial to you, consider carrying out the behavior suggested in the twenty-four hours immediately after or on the date or moment that may have been indicated.

10 Feeling

Story
A long time ago, in a distant town, a story was told about a rich man who searched for happiness. He consulted oracles to find an answer, but none of them made sense to him. He decided to continue seeking as he still felt unhappy.
One day, walking down the street, he passed a woman who had a penetrating gaze that radiated knowledge. He decided to ask her where he could find happiness. She replied that he would find it internally. He responded immediately, saying that in his interior there was not any happiness. The women looked at him fixedly and said: "In one hour, bring me two kilos of flour and half a kilo of sugar and maybe we can find it." The rich man did so even though he was not convinced. When he arrived again, strangely, the woman told him, "Now that you have brought me the flour and sugar, show me the cake." The rich man immediately replied in exasperation, "In order to make cake I first need to knead the flour with the sugar, allow it to rise, bake, and only then can I hand it over to you. I cannot understand what this has to do with happiness?"
The woman then replied smiling that happiness is a decision and, also a process of achievement just like the cake: "It is necessary to decide to bake a cake, knead it, give it sweetness, trust that it is there even when you cannot see it, let it rise, know how to taste the moment, and share it."

"Man now needs for his salvation only one thing: to open his heart to joy."
Bertrand Russell

"Laugh and the world laughs with you."
Ella Wilcox

"I slept and dreamt that life was joy. I awoke and saw that life was service. I acted and behold, service was joy."
Rabindranath Tagore

It is possible that at one time in our lives we have been searching for happiness, just like the character in the story. Did we look for it internally? It is also likely that we wanted an instant formula for happiness. Well, the wise woman in the story spoke of a decision, a process and also an action for the achievement, as well as sharing.
Feelings are a unique dimension in life. They mark and color our day-to- day lives with unparalleled quality, allowing us to imprint subjective impressions in the universe that we inhabit.
The first question I asked myself was, **"Are feelings and emotions the same thing?" No! They are different.**
What is feeling? In a wider sense, it is energy vibrating, consciousness in movement, and light pulsating in the field of consciousness, affecting life.
In addition, it is an affective and subjective impression experienced by a human being supported by the senses. It is also the **language and the "technology of creation," placed at the service of human consciousness for it to build reality.**

What is the origin of feelings? Feelings have their source in the field of unified consciousness, because it is the seat of all life. As fields of human consciousness, we also produce feelings and Earth's field of consciousness also reproduces them and these are the three origins of feelings:

❶ Unified consciousness
❷ Individual consciousness
❸ Planetary consciousness

Strictly speaking, the origin of feeling is just one, the field of unified consciousness, which is the matrix of life in a potential state and also in a manifested state. We merely refer to this tripartition for the sake of exposition and making it understood.

❶ Feeling from the field of unified consciousness

Feeling from the field of unified consciousness is energy in movement, both in a potential as well as in a manifested state, linked to the existing fields of consciousness. It is also pure information, radiating love, beauty and truth for all beings. The feeling that originated in the field of unified consciousness is also primordial light that illuminates the universe.

The human consciousness, in resonance with the field of unified consciousness receives this information, energy and light through the higher senses, namely, empathy, inspiration, intuition, clairvoyance, or the sense of self and the conscious/brain matrix makes it compatible and intelligible so that we can understand it and use it.

Feeling from the field of unified consciousness is **alocal**, able to be "quantumly" represented in two or more locations simultaneously and can be accessed immediately by innumerous conscious beings. Feeling from the field of the unified consciousness is **atemporal**, transcending the limits of linear time, and we are able to access feelings independently of the moment of their occurrence, be it an event in the future or in a distant time (past), and still share them with other beings in the moment we perceive them.

Feeling from the field of consciousness is **holographic**, being represented in the All and in every manifestation of totality that completely mirror itself. Even individualized or divided, this feeling still reunites in itself all the attributes that the field of consciousness has and can be accessed and transmitted immediately in every "focal point." Feeling from the field of unified consciousness can be experienced or shared immediately by innumerous consciences and can also be actualized and retransmitted to other dimensions and beings, emerging from "nothing" and vanishing to "nothing."

Human beings have the faculty of accepting or rejecting feelings that comes from the field of unified consciousness. When you accept it, you feel connected and deeply in communion with the cosmos.

I am going to share an experience that I had, where I experienced a feeling of a loving unity with the field of unified consciousness. I had gone to England to do an internship at the Waldorf school, and was living with a very friendly family in the countryside. After three weeks of an almost monastic life of just going to school, and in spite of the lively family chatting with me on a daily basis, I felt lonely and isolated because there was nothing to see in that little village in the countryside besides one illuminated street and cows. It was the 29th of September, Saint Michael's day, when, at about 5 pm, I went for a walk in the countryside and still felt desolate. I returned home and decided to meditate. I began to meditate to talk to the divine and explain how I felt. I really wanted to be heard, understood and be seen through the eyes of God, because I was not able to see anything worthwhile.

I was affirming internally that I would like to be seen as God saw me with all conviction, when suddenly I felt invaded by a feeling of love and beauty; I saw myself big, luminous and loved by the whole universe. I was ecstatic, deeply moved and connected to a feeling that was "greater" than I was. In fact, I saw myself how God saw me — complete, blessed, healthy, unique—and the love was so strong and intense that my cells were noisy, joyful, and shiny. The light remained inside me and around me, and I felt that everything in me and around me was beautiful. I was in loving unity with life, everything made sense, and was right, and I only had to interact with that love. Time stopped and I could only feel life flowing. I am not sure how long that experience lasted, maybe an hour or more. I know that during the rest of that afternoon and evening, I was expanded, loving and joyful like I had not felt for a long time. After a good dinner, the English family presented me with a piano recital and singing that made me feel at home. Still today, when I remember this episode, I feel invaded by the love and the warmth that this great feeling brought me.

❷ Feeling arising from the individual consciousness

Our consciousness/brain matrix builds feelings through the information it receives via the sixteen senses, processing it, giving it sense and context, and then expressing it in the human energy system. This process of living at the level of the feeling is felt internally both on the level of the soul, the mind, as well as the body. For the production of a feeling, the consciousness/brain matrix entwines the information from a sensation, idea or image in an intelligible form; the feeling is the expression of this cocktail of information. Feelings from the field of human consciousness can be considered as an internally produced ray that discharges light in the energy field, across the body and gives it the indication of a determined, affective, mental and anemic state which is happening. The range of feelings varies greatly from love, truth, and compassion, to sadness or distrust and at each moment, we are choosing the feelings we want to experience.

Feeling from the field of human consciousness is a wave of energy and self-produced light that is in direct communication with the field of unified consciousness and Earth's field of consciousness, affecting both the human energy field as well as the fields of unified and planetary consciousness.

❸ Feeling arising from the planetary consciousness

The planet we inhabit is a consciousness linked to all consciousness existing on it, emitting information to it and to the field of unified consciousness. It also systematically receives information from all human beings and the field of unified consciousness.

A human being, as an intelligent entity with the capacity for creating reality, actively participates in the existing information on Earth, radiating energy, light and information in a constant manner. The feelings, when experienced by each individual or group of human beings, continue to vibrate in Earth's field of consciousness. It accepts these and retransmits them to human beings in the same vibrational frequency, as well as to the field of unified consciousness. Each individual or group of humans, when receiving this information, has the capacity to accept it, change it or reject the information of the feeling evoked, feeding again the planetary consciousness.

Our next step is to better understand the function of feeling in our lives. Let us say, right now that it is **creating reality**.

❤ Stop, Breathe, Love

Feelings are informational vibrations pulsating in the field of unified consciousness, our field and in the planetary field, throughout the day, and allow us to communicate, with ourselves, others, with Earth and the field of unified consciousness.
This exchange of information is being permanently actualized, and informs us, and gives us form and is formative of the reality that is shown to us.

☺ **A feeling informs us** because it is a set of data that we accept and produce in our consciousness/brain matrix and enables ourselves to take a position on it.
☺ **Feeling gives us form** because in the act of processing it, we reorganize ourselves on a number of levels, from physical, mental and spiritual and we notice differences in terms of neural, muscular, hormonal segregations, speed of thought, or our mental images, humor, feelings of connection or separation. The body, mind and spirit make evident the process of feeling and make it clear.
☺ **Feeling is formative of reality** because the field of unified consciousness recognizes the language of feeling, and this information, when emitted, is a force that interferes with the Force, co-linked to the existing fields of energy and information, allowing the manifestation of forms, contexts, events, situations or states.
Feelings are reality interfering with subatomic reality, forming life and we perceive it on various levels.
Before the feeling, the subatomic particles vibrate in a state of indetermination, undulating in our energy field and in the ocean of infinite possibilities. When experiencing a feeling, the subatomic entities assume a position or a defined quality as subatomic particles and enform reality.

Feeling organizes and formats the subatomic reality in accordance with the information and sensation contained in them.
Feelings manifest reality with the contour, quality, color and personal sensibility which is accepted and reproduced by the field of consciousness. This formative act brings people, circumstances, events or objects, who are vibrating in harmony with the waves of form emitted by the feeling, and we see them synchronized in unity with the field of unified and planetary consciousness.
We can meet a family member we have not seen for twenty years, be called for an interview, be grateful for having survived, argue with our mother, or feel jealous because our partner received a phone call, creating realities in every instant.

Feeling is then informing and enforming reality according to personal sensibility or desire, speaking the language and using the "technology of creation."

Discovering Feelings

"Sentiment is that which only we feel."
Dante Milano

"There are times in life when we should be quiet and let silence speak to the heart."
Jacques Prévert

"When the mind is pure, joy follows like a shadow that never leaves."
Buddha

In my discovery of feelings throughout my life, I asked myself many questions, to better understand what I felt and learn how to deal with it. Often, I received immediate responses internally; I had an intuition about what was happening, understood the meaning of the situation and would receive information about how to behave next time.
Other times I had to look further, for example, through meditation, through focusing thought on a subject or through feeling the situation again. I also consulted a lot of scientific research and readings to find the answer I was looking for.
The approach shown here is linear and is summarized because there is much more to be said and practiced. For effect, I have workshops where this information is broadly explained and practiced, and in my next book this topic will be explained more profoundly.
The great majority of us confuse emotions with feelings, and even authors in the field of psychology, neurology or self-help place them all in the same "basket," when they are very distinct things. In effect, both emotion and feeling are information captured by the senses, which is processed by the consciousness/brain matrix, giving it context and significance. As a result of an emotion, or a feeling, we go from one state to another. And both an emotion and a feeling have repercussions in the body, mind and soul.
While an emotion is essentially an automatic response to a given stimulus that has the underlying mechanisms of survival and or adaptation, a feeling is a sensitive cognitive elaboration, much higher than emotion, which is permeated by the affections. Feeling is the imprint of the soul that is neurally woven, expressing itself in the mind and in the sensations, which the body reflects.
Where do we feel emotions and feelings? We feel emotions and feelings in the human energy field; feelings and emotions are experienced simultaneously in the body, causing physical sensations, and we also feel changes on a mental and animic level. For example, we have feelings of hope and notice that we become lighter, expanded, and thoughts or images of hope emerge. Our mood improves, and we gain energy to rise above any situation we may be faced with.
From an evolutionary point of view, human beings first developed emotions, these being the automatic mechanisms of an intelligent response for survival, where the cognitive activity, by itself, was small and routine. Only in more advanced stages, where the survival part was already interiorized, the conditions were created for the

emergence of feelings. **Feelings are a sensitive, intelligent sophistication that result from thoughts and images, entwined with sensations, affections, intuitions and behavioral experiences which are felt in a more embracing and subtle manner.**
Is the process of triggering a feeling or an emotion similar? Yes. That is, both feelings as well as emotions are produced on the level of the consciousness/brain matrix and are triggered based on information that is processed internally. They can be triggered as a result of a thought, an image, a sensation or an experience. For example, we are looking at a photo of our father and feel love and miss him. The issue is that feelings are more intelligent than emotions and take us further as human beings. Feelings are the capacity to use information tempered with sensibility, affection and intelligence. Emotions are basic impulses leading us to a "conditioned" result. The "end" of the emotion is survival, or the adaptation to an environment. On the contrary, the aim of a feeling is the communion, the experience of connection with yourself, with others, with nature and the totality.
It follows that although feelings or emotions are both processed on the level of the consciousness/ brain matrix, the areas dealing with these in the brain are distinct. Actually, from the point of view of the processing of emotions, the areas of the brain that deal with emotional information are more profound areas. The psychologist Daniel Goleman states that it is the reptilian brain, the more primitive brain, which processes emotions such as fear, sadness, disgust or anger. The scientist António Damásio says with a greater precision that emotions are processed on the level of the amygdala and the cingulate cortex, originating responses as a result of *"emotionally competent stimuli"* to trigger emotions. Feelings, as understood by António Damásio, are *"states of mind and the areas concerned with feelings are, namely the superior brainstem and the cerebral cortex."*[1] This permits me to conclude that the areas processing feelings and emotions are different. However, there are emotions and feelings that share the same "places," as in the case of the feeling of compassion and admiration that, in the opinion of António Damásio, occur in the area of the insula, in the anterior cingulate cortex, as well the superior brainstem.[2]
Besides feelings and emotions being processed in different areas of the brain, on an energetic level they are also distinct energies and are dealt with in different "places." We will explain better: from an energetic point of view, a human being is a field of energy and information; it is a universe composed of oscillating energy fields which crisscross and interpenetrate themselves, carrying and exchanging information.
The field of emotional energy is very "close" to the physical body, and is associated with the emotional body (1) and to an energy vortex which is the second chakra (belly—swadhisthana chakra) (2), thus the emotions are experienced rapidly in the body, the whole body, especially on a visceral level.
Yet the energy field of feelings is associated with the astral body (3) and the chakra of the heart (4) seeing that feelings, although capable of being felt throughout the body, have the tendency to be felt more on the chest and also on the frontal and top of the head. Feelings are mediated by the energy of the heart, in correlation with the head. Emotions are associated with the water element and on the level of subtle representation, they are located on the level of the belly (second chakra), more near

---

[1] Damásio, António, *Self Comes to Mind: Constructing the Conscious Brain*, Pantheon, 2010, pg. 151 of the Portuguese edition (Temas e Debates, Círculo de Leitores).
[2] Damásio., *Self Comes to Mind:* de Leitores, pg. 163 of the Portuguese edition.

the feet, of the earth element and are linked to the instinctive component. Yet feelings are associated with the element air, in the chest area closer to the head, the mental part, and are mediated by the wisdom/intelligence of the heart.

On a subtle level, the heart chakra can receive the ascending flow of energy (5) coming from the second chakra (belly swadhisthana chakra) and transforms the emotion into a feeling, just as the heart chakra can receive descending energy flow (6) originating in the chakra of the third eye (7), (mental energy/thought) and transform it into a feeling. It is the chakra of the heart that wisely reconciles the information, expanding it, distributing and storing the information in the human energy field.

1. Emotional body: Subtle energy system that vibrates at a higher speed than the physical body and which has information about the emotions that the person processes and accesses throughout life.
2. Chakra (Sanskrit chakrā) circle or vortex of subtle energy which rotates. The second chakra (belly, swadhisthana chakra), center of energy on the level of the belly which processes, stores and updates the emotional information, distributing it to the physical body.
3. Astral body: System of subtle energy vibrating at a higher speed than the physical body and is associated with the energy of heavenly bodies and to the sensations. The astral body has information about feelings and sensations that the person processes and accesses throughout life.
4. Chakra of the Heart (Anahata): Vortex of vibrating energy located on the level of the chest which processes, stores, distributes and actualizes the information of feelings and distributes to the physical body.
5. Flow of ascending energy: Current of rising energy (In a human being the direction is from the feet up to the head).
6. Flow of descending energy: Current of descending energy. In a human being the direction is from the head down to the feet.
7. Chakra of the third eye (Ajna): Vortex of vibrating energy localized on the level of the forehead, between the eyebrows, which processes, stores, distributes and actualizes the mental information (self-produced thoughts and also intuitions and inspirations) distributing these to the physical body.

Both feelings as well as emotions are energy, information and light vibrating in our field of consciousness, as well as in the field of unified consciousness and the planetary consciousness. They are building tools of reality. Through feelings, we write in the book of life, both our exclusive spelling as well as the unique sensibility that characterizes us. We speak a common language with each other and with the field. We then see woven in the web of life the links and the results that these communications and subtle interactions realized, in a marvelous vital tapestry.

On the Pathway of Feelings

"Do not look for your feelings in others. You will have a full life if you are committed to transforming what you feel in yourself as negative into positive, and a different life if you accept that you are more than that."
Jean, Benedictine Monk

"The worst prison is a closed heart."
Pope John Paul II

"You can complain because roses have thorns, or you can be grateful that thorn bushes have roses."
Tom Wilson

I must confess that since childhood feelings have interested me. Whenever I was sad, I wanted to understand why and free myself from that feeling; whenever I felt happy or loving or being loved, I wanted that feeling to last forever. I thought of feelings as something mysterious and I looked for sense in what I felt and also to find happiness.
Linearly speaking, a feeling is a sensitive intelligent state that moves us internally. A feeling is constructed in the consciousness/brain matrix, which captures information through the senses, for example, vision, smell, touch, empathy or intuition, and processes this data internally. Energetic links are affected and travel through information highways, where informational points (associations) are found. That is, the brain is looking for possibilities of sensations, thoughts, ideas, images or behaviors that we may have experienced. From a perceptual point of view, in case that information has significance and is recognized as valid from the sensitive cognitive point of view, we develop a feeling.
Although what triggers a feeling may originate externally or internally, it is always internally that the feeling occurs and is experienced by us. For example, we see two children playing and caressing each other and we feel the sweetness and beauty in the act. In this case the origin of the feeling was external. If we remembered an occasion from our childhood, playing with our brother, skipping, and feel nostalgic, in this case the origin would be internal.

We know we are facing a feeling because something changed in us in an accentuated or subtle manner. The attention and perception alert us that reality has changed and we have to be present. A feeling is then the sign of presence of the passage from one state to another with immediate repercussions in the body, in the mind and in the spiritual-animic component, in unity with the field of unified and planetary consciousness. In feeling, we inform, are informed and give form to reality in a web of life that changes and is affected at each moment, manifesting our dreams, nightmares, hopes and acts of grandiosity. Feeling is life, participating in life, using the language and The Code of Creation. Any reality can be created.

Feelings are The Code of Creation that allow us to explore and materialize our humanity, feel the divine inside us and share it.

"There is an old tale which says that in the act of creation, the angels got jealous when God gives humans the capacity to feel—because this would be the equivalent of being able to feel God and create with him." However, human beings have not woken up to their divinity, using feelings deliberately to create the life that they desire most. **Who would we be now as men, women, and children, experiencing those geniuses of creation that are feelings? What life would the reader have, using the highest, most loving and sweetest feelings on a daily basis? What reality, what people, things, and events would you have in your life? What miracles would you do in your**

life and in the lives of others?
Think, feel, imagine, and expand your heart at this moment to be able to do this experience... Put the book down if you need to... Feel in the heart, think with the heart, see with your heart... Flow with your heart, love from your heart. You know you can do miracles by feeling them!

♥ Stop, Breathe, Love

We were conceived to feel and does any feeling that we emit or receive affect reality?
Yes, it does because the feeling is reality interfering with the endless possibilities of reality. The nature of reality is one and for feelings as well. Therefore, it is only possible for feelings to interfere with reality, manifesting it, because that is their function, their immanent nature.
A distinct issue is to know if feelings can be different and if they manifest reality differently?
Firstly, feelings are energy, light and information. They simply exist in the field of unified consciousness as possibilities capable of creating reality. Feelings are unity just as unity is, and unity contains diversity. In that sense, there are different feelings and distinct manifestations of reality. This depends on feelings being considered "positive" or "negative," coherent, or incoherent, amongst other things.
Regarding feelings being "positive" or "negative," we reiterate that they are what they are: light, energy and information vibrating; they are reality. "Positive" and "negative" are energetic charges that particles can assume.
On the other hand, positive and negative are perceptions, more appropriately, perceptual and behavioral references by which we are guided at a given moment, as individuals and as a community and to which we give meaning and value and they are always in evolution. Speaking simply, we consider positive what we interpret as such in a given context and it brings results or consequences that we consider beneficial. Negative is the opposite of this.
We considered the feelings associated with the superior pole such as love, joy, trust, peace, hope, compassion, gratitude, forgiveness, altruism, goodness, faith, and admiration, amongst others as positive feelings. Yet the feelings associated with the inferior pole such as lovelessness, hate, sadness, distrust, jealousy, fear, despair, intolerance, ingratitude, egoism, malice, and contempt, amongst others, we consider as negative feelings.
We reiterate that both feelings considered "positive" or "negative" manifest reality. *That is because the nature of feelings is to create. It is both the language as well as the force of creativity in action. A force united to the Force, moving in our energy field and in the field of unified consciousness and the planet, united in the manifestation. Every feeling evokes and inter weaves events, conditions, resources, objects or people aligned with the vibration contained in them. Independently of their polarity "positive" or "negative," the concretization of what is felt, happens. Therefore, take care of what you are feeding with your feelings.*
When we focus the consciousness on "positive" feelings, it is firstly us that are affected positively by this dynamic energy, as well as the people around us and the community we are a part of, as well as the planet and the universe.

On the contrary, if we focus on the "negative," we are immediately creating patterns of interference to experience it in our interior and exterior, and also affecting whoever is receptive to the "negative" vibration, as well as the community we are part of, the planet and Cosmos.

What we feel is "positive" or "negative" about us, others or life, we manifest in our energy field, in the form of events, situations, objects or personal relationships that we are dealing with. The field of unified consciousness, united with our field, makes possible the subatomic rearrangements of feelings that are already experienced and actualizes them as reality, which we interpret as positive or negative.

What do we do when faced by a feeling we consider "negative" that we have or that we receive from someone else or the community that we are a part of?

In case we have the perception that we are having or capturing a feeling that is considered "negative," we can always change it, modifying the perception and the feeling.

There is no one who has more power over our lives or who "controls" us with feelings. Even if we feel fear, malice or intolerance because we generated or accepted these feelings from others or the collective, they can be changed. We can choose to feel love, joy and peace and these feelings dissolve and completely neutralize the negativity.

We are all potent and equal in the light of the field of unified consciousness, and no one has more power than the other does. Only limiting beliefs are able to separate or diminish us. The power that each one of us has is the power of unity and everything is possibly to be transformed. We always have a choice; we are the sovereigns of what we focus on, how we perceive it and what we feel.

One of the possibilities consists in thinking and feeling that *"only love is real"* or "the presence of love is in action, and I am peace and love now," and consciously radiating light which neutralizes any vibration that is different to this one.

 I am going to share an exercise I normally do:

- Purposefully I breathe in and expand myself above my head, feeling full of light.
- At that point, I hold my breath, I feel my heart and think of what I am feeling and then I say "Dissolve."
- I breathe out and let it all go.
- It is wonderful. I feel renewed.
- You can do it too.

Feelings can be coherent or incoherent. In both cases, reality is manifested.

Coherence is the act or effect of "cohering," that is, linking or harmonizing vibrations. From a quantum point of view, coherence can be envisaged as the capacity that subatomic particles have to cooperate and get organized amongst themselves, in such a way that a cohesive entity is manifested. A system is coherent when the entities that make it up have a common end and function consistently, forming ordered patterns, which vibrate coherently and in unison.

Coherent feelings that make harmony and cohesion possible are unity, love, peace, compassion, trust, gratitude, forgiveness and hope, amongst others. These feelings emit coherent light, and the information fields that make them up, vibrate in an orderly way.

Incoherence is the act or effect of "being incoherent," i.e., to disconnect or disharmonize. From a quantum point of view, incoherence can be understood as absence of cooperation and of interrelationship of sub-atomic particles amongst each other. A system is incoherent when the particles are out of phase, the communication and interaction does not have a common end and vibrates in a disordered manner. Incoherent feelings that tend towards disharmony and disconnection /separation are: fear, fighting, intolerance, distrust, ingratitude, and egoism, amongst others. These feelings emit incoherent light, out of phase, and the information fields that make them vibrate in a disorderly way.

We reiterate that both coherent and incoherent feelings manifest reality; they are reality. Since the "informational quality" of both is distinct and the systems of energy and information they are in dialogue and interaction with are different, what they manifest is substantially diverse.

Coherent feelings *make us feel good, expanded, connected, full of energy, clear and inspired. When we experience these feelings, from a neural point of view, the mental images, the thoughts, the words we say, the sensations and the behaviors are in a context of fluidity and of order. The whole organism communicates and cooperates towards a common end: happiness. We are ready to observe life and to cooperate with it in all its variety; we tend toward harmony in our relationships with all beings. From a quantum point of view, coherent feelings probabilize the manifestation of events, developments, objects or people vibrationally aligned with our energy, and manifest the results that we consider good, magic or even miraculous and are for our higher good and for the All.*

Incoherent feelings make us feel bad, contracted, disconnected, discolored, separated from one another and from life. When we live these feelings, we neurologically feed images, sensations, ideas, words and attitudes of tension and disorder. The entire organism is under effort/stress and becomes disorganized. Equilibrium is compromised internally, or is totally lost, and the internal pattern is of tension/stress and unhappiness. We are in a state of struggle, of competition or separation from life. From a quantum point of view, incoherent feelings enable the manifestation of events, situations, things, occurrences or people, which vibrate in the same wave frequency and manifest results that we interpret as bad, unhealthy, impossible or incurable and that can potentially be "absent" from the individual or collective wellbeing.

We feel, and in that moment we are creating/creating reality, and it depends on us choosing what feelings we want to feed. The variety of feelings exists so that we can exercise our free will, taking part in life in accordance with our creativity, imprinting in reality what we feel in partnership with the field of unified and planetary consciousness. The field of consciousness feels us and follows our feelings, giving shape and context to life, so that we can experience them totally.

Here is a testimonial of that creativity:

Testimonial

I had felt unhappy for a long time, without self-confidence, experiencing a feeling of inferiority which prevented me from living naturally. It was so stressful that I thought of myself as ugly, small and incapable of success. I was also not happy with my body,

I avoided my sensuality and was stuck feeling disconnected from happiness.

I knew I could not carry on like this. At thirty-four, it was time that I solved this problem. I looked for a psychologist, but something told me to try another method. Meanwhile, I found the phone number of Susana, I saw her webpage, and I liked it and thought I should ask her for help. I called her, hesitant as normal in my case, but I called. A year later, I am the person that I would like to be: fulfilled, happy, confident, and an adult!

It was during a seminar that there was a click in my interior, liberating myself from sadness and pain. I learned to trust myself, saying openly what I felt, and I have internal confidence. I progressed at work, and in my family, my friendships and in my studies, which I had never thought possible. Today, I feel like a woman, beautiful. I like my body, and I dress tastefully. I discovered my real feelings of love, joy and confidence and I use my mind to remain focused on the positive. My message for anyone I meet now and anyone who complains about life, is that it can change. However bad things look or if they appear without any solution, it is not true. I know through personal experience and I feel good in my skin. The woman I am today is a testimonial of love, authenticity and maturity, who is at peace with life.

Marta Sofia, secretary

Just as Marta decided to change her feelings regarding life and created a different reality for herself, every one of us can do this as well. It may not appear so, especially if we are recycling the cassette of old feelings where the feelings we feel are fear, distrust, fighting or inability. But that is not true; we just have to simultaneously change the quality of our feelings, and the attention we give them for other possibilities to emerge.

In effect, in the process of generating feelings, the information that is neurally received has to be understood as capable of generating a feeling. That is, data is not enough; it has to be data with specific characteristics, qualitatively understood as raw material to trigger a feeling. This selection has to do with the mental filters, images and ideas, humor, sensations and states of the body.

Faced with data considered useful to trigger a feeling, namely on the level of superior brainstem, the information is perceptually analyzed and becomes available, with the person in question being able to relativize the feeling, intensifying it or even taking it out of context and even expressing it or not.

There is an "open space" between the trigger of the feeling and "sensing it" that allows us to change, on a neural level, the perception of the feeling. It is a fraction of a second, where we are aware and interpret the information however we choose at that moment. It is here that we are masters of what we feel or not. This moment constitutes the perceptual turning point, full of possibilities of new forms of feeling or a strengthening of the old way.

The form we observe and interpret will determine the form of how we feel, and this capacity of observation and interpretation is inherent to human beings, it is always available and being actualized at each moment according to the attention and perceptions that we are having. The field of consciousness accepts our feelings and mirrors it immediately.

Here is a simple example so that we can understand this better. A woman is looking in the mirror and decides to put on red lipstick; she looks at her face and she doesn't like it. At that moment, her boyfriend comes in and says, in a critical tone, that he hates to see her with lipstick on. She feels disaffection and disapproval on the part of her boyfriend and thinks: "Damn, you are really ugly and you look horrible with that lipstick." This results in even more disaffection by itself and she feels sad. What triggered this feeling of disaffection and disapproval and sadness was the perception of not liking to see herself, associated with the significance she gives to the comments from her boyfriend and the reinforcement of the perception of being ugly, and that she looks horrible with the lipstick, focusing on those feelings.

If she had put on the lipstick, did not interpret the dislike for the color, in association with the remark from the boyfriend and feeling ugly or looking horrid, she would have a different feeling. She only needed to put her boyfriend's comment in context and respond with humor or look at herself and say "there are other colors that suit me better" and focus her attention on that information or on other things that please her so as to be able to have other feelings and feel good.

Another example, this time the feeling is "positive." You are walking to work and see a child and a grandmother playing in the street. They are singing happily and playing. You remember being that age and the games you played with your grandmother. Internally you see images of games, hear the songs that you used to sing with your grandmother, and you feel happy, light. Unexpectedly, you start singing the song you are hearing and take part in the game. You feel even more joyful and happier, and continue on your way to work, humming the song. What triggered this feeling of happiness was the image of the child and grandmother, which was associated with a memory and interpreted positively, internally activating perceptions and experiences of joy and your focused attention. You became so bound to the feeling that you acted, singing and taking part in the game and fed the feeling, giving it more attention and consistency, when you continued humming on the way to work. This person could, with the same image and memories, have interpreted the scene differently. For example, think it totally ridiculous that a woman that age was playing in the street.

When stating that we have the power and capacity to deal with our feelings and with those of others, it means that all the possibilities are in us when we are faced with a sentimental scenario.

We can both choose to recycle old neural patterns, sensibilities, likes, affections, and experiences, or be open to a new decision with the intelligence of the heart, where reason and intuition communicate, opening a way for a new state, creating a new feeling.

We are the ones who choose our feelings. The observation and the interpretation that we give to the information that is presented to us makes that information gain form and substance in reality.

We are free, and the feelings are also a sovereign act of freedom, uniting us to what makes sense to manifest.

We can decide to love, forgive, be tolerant and are cured instantly, feeding the feelings that are one with the truths that resonate in our hearts. And because of the fundamental interdependence between all things, at that moment the collective of human beings, the planet and the field of unified consciousness expand and vibrate in that feeling with us.

Finding Positive Feelings

"Shared love is duplicated love."
Popular saying

"Whoever is happy will make others happy too."
Mark Twain

"Love is a fire that burns without seeing."
Luís Vaz de Camões

A friend, a doctor by profession, confided in me that she had discovered a secret to feeling good. That now life was better because she was more aware of her feelings; she listened to the messages that the feelings gave her. She told me that once she was going by motorbike to see a patient, and in the middle of traffic, she began to feel very restless and had a sense of ill feeling in her chest. She decided to stop the motorbike and instead of automatically thinking that she may be having a heart attack or something else, she took off her helmet and asked her heart what it was trying to say. Curiously the heart told her that she had left her cell phone at home and she did not have the address of the patient she was going to see with her. She took a deep breath and looked in her bag and confirmed that she had not brought her cell phone with her. At that moment, she experienced a mixture of gratitude, surprise and the connection with something bigger than her. She felt so deeply touched that she needed a few minutes before returning home to fetch her cell phone and see her patient. This friend of mine did not understand intellectually what had happened to her. That feeling coming from nowhere, and without any apparent reason, had saved the day. I was delighted when I heard her, smiling internally, and saying to myself "how I understand you, my friend."
It is probable that we may have had similar experiences; that an unusual feeling gives us vital information that makes all the difference, for the positive in our lives. It is possible that in front of a feeling, that simply "happens to us" (without us consciously having had any direct intervention in its occurrence), we can feel its grandeur, and we can ask ourselves, where do they come from and how can these feelings "happen" more often?
The origin of these feelings is the field of unified consciousness—the seat of all life—and if there are certain "conditions" for these feelings to occur again: these are openness, being receptive to the messages that the field systematically sends us, vibrating on a level of consciousness that accesses this information in a natural manner and also spontaneously accepts the information that is transmitted to us in a nonlinear form.
Besides these feelings that "happen" to us apparently coming from nowhere, in which we download the information on the level of the quantum processor that is the brain, in unity with the heart (which is a very powerful vortex of energy; we will speak about this further on) we self-produce the feelings. We generate feelings in a more or less conscious manner, and we can feed them or not, expressing them or keeping them, according to our decision.
The experience we all have regarding the feelings, and as explained above, we have understood how we trigger feelings and those feelings which are "positive" and

"coherent" allow us, namely, to make life easier and simpler, relativizing the issues we face daily, and experience states of fluidity where we are present and aware. We may even have the feeling that everything is synchronized, and that the universe works in our favor. It is also possible, with a feeling of joy or peace, to do what we need, and have the sensation of involvement and flow and of not getting tired. Faced by the positivity of our feelings, we are able to make clearer decisions, improve the communication and mutual aid and relationships flourish. Health improves and we spread a wave of wellbeing which affects in a beneficial way, the life of those dear to us and the planet.

"Positive" and "coherent" feelings are now on stage.

Love is a feeling that marks our life from the first moment. We are generated in love and the movement of life urges us to love at each instant. It is the sovereign affection that makes a difference in our humanity. Love places in evidence what is most pure and beautiful within us. Through love we surrender, commit ourselves and carry out our greater mission. Loving without limits and simply being who we are. It is love that gives color, context and dimension and also meaning to our existence. In our most significant moments and before going to another life, what we remember is how much we loved and were loved. The mark of love remains timeless and is felt naturally. We have a love radar that detects the presence of love, and in its presence we feel at home. Love is the conscious state of plenitude that we all have and that we resonate with on a more subtle level in our life.

Joy is the feeling of natural vivacity. In it we are animated with energy and we move lightly. Experiencing joy is having internal happiness that irradiates to whoever is around us. The presence of this feeling is a natural stimulus for sharing. We are joyful and we want others to be as well. Spontaneously, we feel the desire to celebrate, to change any act into a rejoicing event. It is also a state of the soul that rejoices and moves in the sense of expansion and of conscious creativity which is infinite. In the presence of joy we face situations with greater lightness, orienting ourselves towards solutions and we feel that we are capable.

Hope is a feeling of waiting for something to happen that has not yet "materialized". It is a desire for a certain manifestation that animates us and keeps us focused on the desired purpose. With hope we take a new breath and we consider other possibilities. For many, this feeling is associated with divine intervention in a project, in health or in the hope for eternal life.
As a general rule, we have hope when we apparently do not possess the means, or resources, conditions, or the results are very unlikely to happen in accordance with our expectations, and in spite of this we persist in trust knowing that it will happen. Hope is an internal quality, where the soul gives us a vision of other possible dimensions and scenarios that we are in resonance with on a conscious level. This feeling is the detonator of internal force and concentration on what is not yet visible or recognizable and that can emerge at any moment.

Gratitude is a feeling of recognition and of reverence for the good that has come to us. It is also an interior quality of contentment where our soul sees a higher purpose underlying things, the events, the people, the phenomena that happen in the reality that we live in. Gratitude is a state of union with the heart, soul and mind that will lead us to give thanks for what we created and for what happens to us. It can be an internal ecstasy where we become aware of the magnificence of creation and how the consciousness, which is all, *is Perfect*. In a state of gratitude, we focus more on blessings and we bring to life the object of our attention. The feelings and everyday life are entwined and dyed with the colors of gratitude at every moment.

Admiration is the feeling of being marveled by life. It is an internal state of awareness, occurring when we are present and allow ourselves to see with the heart. Admiration is observing with delight what emerges daily. It is allowing ourselves to be surprised and see each moment as new and we rejoice with it. It is also an internal quality enabling us to see the "best" in others and feeling touched by their example. We admire Mother Theresa because we acknowledge her special role in changing consciousness and her attitude towards the lepers and the less fortunate in India.
It is a feeling that encourages human excellence and goes in the direction of the sublime that is inherent in the planet and the cosmos in all instants.

Compassion is the feeling of empathizing with another being and being able to feel what he feels and mobilize ourselves to help. It is a state of presence and deep connection with the being, and in this vibration of the "other" is not different from us; he is just consciousness as we are. The openness to the "other" is total. The barriers, the distinctions and the limitations disappear when faced with this feeling of compassion. We are vibrating in a frequency of inclusion, and it accepts and respects all decisions made, enabling changes for the good of all beings. Compassion is also the force that connects us to each other, the planet and the field of unified consciousness, enabling us to evolve.

Faith is a feeling of deep conviction that we nurture. It is an interior unwavering certainty, even if appearances show us something different. It is a quality of consciousness that enables us to absolutely believe in phenomena or unknown realities that the mind would normally reject. It is being innocent, unique and totally available to embrace what we intimately believe. Faith transcends the linear and logical mind, uniting intuition and the heart, which enables us to experience broader perceptions and jump into the unknown. With this feeling, we have vision; we feel the connection and we act animated by this energy. The existence of miracles through faith is the awareness that in the field of infinite possibilities, what we believe already exists and is available for us and can happen immediately.

Kindness is an internal feeling of a disposition towards what is good. It is the attitude of benevolence that allows us to act upon doing good. Kindness has underlying moral values of what is good and for goodness, be it personal, for another person or global. It is the capacity of being present and acting for the benefit of another (and feeling it as a personal achievement), because in fact there is only one of us. It is also an internal state of sharing happily, where we feel abundant to give freely, without any type of expectations or results, we simply hand over the gift and leave it to the receiver to use it as he deems fit. This feeling quickly propels us into action without having to think about the why or the how and we act with conviction and detachment.

Tolerance is a feeling that takes differences into consideration, understanding them as natural and enriching. It is the capacity to allow the liberty of values, references, situations or divergent opinions from those that we have from a personal, social, political, religious or philosophical point of view, giving space, importance and expression to what is diverse. While a state of consciousness, tolerance is simultaneously being open to difference and accepting that we are more than that— we are one. Internally, we have a vision and the wisdom of the wealth that is present in all of the creations that the universe shows us in the most varied forms, and that diversity comes from unity. This feeling expands our perception of reality and reinforces the ties connecting us inexorably to each other, and to the All.

Forgiveness is the feeling of profound deliverance from that which weighs, hurts, saddens and consumes. It is an intelligent act of the heart because it reveals wisdom, flexibility and detachment. Underlying this feeling is a clear conscious decision regarding people, situations or things, and simultaneously, an absolute decision to stop nurturing the old story and its characters. Through it, we re-dimension values and priorities and finally place happiness in the first place. It is a spiritual surgery, where we remove all victimization, guilt, irresponsibility and separation and awaken to the truth: "who I am is "bigger" than this" and "I am free to do the best."
Forgiveness is a quality of consciousness, and at the same time a deliberation and an act of power that only a sovereign, secure being, can practice. The sovereign being perceives that all is his and in him, as well as assuming that the power of powers is not punishing but redeeming, apologizing and evolving. This feeling is the alchemy of the soul par excellence, because we transform lead into gold.
The act of forgiving absolves the internal world of the one who practices it, because it ceases to be in resonance with guilt and fear and instantaneously frees all beings to love. Often it is simply necessary to decide and say internally that it is finished, and selectively, the issue is finished, alchemized in the quantum field. Forgiving is a state of grace that causes us to return to our internal paradise and returns paradise to Earth and to the universe.

Integrity is the feeling of being whole. Being integral is being wise and feeling whole results from the communication between the heart and the mind at the highest level, seeing purity and acting towards goodness. It is also the quality of being firm, secure and behaving accordingly. Imbued in this feeling, we can even be daring and go far on our path and always be coherent. Integrity is a state of consciousness where we perceive ourselves as being part of the whole, and complete in ourselves. We are intact, and the vision of completeness and of perfection accompanies us.

Trust is the feeling of believing intimately in something or someone. It is a conviction that gives us courage and moves us internally and externally into action. Animated by this feeling, we can, namely, deliver things, carry out projects, reveal intimacy or purely and simply relax. When we trust, we are firm, and are relaxed regarding the object of our trust. When we experience this feeling, we are in a state of consciousness, of openness, receptive to the best, and we feel strong and calm that what we focused our attention and conviction on is possible. In the process of believing, we have left behind the resistances, the doubts are overcome, and we give space for what is not yet visible to be manifested. Underlying trust is the state of surrender. Only those who release and really believe, even if they may not know how it is possible from a linear point of view, are really relaxed in the act of trusting.

Appreciation is the feeling of valuing a person, object, entity or event. The act or effect of appreciating something, has underlying it a state of consciousness, of openness to life, naturally finding reasons to consider what we observe, feel, do or receive, as blessings. We can appreciate a sunset, an ice cream, a kiss, a piece of music, help with the shopping, the quality that we have or that another has, etc. Independently of the amount of appreciation, feeling it places us in resonance with what we consider good, beautiful, true, peaceful, important or useful and makes more attention and energy available for our existence.

After briefly explaining some of the positive feelings that exist, and because we already know that they create reality in unity with the field of unified consciousness and bring good to all beings, let us do an exercise.

 Exercise:

Breathe deeply five times. When you breathe in, fill the abdomen and the chest. When you breathe out release the abdomen and the chest. As you consciously breathe, relax. Focus your attention on your chest, namely on your heart. Feel your heart pulsating: the rising and lowering of the chest. Listen to the sound of your heart. Be aware of the heart in totality. Give it all the attention and concentrate on it. Now place your hand over it and feel it. Feel the joy. Let the heart flood itself with that joy and breathe this energy. Remember various moments of joy that you have experienced (a game, a joke, a funny animal, a friend or family member with whom you experienced this feeling or imagine a joyful episode) and nurture it in your heart. Feel it with intensity, see the scene, listen to the comment, move, you can even start laughing. Continue for five minutes to nurture this feeling, and when you are full of it, share it with others. Then, breathe deeply and be thankful for joy being infinite and always joy being at your disposal.

Feelings in Movement

"*When we cannot find* contentment *in ourselves*, it is *useless* to seek it *elsewhere.*"
François La Rochefoucauld

"The real human progress, is achieving happiness."
Master Koot Hoomi

"With an eye made quiet by the power of harmony, and the deep power of joy, we see into the life of things."
William Wordsworth

Breathe deeply. Feel your breathing and in this instant, let yourself simply be. Breathe normally again and feel good... At this moment, what conditions, circumstances or people could appear or disappear, so that your innermost wish for realization could occur? What would you change in your life? What person would you be? What would you like to have or do?

Well, I have good news: you already have in yourself the possibility and the realization of what is meaningful for you. It is true, you have within you the most intelligent form of communicating and the most sophisticated "technology of concretization." It is called feeling; you were born with it and use it 24 hours per day, 365 days per year. You may not have noticed that you own this treasure inside of you, and that at the same time you had the key that gives you access to it. Your challenge is to be aware of your feelings and to use them in a conscious, focused manner, for your good and the good of all. It is an adventure of creation/creation in partnership with the field of unified consciousness.

I am sure you have already used your feelings to manifest small, medium or large concretizations. Who knows... a childhood dream, a common situation or an unexpected wish from your heart? Indeed, the whole of humanity is doing it with you, at this very moment, and sees what we have achieved. From the biggest horrors and also the greatest acts of kindness, love, healing, peace and hope have already happened and continue to happen now.

Whatever has meaning for you (To Be or To Achieve), has in itself, the feeling. That is because it is the essence of life. Any reality is capable of being manifested through feeling, because it is the primordial light of creation, and is endless. It can be a meeting with the higher self, the cure for paralysis, a united and happy family, the car of your dreams, a house in the mountains, or feeding dolphins in the open sea. All these realities are capable of being achieved with feeling.

Feeling is a communication in the scope of the infinite possibilities; it is also the inherent movement of the field itself and the specific concretization of something that until then was only in the kingdom of the potential and then gains form. It is the unity giving life to diversity.
Every feeling is spirit, in spirit, and through spirit becomes flesh, by a selective act of consciousness. *In feeling, we incarnate, and the information becomes incarnated of what we feel in unity with the field of unified consciousness.*

♥ Stop, Breathe, Love

The issue that may emerge is wondering how long it takes to manifest what we are feeling? That is, does it need time or can we manifest immediately what we feel, from moving to a new house, a hug from the woman or the man we love receiving flowers, buying a jacket, speaking to a guardian angel, travelling abroad or for cells to recover? **From a quantum point of view, a feeling can be manifested immediately because it is a wave of possibilities in communication and interaction in the field, and it already exists as reality (although in a potential state) therefore it does not need "any time" because it is already there, it only assumes a particular state.**
From the moment that we feel when we are inwardly united with this state, the

manifestation can happen instantly. This is because we are communicating with the essence of life and it responds and interacts with us in a dance of full potentialities.

Every feeling has a mission and it is always pointing to its realization, and to the extent that it remains coherent, the manifestation has to occur. This coherence can last merely a second, or a few minutes or even days, and in so far as it is present, the field of unified consciousness in unity with us and the planet, makes it visible.

The simplest way to manifest reality, whatever it may be, is feeling it, being it, and embodying it.

Probably the most important question that we can ask ourselves is, **"What feeling serves this reality?"** or **"What feelings make sense for me to be, experience, move or share so that this becomes a reality in my life?"**

The answer is already contained in the question. It is the experience totally felt, embodying the feeling, that actualizes the reality and manifests it immediately. This state is compatible with the infinite possibilities and transforms them into realities immediately and over time.

Feeling is an act of quantum creativity united with the primordial creativity which is underlying the field of unified consciousness, and any reality can be brought to life, because it is already available, in a potential state in the field, capable of being configured in accordance with our heart's desire.

Everything is possible to be manifested, even instantly, both for us and for those to whom we direct our feelings, be it the person we love or a stranger. Our feelings affect us and affect reality at all levels because they already are reality.

Feeling is a language that the field knows, recognizes and responds to, and it is also a "technology of information" that gives form and structures what the feeling conveys; a force in association with the Force, and from the moment we use it, the entire universe mobilizes itself towards concretization.

In fact, life has all that we need, and in the act of feeling it, we actualize numerous probabilities of reality that converge for the concretization of the event, person or circumstance, aligned with our sentimental representation.

The applicability of the feeling is total, be it in the trivial things of everyday life, such as feeling good when waking up, hugging your son at school, or in more elaborate ways, for example, carrying out a mega architectural project, or being able to raise funds for refugees and feed the world. Feeling is present there, giving life to reality. **Therefore, feel it profoundly and MATERIALIZE.**

It does not matter how the feeling is going to be manifested, who is feeling it, or if it is directed to another, if it is going to emerge where we are or will be manifested on the other side of the world, because it can immediately materialize the experience of what is expressed. People can be affected by them in our presence or in another place, be it our city or the globe, objects can appear or disappear, problems can be solved, events emerge in an unexpected manner, illnesses dissolved, relationships cured in the name of a feeling. Feeling is the essence of creation and knows no limits; it is infinitely powerful and is interwoven and evokes any reality in a matrix of perfect life.

Human creativity, united with cosmic creativity can bring to light any possibility that is felt.

Here is a testimonial of an act of creativity, where the feeling interfered with the life of another being and manifested health.

Testimonial

My name is Paula and I have two children. At one of the seminars of Unified Quantum Healing that I attended, my daughter Ana Catarina, ten years old, had a serious problem in her ear. The right eardrum (tympanic membrane) was perforated. This was serious because she had already been subjected to a surgical intervention at the age of three and now imminently needed another surgery. This issue bothered me greatly, because I wanted this imbalance and the complaints from my daughter to stop. I also did not want her to be subjected to another surgery. The doctor told me that it was the only solution. I spoke to Susana during the seminar and she told me that we were in the right place, at the right time, to solve the eardrum issue. After all, "there are always possibilities and the infinite intelligence knows how to solve any issue."

After a wonderful and bombastic healing at the seminar, which ended on Sunday; I felt confident and illuminated. Internally, I knew my daughter was well. A feeling of peace and unwavering trust took me over, and I returned to my family.

A few days later, I took my daughter to the doctor. I was totally sure and confident that the problem with the ear was totally healed. The doctor examined her and was stunned. Her perplexity was so great that she repeated various times: "But I said the eardrum was perforated. It is not possible the eardrum is healed. There is no injury."

Paula Martins, tarot reader

This change from a perforated eardrum to a healthy one was possible through the feeling of unity with health, trust and an open heart and mind, that the possibilities are infinite. From the moment of the heart's wish to establish health, the communication between mother and daughter, Susana and the field of unified consciousness, united and actualized itself in a" focal point" of the field of unified consciousness, a concrete state: a healthy ear.

From a quantum point of view, all possibilities exist simultaneously, and a feeling is a point of infinite possibilities defining a particular state that until then had no form. There is no time nor distance for something that is in an undetermined state to take form, because it is (was and will always be) potentially connected with it. It simply happens. It is.

Some might call the manifestation of a feeling a miracle. I call it "opportunities" always present for the state of openness of the heart and mind, simply allowing life to happen in the field of infinite possibilities.

♥ Stop, Breathe, Love

Returning to the issue of how long does it takes to manifest what we are feeling?

It is our perception of time and space, of being separate from what we feel or intend, which causes the materialization to take a long time or not, to be manifested. For the field of unified consciousness, it is the same to process the information we emit and manifest it immediately (because we have decided and were in alignment) or not manifest it; it respects our will. As long as the language is clear and coherent, the "technology of creation" actualizes reality. The truth is that the field of unified consciousness is open to us, and ready for our active participation through feelings. Sometimes it is only a thousandth of a second or a minute for our feelings to manifest immediately, as in the case above or in other forms. For example, it is probable that we have felt love and we manifested a present that we had wished for. Other times, it is important to feel well, raising the vibration in a constant manner, and mentally accepting the possibility that something is manifested for this or that to emerge in our lives and that can happen in hours, days, weeks or months, depending on each one and the level of energy.

Every person is manifesting what she feels because feeling is reality. The issue here is to manifest what makes sense for us at the moment. Also, if we are truly congruent with what we feel, that is, if we are in total alignment, from the thoughts, words, images and coherent acts with feeling. In case we are, it is simple: the feeling manifests itself. In case we have turbulence, the feeling can be delayed or not even bring to light what we had evoked. It is the distorted and separatist perceptions that we have, the thoughts, images, words, sensations and contradictory behaviors that interfere with the manifestation of what we feel. Because for the field of unified consciousness, any possibility can be materialized.

What are the most common turbulences or incoherencies sabotaging the "positive" and coherent feelings blocking or inhibiting the manifestation of what we evoked for ourselves?

Doubt, distrust, the "how," and insecurity are tensions that interfere negatively. If there is fear, that is the closure of the infinite possibilities, and it builds more fear and limitation. The doubts, distrust, and the "how," the insecurities, and the fear have to do with the perceptions of separation, opposition, difficulty and limitation, be it of the means, the resources, the time, the space or the power that we have. These are visions and linear understandings that reduce the reality that recreates them consecutively, giving us the illusion that reality/ life is like that, when in fact, it is more, much more.

Accepting that we are connected to the infinite intelligence, to the unlimited resources and the endless possibilities and opportunities is an act of intelligence and personal sovereignty, which frees and expands us for personal, family, collective and global materializations. Because that is the truth from a fundamental point of view. That is the truth underlying all of life. Effectively, feeling is a wave of quantum possibilities interacting and communicating with the energy of the field of unified consciousness, behaving in a nonlinear manner, being able to be in superposition in a great number of places at the same time, transcending space and time and manifesting itself physically and instantly with total abundance and creativity.

A feeling is made from the same material that everything is made of, light, energy and information and interacts with it, manifesting any possibility that we focus on.

The field of unified consciousness is complete in itself and unlimited, and whatever we evoke in our communication and interaction with it, is possible for manifestation. From the most sublime feeling, to the most far-fetched detail, including the unexpected and grandiose events in our lives, the probabilities are unlimited.

Therefore, let us leave aside the reductive perceptions when using the language and the "technology of creation" of feeling, since it is possible to materialize what we feel.

What is important is to be clear, detached, and coherent and be open to what may happen, because it can be an even bigger and better than what we felt and idealized. We should remember that the field of unified consciousness is intelligent, sensitive and totally dedicated to serving us. It always manifests perfection united with the feelings that we have. We can relax and be innocent because life is on our side and loves us unconditionally.

Here is a testimonial about quantum creativity on the level of a feeling where love was felt, catapulting gigantic life changes.

Testimonial

Meeting Susana Cor de Rosa was a real blessing. What a great turn my life took... and so many "miracles" happened.... I had a great emptiness and sadness inside me, invading me day after day. I was living all my life for others and never remembered myself. I thought I could be good to all those around me, when in fact, I was not even well myself. The real transformation happened at a seminar whose theme was the "heart." Everything changed. Incredible! My heart was opened; I met someone very special, someone so compatible with me that I could not believe it. I had left a failed marriage, where I had a daughter, and I can say that I was not even able to hug her.

Today I am a very happy man; I feel complete because I found the woman of my dreams. I healed my relationship with my daughter, and now I am a loving, devoted and a more accessible father. I am now able to tell my little princess that I love her, and when we are together, I pamper her with kisses and hugs.

I hold her close to me and we play a lot. This is new because I would have never done this in the past. It was not because I did not want to, but because I was limited.

Today I feel accomplished, because I live in love.

Thank you, Susana, for helping me discover my way of light.

Filipe Nogueira, therapist

With feelings, especially love, it is possible to materialize anything. Opening our hearts to love, and allowing it to guide us, any limitation is dissolved, life gains new colors and we renew strengths, capacities and relationships in a profound manner.

♥ Stop, Breathe, Love

Does a person who is aware of the creative power of feeling and its union with the field of unified consciousness, manifest it immediately or "quicker"?

From the quantum point of view, any feeling has the potential for immediate manifestation, because it already exists in the field of unified consciousness. Feeling is reality linked to all reality, and every person has the same capacity for manifestation. Now the difference lies in the state of consciousness that the person has and nurtures at each moment, because the manifestation can happen in the blink of an eye. It happens to the literate and illiterate alike, for the wise as well as the ignorant, for a man as well as a woman or child. Generally, it is a state of "no mind," of coherence and an open heart, which can happen in a thousandth of a second or need a long time. As it happens, a human being in the act of feeling should be aware that he is communicating and giving form to reality (in unity with the field of unified consciousness and the planet); it is already the manifestation of the feeling. He feels and feels again what he invokes. Internally, he knows that everything is possible and that the materialization has happened because it is united with life.

In this state of clarity and unity, when a person feels, he is immediately witnessing the All and the All responds. Space-time is collapsed in that instant, and any form, object, person or instant is before it, and in it and in everything; because it and the All are just one. He perceives himself as already materialized.

On the other hand, even if the materialization is extended in space-time, the cohesion with the result achieved is maintained. The person behaves as if it has materialized and continues with life in that assumption. The individual can experience this state in a fraction of a second and immediately manifest what he feels, or may do it in minutes, days, weeks, months or even years. For example, manifest the total release of a symptom in a moment, minutes, hours or days or manifest the construction of a hospital which takes years to build. What is important is that the individual knows that the potential for the manifestation is with him, and he can create or recreate always through the focused feeling.

We reiterate that this process normally is a state of no-mind where the heart is open, internally coherent and available for the realization. The feeling when being felt is a wave/drop in the ocean of infinite probabilities that makes it overflow with life. All the masters of this planet used feelings purposefully to create reality. They knew the language and the "technology of creation" and made miracles at all levels. That is, they used the infinite possibilities and transformed them into opportunities, recreating in a new light, people, ideas, events or objects. Also, the reader was conceived and is made of the same "matter" that the masters were made of. You only have to use your innate wisdom and the language and the "subtle technology" of feelings that you now know, to recreate reality. We are active participants in reality and we build it in partnership with the field of unified consciousness that loves us and accepts us completely, mirroring our feelings in the giant screen of life at each instant.

The Timing of Feelings

"I feel myself being born in each moment, in the eternal newness of the world."
Alberto Caeiro, Fernando Pessoa's heteronomous

"The value of things is not in the time they last, but in the intensity with which they happen. Therefore, there are unforgettable moments, unexplained things and incomparable people."
Fernando Pessoa

Presently, we are familiar with feeling. We feel it and we know it is a universal language that we are endowed with at birth to communicate with each other, with the field of unified consciousness and the planet. Furthermore, it is an active force that has the purpose of imprinting our mark on the world and creating reality; from the most intimate and minute feeling to the biggest, it is there animating life with our personal touch, creating/creating the outcomes of our lives.

It can be the hope of a new opportunity in life, trust in ourselves and of those we love, jealousy or sadness of someone we know, or the gratitude of a work colleague. Any feeling is communicating and interacting in a subtle and at the same time profound manner in our life, affecting it and that of other beings, at any moment or place.

Is it possible a feeling to have an impact on space-time reality? Is it possible for feelings to affect the future and even the past that is already consolidated in our lives and transform it? And in the case of it being affirmative, what implications would that have for our lives?

This topic appears to be fiction, maybe from a film where the character "travels" in time and space to find solutions that did not seem to be accessible at the time of making the decision, and in travelling, he can interfere with reality, changing it. In the film *The Terminator*, with Arnold Schwarzeneger, this is virtually explored, and leaves open the fact that we can "travel in time" and create distinct moments and lives.

However this is not fiction, it is very real, and science admits that both the past and the future are available to be affected, as a result of there being "special" subatomic particles, which have the particularity of being bidirectional, travelling in both directions "forward" and "backwards" in space-time, and the movement is due to an act of awareness of the observer, affecting reality at that moment.

It may appear unlikely that the future or the past can be affected by feeling if we consider it as a linear phenomenon, produced locally, in the brain, where chemical electrical impulses transmit information and biological responses are triggered, affecting the mind, body and emotions and are materially limited by the conventional dimensions.

Feeling is confined locally in time and space and its effects are limited to these, not being able to transcend them or interfere with these dimensions.

However, if we see that:

a) There is the field of unified consciousness, the information field, where everything is potentially connected at the same time and at various levels, stretching itself without limits;

b) Understand the brain as a quantum system of energy in correlation and communication with the field of unified consciousness and what exists in it;

c) As well as, if we admit, like the scientific community now admits that there are subatomic particles that are bidirectional, i.e., they move forwards and backwards in space-time, with these being able to interfere at a quantum level with any event;

d) It is possible that these, in their movement change the result at a quantum level, generating a new pattern of energetic coherence.

Feelings, as subatomic waves/particles, communicate and act in an acausal and nonlocal manner, transcending space-time, and can appear on a point of the field of unified consciousness, in the meantime focused by the human consciousness. It can move towards the future, "forward" or towards the past, "backwards" and actualize the quantum potential, individualizing a different state, that is, a new subatomic reality.

The state of consciousness of the observer, his decision and feeling, is the driving force of the creation of the event in unity with the field of unified consciousness.

It is possible to affect a past event through quantum retroaction or affect a future event through quantum progression. Through feeling, we observe a distinct probability, an infinity of possible others, and the field of unified consciousness, in unity with our sentimental communication, actualizes a new state, crystallizing a new reality in accordance with the feeling focused.

For example, in the case of the symptoms of a disease, the cause may be in the past and if we "travel in time" to one day or a month before the first experience of the disease, the collision of the bidirectional particles can possibly unblock the information, and the person becomes automatically healthy again, or in a moment in time, variable with the actualization of the information.

In the case of the future, we may perceive a tendency for disease, the failure of an organ, or even a bad love or business decision. Through the "space time journey" of the bidirectional particles and on a conscious level of total openness, it is possible to make that quantum potential collide and evoke a new possibility: health, love or a different business.

What time is made of—the matter, the events and the feelings—is the same, waves/subatomic particles in movement in the field of unified consciousness and consciousness is infinite and unlimited and is always attentive to any decision we make.

Feeling is capable of creating any reality. It is the creative power in action that is within us and in interaction with the field of unified consciousness. It is the language we speak that the field recognizes, and the "laser technology" of manifestation.

Feeling is energy that interacts with the energy of the totality. In the act of feeling, we specialize our sensibility and world vision in the quantum reality, and this interconnects with the sensitivity and vision of the totality, which emerges manifested in reality.

Independent of the size, context, people, resources or events involved, and even of the space-time, any reality is possible to be manifested at any point or moment.

Feeling works in the scope of infinite possibilities that the field of unified consciousness has in itself and in us as well. We can create, recreate and create without limits, because the possibilities available to us are endless. The field of unified consciousness simply actualizes and inputs the feelings and our creations, "online" in the cosmic internet.

For this phenomenon to happen (we affect events in "the future" or in "the past"), we must be united internally, without any reservations, doubts, attachments and also beyond duality (good/bad, positive/negative) in a state of no mind and with high vibration. Consciously, we are awake in a state of internal cohesion and openness.

Although it may seem strange, the absence of the mental processing, what we want to say is that it is the field of the heart (the vortex of cardiac energy) that commands this interaction in the quantum ocean of all potentialities. The vibration of this field is very high, and the waves of form emitted can vibrate at the speed of light. The energy field of the heart is "five thousand times more powerful than the brain"[3] and is a torsion quantum field, in the form of a donut, reorganizing information, emitting light and energy interactively and functioning in an acausal and nonlocal and holographic manner.

The heart field does not judge, it simply observes and feels in an accurate manner the unity with the field of unified consciousness, moving in it, creating more and

---
[3] Heart Math Institute publications, see also www.hearthmath.org

actualizing new possibilities immediately.

It is only necessary to feel the feeling totally—purely—experiencing it even if it is just for a nanosecond, five minutes, a few days or months for it to happen. Everything is possible.

The energy that the field of the heart processes and is capable of affecting space-time and the events occurring in it is Love; whatever the form that love presents itself in— namely gratitude, appreciation, compassion or forgiveness —it informs and enforms life.

Love is the basic pulsation of the universe, the driving force behind the exchange of information and interaction in the quantum world. It is a hologram of the totality which mirrors the pureness and wholeness of the field of unified consciousness in its manifestations. It is the language, the message and the messenger present in the creation, from the human being to the lizard, and clover, or the supernova and even to what has not yet been created and is merely in a potential state. It is the super structure that builds us and supports the whole, animating us with grace and beauty. **Love is the language and the "subtle technology" of creation in the vanguard of human realization.**

When vibrating in love it is possible to manifest what we feel instantly. We are in a state of inner certainty and innocence where it is only possible for our feelings to happen. We are so internally cohesive and connected therefore it is inevitable that the field of unified consciousness responds in tune with our feelings, which materializes as visible reality. On the other hand, even if the results become visible later on, for example, three days later or in the following week or month, they were triggered by that vibration of love.

What are the implications for the possibility that we can affect both the past as well as the future of our lives?

They are gigantic. First, we begin to perceive as unlimited beings and infinitely expanded in the field of unified consciousness. The boundaries and barriers of space and time which conditioned the perceptions of the impact that we have on reality, disappear, leaving an open space to discover the infinite possibilities. What we feel now is capable of formatting myriad scenarios in an "extended" time of the now, to which we focus our attention and feeling, but which is now already observed by us and woven in our lives. We can have a precognition/premonition of the future, capture it through the higher senses (intuition, clairvoyance etc.) and that precognition/premonition helps us to decide wisely before the events happen. We can forebode and avoid that accident, complete the course, conceive the child that is going to be spiritually illuminated, promote a revolution through flowers, enriching a country, amongst others.

In parallel, we can feel now and that feeling dissolves and actualizes something specific that had been imprinted. A deeply felt look at something that is "there," that potentiates and makes the new scenario available. This retrospective feeling erases and imprints the diversity and gives us the chance of "correcting" the past. A selective "quantum eraser" that gives us the opportunity of a different outcome. It can be to help a relative, telling our mother we love her before she passes, saying yes to an intense passion, making that nation, ending a period of mourning, and in the present feel the effects of thinking back, broadening our horizons and happy experiences.

This probability of affecting time and the respective events in space time places in our hands vast choices and opens many doors, that we resize our place in the world and in the life that is unfolding inside us, around us and in everything this very instant. Instead of spectators of life, we are partners and participants in reality and we create it and recreate it, together with the field of unified consciousness. This requires accountability, and audacity, moderated by good sense in exercising our sovereignty as "kings and queens of our lives," respecting the sovereignty of others and harmonizing it for the good of all.

Besides this, we also become aware that our consciousness is the most sophisticated tool that we have and that feeling, namely love, is the state of consciousness that allows us to transcend the conventional laws of physics and can affect reality multidimensionally. The field of the heart is our laboratory for miracles, allowing us to perform what until then, only imagination or the mystics would say was possible.

In each step of feeling and in each movement in love, there is the possibility of opening multiple other potentialities, in an intricate tapestry, showing outcomes that affect our lives as well as the lives of the rest of the beings.

From a quantum point of view, feeling is a subatomic dance, where there is a sharing of information and interaction of bits of information, of waves of energy and light, in a colorful and gigantic web to which we are all linked and we participate in.

Feeling is an act of conscious sovereignty allowing us to communicate and give form to life in accordance with the authenticity and exclusivity inherent to us, and that the field of unified consciousness subscribes and exhibits.

Feeling is the language and the "subtle technology" that we have at our disposal to transform infinite possibilities into magnificent realities.

♥ Stop, Breathe, Love

Presently, humanity is being called, on a perceptual level, to a gigantic journey where love is the common denominator to perform changes on all levels. And each one of us counts.

It is an illusion to think that we are just by ourselves that we are limited, and that the choices we make do not affect us, and the collective. In fact, our existence affects all existence, and all that we feel, think or imagine, even the simple act of breathing, interferes with all of humanity, with the planet and the universe.

Effectively, one of us is totally sufficient. Furthermore, it is essential for all of life to change, because the universe is only complete with our presence and participation, therefore our love places the universe on another point of creativity and manifestation. Each one of us is powerful, a universe of potentialities affecting other universes with the consciousness.

From a quantum point of view, a minute jump has an overwhelming impact on everything, and that is why each contribution is precious, yours, mine, ours, connected, and makes all the difference. A feeling, a focused intention, felt and maintained by each one of us, is a quantum leap, the revolution we all need.

One of us is the All, and when one of us feels love, the field of unified consciousness reflects it and expands it, informing and giving form to cocreated reality, through the feeling, changing the face of the whole universe, the planet, the community, the families and the individual who generated it.

As already mentioned, only 1% (actually the square root of 1%) of the people in the community are needed, so that through our coherent intentions and feelings, such as love or peace felt and experienced internally, positively and coherently affects the collective consciousness. This number is the trigger of cohesion, connecting and nurturing one another. We create a critical mass and quantum superstructures that sustain the whole community, the globe, and interferes with the cosmos. The more we are aware of this process the better, and the square root of 1% is only a start.

For example, in Portugal, there are 10,427,301 people, 1% is 104,273 people, the square root is even less, 323 people; therefore, it is relatively easy for this number of people to be in love and peace, united towards a common end, for example, improvement of health conditions, or the number of adoptions, or more work and feeling that inside ourselves, affecting the personal and collective reality.

We experience that love makes all the difference because it is the collective cohesive Force, aggregating ordered fields that support the global structure. It is the essence of life, generating more life at each moment. Each one of us, when focused on love, recreates a powerful wave with collective impact.

Being conscious that we are connected with a common purpose, observed and felt by many of us individually, we create and reinvent life, capable of bringing paradise to Earth, and we live in a world and a country where it is good to live.

It is possible now to decide to be focused on internal peace, be it, live in it and allow it to positively affect our lives, work environments, and our families and even massively create a collective intention and feeling, for example, children being successful and happy in school. This may require our total focus, every day for an hour, on this process of being love and internal peace.

Now the next step is even more appetizing and more vibrant. I propose that every day you increase your level of coherence of love and peace; for example, the next day you are in love and peace for two hours, the next day, three hours, and so on until you are in this state for a full day. And then for two days, one week, two weeks, a month, two months, and one year.

This process is going to create a massive turning point, because from the moment we are vibrating the greater part of the time in our day in this coherence, the more love and peaceful coherence we raise. From the moment that we exceed 51% of our time in this state, we grow and cause exponential growth of this love wave, and our life is transformed as well as everyone else's. It is magic and vibrating. We will never be the same; we are transfigured and we transfigure the world. We are requested as humanity, to raise our vibrational level of love above 51% until the total love integrity, so that the personal and planetary leverage occurs rapidly, and we can rise collectively and massively. That is, when human beings irradiate love every day in over 51% of their time, during the day or night, and for each person, situation, event, or object, provoking a gigantic conscious acceleration.

This acceleration changes the field of consciousness and modifies the field of the planet, mirroring holographically in the field of unified consciousness the love we emit, which is exponentially increased causing our bodies, minds, hearts and souls to become increasingly more luminous and in tune with its true essence, which is love and light, creating new manifestations in the collective reality.

Above 51% we create a conscious turning point with individual, global and cosmic implications. This means that every day, at each moment, we have to be aware and choose love; be love, being and acting in it in a coherent and consistent manner. This is completely possible: you, me, we have the strength, the force of love in our hearts to shine and alter reality. Maintain the coherence, deciding now that today for an hour we will be love and whatever happens we will maintain that state. And we celebrate. The following day, we choose to be love for two consecutive hours and celebrate even more, and so forth during a full week. At the end of the week, we will feel a state of grace, rendered to the presence of love and we only want to continue the celebration. If we persist for a full month, our whole life is going to change radically and furthermore all people we interact with will be activated and sensitized for the same transformation in a gigantic wave of love.

This constant loving feeling makes us vibrate consciously in a state of clarity and perfection, communicating and interacting with the field of unified consciousness and with the planet in a synchronized manner, causing the emergence of uncommon realities in the light of conventional laws of physics, often called miracles and they are the law of love in action. Personally, making the turning point, we are also a trampoline so that the whole of humanity, the planet and the universe sing in a single voice.

The calling is for each one of us. Namely for you, reading this chapter now. Because humanity claimed assistance and as the legend says: *"God listened to the request and sent you"* to love intensely and totally at each moment.

It is possible to always give love, because it is present and is abundant in nature. Love is complete in us and generates more love. It moves in us and through us in everything. Love aggregates, includes, accepts, shares, teaches and is supreme intelligence in action.

The love of each one makes all the difference, the impact is real, measurable and totally beneficial and is always available to be exercised, 24 hours per day, 365 days per year, on any continent, in any situation or with any person, animal or event. It always works.

We have the Force in us and we can carry out the revolution of love, believing in its power and realizing its power at any instant for our good and the good of all. Every day and in every instant, we can be, give and make more love, and this feeling places us in an extraordinary vibrational state. As it becomes a constant in our life, our body of light becomes more activated and available to experience higher states of consciousness, affecting all the networks of life on this planet and the Cosmos.

Who Are We? We are butterflies of love clapping our wings in a point of the planet and causing a loving typhoon on the other side of the world. We are beings aware of ourselves and of the dynamic lattice that is life, mutually affecting and creating more love, peace, health, beauty, solidarity and quality of life for all beings in a universal symphony of plenitude and joy. The experience is already happening; it is inside you, me, and us and it is counting on us. Thank you for being love now, for being united in the field of infinite possibilities.

 Key points:
- Feeling is a language through which we communicate with the world and the field. Each feeling creates reality.
- Feeling is an impression of the soul that is neurally woven, expressing itself in the mind and in the sensations, which the body reflects.

- While facing a hard situation raise your energy as soon as you can by remembering this sentence: "Who am I is bigger than this, and this too shall pass. I Trust in the unknown" and feel supported by the field.
- Feelings are like geniuses of creation and you can use them to your advantage.
- Aligning your feelings with the positive results is essential. It can be meeting a friend on the other side of the globe, healing back pain or an autoimmune disease, buy a huge present for your kid or sign an excellent contract. All these realities are available.
- Life has all that we need, and in the act of feeling it, we actualize numerous probabilities of reality that converge for the concretization of the event, person or circumstance, aligned with our sentimental representation.
- Leave aside doubt, fear or tension and be clear about what you want and focus on your results with love and gratitude.
- Be receptive. The results can be even better because the field is generous and loves you.
- It is possible for feelings to affect the future and even the past that is already consolidated in our lives and transform it.
- The most important question that we can ask ourselves is: **What feeling serves this reality?** And then feel it and act.
- Opening our hearts to love, and allowing it to guide us, dissolves any limitation; life gains new colors and we renew strengths, capacities and relationships in a profound manner.
- What kind of man or woman you would like to be? Feel it, embody it and you will transform yourself.

Self-reflection:

❶ What was easiest for you to understand regarding the three origins of feelings?
❷ What feelings do you normally emit for your life and for the planet?
❸ How understanding the importance of "positive" and "coherent" feelings can transform your life?
❹ Which "positive" feelings do you identify most with? Would you add any?
❺ Share to someone you love an experience where you changed the "negative" to the "positive" and what real effects did it have for you.

Exercises:

❶ Remember an experience when an enormously powerful positive feeling flooded you. Write about it in detail and feel it.
Close your eyes and place your attention on your heart and expand that feeling through your chest. Move that feeling upwards to your head, and then to your arms and hands, your abdominals muscles, pelvic area, legs and feet until all your body is permeated with this feeling. Breathe deeply 3 times and maintain this feeling with you.
❷ Describe an experience in your life where you chose to interpret a situation differently (with a person, or an event) and felt good by doing so.
Can you do it today?
With whom?

Describe the feeling, the result you want to feel and go for it.

❸ When something good happens to you intensify it in your mind and heart for 1 min. Expand the energy of that feeling again for 1 min. You are turbocharging yourself, reinforcing neural connections, and creating positive memories.

❹ Today, love intensely. Feel love from the moment you open your eyes in the morning, or step out of bed, answering the phone, eating, in anything you do, sense or think. Merge lovingly with life.

Practice the state of loving coherence for an hour, two hours, one full day, and so forth.

Send us your testimonial about your experiences to: susana@susanacorderosa.com

11 Action

Story

A man was unhappy in his marriage. Arguments and petty quarrels were driving him insane and he decided to leave home. Not quite knowing what to do (as he was feeling drained), he decided to walk. He hoped that during the walk a solution for what was afflicting him would emerge. He walked over mountains and valleys, but his pain followed him. One day, in a village where he stopped to eat, he was told that there was a shrine and whoever went there would be blessed for life. Suddenly, his heart jumped, his eyes were bright and the desire to reach this holy place took over. He quickly set out on his way in the direction he was told. He walked for two weeks continuously, almost without resting, fueled by the internal fire of wanting to reach the place and go in.

As he began to see the shrine ahead, a landslide suddenly came barreling down the side of the mountain. Although he was not harmed, the landslide had blocked his path, preventing him from continuing. What should he do now? He was so close... He observed what had happened from nearby and sat down, falling asleep from exhaustion. He woke up drowsily and went to explore the surrounding site to see if there were other ways that he could take to reach the shrine. At that moment, none seemed secure enough or direct enough to reach it, so he decided to sleep there, to rest and think better on the issue, or even to receive some inspiration. The following morning at sunrise, he saw a rabbit in an illuminated place; he got up, and deciding to have a better look and at that point had a different perspective of the way. He packed his things and walked up the mountain, which led him to another path that would lead him to the shrine. He followed the path all day long and later, at the end of the day, he reached the small walls surrounding the sacred place. He felt very happy; what a breathtaking beauty the place had. He felt so touched for having arrived. Deciding to enter the little chapel to be blessed, he found that the door was closed. At that point, he breathed deeply, looked up to the sky, and understood that it was time to be grateful for everything he had experienced until then.

He surrendered to the presence that animated him and sustained all life. In that instant, time and space disappeared; a golden light absorbed him totally. It was his essence, his home, his hometown and his sea, his family, his wife, his friends, his work and also nature in action. God in everything. He felt so blessed and taken over, so whole, that he could remain there for the rest of his life.

He stayed overnight in that place, serene and confident. Everything was right in his life. In the morning when he woke up, he found that the doors of the chapel were open.

"God wants, man dreams, the work is born."
Fernando Pessoa

"Genius begins great works, labor alone finishes them."
J. Joubert

Are we, like the character, also following a route? Is there someone giving us directions regarding the next stage? Is there a set time to reach the target? And if by chance we had challenges or crossroads, what do we do then? **Action!** What a fantastic way of achieving satisfaction and intervening in life. We consider action to be the act of doing, performing one or various movements in a set direction and with a set end. The activity gives color to everyday life, allowing us to leave our digital imprint on the planet and the universe in which we live.

In a wider sense, what is action? It is energy in movement, light pulsating and conscious information vibrating in an organized manner and with a purpose. It is also **the language and the technology of creation, placed at the service of human consciousness, so that it constructs reality.**

Human action has behavior underlying it, and it can be understood as a way of leading our lives, of our behavior with ourselves and with others. That behavior can be active or passive. **That is, behavior can be action or inaction. Both make sense considering the context.** For example, the act of working is important, but rest and leisure are also essential. Although in the title of the chapter reference is made to action (active behavior) we will also talk about inactive behavior, that is, of "not doing anything." Let us move then.

What is the origin of action? Action, just like inaction, has its source in the field of unified consciousness, which is the base of life. A human being, as a field of consciousness, has behaviors of action and omission. Earth's field of consciousness carries out actions in nature and also reflects human actions. Although we are stating that there are three origins of action (and inaction), the energy of action is one.

❶ Unified consciousness
❷ Individual consciousness
❸ Planetary consciousness

❶ Action from the unified consciousness

It is energy, information and light in movement, organized in an intelligent manner and with a purpose: the construction of reality. The primordial act of the creation of the universe that the field of unified consciousness materialized brought to life what we know as solar systems, water, planets, seasons of the year, humans, cockroaches or flowers.

An action from the field of unified consciousness is **timeless,** able to be represented in quantum terms beyond time, transcending the limits of linear time. This act can be accessed by human beings in the now, and independently of the moment of its occurrence. We can still share this information simultaneously with other human beings, in distinct parts of the globe. For example, in a unified state of consciousness, we can see the works of the present, the past and also of future events, and it can happen individually, in groups, or different places. Various people can simultaneously have access to the same information.

An action from the field of unified consciousness is **holographic,** that is, it is inserted in the whole structure of life and represented in it. However small or big the manifestation, from the germ, to the flea, the cell or a star, all these acts represents the unity and are mirrors of a whole that the human being contains in him, and also has direct access to, on any "focal point" on which the consciousness is focused.

An action of the field of unified consciousness is **alocal,** able to be represented in quantum terms in more than one place in space, namely in parallel universes, and can be accessed and experienced instantaneously by various consciousnesses and be actualized and communicated to other dimensions or beings, emerging from "nothing" and vanishing into "nothing," which the All contains.

The human consciousness in resonance with the field of unified consciousness accesses this information, energy and creative light via the higher senses (namely through inspiration, intuition, clairvoyance), and the consciousness/brain matrix makes it frequencially intelligible so that we can understand it and use it in our life. We have the capacity of accepting or rejecting that energy, information and light. When we accept, we realize inspired works, we have acts of genius, we build forms that have never been seen before and that are profoundly beautiful. They are creative acts full of primordial energy that we use to build reality with perfect forms, and also acts of profound simplicity and wholeness, integrating us with the All, in a constant dialectic. At any instant, we can have glimpses of these acts and we modify our perception of reality, intervening in the world in a unique and intelligent manner.

❷ Action from the individual consciousness

The human consciousness/brain matrix captures information with the sixteen senses, processing, organizing and giving it sense and that information being able to result in an action (an intentional body movement), namely of the upper members and/or the lower members of the body, affecting the personal world and also what surrounds us. In the case of inaction, the internal process happens, but there is no movement. The cause of an action, as a rule, results from thoughts, words, images, emotions or feelings that we experience internally and triggers the action process. We act to change an internal state and also to change the disposition of things, people or events. The action of the field of human consciousness can be seen as a process where a vast electromagnetic energy is produced, just as if it were a great storm, and this energy is channeled to a "focal point" (object, situation, animal or person), with an exchange of energy resulting from that interaction. This energy is self-produced and simultaneously disseminated in waves to the field of unified consciousness and to the field of planetary consciousness, with whom we are in constant communication and interaction, affecting us individually, and to the collective of human beings, to the planet and the All.

❸ Action produced by the planetary consciousness

Earth is a living entity, acting on itself through movements, rhythms, and cycles, creating, destroying and recreating itself, affecting the creatures existing on it. It is also an information field emitting and receiving information systematically to all beings existing on it and sending these vibrations to the unified field of consciousness.

Human beings, through action, affect their lives and the collective, as well as nature. For example, the act of constructing a group of buildings to house 200 families has an impact for all involved in the construction, the resident families, and nature that ceases to be in its initial state.

Each time a human being acts, the planet accepts this information and returns it in the same frequency to its emitter, as well as to all the people who are aligned vibrationally in the same frequency of the wave and also to the field of unified consciousness. Let us imagine the action of helping a child cross the street. The person doing the deed becomes in resonance with all the people in the world that also realized it. The person who is violent, who beats someone up, comes in tune with all the violent people, beating another, on the planet. Earth only returns what it receives.

As it happens, when receiving the vibrations of the acts retransmitted by the planet, we have the power to accept, reject or change them. That is, even if we were in tune with the violence, we can change the energy internally and externally, acting in a different manner, and that act feeds our field, the field of unified consciousness and the planet, which will retransmit to the collective of beings new information, causing a new impact in the chain of actions.

Actions are existing information in the field of unified consciousness, already formatted and in Earth's energy field. They are also condensed energy, in accordance with the form patterns that we self-produce (in our consciousness/ brain matrix) and use every day as well as the energy that we receive. Each action is a point of manifestation that we interpret and use to build reality.

Action is the language and the "technology of creation" at the service of the human being to experience the realization.

From now on we will speak of human action and the innumerable constructions possible that it formats in our personal, collective and cosmic reality. It is our duty to use it for the good of all beings.

The Discovery of Action

"If I knew that the world would end tomorrow, I would still plant a tree today."
Various Authors

"Man is what he himself makes."
André Malraux

"The good deeds are for those who practice them."
Maria Margarida, my grandmother

When we observe behind the scenes of a film, we know that there is always a director. Normally, it is him that says "Action."
Just like in a film, we are the directors of our lives, and also the principal or secondary characters, interacting in a common film that is reality.
What is the function of action?
Action is the instrument of the field of unified consciousness that human beings have and it is multifunctional. It namely enables:

1) **Building reality.** Each time we act, we move in a perceptual state to a direct intervention in things, people, circumstances or events and that leads reality to emerge. For example, the action of weaving, leads to the making of a tapestry. Before going into action, there was an idea, and as a result of various actions, a tapestry is completed.

2) Action changes our vision of the world and also changes the world. When we act, we understand reality in an active manner and the manner we understand the world is permeated with our experience. We see the world in the light of what we realize and our cells integrate that information, which was stored in the memory, and also becoming part of us as lymph, hair, heartbeat, teeth or skin. We assume a body, mind, emotions, and soul in the image of our actions. In parallel, by intervening in the world, we change it. We change the position of where things were, we modify the scenery, we create cooperation between groups, or we create more social justice, amongst other things.

3) We learn quickly through action. When having an experience, the senses and attention are aware of the information and the realization of the activity is rapidly interiorized and we learn. We are involved on various levels, namely the mental and motor parts are activated, and it is easier to understand what functions and how it functions. What makes sense and what does not. What we want and what we do not want. Experience is a great teacher. For example, if we eat something we have never tasted before and we like it, we learn that it tastes good and we can repeat the experience. Another example is when we set up a gadget, we understand how it works much faster than if we had simply read the instructions.

4) Through action, we increase self-confidence. Each time we act, we feel more consistent, capable and complete. We exercise our capabilities, the competencies we already possess and also the ones we want to learn, we expand our perception about what we are able to do and we become full of energy. Acting is the oxygen of self-confidence allowing us to grow and amplify the whole world and the globe.

5) Acting gives us autonomy and freedom to live. When we carry out actions, we use our strength, creativity, intelligence and knowledge, placing our mark on a world that is totally receptive to us. If we do nothing for ourselves and for others, we can lose vitality; we may have the tendency to feel or believe that we are victims of circumstances. The vital force that we possess is available to be put in movement through action, and restraining it is creating resistance to the flow of life.

6) Through action we also build our identity and self-esteem. Each time we act, we inform and give form to Who We Are. Only by acting do we understand what we are capable of, what our convictions and deep emotions are. Without action, we do not assume the name that we were given and the name we want to give ourselves. We are in the virtual world, disassociating ourselves with our role in the world. Self-Esteem is created in the process of intervening in life. Without attitudes, we become fragile, because we do not exercise the power of creating our reality, making it possible to feel that we are at the mercy of others, events or even of time. *Self-Esteem is to value yourself and learn from failures or mistakes, transforming them into the driving force for success and realizing actions. In acting, we reinforce and recreate self-esteem, we become more self-aware, know ourselves better and we support the development of humanity.*

7) In acting, we show what is important to us. Our actions show what we are focusing on, what we are committed to and what we value. When acting, we place our energy on what we want to see manifested and indicate what our priorities are. The behavior shows the project, the person, or the job. Without action, everything is the same and formless.

8) Action makes us visible. It shows us, to others and to the world What We Are at that moment, where we are, and where we want to go. We stop being in the shade and have the spotlight of life shining on us. Action reveals the human facet and leaves its mark.

Existence requires actions and it is vital that we act. That is because acting is effectively modifying our reality and the world through our interaction with the field of unified and planetary consciousness. In each act, we inform, give form and are also enformed by it. In acting, we inform ourselves about the intention, direction and realization of our energy and inform the All when doing it. We also shape what we realize, because through action we sculpture reality, giving it substance and contour. We are also enformed through the actions that we realize because they make us the people we are, and reflect our level of consciousness, as well as the field of unified consciousness gives us form and consistency mirroring the attitudes we took.
Action is the vital expression of what animates us and the potentiality transformed in the act, manifesting reality in unity with the field of unified consciousness. It is the language and the "technology of creation" in the realization.
Through action we can create the construction of a home, launch a rocket to the moon, embroider a tablecloth, bathe your child, ride a motorbike at high speed, play hide and seek, or write a poem. *Any reality is possible.*

 Exercise:
Write down 3 actions that make your heart sing and do them.
Be present while you are involved in them and feel your body.

♥ Stop, Breathe, Love

The human form indicates with evidence the preponderant role of action in existence. Physically, we are what we are, in order to intervene in life, to move and interrelate with it.
The head is small in relationship to the body, and the most prominent and extended parts are the lower and upper members. Regarding the internal organs, the greater majority of them are integrated in the central part of the body until the lower abdomen and in the periphery we have the members. Body movement is a representation and an extension of cosmic movement; in the case of the human being, movement is organized and coordinated in an intelligent form in the cerebral and cardiac center, radiating to the periphery. The peripheral location and the most elongated anatomy, with joints and the softer tissues were conceived to fulfill their function, move, coordinating themselves, being flexible and acting externally. It is with the members that we hug, touch, play football or skip, run, and dig in the garden,

cook or sculpt. We are perfect the way we are, and we were conceived to act in life, changing it and building it up in our image, in partnership with the field of unified and planetary consciousness.

It is in acting that humans make and remake themselves continually, manifesting reality and exemplifying how to proceed in a given moment, bequeathing their property to the world and affecting it, as well as the field of unified consciousness who mirrors it holographically in totality, in a continuous movement, creating and recreating life.

♥ Stop, Breathe, Love

In our day to day lives, we carry out so many actions, many of them routine and linked, that we may have the sensation that we are not creating reality. Like getting out of bed, brushing our teeth, drinking coffee and going to the bus stop, or going by car to work, taking the children to school, doing the same things and taking the same routes. It may seem that life happens and that we are not creating anything, because what we have presently is similar or the same as we have had and we do not like it, giving us the impression that we are being controlled, led or that we have no choice. But this is not true; it is pure illusion. *Our behaviors are always achieving and forming reality.*

We were conceived and structured to participate in life through action. The control is in our hands because we are the being that can realize, undertake, modify, organize and give meaning to reality. This is an innate right of creation that has been present since the beginning of existence.

The issue here is not if we are creating reality through the acts we practice, because that is inborn; it is action fulfilling its function.

The real issue is, **what can we create purposefully, at this moment, through action?** More appropriately, **how can I exercise my innate creativity and choose the behaviors that I practice?**

Deciding to have other behaviors, focusing attention and fulfilling them; being committed to the actions chosen and effectively realizing them.

For example, if your normal behavior was to wear the first thing you saw, have a careless appearance, a different behavior is to choose the clothes that match, and take care of your appearance. If your normal behavior was to read your emails three times per day and you noticed that your time was not well managed, then change your attention, your attitudes and see them only once a day, and focus on priorities. This behavior is to be repeated daily, until it is implemented.

The truth is that we are always deciding, choosing what to do, or not to do at given moment of our lives, thus affecting reality. Distinct actions manifest different realities in any area of our life, from relationships, work, finances, learning or leisure.

From a quantum point of view, each act is a specific energy actualized by the consciousness and is woven on a fundamental level to the whole of existence and communicates and interrelates with it. Each action evokes other events that were in the field of potential, and the field of unified consciousness in the presence of our actions, synchronizes people, events, or situations vibrationally aligned with the action meanwhile realized in a dance of manifestation.

Actions are acts of human creativity in unity with the field of unified consciousness, with immediate impact on reality, modifying it, affecting family, friends, the community, the planet and the cosmos.

Acting is realizing, embodying life in accordance with the decision and with the movement affected, being that reality is permeated with the energy of the author of the act.

Man, molds action and simultaneously molds reality in the field of unified consciousness and the planet. In parallel, action molds man, because he is affected by his acts and is molded automatically by the field of unified consciousness as a result of its essential connection. An act is the most efficient form of making ourselves visible to ourselves, to others, and to all that exists, and communicates what makes sense, at that time, in accordance with our consciousness, putting it into practice. Action revolutionizes and implements the desired changes.

Without action there is no evolution, nor revolution.

The objective now is that you become a cocreator, a "deliberate doer" and organized, instead of a "routine doer," a disorganized creator, using the language and the "technology of creation" of action for the realization of the life of your dreams, which brings wellbeing to the All.

Here is a testimonial of that creativity and of organized and deliberate creation:

Testimonial

My life changed completely after my participation in a workshop of Unified Quantum Healing which took place in Fundão. I thank the universe for the existence of such special and luminous beings such as Susana and also for finally understanding that I am the light and also unique in a certain manner.

Before meeting Susana I liked to do a lot of things, but never managed to do anything. Now I do not say... I do! The day after the seminar, I went to register myself as a volunteer at the hospital, something I had been postponing year after year. At the moment, I am a voluntary worker there. Last week I went to ask if a little boy in a children's foster home could spend a few days at my home. I am waiting for the Court ruling. If the little boy is allowed to come, great, if not, I will go and see him. I have already decided that every week I will visit those wonderful children at the foster home. The day after the seminar, I went to look for work and something extraordinary happened, there was a full-time job offer in my field. Previously I believed that it was difficult to find a full-time job as a physiotherapist. Now that I have changed my beliefs, I saw immediate results. There is work for me, and I can even choose a part time job to reconcile various activities. Before doing the workshop, time seemed to be galloping, I did not have time for anything, and I was always stressed, at the moment, I ask myself if the clock has a battery, because I have so much energy and do so much. It is impressive. The workshop of Unified Quantum Healing was wonderful, and I want to do it again... Thank you so much, Susana, now I know who I am, what my role is in the world and I act confidently.

Heliana Gonçalves, physiotherapist

♥ Stop, Breathe, Love

We have already understood that action manifests reality, more concretely, it is reality and through it we are realized as people and we imprint our mark on the world. But there are so many actions that we can undertake that it is possible sometimes not to know what behavior to opt for.

We may want to know if the action is right or wrong, if it is "positive" or "negative," if it will have the desired results or not, that is, the mind wants answers to act in a certain way. What should we do then?

One of the easiest ways is to ask ourselves, **"Is this what makes sense to experience in reality?" or "Is this the mark that I want to imprint on life?"** If the action is against our personal values, if its results are perceived as confusion, anger, violence, failure or pain, and if the effects are contrary to the motive that has led us to practice this action, then it is preferable to change the behavior.

The action that agrees with personal and universal values, where the results manifested are perceived as valid, positive, clear, and productive and that they are in accordance with the motive by which we realized it, should be maintained.

If we still need greater clarity, the golden rule announced two thousand years ago by Jesus, which is still applicable: *"do unto others as you would have them do unto you,"* and also the new interpretation *"do to ourselves what we would like others to do to us."*

What results can we expect from an action?

It all depends on the act that is practiced and for what end we realize it.

In some actions, we have physical results. For example, chopping firewood or doing the dishes. In others, we feel the effects on the level of emotions or feelings, for example having a bath and have the sensation of pleasure or hug a friend and feel joy in doing so. There are also results on a mental level, for example, the act of studying has the effect of gaining knowledge. We can also experience effects on the level of the soul, for example, the act of meditating illuminates us.

The result we can expect from the action is the one we conceived, wished, felt and realized.

What if the results of our actions are different from what we expected? What shall we do?

1-Have the perception that whatever is happening is for the best. Even if we do not know how and why, the result of the action will bring us a greater good than the one we had initially projected or desired.

There is a gigantic intelligence to which we are connected 24 hours per day, that knows and conceives at the highest level a grandiose result. Normally, we could not even imagine the possibility of such a result, but the field of unified consciousness delivers it when we are receptive. **Therefore, accepting, in the presence of a differentiated result, that what is happening is for the greater good, is fundamental.**

2- Be aware that the differences in the result could also be stages for better clarity, in relation to what we intend to see manifested.

Is it possible to do one thing, but feel another, or have beliefs that are opposite to what we are materializing? It is very likely. But this interferes with the action and makes probable subatomic rearrangements, manifested with distinct effects (rather than the ones intended first), creating turbulence and interfering with the initial clarity.

The reality that we create in harmony with the field of unified consciousness, on the level of action, is linked to the intentions, thoughts, images, words, feelings and emotions that we emit and these waves that we emit create patterns that permit different outcomes. The clearer the action is internally and externally, the more coherent the result is.

3- **Maintain the focus and persist**. Sometimes the effects of the action are not the ones expected because we do not allow the actions to be revealed, or bear fruit, in fact we gave up on them. In the anxiety of seeing immediate results, we forget that it is necessary to have cumulative and directed actions towards the same end, very often until the matter shows us evidence.

This is the result of a "fast food" mentality that is not binding nor disciplined to what is really intended, as well as having our attention dispersed and sabotaging it with negative thoughts, distorted emotions and antagonistic behaviors to whatever you want to see materialized in reality.

How many diets and trips to the gym have been sabotaged this way? Keeping the course of action and continuing to practice it persistently, is vital for the materialization of the result. For example, a famous pianist has thousands of hours of work, dedication and persistence, of love and of positive thoughts and images directed to success. In this case, the lesson is that in the next action with the same motive, we persist.

4-**The action is not a "mean to something" it does not need any result.**
We act with total consciousness that the action is already complete, and the act of realization contains the ideal events or happenings and it is for the good of all beings

♥ Stop, Breathe, Love

Another issue regarding action has to do with the moment of its materialization. That is: **when does action materialize into reality?**

First, it is necessary to understand that action always happens in the now and it is in the moment that we concretize the act that the energy is available for materialization. In this sense, acting is being present and moving the present. The manifestation is immediate.

From the moment we perform a single act or in a set of successive acts, the action is already happening and is materialized.

Another thing is seeing the effect of the action, its result, and that can happen immediately, for example when changing a tire, the action is consummated and is consolidated materially. It can also show itself in what we call the future, for example a job application and starting to work, may not be immediate, or we implement a new measure at work, whose effects will only be seen the following month. Or doing body building at the gym, were the muscles developed will only show months afterwards.

In these cases, a set of events and information linked to the action are being organized on a subtle level and manifest themselves when all the internal and external conditions are met, forming a series of linked steps for the showing of the final result of the action which had been indicated previously but is only subsequently completed.

In parallel, there is also the issue of the limits that we impose on the time that it will "take" until an action is materialized.

Mentally, we decided that we need "more" time, for example, for the house to be found, or to apologize and make up, or to be healed, when in reality, we have all the time on our side and that action may "need no time."

The action may manifest automatically if we so decide and are united with it and receptive to its immediate materialization. That is why there are people who find the right house immediately and solve an emotional issue and are healed instantly. In the field of unified consciousness, such act is already available to gain form; it is only necessary to update our consciousness in tune with that possibility, so that the result becomes visible.

It is the state of internal openness and unity with all the things in which we are vibrating at that moment which brings to life in harmony with the field of unified consciousness and the planet, what we focused and realized. We are creators of reality, in unity with the field of infinite possibilities, and in fact, everything is possible when speaking the language and using the "technology of creation" of action.

Using the words of Thomas Edison: *"If we did all the things we are capable of, we would literally astound ourselves."*

Unfulfilled Action

"Take time to deliberate, but when the time for action has arrived, stop thinking and go in."
Napoleon Bonaparte

"By the street of byandby, one arrives at the house of never."
Miguel Cervantes

"Keep something to eat, but never anything to do."
Portuguese proverb

"True happiness comes from the joy of deeds well done, the zest of creating things new."
Antoine de Saint Exupery

My mother is a very dynamic person, with a very sharp practical sense and therefore was able to raise five children on her own. From the time we were small, she told us, "If you have something to do, do it, and then rest or go and play." This practice was deeply rooted in our house and my brothers and I, even if we tried to run away from it, were quickly confronted with the severity of my mother regarding school and household chores that we were given.

In this manner, the message was passed on to us that we had to assume our responsibilities first, and postpone our fun to a later stage. This way of being was very useful for us, because it trained us to meet our commitments first and then enjoy life, sometimes needing to wait a little for the good things.

Doing first and having fun afterwards can be a good attitude, as long as we do not overload ourselves with activities, and never have time or space for pleasure, because then we become unbalanced.

How many people know that the best thing to do is act, carry out the activity and yet they still avoid it, bypass it and then feel a sensation of impotence and of revolt because they caused the delay. It is called "procrastination," the inertia or escape from activity, through numerous escape mechanisms that then result in irresponsibility.

In general, the internal discourse goes like this: "I will do it later," "Tomorrow, I will feel stronger," "Maybe the weather will get better" "We will see what happens," "I do not feel like it," amongst others.

From the time we repeat this behavior successively, the habit is set, of postponing or even not doing, with negative consequences in our lives.

In truth, inertia is an attitude that leaves side effects in the agent and the community, therefore the decision not to act is in itself an active decision to maintain the status quo. Omitting an action when it is necessary, is negating the position of intervening in the world, allowing disorder to take place by absence.

The usual omissive behavior produces stagnation, creates resistance and disorder in nature, not allowing the revelation of new contexts and states. If Man systematically abstained from acting in the world, he would endanger the very species.

A person that systematically does not act, or that postpones, "*sine die*," the decisions and respective actions, or only acts in cases of extreme necessity, when the circumstances are such that they have to interfere in your life because it is in danger (that it created through inertia) provokes the destruction of the self-confidence, constructs dependency in relation to others. It also creates numerous confusions and difficulties in their lives; having the tendency for blaming others (mother, wife, husband, mother in law, boss, government, past, etc.) as well as, having the tendency to stop investing in himself, in feeling useful, becoming unhappy, not realizing himself or the world through him.

The avoidance of change through inaction does not enable the internal and external revolution nor the respective individual and collective evolution. The tendency to "procrastinate" or not act, produces adverse effects.

What are the causes that underlie this type of behavior which limits or prevents action?

Fear, distrust, insecurity, perfectionism, distorted perceptions in relation to the activity and the lack of habit, are some of them. But first, we need to understand better how **action functions:**

Visualize or imagine the letter V. We have two lines pointing in two opposing directions that have a point of contact in the base. They are united before they branch out. Action can be similar to the V. The starting point of the action is a decision (conscious or unconscious) and from there forces are placed in movement, lines in a given direction, in the space-time that we have to deal with. These forces are apparently dual, but they complement each other.

Every action is made of Risk and Deliverance

RISK is the uncertainty, the possibility of not knowing or of not being able to control

in absolute terms, all the results or effects of our actions. When we act, we run risks: of succeeding or not, of being right or wrong, of being liked or not, the behavior being valid or rejected, etc.

DELIVERANCE consists in the fact that each action, when being realized, is released and takes up its function, leaving us and relaxing us. When we do, we hand over our strengths, our capacities and gifts and they take up their position in the world. The act fulfills itself the moment it is practiced and then belongs to the all.

Although the action is one, it is common to go through this process at the time of its realization. That is, we are aware of the risk and the deliverance that each action carries, and sometimes uncertainty appears in the form of fear, doubt, insecurity or distrust, gaining ground, and then we either postpone or do not do it. At that moment we have lost the train of deliverance because we have not realized it. The V was no longer balanced. Instead of coming out victorious, we became formless.

♥ Stop, Breathe, Love

Returning to procrastination, the 6 most common obstacles that limit or prevent action are:

1-**Fear is the number one cause.** This emotion blocks and contracts the energy field and could prevent us from advancing towards realization. It can be fear of failure, anticipating mentally and emotionally an undesired outcome or remembering an unsuccessful experience. Fear of not being good, capable, intelligent or young enough. For some, it can also be the fear of success, the changes that this may bring on a personal, professional or financial level, the fear of having to maintain or improve performance. There may also be the fear of being judged, assessed or criticized for the initiatives we have, and the fear of being exposed or rejected. Ultimately, many distorted beliefs are fed with images and emotions. The underlying convictions as well as the emotions and the images can be changed so that the act occurs.

2- **Distrust** is also limiting; it is a state of suspicion where we look for what could be wrong or that does not function, or any disability, boycotting the movement.

3- **Insecurity** is a counter power, creating resistance in the action to be taken because it unsettles us, removing "the rug that we want to step on." Feeling insecure, we only do things halfway or we retreat. We don't invest with the internal solidity that we have, and the vital energy becomes tense and dense.

Be careful that we are not denying the value of listening to the emotions and feelings such as fear or distrust because they may have pertinence. In effect, they may be browsing warnings, making us aware of aspects which we should consider. However, if we are vibrating systematically in fear and distrust, if we only act when we are 100% certain, sure, when all the conditions are met, or only when we have the support of others, it is very likely that we will be confined to very little, inclusively becoming depressed due to inaction.

4- **Perfectionism** can be another limitation.
In this society where eccentricity is cultivated, where we want to achieve the

maximum, be the best, and life is centered on results, very often in the short term, perfectionism can be a pothole.

Aiming to reach the highest levels of quality, execution, celebrity or efficiency, excellence can be a great blocker of action. Why? Because we may remain waiting to be excellent, to have the best conditions, living the best moment and it does not happen, or it emerges in an unexpected or a disguised manner, and we miss it completely.

Postponing until we are perfect, or doing it in an excellent manner, is to delay our possibility. In fact, it is losing the present opportunity to act and to grow. In order to move towards perfection we only have to take one step, and then another and so on. But if we do not act because we do not know everything, or we did not realize exactly, or execute the task wonderfully, the probability of being frustrated and not advancing to the following level is high. After all, we have not even given ourselves the opportunity of experimenting, of exercising the action and instead of progressing, we regress. **Perfection is not an isolated action, it is a path.**

Keep in mind that we are in favor of perfect action. We marvel at human excellence in any area of life. Indeed, it is part of human nature to want to transcend and always dare more and be better. The issue is, when seen through that mental filter, we cut ourselves short, we stop ourselves from acting, and we remain entangled in the web of perfectionism and we do not progress. On this subject, a sentence from António Lobo Antunes illustrates well this point of view: *"A fool who walks will get further than an intellectual sitting."*

5- The distorted perception regarding activity and particularly, to work.

From a very young age, we were raised to see activity as an obligation or as a punishment, and that generated antibodies in relation to the action. **For example, our parents told us (and do we replicate it?) that they worked as an obligation. They raise us as an obligation and pay the bills by obligation also. Enough of this kind of talk and subsequent behavior.**

The perception of displeasure, lack of freedom and limitations that we nurture mentally and emotionally regarding obligations, cause our behaviors to be riddled with these vibrations of tension, obligation, implying the tendency of acting against our will. In fact, we are not compelled to do anything; not working, not educating our children, nor paying our bills, not bathing, etc. We are free to do it or not. There are consequences; for example, not having any money at the end of the month, the children not achieving a university degree, electricity being cut off, smelling badly, amongst others. Therefore, the first step is to understand that we are lying to ourselves when we say that it is compulsory. We choose to think, speak, feel and behave in such a way through obligation. There are other alternatives. We can be aware that we have freely decided to work, educate our children, do our daily hygiene, or pay the bills in accordance with the values we nurture such as financial security and the wellbeing of the family, honor our commitments or hygiene. We have the capability of choosing who we want to be, think, say, feel and act at each instant.

Understanding work as punishment is also a barrier to action. The idea of prisoners doing hard labor includes this idea, as well as the idea of punishing us, and having to do, for example, the household chores, or any other activity to teach us a lesson.

I remember once, as a child, being punished and as a result I had to clean the bathroom for a month. What did I think and feel? "Cleaning the bathrooms is bad, very bad; I do not want this for the rest of my life." What a wonderful lesson I got out of the punishment. Evidently my mother was full of good intentions. But was it beneficial associating the task to a punishment? I definitely say no. I am glad that I made peace with cleaning the bathroom, later.

The teaching that links punishment to the activity or tasks is non pedagogical because it discourages the action. We become formatted to associate action, work or activity with displeasure and doing nothing with pleasure. Inertia is placed on a pedestal and worshiped, while action, which makes us grow, improves our self-esteem, gives us maturity and changes us and the world, is relegated to the end, frowned upon and unloved.

Punishing through action only prizes inertia, and from it, generally we do not get good results. No wonder that we then have to relearn to associate work and action with joy, pleasure, vitality, responsibility, maturity and positivity.

On another aspect, it is necessary to connect the concept of being responsible for our actions with the pleasure in acting, and with happiness. Happiness is a state where action has a very important role. It is not enough to decide to be happy; we have to act in accordance with what makes us feel good, of what we want, where we want to go, what we want to achieve and share and also be it.

Instead of waiting for others to act in accordance with what we want, or that they guess our thoughts and feelings, the path of action is much simpler and more direct, as it provides moments of happiness. It is also fantastic to act to give happiness to others, because naturally, we feel doubly blessed.

It is perfectly possible to have pleasure in an action (it can even be fun to get rid of it) and in that state the realization becomes easier. The truth is that we are responsible for the pleasure in our life, even when it is something external to us, or others giving it, it is us who accept it in a neurophysiological manner and process it internally. We accept the idea, the gesture or the feeling and we nurture it. Therefore, it is time to assume that we can give ourselves what we want so much, and what pleasurable attitudes are possible, viable and make a difference in our everyday life and that of others.

Simple acts like playing music while acting, realizing a task faster just for the fun of it, meeting a deadline and feel competent, or seeing a job well done, are just a few of the examples. However, if we need a stimulus for the action, we can ask ourselves, **"What pleasure can we add here?"** It may even be to finish with the issue forever, or know that you do it well, or it helps someone else, etc. **And subsequently we act according to that information and motivation.** We perceive that we are responsible for the pleasure we have in life, that it is available inside us at any moment and that we can channel it to everyday action; it is essential to act with motivation and we become happier, as well as those surrounding us.

6-The lack of action.

The act of postponing a behavior, or not realizing actions in a repeated fashion, produces neural and behavioral links that are assumed as valid and repeated automatically. That is, what we do consecutively becomes a habit and functions in automatic pilot in an unconscious manner, becoming a force in movement. For example, if the first thing we do every day after getting out of bed is drink water, it is natural to do it automatically; we do not even think; we drink the water and that is all. We have a highly functional operating system and it is receptive to routine. Neurally, we link patterns of behavior, of images, of thoughts and sensations, associated to what we normally are and realize, even if it is the omission of behavior or the avoidance of it. Therefore, each time we repeat these attitudes, we strengthen them, and they become familiar ground for us. There is an energetic signal that the cells recognize, sensations, mental and body states that are familiar to us.

The people that systematically postpone action, for example, tidying up the desk, completing the course, answering all the emails, going to the employment center, phoning to solve a serious issue, are in their learned comfort zone. Even if it feels unpleasant, or you criticize yourself for not having done it yet, you are used to it.

Does this have a solution? Yes, of course. Just as we "routinize" flight, avoiding action or inertia, we can also mold ourselves for actions. **And How?**

The answer is making the action "ordinary," acting as much as possible, introducing new habits. Systematically predisposing ourselves for the action and carrying them out effectively. It can be a small and simple thing. For example, tidying up our desk, booking an interview at the employment center, or always placing the car keys in the same place, and leaving the house at 8:00. And we do it. And at night if possible, we write down all we did so that we remember that we acted and we were freed.

The habit of not acting can associated with the need of only doing the important things or very significant ones, or when we are sure of being successful. Here we also turn inaction into routine because from the mental and emotional point of view, it is likely that we are distorting the perception of reality, making any action challenging, however small it may seem.

What to do then? Firstly, try to understand that action "does not bite." And then act, intensely, in the smallest things, that is, make the action so "trivial" and so ordinary that it no longer seems to be a threat, which after all, it is not.

For example: tidying up the clothes, changing the place of objects, going to the bakery to buy bread in the morning and the afternoon; speaking on the phone three people that we normally do not speak with. All this is so we build muscle in the habit of acting. The following day, do the same thing, action for action, without having to think, simply acting, and get involved in the process. And this is repeated the following day. Preferably, this behavior should be repeated for 28 days, the length of the lunar cycle, which is associated with the recording of the habits and the vibrational change of the subconscious. We will be so light and programmed for action that we can engage in any activity without any tension. After this, it is possible that we remember the numerous things that you have pending and get a "shock." It is time to breathe deeply and understand that we only need to do one thing to show the starting point and then, act consecutively.

Planning what to do can be a powerful instrument to give continuity to the action. For example, tomorrow at 15:00, make the phone call to get the quote, or send the email to apply for the job. And at that time have it done. We can tick off the paper where we established the plan and then celebrate the action.

It is very important to rejoice. Jump and say loudly: "I love acting."

With this action, we are associating positive emotions to the realization, and saying internally that you want to be in celebration more often. That is, this is doubling the stimulus and motivation for the action.

Acting and celebrating it is high performance fuel, which gives us more energy for the next activity, making it way easier. In effect, it is a double habit and a positive one, which we are introducing in our energetic system and it will benefit us in the long term. When acting, we are using **the language and the *"technology of creation,"*** and the planet, as well as the field of unified consciousness, mirrors our movement and constructions.

Give

"Be the change you want to see in the world."
Gandhi

"The one who owns plenty can be as rich as the one who gives himself totally and feels total satisfaction, independently of what he has."
Maria Costa

Imagine an overwhelming explosion of light; it is life beginning in a whole universe of which you, I and all of nature are a part of. In a giant leap, we were created and step by step we evolved, and with us, all of existence. What could have triggered this grandiose moment that is still a divine mystery and continues to be studied scientifically, and to a certain extent, we all want to understand?

Now accept this perception. You, I and everything surrounding us are the fruit of an act: **The act of giving.** We are the result of a generous gift, infinitely beautiful, which is life. Giving is the primordial act; it is the first movement of creation and starting with it, worlds are built.

From the moment we are conceived, everything is given to us, and also throughout our existence. The field of unified consciousness, which is our matrix, is available in the most varied manifestations and we share them at each moment. Everything belongs to us, everything was bequeathed to us automatically, including the power to give. Yes, giving life to what we focus through attention, intention, thought, image, word, feeling, emotion and action.

All these instruments construct reality, animate it. Each one of them is in itself and in totality, the language of creation, the unit of creation, and the *"creative technology"* of the human being in the field of unified consciousness and the planetary consciousness.

What significance does it have for us giving, and what is its place in our lives is a question we may ask ourselves and the answers are many.

Giving is, effectively, an act of expression, a manifestation of the will and it is also sharing that we partake in. It is through it that we exercise power, and the height of power is the genuine and unconditional handing over of a gift, of which we are channels. We simply give, and in that way, we are satisfied, and the function of giving is fulfilled.

The place of giving is already defined at birth, it is coded in our DNA, and each cell knows deeply that its mission is to give, communicate and increase more gifts, renewing itself cyclically.

We were conceived to give and we are and have so much at each moment; there is a whole universe available to us, wishing to serve us as it has always done; we merely have to perceive that and act in harmony. And in giving, we receive.

How is this possible? Because there is no separation between the giver and the receiver, or between the giver and the object—we are one—we are united on a fundamental level, woven in the web, and also being the web of life, therefore, everything that has a place on it, is experienced.

The more we give, the more we create, and naturally, the more we experience in that act, and the field reflects the gift meanwhile created immediately, for each existing manifestation at any point of the matrix.

The role that giving has in our lives can also be envisaged as a daily experience. Are we aware of the act of giving and exercise it, or on the contrary, do we not even remember it? Do we mentally create motives such as lack of time, attention or resources to avoid giving?

We can also have the perception of having nothing to give which is illusory and even absurd and is preventing the giving movement. We can also ask: give what, to whom and how?

What can we give? It is almost unlimited, from love, joy, attention, care, cooperation, but also hassles, confusion or violence. We have a choice regarding what we want to give.

To whom do we give? To ourselves, and simultaneously to others, to the planet and the field of unified consciousness.

How do we give? It depends what animates us at the time of the practice. Are we animated by generosity, kindness or by fear or need? The effects of our acts are different according to the animic states we are experiencing at the moment of the practice, whether they are of limitation or fear which causes the contraction of the energy field and the closure of the possibilities for us and the collective or, on the contrary if we are animically open, vibrating with life, which causes expansion of the energy field and numerous possibilities for us and the collective in harmony with the field of unified consciousness.

The capacity to give is inalienable in man, and it can be exercised at any moment in our lives, even in adverse times or in unusual situations, placing our humanity at the service of other beings. And evidently we can use it daily, namely in the metro, the supermarket, when walking the dog, with our husband or wife, with our children, friends or even with strangers.

The time to give is always in the present, and this action resizes us, and actualizes the globe and the All. When giving, we are exercising sovereignty, we become kings and queens, sharing ourselves and the spiritual and material wealth we own. We have a great abundance; we have so much to give, and the results of this donation can be surprising.

We cannot calculate all the outcomes, all the paths a gift may travel and how determinant that action can be in our lives and in the lives of the people that it will affect. Who knows if your smile, or holding a hand, saved the life of that person or even yours? Or who knows that the fact that you stopped to give information to a tourist, resulted in you meeting the great love of your life? Or if that day when you assisted an old lady with her shopping, led you to find money? Or giving a tip at lunch, fed a pet? The unexpected is always on the lookout and blessings are everywhere.

The vital impulse of giving is always current, and the moment is always in the present; give now.

Give as much to others as to yourself, share what you have, what you are, hand yourself over in every act; contribute to the happiness, giving the best of yourself in every instant. Make a difference in the world, contribute to it. Start with yourself, your family, the neighborhood, at work, at the grocers, in public transport, the park, the football stadium, the beach or a rock festival. Give your utmost, because you are giving to yourself, because there is only one of us, one presence, the field of unified consciousness. Infect each place, each person, each thing, each environment and nature with your generous presence. You can give freely, because there is always more to give, because the source in us is endless. Create more love, more joy, more health, more peace, by giving. Experience yourself as the matrix conceived you: powerful, rich and united with it.

We are the flower and the fruit of the gift of a field of consciousness that is nurturing us in every instant, which is infinitely generous, and totally unconditional, not asking for anything in return, and stimulating us to give more, **saying Yes to life.**

Instead of thinking about what we are getting in return when we give, because that creates the tendency of a result that may not be the best, we can free ourselves from the expectations, the need for results, giving genuinely, because it simply makes sense.

This internal clarity in giving without reservations of any kind is so profound that we change the dimension—of giving something—to being the gift. And being it, we are the entirety, the plenitude.

It is from the being that the gift emanates, and the being is all. In this state we are united with ourselves, with the other, with the object, with the planet and with the field of unified consciousness, and automatically the gift is materialized. When we are the gift, surrendering is perfect.

Who Are We? Born givers, always present to rediscover that there is always more to give to life and naturally we grow with what we give. Effectively, WE ARE CREATORS and We are light, We are love, We are peace, We are the ones who save ourselves and also the rescuer of a friend or a stranger, giving ourselves totally and We are happiness in movement deciding and acting accordingly. And therefore, Heaven and Earth sing in unison, and are paradise for all beings. You and I, we, the one, are now a gift in action. Thank you for being united for the same purpose.

Key points:
- Action is the language and the technology of creation, placed at the service of human consciousness, so that it constructs reality.
- Actions are life forces.
- Action is multifunctional. See the 8 functions of it.
- Without action there is neither evolution or revolution in our lives and planet.
- Every action is made of Risk and Deliverance
- RISK is the uncertainty, the possibility of not knowing or of not being able to control in absolute terms, all the results or effects of our actions.
- DELIVERANCE consists in the fact that each action, when being realized, is released and takes up its function, leaving us and relaxing us.
- Before you act, ask yourself: "Is this the mark that I want to imprint on life?" If so, do it.
- Listen to your emotions regarding action, namely fear. But if fear is always

there freezing you, please act.
- Perceptions about work must change in order for us to have better lives and to better raise our children. Work is not an obligation. It gives us purpose and connection to serve others.
- Perfection is not an isolated action, it is a path.
- Planning what to do can be a powerful instrument to give continuity to the action.
- Follow your heart. Inspired actions are available to you.
- Giving is in our nature, and when we give we receive.

Self-reflection:

❶ Have you ever been inspired or have had the intuition to carry out an action? Describe it.
❷ When doing an action, do you normally think about the impact that such behavior has on Earth? If you do not normally think about it, what would change in your attitude?
❸ With what functions of action did you identify?
❹ Is there any another function that you consider important? Describe it.
❺ Draw a V and write the words **Risk** and **Deliverance** in the extremities of the lines. Breathe deeply and feel which of these two aspects of action have you identified with.
❻ Have you identified with any of the aspects that prevented action? Which ones?
❼ Which action or actions have priority for you now?
❽ When will you do them?
❾ How are you going to celebrate them, once done?
❿ REALIZE IT NOW. And describe how you have felt.

Exercise:

❶ Practice 3 acts of kindness this week.
After doing the 3 deeds write down in detail what you have done and especially what you felt. Go deeper and imagine how those actions have affected the human family. Please commit yourself to be consistently kind.

12 The Quantum Leap

Story
A long time ago in the East, there was a peasant; she stood on the shores of a lake, situated in a valley between high mountains; she was contemplating the calm and crystalline water. She attentively observed the reflections of the mountains, the sun, and the trees and also her image mirrored on the water.
She became overwhelmed by the desire to bathe in the water. She entered the lake slowly. She observed herself entering, singing, swirling and swimming and noticed every feature of herself, and all the sounds or movements were reverberated where she was and in the whole lake.
She decided to float, to feel herself and the water in another manner, opening her arms and legs. She closed her eyes.
She floated serenely. The water sustained her on its own; she simply needed to be there, relaxed on the water of the lake.
The peasant could not remember how long she had been floating but there was a moment when she felt that something moved in her, that she was part of it and it was part of her. They were just one.
An immense joy pulsated inside her. She did not know where it came from; she only knew that what she felt was so great that it could cause the mountains to shake. She left the water, smiling and lay down in the sun, absorbing it through every pore...

"There are two ways to live your life. One is as though nothing is a miracle. The other is as though everything is a miracle."
Albert Einstein

"In order to be a realist you must believe in miracles."
David Ben Gurion

Just as the peasant, when floating, became aware that the lake sustained her, moved in her and that she and the lake were one, we also now understand **Who We Are**—the unity of life in movement—in unison with the field of unified consciousness.
We are now perfectly aware of the creative nature that each one of us carries. We now know the place we occupy in the universe. We understand how important we are to life; that it is aligned with us in every instant and what we can realize in it. We are also aware of what the nature of reality is.
We acknowledge that a uterus of primordial energy exists—the field of unified consciousness— where all is conceived, generating any reality. Mine, yours, the neighbor's or of the local community, and also, of the planet and the universe.
We understand how the field of consciousness works, discover how we function and at the same time we also discover by what principles we are governed. On a fundamental level, we are just one; we are intimately connected to one another, with nature, with objects, with the All and it is possible to affect reality, observing it, thinking it or feeling it. The field, as a gigantic hologram, reflects in each part of the whole and in itself the interferences that we provoke in its midst.
Reaching this far, we are aware that life has an infinite source of opportunities and is

open so that we may register in it the decisions, sensations, wishes or activities that make sense for us and with it, we build reality.

We are not predetermined in life, nor fixed with conditions, except by our own limiting beliefs or fears.

We have freedom of choice to decide what we are going to do with our lives and with the whole planet and also with the face of the universe.

In fact, we understand that reality, on a basic level, is insubstantial— waves/particles of energy organized by consciousness—and these are permeable to Who We Are and respond to us. We are having a quantum conversation all the time—we communicate—we are heard and answered and we interfere with all that everything is made of, building life. This happens because we speak a common language that is the **language of creation** and because we are **creators** of reality. We are consciousness in movement, just like the field of unified consciousness is—we work in partnership.

Whether we want to assume it or not, we were conceived to create. The field of consciousness does not ask us if we want to create, because it is immanent to Who We Are; what it asks is **"what are you going to create next?"** so that we can express our natural creativity and sculpt our lives, that of the planet and also the cosmos.

Wherever we are, at any time and independent of the circumstances or who is with us, we are building reality and we do it through Attention, Intention, Thought, Image, Word, Feeling, Emotion and Action. Each one of these eight tools by themselves and all together are **The Code of Creation** that every human being has to conceive and materialize existence.

From the deepest hope we nurture, the most fearful thought, the desire for an ice cream, a joint action to save the rainforest, having an intuition that causes us to say the right word at the meeting, we create and are always creating the web of infinite possibilities.

♥ Stop, Breathe, Love

Who Are We? We are multidimensional beings, gifted with extraordinary capacities that challenge conventional laws, equipped with sixteen senses that allow us to understand realities and conceive and change them in daring ways. It is true that we can know the position of a baby without an ultrasound and know when she/he will be born; it is true that we can intuit the moment to move houses or to propose a marriage; it is real to heal a headache, or leukemia in the wink of an eye; it is possible to know that our dearly beloved is well and in peace and continue on with our life. Furthermore, our children are wise when they say that there are colors around our head and body, when they speak that strange language or bend metal cutlery without quite understanding how. We are like that: telepathic, clairvoyant, intuitive, kinesthetic, empathetic and much more, using the senses we inherited; it is time we acknowledge this, use it and be happy with it.

Effectively we communicate at surprising levels using the technology of the sixteen senses, emitting and receiving information, moving waves/particles of energy with our consciousness and conforming reality to our communication. We witness what we created live and in color, sitting, lying down, standing or in movement and sometimes we see and feel this immediately and we may even be surprised with our creative power in unity with the field of unified consciousness. We can call this a miracle, an accident, a coincidence or even a problem or a crisis, depending on the perception we have. Other times "we need time," to notice the results of what we are doing to ourselves, our family, humanity, to the planet and the All. The truth is that construction proceeds inexorably and that the field of unified consciousness automatically mirrors the data we emit and the forms we crystallized.

In fact, we are called upon in every instant to communicate and participate in existence, to put our digital impression, the quantum impression in every day, from that kiss given in the morning, to the irritating telephone conversation, the moment of peace in the garden, or visiting a friend in hospital.

And each small or big impression is registered simultaneously on Earth and in the universal hologram, in a web of life.

What magnificence we have and what a change in our perception, this relationship of communication, interrelation and creative interdependence with the field of unified consciousness brings to us.

After all, the field listens to us, understands us, recognizes us and values all that we are, what we emit and give form to. This is powerful. All that we emit, for example, a dream, a sigh, a scream, caressing the face of our love or our child and even a shot, is precious for the field of consciousness. It handles every piece of information, every act with the same integrity and importance. The field values us completely. **We have a guaranteed place in the creation of reality—we do it in every instant— and we are always welcomed and accepted. This is magnificent.**

It is important to reiterate this: the field values us completely and at each moment, we are acknowledged and we contribute to life. There is no greater gift in the world than understanding that we are considered on the highest level and that what we bequeath to life, the field of consciousness mirrors fully in our lives, in the planet and the All. It reflects it without judging, prompting us to immediately create the next version of ourselves, the planet and the field, in a triune dance.

This perception is so overwhelming that it finally ends the smallness, the isolation and human irresponsibility. Who Are We? We are grandiose CREATORS, choosing in every instant what we will give to life. Enough of pretending that we do not have the power to change, create life or the world that we desire. We have all the power inside us. We are what everything is; we are Gods in human form, interacting with the *divine unity* in all things and in that which it is.

We are not alone in this grandiose universe; **we are accompanied by the field of unified consciousness. Nor are we separated from one another, from nature or from what exists or will have existence: we are united, we are a field of infinite possibilities.**

The field of unified consciousness acknowledges us as active participants, partners with sensibility and intelligence to inform and enform life. **We were given power— actually we are the power, and it is up to us to honor it**

To be responsible for what we focus on, what we desire, think, verbalize, feel or do. Use our consciousness fully instead of turning the old cassettes into routine. Choose another way of seeing, understanding, supporting and feeling. Therefore, on a day that we may not be at our best, we should remember that there is one more opportunity.

If you are told it is impossible, that there is no cure, that no one has done it before, that it is too much or that we cannot, **we are going to remember that it is possible, because there is always another possibility and another probability and still**

another; there are endless possibilities.
We insist that it is possible, even if at the moment we do not know how, even if we have to do everything differently and even reinvent ourselves, it does not matter, we will find a solution. It exists. It is in the field of unified consciousness and in us, vibrating, we merely need to be open to it. Remember that the quantum lake sustains us, nurtures us, and guides us in the flow of life. There is always more to choose and manifest. The field is limitless and so are we. We have infinite possibilities of perceiving and acting in the world.
Einstein said: *"We will either find a way, or make one,"* we **now know We Are the Way, the Traveler and the Life.** We are the All and it is complete in itself.

♥ Stop, Breathe, Love

Where do we start then, in the process of realizing ourselves and raising all of humanity and the planet in unity with the field of unified consciousness? **With us.**
Each one of us has the mission of being what we are— light, energy, information and also enformation in movement—and to contribute in his way to the world.
Each one of us counts, each one of us is a universe of infinite probabilities, a creator in the quantum network. Let us forget the old story that some are more powerful than others. There is no one more powerful, nor less powerful.
For the field, we are all the same—we are consciousness—and it simply is.
We should open our hearts, minds, and eyes and understanding the miracle. We are the miracle of life in movement, interfering with all that exists in every instant.
We are made of the same matter that everything is made of: information, energy and light vibrating in an ocean of infinite possibilities, and we affect it, change it, and give it contours and substance.
What more do we need to **be the conscious miracle** creating reality in a total manner and for the good of all beings?
Be really happy, open, prosperous, united, innovative and grateful every day.
Persisting moment by moment in being deliberate creators guided and working in a team with the field of unified consciousness. That is possible, it always was, and now that we understand it and practice being it better, let us make it contagious for the entire universe.
Each one of us makes a difference because inside ourselves is the whole—the sacred hologram—and what the holographic principle (that is underlying life) tells us is that a change in any point of the hologram, affects the entire hologram.
Who Are We? We are the ones who can change what we want, innovate, and recreate ourselves in every instant. Life gives us that opportunity at each nanosecond, consistently. Indeed, **we are a vibrating field of infinite opportunities.** It is up to us to use them and modify the face of humanity, the planet and the cosmos.
Furthermore, the truth is that in the present stage of humanity there are increasingly more consciousnesses awakening to the fact that the **language and *"technology of creation"*** exists and they are using it consistently.
This act is accelerating the individual and collective vibration at a great speed, causing the emergence of a critical mass that is elevating the whole planet, making each one accountable for himself and the whole, recalibrating the energy. A critical mass of the square root of 1% of the world's population focused coherently and in a state of unity

with **the system of creation that we have been mentioning** is capable, for example, of restraining an oil spill in the ocean, decreasing the crime rate, bringing peace to an area of the world, or preventing the propagation of an epidemic and healing a great number of people.

What about being part of the 1% now? Better still, increasing the percentage and making it contagious for billions of beings? We already know that it is possible and we have the power in us to affect the web of life. In fact it is our nature. We start where we are at work, in our family, at the football club, at school, at any time, with whoever we are with.

As we choose to feel love in our hearts and in the hearts of the people we work with or we come across in the street, we heal ourselves or we heal family issues and we feed ourselves in a balanced manner; we are necessarily contributing to the human and planetary hologram in unity with the field of unified consciousness, reflecting love, peace, healing and nourishment for all beings.

Imagine what it would be like if each one of us would change one thought, one word, one image, one feeling and one action, every day, in a positive manner and focused on what is good in life?

For example, in the case of Portugal where there are approximately 10 million people, that would be "5 different things" times 10 million. That is 50 million probabilities and functions in a network, automatically vibrating in our energy system, being in resonance with people, events, opportunities and objects in the same positive harmony for our life and country. Truly transformative. In Portugal alone, it would be 50 million opportunities for the manifestation of better lives for ourselves; this is really a lot...

Now multiply 50 million possibilities by the 7 billion human beings that exist on the planet and it will be trillions of trillions. And add our link to the field of unified consciousness. The conscious expansion is tremendous and gigantic and the impact is overwhelming.

Remember that this explosion begins in a simple manner. Each one of us can change what we think, speak, imagine, feel, act and what we focus on, once during the day. This is easy and has this overwhelming impact on our lives and the world.

Now, if we multiply such daily changes (5 things by 10 million in the case of Portugal), it will be 50 million by one year, 365 days, plus the 7 billion people on Earth, we understand the infinitely great impact on the personal, country, planetary and cosmic reality.

That is us functioning in a network and being the power and accountability in the world, in union with the field of unified consciousness. And it started with a small step that caused the change "to the footprint of reality."

For example, each time we think that "life is difficult," we can also think that "easy solutions also exist and can become more visible in our lives." When someone criticizes another in front of us, we can verbalize the positive side of that person. When faced with despair, find courage or motivation. Instead of honking in traffic, we can smile. Or even, for example, when we wake up, feel gratitude for life, open the door for a stranger, work with enthusiasm, forgive the neighbor for shaking the mat over your washing, join our child at play and get all dirty, sing in the street or be able to say no sweetly.

Evidently, besides these steps there are also leaps and these also count for the group of 50 million probabilities of new connections and manifestations in life. Namely, maintaining inner presence when faced with conflict; regarding fear, facing it and removing its burden, holding the hand of a "competitor," forgiving ourselves and forgiving "others" at each moment.

And so many other things we are capable of…

That is inner mastery and it is already with us, capable of being actualized by a decision of consciousness. Because Who We Are is Love, We Are Peace, We Are Light. We Are the Power of Purposeful Change; We Are the Gift; We are the eyes, the ears, the heart and the hands of Christ, of Buddha, of Muhammad or Our Lady in action; magnificent particles of the Divine Unity being expressed here and now in the field of endless opportunities.

We are in the Promised Land, we already live in a magnificent blue planet and paradise is inside us and wherever we choose to experience it. It is up to us to decide at each moment to be a deliberate, organized creator.

When using the language and *"technology of cocreation"* consciously, when sharing it, feeling it and transmitting it happily, Heavens above Heavens are opened for us and a new world emerges in the image and likeness of responsible and happy creators.

This is the information and communication revolution for the 21st century, where the conscious technology is available to everyone, making the miracle happen.

The miracle of using the totality of human potential and of manifesting a humanity complete with values, of sharing and of happy experiences in each one of us, knowing that we are the power, the responsibility and the guardians of life and all of existence to which we are intimately connected. We are Walking Miracles travelling the path of life and life is a miracle in which we operate. Together, we are now making the revolution of consciousness.

In the words of John Lennon, in the song *Imagine*:

"*Imagine all the people living life in peace (…)*
You may say I'm a dreamer, but I'm not the only one.
I hope, someday you'll join us and the world will be as one."

This is not imagination, it is possible.

We live in the "Land Where Everything Is Possible." It is happening now, thanks to each one of us who uses the Code of Creation and knows after all, Who We Are.

Many blessings for you my friend, my consciousness. Be happy, united.
Gratefully,

Susana Cor de Rosa

We have a present for you: "Who We Are" special meditation. Please visit www.susanacorderosa.com and receive your free gift.

Bibliography

Aspect, A., Dalibard, J., and Roger, G., "Experimental Test of Bell's Inequalities Using Time-Varying Analyzers" *Physical Review Letters 49* (1982), summarized from pgs. 1804-7.

Backster, C., "Evidence of a Primary Perception in Plant Life," *International Journal of Parapsychology*, Vol 10, Winter, 1968, N° 4.

Bhom, David, *Wholeness and the Implicate Order* (London: Routlegde & Kegan Paul, 1980).

Binkofski, F. and Buccino, G., Scientific American magazine - *Mente e Cérebro*, Brazilian Edition 171, April 2007, Duetto Editorial. If you would like to read the original article in English, please see, Binkofski, F. and Buccino, G., "Therapeutic Reflection," *Scientific American Magazine –Mind*, Edition 171, June/July 2007.

Braud, W.G., *Distant Mental influence: Its Contribution to Science, Healing, and Human Interactions.* Hampton Roads Publishing, December 2003.

Braud, W., *Mental Influence Research*, Hampton Road Publishing. Also see, Braud, W. Et al, "Attention focusing facilitated through remote mental interaction," Journal of the American Society for Psychic Research, 89, 1995, pgs 103-115.

Braud, W.G., Schlitz, M.J., "Consciousness Interactions with Remote Biological Systems: Anomalous Intentionality Effects." *Subtle Energies*, Vol. 2, 1991, , pg. 1-46, summarized from pg. 28 and following pages.

Byrd, R., "Positive Therapeutic Effects of Intercessory Prayer in a Coronary Care Unit Population, Summarized from" *Southern Medical Journal*, July 1988, Vol. 81:826-828.

Capra, F., *The Tao of Physics; An Exploration of the Parallels Between Modern Physics and Eastern Mysticism*, Flamingo, 1992.

Chesney, M.A. and Rosenman, R.H. (eds), *Anger and Hostility in Cardiovascular and Behavioural Disorders*, Hemisphere/McGraw Hill, London, 1985.

Damásio, A., *Self Comes to Mind: Constructing the Conscious Brain*, Pantheon, 2010, pg. 151and 163, of the Portuguese version.

Eatherley, D., *How Pet Dogs face up to your moods*, "New Scientist, 29", October 2008, based on the work of Guo, K., "Left gaze bias in humans, rhesus monkeys and domestic dogs," *Animal Cognition*, May 2009, Vol. 12 Issue 3, pg. 409-418.

Ekman, P., "Facial Expressions of Emotion: New Findings, New Questions" *Psychological Science*, Vol. 3, No. 1, 1992, pg. 34-38.

Emoto, M., *The Miracle of Water*, Simon and Shuster, 2010, pg.32, 124 of the Portuguese Edition.

Fussell, J. H, 'Where is Science Going?: Review and Comment", *Theosophical Path Magazine, January to December 1933* (2003), 199. Quoted in *The Observer* (25th January 1931).

Gerber, R., *Vibrational Medicine: New Choices for Healing Ourselves*, Bear and Company, 1996, summarized from pg. 257 of the Portuguese edition.

Goswami, A., *The Self-Aware Universe: How Consciousness Creates the Material World*, Putnam's Son, 1995, pg. 130.

Goswami, A. *Visionary Window: A Quantum Physicist's Guide to Enlightenment*,

Portuguese edition (Editora Cultrix), pgs. 42, 53, 79.
Grad, B., "The Biological Effects of the "Laying On Of Hands" on Animals and Plants: Implications for Biology," In Schmeider, G, ed.; *Parapsychology: Its Relation to Physics, Biology, and Psychiatry*, Metuchen, NJ: Scarecrow Press, 1976: 75-89.
Graham, B., *The Holy Spirit: Activating God's Power in Your Life*, adaptation from variations of a popular story - pg. 92
Grinberg-Zylberbaum, J., Delaflor, M., Attie, L., and Goswami A., "The Einstein-Podolsky-Rosen Paradox in the Brain: The Transferred Potential," *Physical Essays*, Vol.7, No 4, 1994 (summarized from pgs. 422-428).
Hamilton, D., Digital Magazine, *Whole Science*, August 21, 2009. See also, Dr. David Hamilton website: http://drdavidhamilton.com/category/visualization-2/page/2/.
Harris, W.S., "A Randomized, Controlled Trial of the Effects of Remote, Intercessory Prayer on Outcomes in Patients Admitted to the Coronary Care Unit," *Archives of Internal Medicine*, 1999; 159(19), 2273-8.
Heart Math Institute publications, see also www.hearthmath.org.
Hirschberg, C. & O'Regan, B., summarized from: *Spontaneous Remission: An Annotated Bibliography*, Institute of Noetic Sciences, 1993.
Journal of Mind and Behavior, 8(1), 67-104, 1987, "Consciousness as a field: The Transcendental Meditation and TM-Sidhi program and changes in social indicators.
Langford, M., *Fotografia Básica*, (Basic photography), Portuguese 5th edition, 2003, Dinalivro.
Laszlo, E., *The Whispering Pond: A Personal Guide to the Emerging Vision of Science*, Element, 1996, summarized from pgs. 135 - 136 of the Portuguese edition.
Leibniz, G. W., "*Essays on the Goodness of God, the Freedom of Man and the Origin of Evil*".
Marcikic, I, de Riedmatten, H., Tittel, W., Zbinden, h., Legré, M., Gisin, N Demonstration of Quantum Correlations over more than 10 km," *Physical Review A*, Vol. 57, No. 5, 1998. Letters, 93 (2004). Distribution of time-bin entangled qubits over 50km of optic fiber. Physical Review Letter, 93.
Maxwell J. and Faraday M. - see electromagnetic theory
McTaggart, L., "*The Field*; The Quest for the Secret Force of The Universe", Element, HarperCollins Publishers 2003, pp. 138, 242.
Mermin, D., *Boojums All the Way Through: Communicating Science in a Prosaic Age*. Cambridge University Press, 1990, pg. 119.
Moody, R., *Life After Life: The Investigation of a Phenomenon-Survival of Bodily Death*, Bantam Books, 1976.
Mora, J. F., *Dictionary of Philosophy*, José Ferrater, Allianza Editora, pg. 2997.
Planck, M., "Discourse of Max Planck about the nature of matter," Archiv zur Geschichte der Max-Planck-Gesellschaft, Abt. Va, Rep. 11 Planck, Nr. 1797.
Planck, M., *Religion und Naturwissenschaft*, Leipzig: Johann Ambrosius Barth Verlag, 1958, 27.
Planck, M., – Quantum theory.
Plato, *Cratylus*, ([391e and b])
Plessinger, A., "The Effects of Mental Imagery on Athletic Performance," published by the Psychology Department of Vanderbilt University.
Portuguese dictionary, Porto Editora
Pribram, K.H., *Brain and Perception: Holonomy and Structure in Figural Processing*,

Hillsdale, NJ, Lawrence Eribaum, 1991.

Puthoff, H., "CIA-Initiated Remote Viewing at Stanford Research Institute" paper, 1996

Rein, G., Atkinson, M., and McCraty, R., "Physiological and Psychological Effects of Compassion and Anger," Summarized from *Journal of Advancement in Medicine*, Vol. 8, No. 2, Summer 1995.

Siegel, B. S., *Love, Medicine and Miracles, lessons learned about self-healing from a surgeon´s experience with exceptional patients*, Harper Collins, 1990, summarized from pg. 53, 76, 191 of the Portuguese edition.

Simonton, O.C., M.D., James Creighton, Ph.D., Matthews S.,. *Getting Well Again*, Bantam, April 01, 1992, and www.simontoncenter.com.

Sheldrake, R., *Seven Experiments that Could Change the World*, Riverhead Books, 1995, Summarized from pgs. 268, 272 of the Portuguese edition.

Sheldrake, R., Morphic field, concept in "Morphic Field is a vital model of organization". For more information please see www.sheldrake.org/research/glossary.

Schmidt, H., "*Mental Influence on random events*", New Scientist 24 June 1971, ca. pg 757.

Solfvin, G. F., "PSI expectancy effects in psychic healing studies with malarial mice," *European Journal of Parapsychology*, 1982 N° 4, pp 160-97.

Stanford, R., "Associative activation of the unconscious," and "visualization" as a method for influencing the PK target" *Journal of the American Society for Psychical Research*, 1969; 63: summarized from pg. 338-51.

Stapp, H. P., *Mind, Matter, and Quantum Mechanics*, Springer Verlag, New York, 1993.

Steiner, R., "The Riddle of Humanity," (GA 170), Conference at Dornach (1916).

Targ, R. and Puthoff, H., *Mind-Reach: Scientists Look at Psychic Abilities*, Delacorte Press, 1977, summarized from text.

Targ, R., and Harary, K., *The Mind Race: Understanding and Using Psychic Abilities*, Villard Books, 1984.

Tart, C., "Physiological Correlates of PSI Cognition," *International Journal of Parapsychology*, Vol. 5, No. 4, 1963, summarized from pgs. 375-86.

The Bible - Matthew 18:20

The *Maharishi Effect*, published in *Scientific Research* on Maharishi's *Transcendental Meditation and TM-Sidhi Program*: Increased Progress towards Peaceful Resolution of Conflict; *Collected Papers*, Vol. 4: 335, Lebanon; 337.

Tompkins, P. & Bird, C., *The Secret Life of Plants*, 1973, Harper & Row.

Wieder, M. with Raj-Bhavsar—Dream University 2010/2011, please see www.dreamuniversity.com. Interview with Marylin King, Dream University, 2010/2011

Tables and illustrations captions (number in sequence)

The source of the 2 images from chapter 3 is:
https://images.search.yahoo.com/search/images;_ylt=A2KIbZzfAlt b8.wA6yFXNyoA;_ylu=X3oDMTEyanNvNWYzBGNvbG8DYmYxBHBvcw MxBHZ0aWQDQjQ4NTNfMQRzZWMDc2M?p=free+images+interferenc e+patterns&fr=mc afee_uninternational

Susana Cor de Rosa's bio and activities

Susana was born in Lisbon on May 30th, 1969.
She has a university degree and a Post-Graduate degree in Law. At the age of 30, she felt an inner calling to expand her consciousness and to change the direction of her life – to teach, heal and re-educate human beings to live aligned with their innate happiness.
She has travelled the world and trained in various fields such as Quantum Physics, Shamanism, Alternative Therapies and Waldorf Pedagogy.
Susana is dedicated to expanding consciousness, healing, teaching and re-educating human beings towards self-empowerment, happiness and growth. She spreads this message and practices her work all over the world in the areas of personal and spiritual development.
To that effect, she provides workshops, retreats, lectures, private consultations, and development programs for individuals, groups, and organizations all over the world.
To better know her work and to get more information, please visit: susanacorderosa.com/en
Email: susana@susanacorderosa.com
Cell phone: +351.923.015.310

Workshops and Retreats

- Unified Quantum Healing (1, 2 and 3)
- Subtle Activation DNA (Retreat)
- Silence Retreat
- Healthy Relationships
- Confidence
- Soul's Map

Consultations
Unified Quantum Healing
This is a transformational and profound session to heal your body, mind and soul.

You will be connected to the quantum field and your patterns of energy, light and information will be enhanced so healing and communication can occur at all levels of your being.

Relationships

To solve relationship issues and build healthy relationships with yourself, your partner, your family members or work colleagues.

We provide you with support so that you can expand your awareness, raise your energy and find new ways to express yourself and connect with others.

We explore new possibilities for you to change, activate your own resources, strategies and energetic skills to help you be at your best.

Soul's Map

Discover the territory of your soul and map your energy so you can fulfill your life's purpose.

Access the higher vision of your life and understand the signs that your path has shown you.

Be guided throughout your life cycles and be empowered by your soul to put into practice your unique strengths and skills to contribute to the world.

VIP day

One day with Susana Cor de Rosa to go deeper in your inner transformation. You will breakthrough whatever has been holding you back in life and expand the unlocked resources within you to make it happen, maintaining your soul connection. This day is often done for individuals or companies.

Susana Cor de Rosa Products

"The Land Where Everything is Possible"

An inspiring story about Happiness, the Power of Dreams, Magic and the Meaning of life. To read, dream, talk and grow.
From ages 8 to 98.
Portuguese and other versions also available.

"Who We Are: The Code of Creation" Portuguese and other versions: All books are available at bookstores and at www.susanacacorderosa.com

The Wisdom of Infinite Possibilities
A transformational book to expand your energy, connection, inner wisdom and power to achieve your dreams.

MP3-Infinite Force: Five-week Mediation Programme.
Meditation and energetic programming for the body, emotion, mind and soul.
Infinite Force is an experience full of energy and joy that will surprise you. Each day and week you become more conscious of yourself, with greater confidence, freedom, clarity, health, peace, joy and determination. Achieve more personal satisfaction and results in all areas of your life.
During and after this journey you will communicate with the Infinite Force, and feel completely connected with it, entering the field of miracles.
Available at www.cdbaby.com. Portuguese version also available at www.susanacordeosa.com

To know more about these products or Susana's work visit:
www.susanacorderosa.com/en
Please feel free to contact Susana by email: susana@susanacorderosa.com or by phone +351 929015310

Synopsis

The book you have in your hands is revolutionary and it will resonate profoundly within you. It provides you a fresh and empowering vision of Who You Are, the role you play on this Earth and what you can accomplish. It also provides you a different perspective of the Universe, the power you share with it and the power it shares with you, and how you use this power, even though you are not aware of it.

With this book, you will rediscover your essence, the bond and communication you have with everything that exists: a tree, a person you love, your pet, a distant friend, or the universe or even the mobile phone you use. And you will learn how to use this bond to create any reality, because EVERYTHING IS POSSIBLE.

You will understand that you're speaking, at each instant, a language the Universe knows and it answers to: your thoughts, wishes, words, fears, loves or gestures. It shows you that you are not alone, that you have the force of creation, the force of change within you and you affect your family, friends, community, planet, and the Cosmos at every nano-second.

You will understand that you have extraordinary, innate capabilities, and you can use them, for example, to resolve an issue at work, receive news from your child who lives on a different continent, heal yourself, contribute to clean the oceans, or feed the world.

This work connects science and spirituality and it presents healing as a natural part of each one of us, and we can use it always. It also makes us rethink old and limiting beliefs by reprogramming ourselves towards freedom and who we really are: Consciousness. We Are Unlimited, Powerful, and Creative Beings who are totally capable of being happy and sharing happiness.

Notes:

www.ingramcontent.com/pod-product-compliance
Lightning Source LLC
Chambersburg PA
CBHW071111160426
43196CB00013B/2536